On This Date . . .

A Day-by-Day Listing of Holidays,
Birthdays and Historic Events and
Special Days, Weeks and Months

COMPILED BY SANDY WHITELEY

Contemporary Books

Chicago   New York   San Francisco   Lisbon   London   Madrid   Mexico City
Milan   New Delhi   San Juan   Seoul   Singapore   Sydney   Toronto

Library of Congress Cataloging-in-Publication Data

On this date— : a day-by-day listing of holidays, birthdays and historic events and special days, weeks and months / compiled by Sandy Whiteley.

      p.   cm.
    Includes index.
    ISBN 0-07-139827-9
    1. Holidays.   2. Days.   I. Whiteley, Sandy.

  GT3930 .O5   2002
  394.26—dc21   2002074083

1 2 3 4 5 6 7 8 9 0   AGM/AGM   1 0 9 8 7 6 5 4 3 2

ISBN 0-07-139827-9

McGraw-Hill books are available at special quantity discounts to use as premiums and sales promotions, or for use in corporate training programs. For more information, please write to the Director of Special Sales, Professional Publishing, McGraw-Hill, Two Penn Plaza, New York, NY 10121-2298. Or contact your local bookstore.

This book is printed on acid-free paper.

Contents

Introduction

Welcome to *On This Date . . . A Day-by-Day Listing of Holidays, Birthdays and Historic Events and Special Days, Weeks and Months*. This book contains more than 2,000 historical events and special days, as well as the birth dates and places of all sorts of interesting people. These entries, arranged from January 1 through December 31, have been selected from the 12,000+ entries in *Chase's Calendar of Events*, an annual reference book, which for almost 50 years has provided information arranged day-by-day for librarians, the media, public relations firms and anyone else interested in the calendar. *On This Date . . .* pulls together the best, most exciting, interesting and thought-provoking of those events for your use.

This volume lists only events that occur on a fixed date. For holidays that have dates that change each year, we've pulled together tables of those dates for the next five years and you'll find those at the back of this book.

How have the special days, weeks and months in *On This Date . . .* been declared? The president of the United States has the authority to issue a presidential proclamation to commemorate an event or person, but the president issues only about 100 proclamations a year. Until 1995, members of the Senate and the House of Representatives could introduce legislation for special observances to commemorate people and events they thought worthy of national recognition. Because these bills took up a lot of time on the part of Congress, when Congress reformed its rules and procedures in 1995, the decision was made to discontinue this practice. Today the Senate may pass resolutions commemorating special days, weeks and months but these resolutions do not have the force of law.

It is not necessary to have a public official declare a special day, week or month—many of the events in *On This Date . . .* have been declared only by their sponsoring organizations. Please contact those sponsoring organizations if you need more information.

Also listed are various historic anniversaries, folkloric events and birthdays. Dates for these entries have been gathered from a wide range of reference books. Dates for historic events can be assumed to be Gregorian calendar (New Style) dates unless (OS) appears after the date. This means it is an Old Style or Julian date. Most of America's founding fathers were born before 1752, when Great Britain and its colonies adopted the Gregorian calendar. As an example of this, we list George Washington's birthday as Feb 22, 1732, the Gregorian or New Style date. However, when he was born Great Britain and its colonies began the year on Mar 25, not Jan 1, so his Julian birthdate was Feb 11, 1731.

One of the founders of *Chase's Calendar of Events*, William D. Chase, gave us the following philosophy: "As wise men have observed, festivity and celebration are unique to mankind. No other creature enjoys them. And enjoying them to the fullest degree seems to me to be a worthy undertaking. *Chase's Calendar* provides the map of time on which all the wonderful celebrations can be located. It has been our aim to fill the calendar with times to recognize, to learn from and to enjoy." We hope that our new book, *On This Date . . .* , also gives you something to commemorate or celebrate every day of the year!

Sandy Whiteley, Compiler, *On This Date . . .*

January

January 1

JANUARY ONE—NEW YEAR'S DAY. Jan 1. First day of the first month of the Gregorian calendar year. New Year's Day is a public holiday in the US and in many other countries. Traditionally, it is a time for personal stocktaking, for making resolutions for the coming year and sometimes for recovering from the festivities of New Year's Eve. Financial accounting begins anew for businesses and individuals whose fiscal year is the calendar year. Jan 1 has been observed as the beginning of the year in most English-speaking countries since the British Calendar Act of 1751, prior to which the New Year began Mar 25 (approximating the vernal equinox). Earth begins another orbit of the sun, during which it, and we, will travel some 583,416,000 miles in 365.2422 days. New Year's Day has been called "Everyman's Birthday," and in some countries a year is added to everyone's age Jan 1 rather than on the anniversary of each person's birth. The world's most widely celebrated holiday.

AUSTRALIA: COMMONWEALTH FORMED: ANNIVERSARY. Jan 1, 1901. On this day, the six colonies of Victoria, New South Wales, Queensland, South Australia, Western Australia and Northern Territory were united into one nation. The British Parliament had passed the Commonwealth Constitution Bill in the spring of 1900, and Queen Victoria signed the document Sept 17, 1900.

BONZA BOTTLER DAY™. Jan 1. (also Feb 2, Mar 3, Apr 4, May 5, June 6, July 7, Aug 8, Sept 9, Oct 10, Nov 11 and Dec 12). To celebrate when the number of the day is the same as the number of the month. Bonza Bottler Day™ is an excuse to have a party at least once a month. For info: Gail M. Berger. E-mail: gberger5@aol.com.

CUBA: ANNIVERSARY OF THE REVOLUTION AND LIBERATION DAY. Jan 1. National holiday celebrating the overthrow of the government of Fulgencio Batista in 1959 by the revolutionary forces of Fidel Castro, which had begun a civil war in

1956. Also a national holiday that celebrates the end of Spanish rule in 1899. Cuba, the largest island of the West Indies, was a Spanish possession from its discovery by Columbus (Oct 27, 1492) until 1899. Under US military control 1899–1902 and 1906–09, a republican government took over Jan 28, 1909, and controlled the island until overthrown Jan 1, 1959, by Fidel Castro's revolutionary movement.

CZECH-SLOVAK DIVORCE: ANNIVERSARY. Jan 1, 1993. As Dec 31, 1992, gave way to Jan 1, 1993, the 74-year-old state of Czechoslovakia separated into two nations—the Czech and Slovak Republics. The nation of Czechoslovakia ended peacefully though polls showed that most Slovaks and Czechs would have preferred that it survive. Before the split Czech Prime Minister Vaclav Klaus and Slovak Prime Minister Vladimir Meciar reached an agreement on dividing everything from army troops and gold reserves to the art on government building walls.

ELLIS ISLAND OPENED: ANNIVERSARY. Jan 1, 1892. Over the years more than 20 million individuals were processed through the immigration stations at Ellis Island. The island was used as a point of deportation as well: in 1932 alone, 20,000 people were deported from Ellis Island. When the US entered World War II in 1941, Ellis Island became a US Coast Guard Station. It closed Nov 12, 1954, and was declared a national park in 1956. After years of disuse it was restored and in 1990 reopened as a museum.

EURO INTRODUCED: ANNIVERSARY. Jan 1, 1999. The euro, the common currency of members of the European Union, was introduced for use by financial institutions. The value of the currencies of the 11 nations (Austria, Belgium, Finland, France, Germany, Ireland, Italy, Luxembourg, the Netherlands, Portugal and Spain) was locked in at a permanent conversion rate to the euro. Greece joined the eurozone the following year. On Jan 1, 2002, euro bills and coins began circulating; other currencies were phased out as of Feb 28, 2002.

FIRST BABY BOOMER BORN: ANNIVERSARY. Jan 1, 1946. Kathleen Casey Wilkens, born at one minute after midnight in Philadelphia, PA, was decreed the first of the almost 78 million baby boomers born between 1946 and 1964.

HAITI: INDEPENDENCE DAY. Jan 1. A national holiday commemorating the proclamation of independence in 1804. Haiti, occupying the western third of the island Hispaniola (second largest of the West Indies), was a Spanish colony from the time of its discovery by Columbus in 1492 until 1697, then a French colony until the proclamation of independence in 1804.

NATIONAL GLAUCOMA AWARENESS MONTH. Jan 1–31. Between 2 and 3 million people suffer from glaucoma. Nearly half do not know they have the disease—it causes no early symptoms. Prevent Blindness America provides valuable information about this "sneak thief of sight." For info: Prevent Blindness America®. Web: www.preventblindness.org.

NATIONAL HOT TEA MONTH. Jan 1–31. To celebrate one of nature's most popular, soothing and relaxing beverages; the only beverage in America commonly served hot or iced, anytime, anywhere, for any occasion. For info: The Tea Council of the USA. Web: www.teausa.com.

NATIONAL MAILORDER GARDENING MONTH. Jan 1–31. There's no better way to beat the winter "blahs" than by curling up with a few colorful garden catalogs and spending some time dreaming and scheming about next spring's garden. Many catalogs offer tips and information on how to create a beautiful garden. For info: Mailorder Gardening Association. Web: www .mailordergardening.com.

NATIONAL POVERTY IN AMERICA AWARENESS MONTH. Jan 1–31. To promote public awareness of the continuing existence of poverty and social injustice in America. Individuals are encouraged to support efforts to eradicate poverty by increasing their understanding of the causes and practical solutions and by active participation and support for antipoverty programs. For info: Catholic Campaign for Human Development,

US Conference of Catholic Bishops. Web: www.povertyusa.org.

OATMEAL MONTH. Jan 1–31. Celebrate oatmeal, a low-fat, sodium-free, whole grain. When eaten daily as a part of a diet that's low in saturated fat and cholesterol, oatmeal may help reduce the risk of heart disease. For info: The Oat Expert. Web: www.quakeroatmeal.com.

ROSE BOWL GAME—TOURNAMENT OF ROSES PARADE. Jan 1. Pasadena, CA. Football conference champions from the Big Ten and Pacific-10 meet in the Rose Bowl game. Tournament of Roses has been an annual New Year's event since 1890; Rose Bowl football game since 1902. Michigan defeated Stanford 49–0 in what was the first postseason football game. Called the Rose Bowl since 1923, it is preceded each year by the Tournament of Roses Parade. Estimated attendace: 100,000. For info: Rose Bowl. Web: www.tournamentofroses.com.

ROSS, BETSY: BIRTH ANNIVERSARY. Jan 1, 1752 (OS). According to legend based largely on her grandson's revelations in 1870, needleworker Betsy Ross created the first stars and stripes flag in 1775, under instructions from George Washington. Her sewing and her making of flags were well known, but there is little corroborative evidence of her role in making the first Stars and Stripes. The account is generally accepted, however, in the absence of any documented claims to the contrary. She was born Elizabeth Griscom at Philadelphia, PA, and died there Jan 30, 1836.

SOLEMNITY OF MARY, MOTHER OF GOD. Jan 1. Holy Day of Obligation in Roman Catholic Church since calendar reorganization of 1969, replacing the Feast of the Circumcision, which had been recognized for more than 14 centuries.

Z DAY. Jan 1. To give recognition on the first day of the year to all persons and places whose names begin with the letter "Z" and who are always listed or thought of last in any alphabetized list. For info: Tom Zager. E-mail: tee_zee @excite.com.

★ Birthdays ★

Frank Langella, actor (*The Beast, Dracula*), born Bayonne, NJ, Jan 1, 1940.

January 2

55-MPH SPEED LIMIT: ANNIVERSARY. Jan 2, 1974. President Richard Nixon signed a bill requiring states to limit highway speeds to a maximum of 55 miles per hour. This measure was meant to conserve energy during the crisis precipitated by the embargo imposed by the Arab oil-producing countries. A plan used by some states limited sale of gasoline on odd-numbered days for cars whose plates ended in odd numbers and even-numbered days for even-numbered plates. Some states limited purchases to $2–$3 per auto, and lines as long as six miles resulted in some locations.

GEORGIA: RATIFICATION DAY. Jan 2, 1788. By unanimous vote, Georgia became the fourth state to ratify the Constitution.

★ Birthdays ★

Cuba Gooding, Jr, actor (*Jerry Maguire, As Good as It Gets*), born the Bronx, NY, Jan 2, 1968.

January 3

ALASKA: ADMISSION DAY: ANNIVERSARY. Jan 3. Alaska, which had been purchased from Russia in 1867, became the 49th state in 1959. The area of Alaska is nearly one-fifth the size of the rest of the US.

CONGRESS ASSEMBLES. Jan 3. The Constitution provides that "the Congress shall assemble at least once in every year, . . ." and the 20th

Amendment specifies "and such meeting shall begin at noon on the 3rd day of January, unless they shall by law appoint a different day."

HOBBIT DAY: ANNIVERSARY. Jan 3, 1892. To celebrate the birthday of John Ronald Reuel Tolkien, author of *The Hobbit* (1937) and the trilogy *The Lord of the Rings.* Though best known for his fantasies, Tolkien was also a serious philologist. Born at Bloemfontein, South Africa, he died at Bournemouth, England, Sept 2, 1973.

★ Birthdays ★

Dabney Coleman, actor ("Buffalo Bill," *Nine to Five, Tootsie*), born Austin, TX, Jan 3, 1932.
Mel Gibson, actor (*Braveheart, Lethal Weapon*), born Peekskill, NY, Jan 3, 1956.
Robert Marvin (Bobby) Hull, Hockey Hall of Fame left wing, born Point Anne, ON, Canada, Jan 3, 1939.

January 4

AMNESTY FOR POLYGAMISTS: ANNIVERSARY. Jan 4, 1893. President Benjamin Harrison issued a proclamation granting full amnesty and pardon to all persons who had since Nov 1, 1890, abstained from unlawful cohabitation of a polygamous marriage. The practice of polygamy was a factor interfering with attainment of statehood for Utah.

BRAILLE, LOUIS: BIRTH ANNIVERSARY. Jan 4, 1809. The inventor of a widely used touch system of reading and writing for the blind was born at Coupvray, France. Permanently blinded at the age of three by a leather-working awl in his father's saddle-making shop, Braille developed a system of writing that used, ironically, an awl-like stylus to punch marks in paper that could be felt and interpreted by the blind. The system was largely ignored until after Braille died in poverty, suffering from tuberculosis, at Paris, France, Jan 6, 1852.

NEWTON, ISAAC: BIRTH ANNIVERSARY. Jan 4, 1643. Sir Isaac Newton was the chief figure of the scientific revolution of the 17th century, a physicist and mathematician who laid the foundations of calculus, studied the mechanics of planetary motion and discovered the law of gravitation. Born at Woolsthorpe, England, he died at London, England, Mar 31, 1727.

POP MUSIC CHART INTRODUCED: ANNIVERSARY. Jan 4, 1936. *Billboard* magazine published the first list of best-selling pop records, covering the week that ended Dec 30, 1935. On the list were recordings by the Tommy Dorsey and the Ozzie Nelson orchestras.

UTAH: ADMISSION DAY: ANNIVERSARY. Jan 4. Utah became the 45th state in 1896.

★ *Birthdays* ★

Dyan Cannon, actress (Oscar nominations for *Heaven Can Wait, Bob and Carol and Ted and Alice*), born Tacoma, WA, Jan 4, 1937.

Donald Francis (Don) Shula, Pro Football Hall of Fame coach and player, born Painesville, OH, Jan 4, 1930.

January 5

"ALL MY CHILDREN" TV PREMIERE: ANNIVERSARY. Jan 5, 1970. This ABC show became TV's top-rated soap opera by the 1978–79 season, and it still keeps viewers glued to the screen. "All My Children" was created by Agnes Nixon, who had written for "Search for Tomorrow," "Another World" and "One Life to Live." Cast member Susan Lucci, who became one of daytime TV's most popular actresses, had been nominated more than a dozen times for an Emmy and finally won one in 1999.

CARVER, GEORGE WASHINGTON: DEATH ANNIVERSARY. Jan 5, 1943. Black American agricultural scientist, author, inventor and teacher. Born into slavery at Diamond Grove, MO, probably in 1864. His research led to the creation of synthetic products made from peanuts, potatoes and wood. Carver died at Tuskegee, AL. His birthplace became a national monument in 1953.

FIVE-DOLLAR-A-DAY MINIMUM WAGE: ANNIVERSARY. Jan 5, 1914. Henry Ford announced that all worthy Ford Motor Company employees would receive a minimum wage of $5 a day. Ford explained the policy as "profit sharing and efficiency engineering." The more cynical attributed it to an attempt to prevent unionization and to obtain a docile workforce that would accept job speedups. To obtain this minimum wage an employee had to be of "good personal habits." Whether an individual fit these criteria was determined by a new office created by Ford Motor Company—the Sociological Department.

TWELFTH NIGHT. Jan 5. Evening before Epiphany. Twelfth Night marks the end of medieval Christmas festivities and the end of Twelfthtide (the 12-day season after Christmas ending with Epiphany). Also called Twelfth Day Eve.

★ *Birthdays* ★

Robert Duvall, actor (*A Civil Action, The Godfather*), born San Diego, CA, Jan 5, 1931.

Diane Keaton, actress (Oscar for *Annie Hall; The First Wives Club, The Other Sister*), born Diane Hall at Los Angeles, CA, Jan 5, 1946.

January 6

CARNIVAL SEASON. Jan 6. A secular festival preceding Lent. A time of merrymaking and feasting before the austere days of Lenten fasting and penitence. The word *carnival* probably is derived from the Latin *carnem levare,* meaning "to remove meat." Depending on local custom, the carnival season may start any time between Jan 6 and Shrove Tuesday. Conclusion of the season is much less variable, being the close of Shrove Tuesday in most places. Celebrations vary considerably, but the festival often includes many theatrical aspects (masks, costumes and songs) and has given its name (in the US) to traveling amusement shows that may be seen throughout the year.

EPIPHANY or TWELFTH DAY—THREE KINGS DAY. Jan 6. Known also as Old Christmas Day and Twelfthtide. On the 12th day after Christmas, Christians celebrate the visit of the Magi, the first Gentile recognition of Christ. Epiphany of Our Lord, one of the oldest Christian feasts, is observed in Roman Catholic churches in the US on a Sunday between Jan 2 and 8. Three Kings Day is observed in many parts of the world with gifts, feasting, last lighting of Christmas lights and burning of Christmas greens. Twelfth and last day of the Feast of the Nativity. Commemorates visit of the Three Wise Men (Kings or Magi) to Bethlehem.

"HALLMARK HALL OF FAME" TV PREMIERE: ANNIVERSARY. Jan 6, 1952. Carried at different times by ABC, CBS, NBC and PBS, this was a top-quality dramatic anthology series with splendid performances by many acclaimed actors. Originally titled "Hallmark Television Playhouse," the program was sponsored by Hallmark Cards and hosted by Sarah Churchill until 1955. A few of the presentations: *Hamlet,* with Maurice Evans and Ruth Chatterton (1953); *Macbeth,* with Maurice Evans and Dame Judith Anderson (1954); *Alice in Wonderland,* with Eva LeGallienne and Elsa Lanchester (1955).

NEW MEXICO: ADMISSION DAY: ANNIVERSARY. Jan 6, 1912. Became 47th state in 1912.

SANDBURG, CARL: BIRTH ANNIVERSARY. Jan 6, 1878. American poet, biographer of Lincoln, historian and folklorist, born at Galesburg, IL. Died at Flat Rock, NC, July 22, 1967.

SPACE MILESTONE: *LUNAR EXPLORER* (US). Jan 6, 1998. NASA headed back to the moon for the first time since the *Apollo 17* flight 25 years before. This unmanned probe searched for evidence of frozen water on the moon and found evidence of ice in late 1998.

"WHEEL OF FORTUNE" TV PREMIERE: ANNIVERSARY. Jan 6, 1975. This daytime quiz show was originally hosted by Chuck Woolery. In 1981 Pat Sajak became host, assisted by Vanna White. A nighttime version was added in 1983.

★ *Birthdays* ★

Rowan Atkinson, British actor ("Mr Bean," "Blackadder"), born Newcastle-upon-Tyne, England, Jan 6, 1955.
Howard M. (Howie) Long, sportscaster, Hall of Fame football player, born Somerville, MA, Jan 6, 1960.

January 7

FILLMORE, MILLARD: BIRTH ANNIVERSARY. Jan 7, 1800. The 13th president of the US (July 10, 1850–Mar 3, 1853). Fillmore succeeded to the presidency upon the death of Zachary Taylor, but he did not get the hoped-for nomination from his party in 1852. He ran for president unsuccessfully in 1856 as candidate of the "Know-Nothing Party," whose platform demanded, among other things, that every government employee (federal, state and local) should be a native-born citizen. Fillmore was born at Summerhill, NY, and died at Buffalo, NY, Mar 8, 1874.

OLD CALENDAR ORTHODOX CHRISTMAS. Jan 7. Some Orthodox churches celebrate Christmas on the "old" (Julian) calendar date.

TRANSATLANTIC PHONING: ANNIVERSARY. Jan 7, 1927. Commercial transatlantic telephone service between New York and London was inaugurated. There were 31 calls made the first day.

★ *Birthdays* ★

Nicolas Cage, actor (*Leaving Las Vegas, Con Air*), born Long Beach, CA, Jan 7, 1964.
Katie Couric, cohost ("Today"), born Arlington, VA, Jan 7, 1957.

January 8

AT&T DIVESTITURE: ANNIVERSARY. Jan 8, 1982. In the most significant antitrust suit since the breakup of Standard Oil in 1911, American Telephone and Telegraph agreed to give up its 22 local Bell System companies ("Baby Bells"). These companies represented 80 percent of AT&T's assets. This ended the corporation's virtual monopoly on US telephone service.

BATTLE OF NEW ORLEANS: ANNIVERSARY. Jan 8, 1815. British forces suffered crushing losses (more than 2,000 casualties) in an attack on New Orleans, LA. Defending US troops were led by General Andrew Jackson, who became a popular hero as a result of the victory. Neither side knew that the War of 1812 had ended two weeks previously with the signing of the Treaty of Ghent, Dec 24, 1814. Battle of New Orleans Day is observed in Louisiana.

DOW-JONES TOPS 2,000: ANNIVERSARY. Jan 8, 1987. The Dow-Jones Index of 30 major industrial stocks topped the 2,000 mark for the first time.

EARTH'S ROTATION PROVED: ANNIVERSARY. Jan 8, 1851. Using a device now known as Foucault's pendulum in his Paris home, physicist Jean Foucault demonstrated that Earth rotates on its axis.

PRESLEY, ELVIS AARON: BIRTH ANNIVERSARY. Jan 8, 1935. Popular American rock singer, born at Tupelo, MS. Elvis Presley was pronounced dead at the Memphis Baptist Hospital at 3:30 PM, Aug 16, 1977, at age 42. The anniversary of his death is an occasion for pilgrimages by admirers to Graceland, his home and gravesite at Memphis, TN.

WAR ON POVERTY: ANNIVERSARY. Jan 8, 1964. President Lyndon Johnson declared a War on Poverty in his State of the Union address. He stressed improved education as one of the cor-

nerstones of the program. The following Aug 20, he signed a $947.5 million antipoverty bill designed to assist more than 30 million citizens.

★ *Birthdays* ★

David Bowie, musician, actor (*The Labyrinth*), born David Robert Jones, London, England, Jan 8, 1947.
Charles Osgood, CBS newsman, born New York, NY, Jan 8, 1933.

January 9

CONNECTICUT RATIFIES CONSTITUTION: ANNIVERSARY. Jan 9, 1788. By a vote of 128 to 40, Connecticut became the fifth state to ratify the Constitution.

NIXON, RICHARD MILHOUS: BIRTH ANNIVERSARY. Jan 9, 1913. Richard Nixon served as 36th vice president of the US (under President Dwight D. Eisenhower) Jan 20, 1953, to Jan 20, 1961. He was the 37th president of the US, serving Jan 20, 1969, to Aug 9, 1974, when he resigned the presidency while under the threat of impeachment. First US president to resign that office. He was born at Yorba Linda, CA, and died at New York, NY, Apr 22, 1994.

"3rd ROCK FROM THE SUN" TV PREMIERE: ANNIVERSARY. Jan 9, 1996. In this comedy a quartet of space aliens who had taken on human form came to Earth to spy on its natives. They were led by Dick Solomon, played by John Lithgow, who fell in love with earthling Mary Albright, played by Jane Curtin. Other cast members included Kristen Johnston, French Stewart and Joseph Gordon-Levitt. On May 22, 2001, Commander Solomon was ordered to conclude the mission and bring his crew home. Though it won a slew of Emmys, NBC bounced the series around to more than a dozen time slots, damaging the ratings, and finally pulled the show after six seasons.

★ *Birthdays* ★

Joan Baez, folksinger, born Staten Island, NY, Jan 9, 1941.

Byron Bartlett (Bart) Starr, former football coach, Hall of Fame football player, born Montgomery, AL, Jan 9, 1934.

January 10

***COMMON SENSE* PUBLISHED: ANNIVERSARY.** Jan 10, 1776. More than any other publication, *Common Sense* influenced the authors of the Declaration of Independence. Thomas Paine's 50-page pamphlet sold more than 500,000 copies within a few months of its first printing.

LEAGUE OF NATIONS FOUNDING: ANNIVERSARY. Jan 10, 1920. Through the Treaty of Versailles, the League of Nations came into existence. Fifty nations entered into a covenant designed to avoid war. The US never joined the League of Nations, which was dissolved Apr 18, 1946.

"MASTERPIECE THEATRE" TV PREMIERE: ANNIVERSARY. Jan 10, 1971. Television at its best, PBS's long-running anthology series consists of many highly acclaimed original and adapted dramatizations. Many are produced by the BBC. Alistair Cooke and Russell Baker have hosted the program. The first presentation was "The First Churchills." Other notable programs include: "The Six Wives of Henry VIII" and "Elizabeth R" (1972); "Upstairs, Downstairs" (1974–77); "I, Claudius" (1978); "The Jewel in the Crown" (1984); "Bleak House" (1985); "Sharpe" (1993–95) and "David Copperfield" (2001).

UNITED NATIONS GENERAL ASSEMBLY: ANNIVERSARY. Jan 10, 1946. On the 26th anniversary of the establishment of the unsuccessful League of Nations, delegates from 51 nations met at London, England, for the first meeting of the United Nations General Assembly.

WOMEN'S SUFFRAGE AMENDMENT INTRODUCED IN CONGRESS: ANNIVERSARY. Jan 10, 1878. Senator A.A. Sargent of California, a close friend of Susan B. Anthony, introduced into the US Senate a women's suffrage amendment known as the Susan B. Anthony Amendment. It wasn't until Aug 26, 1920, 42 years later, that the amendment was signed into law.

★ Birthdays ★

George Edward Foreman, boxer, born Marshall, TX, Jan 10, 1949.

Rod Stewart, singer ("Maggie May"), born London, England, Jan 10, 1945.

★ Birthdays ★

Mary J. Blige, pop singer, born the Bronx, NY, Jan 11, 1971.

Jean Chretien, 20th prime minister of Canada, born Shawinigan, QC, Canada, Jan 11, 1934.

January 11

"DESIGNATED HITTER" RULE ADOPTED: ANNIVERSARY. Jan 11, 1973. American League adopted the "designated hitter" rule, whereby an additional player is used to bat for the pitcher.

HAMILTON, ALEXANDER: BIRTH ANNIVERSARY. Jan 11, 1755. American statesman, an author of *The Federalist* papers, first secretary of the treasury, born at British West Indies. Engaged in a duel with Aaron Burr the morning of July 11, 1804, at Weehawken, NJ. Mortally wounded there and died July 12, 1804.

MOROCCO: INDEPENDENCE DAY. Jan 11. National holiday. Commemorates the date in 1944 when the Independence Party submitted a memo to the Allied authorities asking for independence under a constitutional regime. Morocco gained independence from France in 1956.

US SURGEON GENERAL DECLARES CIGARETTES HAZARDOUS: ANNIVERSARY. Jan 11, 1964. US Surgeon General Luther Terry issued the first government report saying that smoking may be hazardous to one's health.

January 12

"ALL IN THE FAMILY" TV PREMIERE: ANNIVERSARY. Jan 12, 1971. Based on the success of a British comedy, Norman Lear created CBS's controversial sitcom "All in the Family." The series was the first of its kind to realistically portray the prevailing issues and taboos of its time with a wickedly humorous bent. Ultraconservative Archie Bunker (played by Carroll O'Connor) held court from his recliner, spewing invective at any who disagreed with him. Jean Stapleton portrayed Archie's dutiful wife, Edith. Sally Struthers and Rob Reiner rounded out the cast as Archie's liberal daughter and son-in-law, Gloria and Mike "Meathead" Stivic. The series had a 12-year run.

"BATMAN" TV PREMIERE: ANNIVERSARY. Jan 12, 1966. ABC's crime-fighting show gained a place in Nielsen's top ten ratings in its first season. The series was based on the DC Comics characters created by Bob Kane in 1939. Adam

West starred as Batman. Burt Ward costarred as Robin, the Boy Wonder. An assortment of villains guest-starring each week included Cesar Romero as the Joker, Eartha Kitt and Julie Newmar as Catwoman, Burgess Meredith as the Penguin and Frank Gorshin as the Riddler. Some other stars making memorable appearances included Liberace, Vincent Price, Milton Berle, Tallulah Bankhead and Ethel Merman. Although the last telecast was Mar 14, 1968, "Batman" can be seen today with some 120 episodes in syndication. Many Batman movies have been made, the first in 1943. The most recent was *Batman & Robin*, released in 1997 and starring George Clooney and Chris O'Donnell.

"DYNASTY" TV PREMIERE: ANNIVERSARY. Jan 12, 1981. The popular ABC prime-time serial focused on the high-flying exploits of the Denver-based Carrington family. The series had a weekly wardrobe budget of $10,000 with many elegant costumes designed by Nolan Miller. Many tuned in worldwide to view the palatial mansions and lavish sets as well as the juicy story lines. John Forsythe played patriarch Blake Carrington with Linda Evans as his wife, Krystle. Joan Collins played Alexis, Blake's scheming ex-wife and arch business rival.

FIRST ELECTED WOMAN SENATOR: ANNIVERSARY. Jan 12, 1932. Hattie W. Caraway, a Democrat from Arkansas, was the first woman elected to the US Senate. Born in 1878, Caraway was appointed to the Senate on Nov 13, 1931, to fill out the term of her late husband, Senator Thad-deus Caraway. On Jan 12, 1932, she won a special election to fill the remaining months of his term. Subsequently elected to two more terms, she served in the Senate until January 1945. She was an adept and tireless legislator (once introducing 43 bills on the same day) who worked for women's rights and supported New Deal policies. She died Dec 21, 1950, at Falls Church, VA. The first woman appointed to the Senate was Mrs W.H. Felton, who served for two days in 1922. The first woman to be elected to the Senate without having been appointed first was Margaret Chase Smith of Maine, who had served first in the House. She was elected to the Senate in 1948.

HANCOCK, JOHN: BIRTH ANNIVERSARY. Jan 12, 1737 (OS). American patriot and statesman, first signer of the Declaration of Independence. Born at Braintree, MA, he died at Quincy, MA, Oct 8, 1793. Because of his conspicuous signature on the Declaration, Hancock's name has become part of the American language, referring to any handwritten signature, as in "Put your John Hancock on that!" Observed as National Handwriting Day.

LONDON, JACK: BIRTH ANNIVERSARY. Jan 12, 1876. American author of more than 50 books: short stories, novels and travel stories of the sea and of the far north, many marked by brutal realism. His most widely known work is *The Call of the Wild,* the great dog story published in 1903. London was born at San Francisco, CA. He died by suicide Nov 22, 1916, near Santa Rosa, CA.

★ Birthdays ★

Kirstie Alley, actress (Emmy for "Cheers"; *Look Who's Talking*, "Veronica's Closet"), born Wichita, KS, Jan 12, 1955.
Rush Limbaugh, talk-show host ("The Rush Limbaugh Show"), born Cape Girardeau, MO, Jan 12, 1951.

January 13

ALGER, HORATIO, JR: BIRTH ANNIVERSARY. Jan 13, 1834. American clergyman and author of more than 100 popular books for boys (some 20 million copies sold). Honesty, frugality and hard work assured that the heroes of his books would find success, wealth and fame. Born at Revere, MA, he died at Natick, MA, July 18, 1899.

RADIO BROADCASTING: ANNIVERSARY. Jan 13, 1910. Radio pioneer and electron tube inventor Lee De Forest arranged the world's first radio broadcast to the public at New York, NY. He succeeded in broadcasting the voice of Enrico Caruso along with other stars of the Metropolitan Opera to several receiving locations in the city where listeners with earphones marveled at wireless music from the air. Though only a few were equipped to listen, it was the first broadcast to reach the public and the beginning of a new era in which wireless radio communication became almost universal. See also: "First Scheduled Radio Broadcast: Anniv" (Nov 2).

STEPHEN FOSTER MEMORIAL DAY. Jan 13. The anniversary of Foster's death in 1864 at New York, NY, has been observed as Stephen Foster Memorial Day by Presidential Proclamation since 1952. Foster, one of America's most famous and most-beloved songwriters, was born July 4, 1826, at Lawrenceville, PA. Among his nearly 200 songs: "Oh! Susanna," "Camptown Races," "Old Folks at Home" ("Swanee River"), "Jeanie with the Light Brown Hair," "Old Black Joe" and "Beautiful Dreamer."

★ Birthdays ★

Julia Louis-Dreyfus, actress ("Seinfeld"), born New York, NY, Jan 13, 1961.
Penelope Ann Miller, actress (*The Freshman, Carlito's Way*), born Los Angeles, CA, Jan 13, 1964.

January 14

ARNOLD, BENEDICT: BIRTH ANNIVERSARY. Jan 14, 1741 (OS). American officer who deserted to the British during the Revolutionary War and whose name has since become synonymous with treachery. Born at Norwich, CT. Died June 14, 1801, at London, England.

RATIFICATION DAY. Jan 14, 1784. Anniversary of the act that officially ended the American Revolution and established the US as a sovereign power. On Jan 14, 1784, the Continental Congress, meeting at Annapolis, MD, ratified the Treaty of Paris, thus fulfilling the Declaration of Independence of July 4, 1776.

"SANFORD AND SON" TV PREMIERE: ANNIVERSARY. Jan 14, 1972. NBC sitcom that gained immediate popularity depicting an African American father and son engaged in the junkyard business. Comedian Redd Foxx played Fred Sanford. His son, Lamont, was played by Demond Wilson. Others appearing on the show were Whitman Mayo as Grady, Slappy White as Melvin and LaWanda Page as Aunt Esther. The last telecast was Sept 2, 1977.

"TODAY" TV PREMIERE: ANNIVERSARY. Jan 14, 1952. NBC program that started the morning news format we know today. Hosted by Dave Garroway, the show was segmented with bits of news, sports, weather, interviews and other features that were repeated so that viewers did not have to stop their morning routine to watch. The addition of chimpanzee J. Fred Muggs in 1953 helped push ratings up. There have been a number of hosts over the years, from John Chancellor and Hugh Downs to Tom Brokaw, Bryant Gumbel and Matt Lauer. Female hosts (originally called "Today Girls") include Betsy

Palmer, Florence Henderson, Barbara Walters, Jane Pauley and Katie Couric.

★ Birthdays ★

Faye Dunaway, actress (*Bonnie and Clyde, Chinatown*; Oscar for *Network*), born Bascom, FL, Jan 14, 1941.

Emily Watson, actress (*Angela's Ashes, Gosford Park*), born London, England, Jan 14, 1967.

January 15

FIRST SUPER BOWL: ANNIVERSARY. Jan 15, 1967. The Green Bay Packers won the first NFL–AFL World Championship Game, defeating the Kansas City Chiefs, 35–10, at the Los Angeles Memorial Coliseum. Packers quarterback Bart Starr was named the game's Most Valuable Player. Pro football's title game later became known as the Super Bowl and is now played on the last Sunday in January.

"HAPPY DAYS" TV PREMIERE: ANNIVERSARY. Jan 15, 1974. This nostalgic comedy set in Milwaukee in the 1950s starred Ron Howard as teenager Richie Cunningham with Anson Williams and Don Most as his best friends "Potsie" Weber and Ralph Malph. Tom Bosley and Marion Ross played Richie's parents, and his sister Joanie was played by Erin Moran. The most memorable character was The Fonz—Arthur "Fonzie" Fonzarelli—played by Henry Winkler. "Happy Days" remained on the air until July 12,

1984, and has been in syndication ever since. "Laverne and Shirley" was a spin-off.

"HILL STREET BLUES" TV PREMIERE: ANNIVERSARY. Jan 15, 1981. Immensely popular NBC police scrics that focuscd morc on policc officcrs than on crime. The show was realistic and highly praised by real police officers. It won a slew of Emmys and ran for seven seasons. Cast: Daniel J. Travanti as Captain Frank Furillo, Veronica Hamel as public defender Joyce Davenport, Michael Conrad as Sergeant Phil "Let's be careful out there" Esterhaus, Barbara Bosson as Fay Furillo, and as the wonderfully drawn cops, Bruce Weitz (Mick Belker), Taurean Blacque (Neal Washington), Kiel Martin (Johnny LaRue), Joe Spano (Henry Goldblume), James B. Sikking (Howard Hunter), René Enríquez (Ray Calletano), Michael Warren (Bobby Hill), Betty Thomas (Lucy Bates), Ed Marinaro (Joe Coffey) and Charles Haid (Andy Renko). The last telecast was May 19, 1987.

KING, MARTIN LUTHER, JR: BIRTH ANNIVERSARY. Jan 15, 1929. Black civil rights leader, minister, advocate of nonviolence and recipient of the Nobel Peace Prize (1964). Born at Atlanta, GA, he was assassinated at Memphis, TN, Apr 4, 1968. After his death many states and territories observed his birthday as a holiday. In 1983 the Congress approved House Resolution 3706, "A bill to amend Title 5, United States Code, to make the birthday of Martin Luther King, Jr, a legal public holiday." Signed by the president on Nov 2, 1983, it became Public Law 98–144, which sets the third Monday in January for observance of King's birthday. First observance was Jan 20, 1986.

PENTAGON COMPLETED: ANNIVERSARY. Jan 15, 1943. The world's largest office building with 6.5 million square feet of usable space, the Pentagon is located in Virginia across the Potomac River from Washington, DC, and serves as headquarters for the Department of Defense.

★ *Birthdays* ★

Andrea Martin, actress, (*Wag the Dog, Hedwig and the Angry Inch*), born Portland, ME, Jan 15, 1947.

Margaret O'Brien, actress (*Meet Me in St. Louis, Little Women*), born San Diego, CA, Jan 15, 1937.

January 16

DEAN, DIZZY: BIRTH ANNIVERSARY. Jan 16, 1911. Jay Hanna "Dizzy" Dean, major league pitcher (St. Louis Cardinals) and Baseball Hall of Fame member, was born at Lucas, AR. Following his baseball career, Dean established himself as a radio and TV sports announcer and commentator, becoming famous for his innovative delivery. "He slud into third," reported Dizzy, who on another occasion explained that "Me and Paul [baseball player brother Paul "Daffy" Dean] . . . didn't get much education." Died at Reno, NV, July 17, 1974.

NATIONAL NOTHING DAY: ANNIVERSARY. Jan 16. Anniversary of National Nothing Day, an event created by the late newspaperman Harold Pullman Coffin and first observed in 1973 "to provide Americans with one national day when they can just sit without celebrating, observing or honoring anything." Since 1975, though many other events have been listed on this day, lighthearted traditional observance of Coffin's idea has continued.

PERSIAN GULF WAR BEGINS: ANNIVERSARY. Jan 16, 1991. Allied forces launched a major air offensive against Iraq to begin the Gulf War. The strike was designed to destroy Iraqi air defenses, command, control and communication centers. As Desert Shield became Desert Storm, the world was able to see and hear for the first time an initial engagement of war as CNN broadcasters, stationed at Baghdad, covered the attack live.

PROHIBITION (EIGHTEENTH) AMENDMENT: ANNIVERSARY. Jan 16, 1919. Nebraska became the 36th state to ratify the Prohibition amendment, and the 18th Amendment became part of the US Constitution. One year later, Jan 16, 1920, the 18th Amendment took effect, and the sale of alcoholic beverages became illegal in the US with the Volstead Act providing for enforcement. This was the first time that an amendment to the Constitution dealt with a social issue. The 21st Amendment, repealing the 18th, went into effect Dec 6, 1933.

RELIGIOUS FREEDOM DAY. Jan 16, 1786. The legislature of Virginia adopted a religious freedom statute that protected Virginians against any requirement to attend or support any church and against discrimination. This statute, which had been drafted by Thomas Jefferson and introduced by James Madison, later was the model for the First Amendment to the US Constitution.

★ Birthdays ★

Debbie Allen, dancer, choreographer, singer, actress ("Fame"), born Houston, TX, Jan 16, 1950.

Eartha Kitt, singer ("Santa Baby"), born North, SC, Jan 16, 1928.

January 17

FIRST NUCLEAR-POWERED SUBMARINE VOYAGE: ANNIVERSARY. Jan 17, 1955. At 11 AM, EST, the commanding officer of the world's first nuclear-powered submarine, the *Nautilus,* ordered all lines cast off and sent the historic message: "Under way on nuclear power." It now forms part of the *Nautilus* Memorial Submarine Force Library and Museum at the Naval Submarine Base at Groton, CT.

FRANKLIN, BENJAMIN: BIRTH ANNIVERSARY. Jan 17, 1706. "Elder statesman of the American Revolution," oldest signer of both the Declaration of Independence and the Constitution, scientist, diplomat, author, printer, publisher, philosopher, philanthropist and self-made, self-educated man. Author, printer and publisher of *Poor Richard's Almanack* (1733–58). Born at Boston, MA, Franklin died at Philadelphia, PA, Apr 17, 1790. In 1728 Franklin wrote a premature epitaph for himself: "The Body of BENJAMIN FRANKLIN/Printer/Like a Covering of an old Book/Its contents torn out/And stript of its Lettering and Gilding,/Lies here, Food for Worms;/But the work shall not be lost,/It will (as he believ'd) appear once more/In a New and more beautiful Edition/Corrected and amended/By the Author."

IKE'S FAREWELL: ANNIVERSARY. Jan 17, 1961. President Dwight D. Eisenhower, in his farewell address to the nation on national radio and television, spoke the sentences that would be the most quoted and remembered of his presidency. In a direct warning, he said, "In the councils of government, we must guard against the acquisition of unwarranted influence, whether sought or unsought, by the military-industrial complex. The potential for the disastrous rise of misplaced power exists and persists."

PGA OF AMERICA FOUNDED: ANNIVERSARY. Jan 17, 1916. Golf great Walter Hagen and some 30 other pro golfers met and formed the Professional Golfers' Association of America and also developed the idea for a national championship.

Rodman Wanamaker provided the trophy and the $2,580 purse for the first PGA Championship, which was played Apr 10, 1916, at the Siwanoy course at Bronxville, NY. The winner was British golfer Jim Barnes, who also won the second competition held in 1919. In 1921 Walter Hagen became the first American to win, a feat he accomplished four more times—in 1924, '25, '26 and '27.

SOUTHERN CALIFORNIA EARTHQUAKE: ANNIVERSARY. Jan 17, 1994. An earthquake measuring 6.6 on the Richter scale struck the Los Angeles area about 4:20 AM. The epicenter was at Northridge in the San Fernando Valley, about 20 miles northwest of downtown Los Angeles. A death toll of 51 was announced Jan 20. Sixteen of the dead were killed in the collapse of one apartment building. More than 25,000 people were made homeless by the quake and 680,000 lost electric power. Many buildings were destroyed and others made uninhabitable due to structural damage. A section of the Santa Monica Freeway, part of the Simi Valley Freeway and three major overpasses collapsed. Hundreds of aftershocks occurred in the following several weeks. Costs to repair the damages were estimated at 15–30 billion dollars.

★ *Birthdays* ★

Muhammad Ali, former heavyweight champion boxer, who changed his name after converting to Islam, born Cassius Marcellus Clay, Jr, at Louisville, KY, Jan 17, 1942.

Jim Carrey, actor (*Dumb and Dumber, The Truman Show, Ace Ventura*), comedian ("In Living Color"), born Newmarket, ON, Canada, Jan 17, 1962.

James Earl Jones, actor (*The Great White Hope, Field of Dreams, Roots: The Next Generations;* voice of Darth Vader in the *Star Wars* movies), born Arkabutla, MS, Jan 17, 1931.

January 18

FIRST BLACK US CABINET MEMBER: ANNIVERSARY. Jan 18, 1966. Robert Clifton Weaver was sworn in as US Secretary of Housing and Urban Development, becoming the first black cabinet member in US history. He was nominated by President Lyndon Johnson. Born Dec 29, 1907, at Washington, DC, Weaver died at New York, NY, July 17, 1997.

GRANT, CARY: BIRTH ANNIVERSARY. Jan 18, 1904. Known as a romantic leading actor, Grant was born at Bristol, England. For more than three decades Grant entertained with his wit, charm, sophistication and personality. His films include *Topper, The Awful Truth, Bringing Up Baby* and *Holiday.* Died at Davenport, IA, Nov 29, 1986.

"THE JEFFERSONS" TV PREMIERE: ANNIVERSARY. Jan 18, 1975. CBS sitcom about an African American family (formerly neighbors of the Bunkers on "All in the Family") who moved to Manhattan's East Side, thanks to the success of George Jefferson's chain of dry cleaning stores. Having a format similar to "All in the Family," the show featured a black bigot, George Jefferson. The show was able to humorously introduce subjects such as mixed marriage on a prime-time series. Cast included Sherman Hemsley as George Jefferson, Isabel Sanford as Louise Jefferson, Mike Evans and Damon Evans as Lionel and Franklin Cover and Roxie Roker as Tom and Helen Willis. The last episode aired July 23, 1985.

KAYE, DANNY: BIRTH ANNIVERSARY. Jan 18, 1913. American entertainer Danny Kaye was born David Daniel Kaminski at Brooklyn, NY. Kaye became a star in films, international stage performances and television. His most notable films are *The Secret Life of Walter Mitty* (1947) and *Hans Christian Andersen* (1952), as well as the classic *White Christmas.* He hosted the television show "The Danny Kaye Show" in the 1960s. In addition, Kaye helped raise millions of dollars for the United Nations International Children's Emergency Fund (UNICEF). He died Mar 3, 1987, at Los Angeles, CA.

POOH DAY: A.A. MILNE: BIRTH ANNIVERSARY. Jan 18, 1882. Anniversary of the birth of A(lan) A(lexander) Milne, English author, especially remembered for his children's stories *Winnie the Pooh* and *The House at Pooh Corner.* Also the author of *When We Were Very Young* and *Now We Are Six.* Born at London, England, died at Hartfield, England, Jan 31, 1956.

★ Birthdays ★

Kevin Costner, actor (*Field of Dreams, Dances with Wolves* [Oscar for directing], *Bull Durham*), born Compton, CA, Jan 18, 1955.
Jesse L. Martin, actor ("Law & Order," "Ally McBeal"), born Rocky Mountain, VA, Jan 18, 1969.

January 19

CÉZANNE, PAUL: BIRTH ANNIVERSARY. Jan 19, 1839. Post-Impressionist painter, born at Aix-en-Provence, France. Still lifes and landscapes were his preferred subjects. Cézanne died Oct 23, 1906, at Aix.

"48 HOURS" TV PREMIERE: ANNIVERSARY. Jan 19, 1988. CBS prime-time newsmagazine program airing each week with Dan Rather as anchor and Bernard Goldberg as main correspondent.

LEE, ROBERT E.: BIRTH ANNIVERSARY. Jan 19, 1807. Greatest military leader of the Confederacy, son of Revolutionary War General Henry (Light Horse Harry) Lee. His surrender Apr 9, 1865, to Union General Ulysses S. Grant brought an end to the Civil War. Born at Westmoreland County, VA, he died at Lexington, VA, Oct 12, 1870. His birthday is observed in Florida, Kentucky, Louisiana, South Carolina and Tennessee. Observed on third Monday in January in Alabama, Arkansas and Mississippi.

POE, EDGAR ALLAN: BIRTH ANNIVERSARY. Jan 19, 1809. American poet and story writer, called "America's most famous man of letters." Born at Boston, MA, he was orphaned in dire poverty in 1811 and was raised by Virginia merchant John Allan. A magazine editor of note, he is best remembered for his poetry (especially "The Raven") and for his tales of suspense. Died at Baltimore, MD, Oct 7, 1849.

TIN CAN PATENT: ANNIVERSARY. Jan 19, 1825. Ezra Daggett and Thomas Kensett obtained a patent for a process for storing food in tin cans.

★ Birthdays ★

Dolly Parton, singer ("Jolene"), actress (*Nine to Five*), born Sevier County, TN, Jan 19, 1946.
Jean Stapleton, actress (*Klute*; Emmy for "All in the Family"), born Jeanne Murray, New York, NY, Jan 19, 1923.

January 20

AQUARIUS, THE WATER CARRIER. Jan 20–Feb 19. In the astronomical/astrological zodiac, which divides the sun's apparent orbit into 12 segments, the period Jan 20–Feb 19 is identified, traditionally, as the sun sign of Aquarius, the Water Carrier. The ruling planet is Uranus or Saturn.

BURNS, GEORGE: BIRTH ANNIVERSARY. Jan 20, 1896. Comedian George Burns was born at New York City. He began in vaudeville without much success until he teamed up with Gracie Allen, who became his wife. As Burns and Allen, the two had a long career on radio, in film and with their hit TV show, "The George Burns and Gracie Allen Show." More recently he played the role of God and the Devil in the *Oh, God!* movies. He lived to be 100 and died Mar 9, 1996, at Los Angeles, CA.

CAMCORDER DEVELOPED: ANNIVERSARY. Jan 20, 1982. Five companies (Hitachi, JVC, Philips, Matsushita and Sony) agreed to cooperate on the construction of a camera with a built-in videocassette recorder.

★ *Birthdays* ★

Edwin "Buzz" Aldrin, former astronaut, one of first three men on moon, born Montclair, NJ, Jan 20, 1930.
Bill Maher, comedian, TV host ("Politically Incorrect with Bill Maher"), born New York, NY, Jan 20, 1956.

January 21

FIRST CONCORDE FLIGHT: ANNIVERSARY. Jan 21, 1976. The supersonic Concorde airplane was put into service by Britain (from London to Bahrain) and France (Paris to Rio).

JACKSON, THOMAS JONATHAN "STONEWALL": BIRTH ANNIVERSARY. Jan 21, 1824. Confederate general and one of the most famous soldiers of the American Civil War, best known as "Stonewall" Jackson. Born at Clarksburg, VA (now WV). He died of wounds received in battle near Chancellorsville, VA, May 10, 1863.

★ *Birthdays* ★

Geena Davis, actress (Oscar for *The Accidental Tourist; Thelma and Louise*, "Buffalo Bill"), born Ware, MA, Jan 21, 1957.
Placido Domingo, opera singer, one of the "Three Tenors," born Madrid, Spain, Jan 21, 1941.
Jack William Nicklaus, golfer, born Columbus, OH, Jan 21, 1940.

January 22

"LAUGH-IN" TV PREMIERE: ANNIVERSARY. Jan 22, 1968. Actually the name of this NBC comedy was "Rowan and Martin's Laugh-In." Funny men Dan Rowan and Dick Martin hosted the show, but they seemed staid next to the show's other regulars, including Dennis Allen, Chelsea Brown, Judy Carne, Ruth Buzzi, Ann Elder, Richard Dawson, Teresa Graves, Arte Johnson, Goldie Hawn, Alan Sues, Jo Anne Worley and Lily Tomlin. The show moved fast from gag to gag, bringing a new energy to comedy as well as new phrases to our vocabulary ("You bet your sweet bippy," "Sock it to me"). The last telecast was May 14, 1973.

QUEEN VICTORIA: DEATH ANNIVERSARY. Jan 22, 1901. Queen Victoria died at age 82 after a reign of 64 years, the longest in British history. She had ruled over the one-quarter of the world that was the British Empire. Born May 24, 1819, at London, she died at Osborne, England.

***ROE v WADE* DECISION: ANNIVERSARY.** Jan 22, 1973. In the case of *Roe v Wade*, the US Supreme Court struck down state laws restricting abortions during the first six months of pregnancy. In the following three decades debate has continued to rage between those who believe a woman has a right to choose whether to continue a pregnancy and those who believe that aborting such a pregnancy is murder of an unborn child.

★ *Birthdays* ★

Linda Blair, actress (*The Exorcist, Airport*), born Westport, CT, Jan 22, 1959.
John Hurt, actor ("And the Band Played On," *The Elephant Man*), born Lincolnshire, England, Jan 22, 1940.

January 23

"BARNEY MILLER" TV PREMIERE: ANNIVERSARY. Jan 23, 1975. ABC sitcom about a New York precinct captain starred Hal Linden as Captain Barney Miller. The 12th Precinct gang included Barbara Barrie as Miller's wife, Abe Vigoda as Detective Phil Fish, Max Gail as Sergeant Stan Wojciehowicz, Gregory Sierra as Sergeant Chano Amenguale, Jack Soo as Sergeant Nick Yemana and Ron Glass as Detective Ron Harris. The last episode aired in 1982.

MANET, ÉDOUARD: BIRTH ANNIVERSARY. Jan 23, 1832. Painter, born at Paris, France. Among his best-known paintings are *Olympia* and *Déjeuner sur l'herbe*. Manet died Apr 30, 1883, at Paris.

TWENTIETH AMENDMENT TO US CONSTITUTION RATIFIED: ANNIVERSARY. Jan 23, 1933. The 20th Amendment was ratified, fixing the date of the presidential inauguration at the current Jan 20 instead of the previous Mar 4. It also specified that were the president-elect to die before taking office, the vice-president-elect would succeed to the presidency. In addition, it set Jan 3 as the official opening date of Congress each year.

TWENTY-FOURTH AMENDMENT TO US CONSTITUTION RATIFIED: ANNIVERSARY. Jan 23, 1964. Poll taxes and other taxes were eliminated as a prerequisite for voting in all federal elections by the 24th Amendment.

★ *Birthdays* ★

Richard Dean Anderson, actor ("MacGyver"), born Minneapolis, MN, Jan 23, 1950.
Mariska Hargitay, actress ("Law & Order: Special Victims Unit"), born Los Angeles, CA, Jan 23, 1964.

January 24

BELUSHI, JOHN: BIRTH ANNIVERSARY. Jan 24, 1949. Actor, comedian ("Saturday Night Live," *Animal House, The Blues Brothers*), born at Chicago, IL. Died Mar 5, 1982, at Hollywood, CA.

CALIFORNIA GOLD DISCOVERY: ANNIVERSARY. Jan 24, 1848. James W. Marshal, an employee of John Sutter, accidentally discovered gold while building a sawmill near Coloma, CA. Efforts to keep the discovery secret failed, and the gold rush of 1849 was under way.

FIRST CANNED BEER: ANNIVERSARY. Jan 24, 1935. Canned beer went on sale for the first time, at Richmond, VA.

★ *Birthdays* ★

Neil Diamond, singer, composer ("Cracklin' Rosie," "Song Sung Blue"), born Coney Island, NY, Jan 24, 1941.
Matthew Lillard, actor (*Scream*), born Lansing, MI, Jan 24, 1970.

January 25

CAPONE, AL: DEATH ANNIVERSARY. Jan 25, 1947. Gangster Alphonse ("Scarface") Capone, who dominated organized crime in Chicago throughout Prohibition, died at age 48 at Miami after suffering from syphilis. Capone was born Jan 17, 1899, at Naples, Italy, and moved with his family to Brooklyn, NY.

FIRST SCHEDULED TRANSCONTINENTAL FLIGHT: ANNIVERSARY. Jan 25, 1959. American Airlines opened the jet age in the US with the first scheduled transcontinental flight on a Boeing 707 nonstop from California to New York.

FIRST TELEVISED PRESIDENTIAL NEWS CONFERENCE: ANNIVERSARY. Jan 25, 1961. Beginning a tradition that survives to this day, John F.

Kennedy held the first televised presidential news conference five days after being inaugurated the 35th president.

FIRST WINTER OLYMPICS: ANNIVERSARY. Jan 25, 1924. The first Winter Olympic Games opened in Chamonix, France, with athletes representing 16 nations. The ski jump, previously unknown, thrilled spectators. The Olympics offered a boost to skiing, which would make enormous strides in the next decade.

MACINTOSH DEBUTS: ANNIVERSARY. Jan 25, 1984. Apple's Macintosh computer went on sale this day for $2,495. It wasn't until mid-1985, however, that sales began to take off and this computer began to replace the Apple II model.

A ROOM OF ONE'S OWN DAY. Jan 25. For anyone who knows or longs for the sheer bliss and rightness of having a private place, no matter how humble, to call one's own. On the birthday of Virginia Woolf, author of *A Room of One's Own*. [©2001 by WH.] For info: Wellcat Holidays. Web: www.wellcat.com.

★ *Birthdays* ★

Alicia Keys, singer, born Alicia Cook, New York, NY, Jan 25, 1981.
Dinah Manoff, actress (Tony Award for *I Ought to Be in Pictures* [stage]; *Grease,* "Empty Nest"), born New York, NY, Jan 25, 1958.

January 26

AUSTRALIA: AUSTRALIA DAY. Jan 26, 1788. A shipload of convicts arrived briefly at Botany Bay (which proved to be unsuitable) and then at Port Jackson (later the site of the city of Sydney). Establishment of an Australian prison colony, the first British settlement in Australia, was to relieve crowding of British prisons. Australia Day, formerly known as Foundation Day or Anniversary Day, has been a public holiday since 1838.

LOTUS 1-2-3 RELEASED: ANNIVERSARY. Jan 26, 1983. This spreadsheet software drove demand for the IBM PC, just as the introduction of VisiCalc had for the Apple II in 1979.

MacARTHUR, DOUGLAS: BIRTH ANNIVERSARY. Jan 26, 1880. US general and supreme commander of Allied forces in the Southwest Pacific during World War II. Born at Little Rock, AR, he served as commander of the Rainbow Division's 84th Infantry Brigade in World War I, leading it in the St. Mihiel, Meuse-Argonne and Sedan offensives. Remembered for his "I shall return" prediction when forced out of the Philippines by the Japanese during World War II, a promise he fulfilled. Relieved of Far Eastern command by President Harry Truman on Apr 11, 1951, during the Korean War. MacArthur died at Washington, DC, Apr 5, 1964.

MICHIGAN: ADMISSION DAY: ANNIVERSARY. Jan 26. Became 26th state in 1837.

★ Birthdays ★

Ellen DeGeneres, comedienne, actress ("Ellen"), born New Orleans, LA, Jan 26, 1958.

Wayne Gretzky, Hall of Fame hockey player, born Brantford, ON, Canada, Jan 26, 1961.

Paul Newman, actor (Oscar for *The Color of Money; Cat on a Hot Tin Roof, Butch Cassidy and the Sundance Kid*), director (*Rachel, Rachel; The Glass Menagerie*), born Cleveland, OH, Jan 26, 1925.

January 27

***APOLLO I*: SPACECRAFT FIRE: ANNIVERSARY.** Jan 27, 1967. Three American astronauts, Virgil I. Grissom, Edward H. White and Roger B. Chaffee, died when fire suddenly broke out at 6:31 PM in *Apollo I* during a launching simulation test, as it stood on the ground at Cape Kennedy,

FL. First launching in the Apollo program had been scheduled for Feb 27, 1967.

CARROLL, LEWIS (CHARLES LUTWIDGE DODGSON): BIRTH ANNIVERSARY. Jan 27, 1832. English mathematician and author, best known by his pseudonym, Lewis Carroll, creator of *Alice's Adventures in Wonderland,* was born at Cheshire, England. *Alice* was written for Alice Liddell, daughter of a friend, and first published in 1886. *Through the Looking-Glass,* a sequel, and *The Hunting of the Snark* followed. Carroll's books for children proved equally enjoyable to adults, and they overshadowed his serious works on mathematics. He died at Guildford, Surrey, England, Jan 14, 1898.

MOZART, WOLFGANG AMADEUS: BIRTH ANNIVERSARY. Jan 27, 1756. One of the world's greatest music makers. Born at Salzburg, Austria, into a gifted musical family, Mozart began performing at age three and composing at age five. Some of the best known of his more than 600 compositions include the operas *Marriage of Figaro, Don Giovanni, Cosi fan tutte* and *The Magic Flute,* his unfinished Requiem Mass, his C major symphony known as the "Jupiter" and many of his quartets and piano concertos. He died at Vienna, Austria, Dec 5, 1791.

THOMAS CRAPPER DAY. Jan 27, 1910. Born at Thorne, Yorkshire, England, in 1836 (exact date unknown), Crapper is often described as the prime developer of flush toilet mechanism as it is known today. The flush toilet had been in use for more than 100 years; Crapper perfected it. He founded Thomas Crapper & Co in London in 1861, which later patented and manufactured sanitary appliances. Died Jan 27, 1910.

VIETNAM PEACE AGREEMENT SIGNED: ANNIVERSARY. Jan 27, 1973. US and North Vietnam, along with South Vietnam and the Vietcong, signed an "Agreement on ending the war and restoring peace in Vietnam." Signed at Paris, France, to take effect Jan 28 at 8 AM Saigon time, thus ending US combat role in a war that had involved American personnel stationed in Vietnam since defeated French forces had departed under terms of the Geneva Accords in 1954. This was the longest war in US history, with more than 1 million combat deaths (US: 47,366). However, within weeks of the departure of American troops the war between North and South Vietnam resumed. For the Vietnamese, the war didn't end until Apr 30, 1975, when Saigon fell to Communist forces.

★ *Birthdays* ★

Mikhail Baryshnikov, ballet dancer, actor (*White Nights, The Turning Point*), born Riga, Latvia, USSR, Jan 27, 1948.

Bridget Fonda, actress (*Single White Female, Lake Placid*), daughter of Peter Fonda, born Los Angeles, CA, Jan 27, 1964.

January 28

***CHALLENGER* SPACE SHUTTLE EXPLOSION: ANNIVERSARY.** Jan 28, 1986. At 11:39 AM, EST, the space shuttle *Challenger STS-51L* exploded, 74 seconds into its flight and about ten miles above Earth. Hundreds of millions around the world watched television replays of the horrifying event that killed seven people, destroyed the billion-dollar craft, suspended all shuttle flights and halted, at least temporarily, much of the US manned space flight program. Killed were teacher Christa McAuliffe (who was to have been the first ordinary citizen in space) and six crew members: Francis R. Scobee, Michael J. Smith, Judith A. Resnik, Ellison S. Onizuka, Ronald E. McNair and Gregory B. Jarvis.

"FANTASY ISLAND" TV PREMIERE: ANNIVERSARY. Jan 28, 1978. You knew you were a bona fide "star" in the '70s when you received a casting call from "Fantasy Island." Young and old stayed home on Saturday night to watch Mr Roarke introduce guest stars eager to live out their fantasies in camp splendor. Ricardo Montalban starred as our prescient guide, Mr Roarke, with

Hervé Villechaize as Tattoo. The show's run of 130 episodes ended on Aug 18, 1984. Who can forget Tattoo's opening lines each week, "De plane, de plane!"

★ Birthdays ★

Alan Alda, actor (*Paper Lion, The Four Seasons,* "M*A*S*H"), director, born Alphonso D'Abruzzo at New York, NY, Jan 28, 1936.
Elijah Wood, actor (*The Lord of the Rings: The Fellowship of the Ring, The Good Son*), born Cedar Rapids, IA, Jan 28, 1981.

January 29

KANSAS: ADMISSION DAY: ANNIVERSARY. Jan 29. Became the 34th state in 1861.

McKINLEY, WILLIAM: BIRTH ANNIVERSARY. Jan 29, 1843. Twenty-fifth president of the US (1897–1901), born at Niles, OH. Died in office, at Buffalo, NY, Sept 14, 1901, as the result of a gunshot wound by an anarchist assassin Sept 6, 1901, while he was attending the Pan-American Exposition. Vice President Teddy Roosevelt became president.

★ Birthdays ★

Tom Selleck, actor ("Magnum, PI," *Three Men and a Baby, Mr Baseball*), born Detroit, MI, Jan 29, 1945.
Oprah Winfrey, TV talk-show host (Emmys for "The Oprah Winfrey Show"), actress (*The*

Color Purple), producer (owner of Harpo Studios), born Kosciusko, MS, Jan 29, 1954.

January 30

NATIONAL INANE ANSWERING MESSAGE DAY. Jan 30. Annually, the day set aside to change, shorten, replace or delete those ridiculous and/or annoying answering machine messages that waste the time of anyone who must listen to them. [©2001 by WH.] For info: Wellcat Holidays. Web: www.wellcat.com.

ROOSEVELT, FRANKLIN DELANO: BIRTH ANNIVERSARY. Jan 30, 1882. Thirty-second president of the US (Mar 4, 1933–Apr 12, 1945). The only president to serve more than two terms, FDR was elected four times. He supported the Allies in World War II before the US entered the struggle by supplying them with war materials through the Lend-Lease Act; he became deeply involved in broad decision making after the Japanese attack on Pearl Harbor Dec 7, 1941. Born at Hyde Park, NY, he died a few months into his fourth term at Warm Springs, GA, Apr 12, 1945.

TET OFFENSIVE BEGINS: ANNIVERSARY. Jan 30, 1968. After calling for a cease-fire during the Tet holiday celebrations, North Vietnam and the National Liberation Front launched a major offensive throughout South Vietnam on that holiday. The Vietcong attacked the US embassy in Saigon, Tan Son Nhut Air Base and the presidential palace. Costing as many as 40,000 battlefield deaths, the offensive was a tactical defeat for the Vietcong and North Vietnam. The South Vietnamese held their ground, and the US was able to airlift troops into the critical areas and quickly regain control. However, the offensive is credited as a strategic success in that it continued the demoralization of American public opinion. After Tet, American policy toward Vietnam shifted from winning the war to seeking an honorable way out.

★ Birthdays ★

Richard (Dick) Cheney, 46th vice president of the US, born Lincoln, NE, Jan 30, 1941.
Phil Collins, musician, singer, songwriter, born Chiswick, England, Jan 30, 1951.
Gene Hackman, actor (*The French Connection, Bonnie and Clyde, Unforgiven*), born San Bernardino, CA, Jan 30, 1930.

January 31

FIRST SOCIAL SECURITY CHECK ISSUED: ANNIVERSARY. Jan 31, 1940. Ida May Fuller of Ludlow, VT, received the first monthly retirement check in the amount of $22.54. Ms Fuller had worked for three years under the Social Security program (which had been established by legislation in 1935). The accumulated taxes on her salary over those three years were $24.75. She lived to be 100 years old, collecting $22,888 in Social Security benefits. See also: "Social Security Act: Anniv" (Aug 14).

ROBINSON, JACKIE: BIRTH ANNIVERSARY. Jan 31, 1919. Jack Roosevelt Robinson, athlete and business executive, first black to enter professional major league baseball (Brooklyn Dodgers, 1947–56). Voted National League's Most Valuable Player in 1949 and elected to the Baseball Hall of Fame in 1962. Born at Cairo, GA, Jackson died at Stamford, CT, Oct 24, 1972.

SPACE MILESTONE: *EXPLORER 1* (US). Jan 31, 1958. The first successful US satellite. Although launched four months later than the Soviet Union's *Sputnik*, *Explorer 1* reached a higher altitude and detected a zone of intense radiation inside Earth's magnetic field. This was later named the Van Allen radiation belts. More than 65 subsequent *Explorer* satellites were launched through 1984.

SPACE MILESTONE: PROJECT MERCURY TEST (US). Jan 31, 1961. A test of Project Mercury spacecraft accomplished the first US recovery of a large animal from space. Ham, the chimpanzee, successfully performed simple tasks in space.

★ *Birthdays* ★

Ernest (Ernie) Banks, Hall of Fame baseball player, born Dallas, TX, Jan 31, 1931.
Minnie Driver, actress (*Grosse Pointe Blank, Good Will Hunting*), born London, England, Jan 31, 1971.
Nolan Ryan, Hall of Fame baseball player, born Refugio, TX, Jan 31, 1947.

February

February 1

AMERICAN HEART MONTH. Feb 1–28. Volunteers across the country spend one to four weeks canvassing neighborhoods and providing educational information about heart disease and stroke. Know the warning signs of a heart attack. Call 911. Give CPR. For info: American Heart Association. Web: www.american heart.org.

CAR INSURANCE FIRST ISSUED: ANNIVERSARY. Feb 1, 1898. Travelers Insurance Company issued the first car insurance against accidents with horses.

FIRST SESSION OF SUPREME COURT: ANNIVERSARY. Feb 1, 1790. The Supreme Court of the United States met for the first time in New York City with Chief Justice John Jay presiding.

GABLE, CLARK: BIRTH ANNIVERSARY. Feb 1, 1901. Actor William Clark Gable's first films were made in the era when talking films were replacing silent films. He won an Academy Award for his role in the comedy *It Happened One Night*. Other films included *Mutiny on the Bounty* and *Gone with the Wind*, for which his casting as Rhett Butler seemed a foregone conclusion due to his popularity as the acknowledged "King of Movies." Gable was born at Cadiz, OH, and died Nov 16, 1960, at Hollywood, CA.

GREENSBORO SIT-IN: ANNIVERSARY. Feb 1, 1960. Commercial discrimination against blacks provoked a nonviolent protest. At Greensboro, NC, four students from the Agricultural and Technical College (Ezell Blair, Jr, Franklin McCain, Joseph McNeill and David Richmond) sat down at a Woolworths store lunch counter and ordered coffee. Refused service, they remained all day. The following days similar sit-ins took place at the Woolworths lunch counter. Before the week was over the protesters were joined by a few white students. The protest spread rapidly, especially in Southern states. More than 1,600 people were arrested before the year was over for participating in sit-ins. Civil rights for all became a cause for thousands of students and activists. In response, equal accommodation regardless of race became the rule in business establishments in thousands of places.

HUGHES, LANGSTON: BIRTH ANNIVERSARY. Feb 1, 1902. African American poet and author, born at Joplin, MO. Among his works are the poetry collection *Montage of a Dream Deferred*, plays, a novel and short stories. Hughes died May 22, 1967, at New York, NY.

"LATE NIGHT WITH DAVID LETTERMAN" TV PREMIERE: ANNIVERSARY. Feb 1, 1982. This is when it all began: the stupid pet tricks and the legendary top ten lists. "Late Night" premiered on NBC as a talk/variety show appearing after "The Tonight Show with Johnny Carson." The offbeat show attained cult status among college crowds and insomniacs, as many tuned in to see a Velcro-suited Letterman throw himself against a wall. In 1993, Letterman made a highly publicized exit from NBC and began hosting "The Late Show" on CBS.

NATIONAL CHILDREN'S DENTAL HEALTH MONTH. Feb 1–28. To increase dental awareness and stress the importance of regular dental care. For info: American Dental Association. Web: www .ada.org.

NATIONAL SIGN UP FOR SUMMER CAMP MONTH. Feb 1–28. Every year more than 9 million children continue a national tradition by attending day or resident camps. Building self-confidence, learning new skills and making memories that last a lifetime are just a few examples of what makes camp special and why camp does children a world of good. To find the right program, parents begin looking at summer camps during this month—and sign their children up while there are still vacancies. For info: American Camping Association. Web: www.ACA camps.org.

ROBINSON CRUSOE DAY. Feb 1, 1709. Anniversary of the rescue of Alexander Selkirk, Scottish sailor who had been put ashore (in September 1704) on an uninhabited island, Juan Fernandez, at his own request after a quarrel with his captain. His adventures formed the basis for Daniel Defoe's book *Robinson Crusoe*. A day to be adventurous and self-reliant.

★ Birthdays ★

Sherilyn Fenn, actress ("Twin Peaks," *Wild at Heart*), born Detroit, MI, Feb 1, 1965.
Sherman Hemsley, actor ("The Jeffersons," "Amen"), born Philadelphia, PA, Feb 1, 1938.

February 2

BASEBALL HALL OF FAME ESTABLISHED: ANNIVERSARY. Feb 2, 1936. The five charter members of the brand-new Baseball Hall of Fame at Cooperstown, NY, were announced. Of 226 ballots cast, Ty Cobb was named on 222, Babe Ruth on 215, Honus Wagner on 215, Christy Mathewson on 205 and Walter Johnson on 189.

BONZA BOTTLER DAY™. Feb 2. To celebrate when the number of the day is the same as the number of the month. Bonza Bottler Day™ is an excuse to have a party at least once a month. For info: Gail M. Berger. E-mail: gberger5@aol.com.

CANDLEMAS DAY or PRESENTATION OF THE LORD. Feb 2. Observed in Roman Catholic and Eastern Orthodox churches. Commemorates presentation of Jesus in the temple and the purification of Mary 40 days after his birth. Candles have been blessed since the 11th century. This marks the end of the Christmas liturgical season. Old Scottish couplet proclaims: "If Candlemas is fair and clear/There'll be two winters in the year."

GROUNDHOG DAY. Feb 2. Old belief that if the sun shines on Candlemas Day, or if the groundhog sees his shadow when he emerges on this day, six weeks of winter will ensue. A groundhog named Phil sometimes appears in Punxsutawney, PA.

GROUNDHOG JOB SHADOW DAY. Feb 2. Students spend part of the day in the workplace "shadowing" an employee as he or she goes through a normal day on the job. Job Shadow Day demonstrates the connection between academics and careers and introduces students to the requirements of professions and industries. For info: Groundhog Job Shadow Day. Web: www.jobshadow.org.

★ Birthdays ★

Christie Brinkley, model, born Monroe, MI, Feb 2, 1953.
Farrah Fawcett, model, actress ("Charlie's Angels," *The Burning Bed*), born Corpus Christi, TX, Feb 2, 1947.

February 3

"THE DAY THE MUSIC DIED": ANNIVERSARY. Feb 3, 1959. The anniversary of the death of rock-and-roll legend Charles Hardin "Buddy" Holly. "The Day the Music Died," so-called in singer Don McLean's song "American Pie," is the date on which Holly was killed in a plane crash in a cornfield near Mason City, IA, along with J.P. Richardson (otherwise known as "the Big Bopper") and Richie Valens. Holly was born Sept 7, 1936, at Lubbock, TX.

FIFTEENTH AMENDMENT TO US CONSTITUTION RATIFIED: ANNIVERSARY. Feb 3, 1870. The 15th Amendment granted that the right of citizens to vote shall not be denied on account of race, color or previous condition of servitude.

FOUR CHAPLAINS MEMORIAL DAY. Feb 3, 1943. Commemorates four chaplains (George Fox, Alexander Goode, Clark Poling, John Washington) who sacrificed their life belts and lives when the SS *Dorchester* was torpedoed off Greenland during World War II.

INCOME TAX BIRTHDAY: SIXTEENTH AMENDMENT TO US CONSTITUTION RATIFIED: ANNIVERSARY. Feb 3, 1913. The 16th Amendment was ratified, granting Congress the authority to levy taxes on income. (Church bells did not ring throughout the land, and no dancing in the streets was reported.)

NORTH AMERICA'S COLDEST RECORDED TEMPERATURE: ANNIVERSARY. Feb 3, 1947. At Snag, in Canada's Yukon Territory, a temperature of 81 degrees below zero (Fahrenheit) was recorded on this date, a record low for all of North America.

ROCKWELL, NORMAN: BIRTH ANNIVERSARY. Feb 3, 1894. American artist and illustrator especially noted for his realistic and homey magazine cover art for the *Saturday Evening Post*. Born at New York, NY, he died at Stockbridge, MA, Nov 8, 1978.

SPACE MILESTONE: *CHALLENGER STS-10* (US). Feb 3, 1984. Shuttle *Challenger* launched from Kennedy Space Center, FL, with a crew of five (Vance Brand, Robert Gibson, Ronald McNair, Bruce McCandless and Robert Stewart). On Feb 7 two astronauts became the first to fly freely in space (propelled by their backpack jets), untethered to any craft. Landed at Cape Canaveral, FL, Feb 11.

★ *Birthdays* ★

Blythe Danner, actress (*Butterflies Are Free, Brighton Beach Memoirs, Mr and Mrs Bridge*), born Philadelphia, PA, Feb 3, 1943.
Nathan Lane, actor (Tony Awards for *A Funny Thing Happened on the Way to the Forum, The Producers*; *The Birdcage*, "Encore! Encore!"), born Jersey City, NJ, Feb 3, 1956.
Francis Asbury (Fran) Tarkenton, Hall of Fame football player, born Richmond, VA, Feb 3, 1940.

February 4

APACHE WARS BEGAN: ANNIVERSARY. Feb 4, 1861. The period of conflict known as the Apache Wars began at Apache Pass, AZ, when army lieutenant George Bascom arrested Apache chief Cochise for raiding a ranch. Cochise escaped and declared war. The wars lasted 25 years under the leadership of Cochise and, later, Geronimo.

SRI LANKA: INDEPENDENCE DAY. Feb 4. Democratic Socialist Republic of Sri Lanka observes National Day. On Feb 4, 1948, Ceylon (as it was then known) obtained independence from Great Britain. The country's name was changed to Sri Lanka in 1972.

★ Birthdays ★

Betty Friedan, author (*The Feminine Mystique*), founder, the National Organization for Women (NOW), born Peoria, IL, Feb 4, 1921.
Lawrence Taylor, Hall of Fame football player, born Williamsburg, VA, Feb 4, 1959.

February 5

FAMILY-LEAVE BILL: ANNIVERSARY. Feb 5, 1993. President William Clinton signed legislation requiring companies with 50 or more employees (and all government agencies) to allow employees to take up to 12 weeks unpaid leave in a 12-month period to deal with the birth or adoption of a child or to care for a relative with a serious health problem. The bill became effective Aug 5, 1993.

WEATHERMAN'S [WEATHERPERSON'S] DAY. Feb 5. Commemorates the birth of one of America's first weathermen, John Jeffries, a Boston physician who kept detailed records of weather conditions, 1774–1816. Born at Boston, Feb 5, 1744, and died there Sept 16, 1819.

★ Birthdays ★

Jennifer Jason Leigh, actress (*Miami Blues, Rush, Backdraft*), born Los Angeles, CA, Feb 5, 1962.
Laura Linney, actress (*The Truman Show, You Can Count on Me*), born New York, NY, Feb 5, 1964.
Roger Thomas Staubach, Hall of Fame football player, born Cincinnati, OH, Feb 5, 1942.

February 6

ACCESSION OF QUEEN ELIZABETH II: ANNIVERSARY. Feb 6, 1952. Princess Elizabeth Alexandra Mary succeeded to the British throne (becoming Elizabeth II, Queen of the United Kingdom of Great Britain and Northern Ireland and Head of the Commonwealth) upon the death of her father, King George VI, Feb 6, 1952. Her coronation took place June 2, 1953, at Westminster Abbey at London.

BURR, AARON: BIRTH ANNIVERSARY. Feb 6, 1756. Third vice president of the US (Mar 4, 1801–Mar 3, 1805). While vice president, Burr challenged political enemy Alexander Hamilton to a duel and mortally wounded him July 11, 1804, at Weehawken, NJ. Indicted for the challenge and for murder, he returned to Washington to complete his term of office (during which he presided over the impeachment trial of Supreme Court Justice Samuel Chase). In 1807 Burr was arrested, tried for treason (in an alleged scheme to invade Mexico and set up a new nation in the West) and acquitted. Born at Newark, NJ, he died at Staten Island, NY, Sept 14, 1836.

MARLEY, BOB: BIRTH ANNIVERSARY. Feb 6, 1945. With his group, The Wailers, Bob Marley was one of the most popular and influential performers of reggae music, an "off-beat-accented Jamaican" music closely associated with the political/religious Rastafarian movement (admirers of the late Ethiopian emperor Haile Selassie, who was formerly called Ras Tafari). Marley was born at Rhoden Hall in northern Jamaica. Died of cancer at Miami, FL, May 11, 1981.

MASSACHUSETTS RATIFIES CONSTITUTION: ANNIVERSARY. Feb 6, 1788. By a vote of 187 to 168, Massachusetts became the sixth state to ratify the Constitution.

RUTH, "BABE": BIRTH ANNIVERSARY. Feb 6, 1895. One of baseball's greatest heroes, George Herman "Babe" Ruth was born at Baltimore, MD.

The left-handed pitcher—"the Sultan of Swat"—hit 714 home runs in 22 major league seasons of play and played in ten World Series. Died at New York, NY, Aug 16, 1948.

★ Birthdays ★

Tom Brokaw, journalist, born Yankton, SD, Feb 6, 1940.
Natalie Cole, singer ("This Will Be," "Unforgettable"), born Los Angeles, CA, Feb 6, 1950.
Ronald Reagan, 40th president of the US, born Tampico, IL, Feb 6, 1911.

February 7

BLAKE, EUBIE: BIRTH ANNIVERSARY. Feb 7, 1883. James Hubert "Eubie" Blake, American composer and pianist, writer of nearly 1,000 songs (including "I'm Just Wild About Harry" and "Memories of You"). Born at Baltimore, MD. Recipient of the Presidential Medal of Freedom in 1981. Last professional performance was in January 1982. Died at Brooklyn, NY, five days after his 100th birthday, Feb 12, 1983.

DICKENS, CHARLES: BIRTH ANNIVERSARY. Feb 7, 1812. English social critic and novelist, born at Portsmouth, England. Among his most successful books: *Oliver Twist, The Posthumous Papers of the Pickwick Club, Tale of Two Cities, David Copperfield* and *A Christmas Carol.* Died at Gad's Hill, England, June 9, 1870, and was buried at Westminster Abbey.

ELEVENTH AMENDMENT TO US CONSTITUTION (SOVEREIGNTY OF THE STATES) RATIFIED: ANNIVERSARY. Feb 7, 1795. The 11th Amendment to the Constitution was ratified, curbing the powers of the federal judiciary in relation to the states. The amendment reaffirmed the sovereignty of the states by prohibiting suits against them.

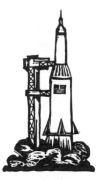

SPACE MILESTONE: *STARDUST* **(US).** Feb 7, 1999. *Stardust* began its 3 billion-mile journey to collect comet dust on this date. The unmanned mission is to meet up with Comet Wild–2 in January 2004 and the comet samples will reach Earth in January 2006. This is the first US mission devoted solely to a comet. NASA plans three more over a four-year period.

★ *Birthdays* ★

Garth Brooks, singer ("Friends in Low Places"), born Tulsa, OK, Feb 7, 1962.
Juwan Howard, basketball player, born Chicago, IL, Feb 7, 1973.
Pete Postlethwaite, actor (*Amistad, The Lost World: Jurassic Park, Brassed Off*), born London, England, Feb 7, 1945.

February 8

BOY SCOUTS OF AMERICA FOUNDED: ANNIVERSARY. Feb 8, 1910. The Boy Scouts of America was founded at Washington, DC, by William Boyce, based on the work of Sir Robert Baden-Powell with the British Boy Scout Association.

DEAN, JAMES: BIRTH ANNIVERSARY. Feb 8, 1931. American stage, film and television actor who achieved immense popularity during a brief career. Born at Fairmont, IN. Best remembered for his role in *Rebel Without a Cause*. Died in an automobile accident near Cholame, CA, Sept 30, 1955, at age 24.

LEMMON, JACK: BIRTH ANNIVERSARY. Feb 8, 1925. Stage, screen and television actor, born John Uhler Lemmon III at Boston, MA. He was nominated for seven Academy Awards, winning in 1955 for his supporting role in *Mister Roberts* and in 1974 for his leading role in *Save the Tiger*. Other films included *Some Like It Hot* and *Days of Wine and Roses*. Frequently paired with actor Walter Matthau, they starred in several highly popular films such as *The Odd Couple* and *Grumpy Old Men*. Lemmon also starred in television versions of *Twelve Angry Men* and won an Emmy in 2000 for the TV movie *Tuesdays with Morrie*. He died at Los Angeles, CA, June 27, 2001.

VERNE, JULES: BIRTH ANNIVERSARY. Feb 8, 1828. French writer, sometimes called "the father of science fiction," born at Nantes, France. Author of *Around the World in Eighty Days* and *Twenty*

Thousand Leagues Under the Sea. Died at Amiens, France, Mar 24, 1905.

★ Birthdays ★

Ted Koppel, journalist (anchor of "Nightline"), born Lancashire, England, Feb 8, 1940.

Nick Nolte, actor (*48 HRS, Grace Quigley, Prince of Tides*, "Rich Man, Poor Man"), born Omaha, NE, Feb 8, 1941.

February 9

HARRISON, WILLIAM HENRY: BIRTH ANNIVERSARY. Feb 9, 1773. Ninth president of the US (Mar 4–Apr 4, 1841). His term of office was the shortest in our nation's history—32 days. He was the first president to die in office (of pneumonia contracted during inaugural ceremonies). Born at Berkeley, VA, he died at Washington, DC, Apr 4, 1841. His grandson, Benjamin Harrison, was the 23rd president of the US.

★ Birthdays ★

Mia Farrow, actress ("Peyton Place," *Rosemary's Baby, Hannah and Her Sisters*), born Maria de Lourdes Villers at Los Angeles, CA, Feb 9, 1945.

Joe Pesci, actor (*Raging Bull, Goodfellas, My Cousin Vinny*), born Newark, NJ, Feb 9, 1943.

Mena Suvari, actress (*American Beauty, Loser*), born Newport, RI, Feb 9, 1979.

February 10

PLIMSOLL DAY. Feb 10, 1824. A day to remember Samuel Plimsoll, "The Sailor's Friend," a coal merchant turned reformer and politician, who was elected to the British Parliament in 1868. He attacked the practice of overloading heavily insured ships, calling them "coffin ships." The Plimsoll Line, named for him, is a line on the side of ships marking maximum load allowed by law. Born at Bristol, England, Feb 10, 1824. Died at Folkestone, England, June 3, 1898.

TREATY OF PARIS ENDS FRENCH AND INDIAN WAR: ANNIVERSARY. Feb 10, 1763. Known in Europe as the Seven Years' War, this conflict ranged from North America to India, with many European nations involved. In North America French expansion in the Ohio River Valley in the 1750s led to conflict with Great Britain. Some Indians fought alongside the French; a young George Washington fought for the British. As a result of the signing of the Treaty of Paris, France lost all claims to Canada and had to cede Louisiana to Spain. Fifteen years later French bitterness over the loss of its North

American colonies to Britain contributed to its supporting the colonists in the American Revolution.

TWENTY-FIFTH AMENDMENT TO US CONSTITUTION (PRESIDENTIAL SUCCESSION, DISABILITY) RATIFIED: ANNIVERSARY. Feb 10, 1967. Procedures for presidential succession were further clarified by the 25th Amendment, along with provisions for continuity of power in the event of a disability or illness of the president.

★ *Birthdays* ★

Laura Dern, actress (*Blue Velvet, Rambling Rose*), born Los Angeles, CA, Feb 10, 1967.
Robert Wagner, actor ("It Takes a Thief," "Hart to Hart"), born Detroit, MI, Feb 10, 1930.

February 11

EDISON, THOMAS ALVA: BIRTH ANNIVERSARY. Feb 11, 1847. American inventive genius and holder of more than 1,200 patents (including the incandescent electric lamp, phonograph, electric dynamo and key parts of many now-familiar devices such as the movie camera, telephone transmitter, etc). Edison said, "Genius is 1 percent inspiration and 99 percent perspiration." His birthday is now widely observed as Inventor's Day. Born at Milan, OH, and died at Menlo Park, NJ, Oct 18, 1931.

IRAN: NATIONAL DAY. Feb 11. National holiday. Commemorates the revolution that overthrew the Shah in 1979.

MANDELA, NELSON: PRISON RELEASE: ANNIVERSARY. Feb 11, 1990. After serving more than 27½ years of a life sentence (convicted, with eight others, of sabotage and conspiracy to overthrow the government), South Africa's Nelson Mandela, 71 years old, walked away from the Victor Verster prison farm at Paarl, South Africa, a free man. He had survived the governmental system of apartheid. Mandela greeted a cheering throng of well-wishers, along with hundreds of millions of television viewers worldwide, with demands for an intensification of the struggle for equality for blacks, who make up nearly 75 percent of South Africa's population.

SATISFIED STAYING SINGLE DAY. Feb 11. As Valentine's Day approaches, some single folks would like to point out that they're quite content buying candy and flowers for no one but themselves. Live it up. Shadow dance! [©2001 by WH.] For info: Wellcat Holidays. Web: www.wellcat.com.

SPACE MILESTONE: *ENDEAVOUR* **MAPPING MISSION (US).** Feb 11, 2000. This manned flight, the

Shuttle Radar Topography Mission, spent 11 days in space creating a 3-D map of more than 70 percent of Earth's surface. It is the most accurate and complete topographic map of Earth ever produced.

★ *Birthdays* ★

Jennifer Aniston, actress ("Friends," *Picture Perfect*), born Sherman Oaks, CA, Feb 11, 1969.
Burt Reynolds, actor (*Hooper, Deliverance, Cannonball Run*, "Evening Shade"), born Waycross, GA, Feb 11, 1936.

February 12

DARWIN, CHARLES ROBERT: BIRTH ANNIVERSARY. Feb 12, 1809. Author and naturalist, born at Shrewsbury, England. Best remembered for his books *On the Origin of Species by Means of Natural Selection, or the Preservation of Favoured Races in the Struggle for Life* and *The Descent of Man and Selection in Relation to Sex*. Died at Down, Kent, England, Apr 19, 1882.

LINCOLN, ABRAHAM: BIRTH ANNIVERSARY. Feb 12, 1809. Sixteenth president of the US (Mar 4, 1861–Apr 15, 1865) and the first to be assassinated (on Good Friday, Apr 14, 1865, at Ford's Theatre at Washington, DC). His presidency encompassed the tragic Civil War. Especially remembered are his Emancipation Proclamation (Jan 1, 1863), his Gettysburg Address (Nov 19, 1863) and his proclamation establishing the last Thursday of November as Thanksgiving Day. Born at Hardin County, KY, he died at Washington, DC, Apr 15, 1865. Lincoln's birthday is observed as part of Presidents' Day on the third Monday in February in most states but is a legal holiday in Illinois and an optional bank holiday in Iowa, Maryland, Michigan, Pennsylvania, Washington and West Virginia.

NAACP FOUNDED: ANNIVERSARY. Feb 12, 1909. The National Association for the Advancement of Colored People was founded by W.E.B. Du Bois and Ida Wells-Barnett, among others, to wage a militant campaign against lynching and other forms of racial oppression. Its legal wing brought many lawsuits that successfully challenged segregation in the 1950s and '60s.

★ *Birthdays* ★

Arsenio Hall, comedian, actor (*Coming to America*), former TV talk-show host, born Cleveland, OH, Feb 12, 1955.
Christina Ricci, actress (*Ice Storm, Addams Family Values*), born Santa Monica, CA, Feb 12, 1980.
William Felton (Bill) Russell, Hall of Fame basketball player and coach, born Monroe, LA, Feb 12, 1934.

February 13

DOW-JONES TOPS 7,000: ANNIVERSARY. Feb 13, 1997. The Dow-Jones Index of 30 major industrial stocks topped the 7,000 mark for the first time.

FIRST MEDAL OF HONOR: ANNIVERSARY. Feb 13, 1861. Colonel Bernard Irwin distinguished himself while leading troops in a battle with Chiricahua Apache Indians at Apache Pass, AZ (at the time part of the territory of New Mexico). For those actions Irwin became the first person awarded the new US Medal of Honor, although he didn't actually receive it until three years later (Jan 24, 1864).

WOOD, GRANT: BIRTH ANNIVERSARY. Feb 13, 1892. American artist, especially noted for his powerful realism and satirical paintings of the American scene, was born near Anamosa, IA. He was a printer, sculptor, woodworker and teacher. Among his best-remembered works are *American Gothic, Fall Plowing* and *Stone City.* Died at Iowa City, IA, Feb 12, 1942.

★ Birthdays ★

Stockard Channing, actress (*Six Degrees of Separation, The House of Blue Leaves,* "The West Wing"), born Susan Stockard at New York, NY, Feb 13, 1944.

George Segal, actor (*A Touch of Class,* "Just Shoot Me"), born Great Neck, NY, Feb 13, 1934.

February 14

ARIZONA: ADMISSION DAY: ANNIVERSARY. Feb 14. Became 48th state in 1912.

ENIAC COMPUTER INTRODUCED: ANNIVERSARY. Feb 14, 1946. J. Presper Eckert and John W. Mauchly demonstrated the Electronic Numerical Integrator and Computer (ENIAC) for the first time at the University of Pennsylvania. This was the first electronic digital computer. It occupied a room the size of a gymnasium and contained nearly 18,000 vacuum tubes. The US Army commissioned the computer to speed the calculation of firing tables for artillery. By the time the computer was ready, World War II was over. However, ENIAC prepared the way for future generations of computers.

FERRIS WHEEL DAY. Feb 14, 1859. Anniversary of the birth of George Washington Gale Ferris, American engineer and inventor, at Galesburg, IL. Among his many accomplishments as a civil engineer, Ferris is best remembered as the inventor of the Ferris wheel, which he developed for the World's Columbian Exposition at Chicago, IL, in 1893. Built on the Midway Plaisance, the 250-feet-in-diameter Ferris wheel (with 36 coaches, each capable of carrying 40 passengers), proved one of the greatest attractions of the fair. It was America's answer to the Eiffel Tower of the Paris International Exposition of 1889. Ferris died at Pittsburgh, PA, Nov 22, 1896.

FIRST PRESIDENTIAL PHOTOGRAPH: ANNIVERSARY. Feb 14, 1849. President James Polk became the first US president to be photographed while in office. The photographer was Mathew B. Brady, who would become famous for his photography during the American Civil War.

OREGON: ADMISSION DAY: ANNIVERSARY. Feb 14. Became 33rd state in 1859.

SPACE MILESTONE: 100th SPACE WALK. Feb 14, 2001. Two astronauts from the space shuttle *Atlantis* took the 100th space walk; the first had been taken by American Edward White in 1965. On their excursion Thomas Jones and Robert Curbeam, Jr, put the finishing touches on the International Space Station's new science lab *Destiny*. See also: "Space Milestone: *Gemini 4*" (June 3).

VALENTINE'S DAY. Feb 14. St. Valentine's Day celebrates the feasts of two Christian martyrs of this name. One, a priest and physician, was beaten and beheaded on the Flaminian Way at Rome, Italy, Feb 14, AD 269, during the reign of Emperor Claudius II. Another Valentine, the Bishop of Terni, is said to have been beheaded, also on the Flaminian Way at Rome, Feb 14 (possibly in a later year). Both history and leg-

end are vague and contradictory about details of the Valentines, and some say that Feb 14 was selected for the celebration of Christian martyrs as a diversion from the ancient pagan observance of Lupercalia. An old legend has it that birds choose their mates on Valentine's Day. Now it is one of the most widely observed unofficial holidays. It is an occasion for the exchange of gifts (usually books, flowers or sweets) and greeting cards with affectionate or humorous messages.

VALENTINE'S DAY MASSACRE: ANNIVERSARY. Feb 14, 1929. Anniversary of Chicago gangland executions, when gunmen posing as police shot seven members of the George "Bugs" Moran gang.

★ *Birthdays* ★

Drew Bledsoe, football player, born Ellensburg, WA, Feb 14, 1972.
Gregory Hines, dancer, actor (*Tap, White Nights*, "The Gregory Hines Show"), born New York, NY, Feb 14, 1946.

February 15

CANADA: MAPLE LEAF FLAG ADOPTED: ANNIVERSARY. Feb 15, 1965. The new Canadian national flag was raised in Ottawa, Canada's capital, on this day. The red-and-white flag with a red maple leaf in the center replaced the Red Ensign flag, which had the British Union Jack in the upper left-hand corner.

GALILEI, GALILEO: BIRTH ANNIVERSARY. Feb 15, 1564. Physicist and astronomer who helped overthrow medieval concepts of the world, born at Pisa, Italy. He proved the theory that all bodies, large and small, descend at equal speed and gathered evidence to support Copernicus's theory that Earth and other planets revolve around the sun. Galileo died at Florence, Italy, Jan 8, 1642.

REMEMBER THE *MAINE* DAY: ANNIVERSARY. Feb 15, 1898. American battleship *Maine* was blown up while at anchor in the Havana harbor, at 9:40 PM, on this day in 1898. The ship, under the command of Captain Charles G. Sigsbee, sank quickly, and 260 members of its crew were lost. Inflamed public opinion in the US ignored the lack of evidence to establish responsibility for the explosion. "Remember the *Maine*" became the war cry, and a formal declaration of war against Spain followed on Apr 25, 1898, beginning the Spanish-American War.

★ Birthdays ★

Matt Groening, cartoonist ("The Simpsons"), born Portland, OR, Feb 15, 1954.
Jane Seymour, actress (Emmy for "East of Eden"; "Dr. Quinn: Medicine Woman"), born Hillingdon, England, Feb 15, 1951.

February 16

LITHUANIA: INDEPENDENCE DAY. Feb 16. National Day. The anniversary of Lithuania's declaration of independence in 1918 is observed as the Baltic state's Independence Day. In 1940, Lithuania became a part of the Soviet Union under an agreement between Joseph Stalin and Adolf Hitler. On Mar 11, 1990, Lithuania declared its independence from the Soviet Union, the first of the Soviet republics to do so. In the wake of the failed coup attempt in Moscow on Aug 19, 1991, Lithuanian independence finally was recognized.

★ Birthdays ★

LeVar Burton, actor ("Roots," "Star Trek: The Next Generation"), host ("Reading Rainbow"), born Landsthul, West Germany, Feb 16, 1957.
John McEnroe, Jr, former tennis player, born Wiesbaden, West Germany, Feb 16, 1959.

February 17

BARBER, WALTER LANIER "RED": BIRTH ANNIVERSARY. Feb 17, 1908. One of the first broadcasters inducted into the Baseball Hall of Fame, "Red" Barber was born at Columbus, MS. Barber's first professional play-by-play experience was announcing the Cincinnati Reds opening day on radio in 1934. That game was also the first major league game he had ever seen. He broadcast baseball's first night game on Aug 26, 1939, the 1947 game in which Jackie Robinson broke the color barrier, and Roger Maris's 61st home run in 1961. "Red" Barber died Oct 22, 1992, at Tallahassee, FL.

GERONIMO: DEATH ANNIVERSARY. Feb 17, 1909. American Indian of the Chiricahua (Apache) tribe was born about 1829 in Arizona. He was the leader of a small band of warriors whose devastating raids in Arizona, New Mexico and Mexico caused the US Army to send 5,000 men to recapture him after his first escape. He was confined at Fort Sill, OK, where he died Feb 17, 1909, after dictating the story of his life for publication.

MALTHUS, THOMAS: BIRTH ANNIVERSARY. Feb 17, 1766. English economist, author and demographer, born near Dorking, England. Malthusian population theories (especially that population growth exceeds growth of production) provoked great controversy when published in 1798. Died near Bath, England, Dec 23, 1834.

NATIONAL PTA FOUNDERS' DAY: ANNIVERSARY. Feb 17, 1897. Celebrates the PTA's founding by Phoebe Apperson Hearst and Alice McLellan Birney. For info: National PTA. Web: www.pta.org.

"A PRAIRIE HOME COMPANION" PREMIERE: ANNIVERSARY. Feb 17, 1979. This popular live variety show debuted locally on Minnesota Public Radio in 1974 and was first broadcast nationally on Feb 17, 1979, as part of National Public Radio's Folk Festival USA. It became a regular Saturday night program in early 1980. Host Garrison Keillor's monologues about the mythical Lake Wobegon and his humorous ads for local businesses such as Bertha's Kitty Boutique, Powdermilk Biscuits and the Chatterbox Cafe are accompanied by various musical groups.

★ Birthdays ★

Michael Jordan, basketball player, former minor league baseball player, born Brooklyn, NY, Feb 17, 1963.

Lou Diamond Phillips, actor (*La Bamba, Stand and Deliver*), born Corpus Christi, TX, Feb 17, 1962.

Rene Russo, actress (*Lethal Weapon 3, Ransom*), born Burbank, CA, Feb 17, 1954.

February 18

GAMBIA: INDEPENDENCE DAY. Feb 18, 1965. National holiday. Independence from Britain granted. Referendum in April 1970 established Gambia as a republic within the Commonwealth.

PLANET PLUTO DISCOVERY: ANNIVERSARY. Feb 18, 1930. Pluto, the ninth planet, was discovered by astronomer Clyde Tombaugh at the Lowell Observatory at Flagstaff, AZ. It was given the name of the Roman god of the underworld. Some astronomers don't accept Pluto as a planet.

TIFFANY, LOUIS COMFORT: BIRTH ANNIVERSARY. Feb 18, 1848. American artist, son of famed jeweler Charles L. Tiffany. Best remembered for his remarkable work with decorative iridescent "favrile" glass. Born at New York, NY; died there Jan 17, 1933.

★ Birthdays ★

Toni Morrison, Nobel Prize–winning novelist (*Beloved, Jazz, Tar Baby, Sula*), born Chloe Anthony Wofford, Lorain, OH, Feb 18, 1931.

Cybill Shepherd, actress (*The Last Picture Show,* "Moonlighting," "Cybill"), born Memphis, TN, Feb 18, 1950.

John Travolta, actor (*Pulp Fiction, Urban Cowboy, Saturday Night Fever,* "Welcome Back Kotter"), born Englewood, NJ, Feb 18, 1955.

February 19

COPERNICUS, NICOLAUS: BIRTH ANNIVERSARY. Feb 19, 1473. Polish astronomer and priest who revolutionized scientific thought with what came to be called the Copernican theory that placed the sun instead of Earth at the center of our planetary system. Born at Torun, Poland, he died at East Prussia, May 24, 1543.

***THE FEMININE MYSTIQUE* PUBLISHED: ANNIVERSARY.** Feb 19, 1963. Betty Friedan published *The Feminine Mystique* this month, a call for women to achieve their full potential. Her book generated enormous response and revitalized the women's movement in the US.

JAPANESE INTERNMENT: ANNIVERSARY. Feb 19, 1942. As a result of President Franklin Roosevelt's Executive Order 9066, some 110,000 Japanese-Americans living in coastal Pacific areas were placed in concentration camps in remote areas of Arizona, Arkansas, inland California, Colorado, Idaho, Utah and Wyoming. The interned Japanese-Americans (two-thirds were US citizens) lost an estimated $400 million in property. They were allowed to return to their homes Jan 2, 1945.

★ *Birthdays* ★

Jeff Daniels, actor (*The Purple Rose of Cairo, Something Wild, Dumb and Dumber*), born Chelsea, MI, Feb 19, 1955.
Benicio Del Toro, actor (*Traffic, The Usual Suspects*), born Santurce, Puerto Rico, Feb 19, 1967.

February 20

ADAMS, ANSEL: BIRTH ANNIVERSARY. Feb 20, 1902. American photographer, known for his photographs of Yosemite National Park, born at San Francisco, CA. Adams died at Monterey, CA, Apr 22, 1984.

DOUGLASS, FREDERICK: DEATH ANNIVERSARY. Feb 20, 1895. American journalist, orator and anti-slavery leader. Born at Tuckahoe, MD, probably in February 1817. Died at Anacostia Heights, DC. His original name before his escape from slavery was Frederick Augustus Washington Bailey.

PISCES, THE FISH. Feb 20–Mar 20. In the astronomical/astrological zodiac, which divides the sun's apparent orbit into 12 segments, the period Feb 20–Mar 20 is identified, traditionally, as the sun sign of Pisces, the Fish. The ruling planet is Neptune.

SPACE MILESTONE: *FRIENDSHIP 7* (US): FIRST AMERICAN TO ORBIT EARTH. Feb 20, 1962. John Herschel Glenn, Jr, became the first American, and the third person, to orbit Earth. Aboard the capsule *Friendship 7*, he made three orbits of Earth. Spacecraft was *Mercury-Atlas 6*. In 1998 the 77-year-old Glenn went into space again on the space shuttle *Discovery* to test the effects of aging.

SPACE MILESTONE: *MIR* SPACE STATION (USSR). Feb 20, 1986. A "third-generation" orbiting space station, *Mir* (Peace), was launched without crew from the Baikonur space center at Leninsk, Kazakhstan. Both Russian and American crews used the station. After many equipment failures and financial problems, the Russians took *Mir* out of service Mar 23, 2001.

★ *Birthdays* ★

Charles Barkley, former basketball player, born Leeds, AL, Feb 20, 1963.
Cindy Crawford, model, actress, born DeKalb, IL, Feb 20, 1966.
Sidney Poitier, actor (*In the Heat of the Night*; Oscar for *Lilies of the Field*), born Miami, FL, Feb 20, 1927.

February 21

BATTLE OF VERDUN: ANNIVERSARY. Feb 21, 1916. The German High Command launched an offensive on the Western Front at Verdun, France, which became World War I's single longest battle. An estimated 1 million men were killed, decimating both the German and French armies, before the battle ended on Dec 15, 1916.

MALCOLM X: ASSASSINATION ANNIVERSARY. Feb 21, 1965. Malcolm X, a black leader who renounced the Black Muslim sect to form the Organization of Afro-American Unity and to practice a more orthodox form of Islam, was shot and killed as he spoke to a rally at the Audubon Ballroom at New York, NY. Three men were convicted of the murder in 1966 and sentenced to life in prison. Malcoln X was born Malcolm Little, the son of a Baptist preacher, at Omaha, NE, May 19, 1925.

***NEW YORKER* PUBLISHED: ANNIVERSARY.** Feb 21, 1925. First issue of the magazine published on this date.

UNITED NATIONS: INTERNATIONAL MOTHER LANGUAGE DAY. Feb 21. To help raise awareness among all peoples of the distinct and enduring value of their languages. For info: United Nations. Web: www.un.org.

WASHINGTON MONUMENT DEDICATED: ANNIVERSARY. Feb 21, 1885. Monument to the first president was dedicated at Washington, DC.

★ *Birthdays* ★

Charlotte Church, singer (*Voice of an Angel*), born Llandaff, Cardiff, Wales, Feb 21, 1986.
Tyne Daly, actress ("Judging Amy"; Emmy for "Cagney and Lacey"; *Gypsy*), born Madison, WI, Feb 21, 1947.
Kelsey Grammer, actor ("Cheers," "Frasier"), born St. Thomas, US Virgin Islands, Feb 21, 1955.

February 22

FLORIDA ACQUIRED BY US: ANNIVERSARY. Feb 22, 1819. Secretary of State John Quincy Adams signed the Florida Purchase Treaty under which Spain ceded Florida to the US. As payment, the US assumed $5 million of claims by US citizens against Spain. Florida became a state in 1845.

WADLOW, ROBERT PERSHING: BIRTH ANNIVERSARY. Feb 22, 1918. Tallest man in recorded history, born at Alton, IL. Though only nine pounds at birth, by age ten Wadlow already stood over six feet tall and weighed 210 pounds. When Wadlow died at age 22, he was a remarkable eight feet 11.1 inches tall, 490 pounds. His gentle, friendly manner in the face of constant public attention earned him the name "Gentle Giant." Wadlow died July 15, 1940, at Manistee, MI, of complications resulting from a foot infection.

WASHINGTON, GEORGE: BIRTH ANNIVERSARY. Feb 22, 1732. First president of the US ("First in war, first in peace and first in the hearts of his countrymen" in the words of Henry "Light Horse Harry" Lee). Born at Westmoreland County, VA, Feb 22, 1732 (New Style). However, the Julian (Old Style) calendar was still in use in the colonies when he was born and the year began in March, so the date on the calendar when he was born was Feb 11, 1731. He died at Mount Vernon, VA, Dec 14, 1799. Washington's birthday is a federal holiday commemorated on the third Monday in February. In many states his birthday is celebrated as Presidents' Day.

WOOLWORTHS FIRST OPENED: ANNIVERSARY. Feb 22, 1879. First chain store, Woolworths, opened at Utica, NY. In 1997, the closing of the chain of "5 and 10 cent" stores was announced.

★ Birthdays ★

Drew Barrymore, actress (*E.T. the Extra-Terrestrial, Ever After, Charlie's Angels*), born Los Angeles, CA, Feb 22, 1975.
Julius Winfield "Dr. J" Erving, Hall of Fame basketball player, born Roosevelt, NY, Feb 22, 1950.

February 23

DIESEL ENGINE PATENTED: ANNIVERSARY. Feb 23, 1983. Rudolf Diesel received a patent in Germany for the engine that bears his name. The diesel engine burns fuel oil rather than gasoline and is used in trucks and heavy industrial machinery.

DOW-JONES TOPS 4,000: ANNIVERSARY. Feb 23, 1995. The Dow-Jones Index of 30 major industrial stocks topped the 4,000 mark for the first time.

Du BOIS, W.E.B.: BIRTH ANNIVERSARY. Feb 23, 1868. William Edward Burghardt Du Bois, American educator and leader of the movement for black equality. Born at Great Barrington, MA, he died at Accra, Ghana, Aug 27, 1963. "The cost of liberty," he wrote in 1909, "is less than the price of repression."

FIRST CLONING OF AN ADULT ANIMAL: ANNIVERSARY. Feb 23, 1997. Researchers in Scotland announced the first cloning of an adult animal, a lamb they named Dolly with a genetic makeup identical to that of her mother. This led to worldwide speculation about the possibility of human cloning. On Mar 4, President Clinton imposed a ban on the federal funding of human cloning research.

GROUND WAR AGAINST IRAQ BEGINS: ANNIVERSARY. Feb 23, 1991. After an air campaign lasting slightly more than a month, Allied forces launched the ground offensive against Iraqi forces as part of Desert Storm. The relentless air attacks had devastated troops and targets in both Iraq and Kuwait. A world that had watched and anticipated "the Mother of All Battles" was surprised at the swiftness and ease with which Allied forces were able to subdue Iraqi forces in 100 hours.

HANDEL, GEORGE FREDERICK: BIRTH ANNIVERSARY. Feb 23, 1685 (OS). Born at Halle, Saxony, Germany, Handel was perhaps the greatest master of Baroque music. Handel's most frequently performed work is the oratorio *Messiah*, which was first heard in 1742. He died at London, England, Apr 14, 1759.

JAPANESE ATTACK US MAINLAND: ANNIVERSARY. Feb 23, 1942. In the first attack on the US mainland, a Japanese submarine fired 25 shells at an oil refinery at the edge of Ellwood Oil Field 12 miles west of Santa Barbara, CA. One shell made a direct hit on the rigging, causing minor damage. President Roosevelt was giving a fireside chat at the time of the attack.

★ *Birthdays* ★

Peter Fonda, actor (*Easy Rider, Ulee's Gold*), born New York, NY, Feb 23, 1939.
Patricia Richardson, actress ("Double Trouble," "Home Improvement"), born Bethesda, MD, Feb 23, 1951.

February 24

ESTONIA: INDEPENDENCE DAY. Feb 24. National holiday. Commemorates declaration of independence from Soviet Union in 1918. Independence was brief, however; Estonia was again under Soviet control until 1991.

JOHNSON IMPEACHMENT PROCEEDINGS: ANNIVERSARY. Feb 24, 1867. In a showdown over reconstruction policy following the Civil War, the House of Representatives voted to impeach President Andrew Johnson. Congress had passed the Reconstruction Act that divided the South into five military districts headed by officers who were to take their orders from General Grant, the head of the army, instead of from President Johnson. In addition, Congress passed the Tenure of Office Act, which required Senate approval before Johnson could remove any official whose appointment was originally approved by the Senate. To test the constitutionality of the act, Johnson dismissed Secretary of War Edwin Stanton, triggering the impeachment vote. On Mar 5, 1868, the Senate convened as a court to hear the charges against the president. The Senate vote of 35–19 fell one vote short of the two-thirds majority needed for impeachment.

★ *Birthdays* ★

Barry Bostwick, actor (*The Rocky Horror Picture Show*, "Spin City"), born San Mateo, CA, Feb 24, 1945.

Edward James Olmos, actor (*Stand and Deliver*; Emmy for "Miami Vice"), born East Los Angeles, CA, Feb 24, 1947.

Paula Zahn, newscaster, host ("CNN American Morning"), born Naperville, IL, Feb 24, 1956.

February 25

CLAY BECOMES HEAVYWEIGHT CHAMP: ANNIVERSARY. Feb 25, 1964. Twenty-two-year-old Cassius Clay (later Muhammad Ali) became world heavyweight boxing champion by defeating Sonny Liston. At the height of his athletic career Ali was well known for both his fighting ability and personal style. His most famous saying was, "I am the greatest!" In 1967 he was convicted of violating the Selective Service Act and was stripped of his title for refusing to be inducted into the armed services during the Vietnam War. Ali cited religious convictions as his reason for refusal. In 1971 the Supreme Court reversed the conviction. Ali is the only fighter to win the heavyweight fighting title three separate times. He defended that title nine times.

FIRST NATIONAL BANK CHARTERED BY CONGRESS: ANNIVERSARY. Feb 25, 1791. The First Bank of the US at Philadelphia, PA, was chartered. Proposed as a national bank by Alexander Hamilton, it lost its charter in 1811. The Second Bank of the US received a charter in 1816, which expired in 1836. Since that time, the US has had no central bank. Central banking functions are carried out by the Federal Reserve System, established in 1913. See also: "Federal Reserve System: Anniversary" (Dec 23).

RENOIR, PIERRE AUGUSTE: BIRTH ANNIVERSARY. Feb 25, 1841. Impressionist painter, born at Limoges, France. Renoir's paintings are known for their joy and sensuousness as well as the light techniques he employed in them. In his later years he was crippled by arthritis and would paint with the brush strapped to his hand. He died at Cagnes-sur-Mer, Provence, France, Dec 17, 1919.

★ Birthdays ★

Tea Leoni, actress ("The Naked Truth," *Deep Impact*), born New York, NY, Feb 25, 1966.

Sally Jessy Raphael, talk-show host, born Easton, PA, Feb 25, 1943.

February 26

COMMUNIST MANIFESTO PUBLISHED: ANNIVERSARY. Feb 26, 1848. Published by Karl Marx and Friedrich Engels on the eve of the revolutions of 1848, the *Manifesto* provided ideas for Socialist and Communist movements.

FEDERAL COMMUNICATIONS COMMISSION CREATED: ANNIVERSARY. Feb 26, 1934. President Franklin D. Roosevelt ordered the creation of a Communications Commission, which became the FCC. It was created by Congress June 19, 1934, to oversee communication by radio, wire or cable. TV and satellite communication later became part of its charge.

FOR PETE'S SAKE DAY. Feb 26. A world wonders: after all these years, who is Pete and why do we do or not do things for his sake? [©2001 by WH.] For info: Wellcat Holidays. Web: www.wellcat.com.

GRAND CANYON NATIONAL PARK ESTABLISHED: ANNIVERSARY. Feb 26, 1919. By an act of Congress, Grand Canyon National Park was established. An immense gorge cut through the high plateaus of northwest Arizona by the raging Colorado River and covering 1,218,375 acres, Grand Canyon National Park is considered one of the most spectacular natural phenomena in the world. Web: www.nps.gov/grca.

STRAUSS, LEVI: BIRTH ANNIVERSARY. Feb 26, 1829. Bavarian immigrant Levi Strauss created the world's first pair of jeans—Levi's 501 jeans—for California's gold miners in 1850. Born at Buttenheim, Bavaria, Germany, he died in 1902.

★ *Birthdays* ★

Johnny Cash, singer ("Guess Things Happen That Way," "Ring of Fire"), born Kingsland, AR, Feb 26, 1932.
Marshall Faulk, football player, born New Orleans, LA, Feb 26, 1973.

February 27

DOMINICAN REPUBLIC: INDEPENDENCE DAY. Feb 27. National Day. Independence gained in 1844 with the withdrawal of Haitians, who had controlled the area for 22 years.

KUWAIT LIBERATED AND 100-HOUR WAR ENDS: ANNIVERSARY. Feb 27, 1991. Allied troops entered Kuwait City, Kuwait, four days after launching a ground offensive. President George Bush declared Kuwait to be liberated and ceased all offensive military operations in the Gulf War. The end of military operations at midnight EST came 100 hours after the beginning of the land attack. Feb 26 is commemorated as Liberation Day in Kuwait.

LONGFELLOW, HENRY WADSWORTH: BIRTH ANNIVERSARY. Feb 27, 1807. American poet and writer, born at Portland, ME. He is best remembered for his classic narrative poems, such as *The Song of Hiawatha, Paul Revere's Ride* and *The Wreck of the Hesperus.* Died at Cambridge, MA, Mar 24, 1882.

TWENTY-SECOND AMENDMENT TO US CONSTITUTION (TWO-TERM LIMIT) RATIFIED: ANNIVERSARY. Feb 27, 1950. After the four successive presidential terms of Franklin Roosevelt, the 22nd Amendment limited the tenure of presidential office to two terms.

★ Birthdays ★

Ralph Nader, consumer advocate, lawyer, presidential candidate, born Winsted, CT, Feb 27, 1934.
Elizabeth Taylor, actress (Oscar for *Who's Afraid of Virginia Woolf?; National Velvet, Cleopatra, Cat on a Hot Tin Roof*), AIDS activist, born London, England, Feb 27, 1932.

February 28

USS *PRINCETON* EXPLOSION: ANNIVERSARY. Feb 28, 1844. The newly built "war steamer," USS *Princeton*, cruising on the Potomac River with top government officials as its passengers, fired one of its guns (known, ironically, as the "Peacemaker") to demonstrate the latest in naval armament. The gun exploded, killing Secretary of State Abel P. Upshur, Secretary of the Navy Thomas W. Gilmer, David Gardiner of Gardiners Island, NY, and several others. Many were injured. The president of the US, John Tyler, was on board and narrowly escaped death.

★ Birthdays ★

Robert Sean Leonard, actor (*The Manhattan Project, Dead Poets Society*), born Westwood, NJ, Feb 28, 1969.
Eric Lindros, hockey player, born London, ON, Canada, Feb 28, 1973.
Bernadette Peters, singer, actress (*Dames at Sea, Annie Get Your Gun*), born Queens, NY, Feb 28, 1944.

March

March 1

BOSNIA AND HERZEGOVINA: INDEPENDENCE DAY. Mar 1. Commemorates independence in 1992 with the breakup of Yugoslavia.

IRISH-AMERICAN HERITAGE MONTH. Mar 1–31. Presidential Proclamation called for by House Joint Resolution 401 (Public Law 103–379).

LAND MINE BAN: ANNIVERSARY. Mar 1, 1999. A United Nations treaty banning land mines took effect on this date. More than 130 nations signed the treaty; the US, Russia and China did not.

MENTAL RETARDATION AWARENESS MONTH. Mar 1–31. To educate the public about the needs of this nation's more than 7 million citizens with mental retardation and about ways to prevent retardation. The Arc is a national organization on mental retardation, formerly the Association for Retarded Citizens. For info: The Arc. Web: www.thearc.org.

MILLER, GLENN: BIRTH ANNIVERSARY. Mar 1, 1904. American bandleader and composer (Alton) Glenn Miller was born at Clarinda, IA. He enjoyed great popularity preceding and during World War II. His hit recordings included "Moonlight Serenade," "String of Pearls," "Jersey Bounce" and "Sleepy Lagoon." Major Miller, leader of the US Army Air Force band, disappeared Dec 15, 1944, over the English Channel, on a flight to Paris where he was scheduled to give a show. There were many explanations of his disappearance, but 41 years later, in December 1985, crew members of an aborted Royal Air Force bombing said they believed they had seen Miller's plane go down, the victim of bombs being jettisoned by the RAF over the English Channel.

MUSIC IN OUR SCHOOLS MONTH. Mar 1–31. To increase public awareness of the importance of music education as part of a balanced curriculum. For info: Music Educators National Conference. Web: www.menc.org.

NATIONAL COLORECTAL CANCER AWARENESS MONTH. Mar 1–31. To generate widespread awareness about colorectal cancer and to encourage people to learn more about how to prevent the disease through a healthy lifestyle and regular screening. Founding partners include the Cancer Research Foundation of America, the National Colorectal Cancer Roundtable and the Foundation for Digestive Health and Nutrition. For info: Cancer Research Foundation of America. Web: www .preventcancer.org/colorectal.

NATIONAL CRAFT MONTH. Mar 1–31. Promoting the fun and creativity of hobbies and crafts. For info: Hobby Industry Association. Web: www .i-craft.com.

NATIONAL FROZEN FOOD MONTH. Mar 1–31. Promotes national awareness of the economical and nutritional benefits of frozen foods. For info: National Frozen Food Association. Web: www .nffa.org.

NATIONAL KIDNEY MONTH. Mar 1–31. Kidney disease often may be silent for many years, until it has reached an advanced stage. The National Kidney Foundation urges everyone to get regular checkups that include tests for blood pressure, blood sugar, urine protein and kidney function. For info: National Kidney Foundation. Web: www.kidney.org.

NATIONAL NUTRITION MONTH®. Mar 1–31. To educate consumers about the importance of good nutrition by providing the latest practical information on how simple it can be to eat healthfully. For info: American Dietetic Association. Web: www.eatright.org.

NATIONAL PROFESSIONAL SOCIAL WORK MONTH. Mar 1–31. To honor the social work profession and to recognize the contributions social workers and concerned citizens make within their communities. For info: National Association of Social Workers. Web: www.socialworkers.org.

NATIONAL UMBRELLA MONTH. Mar 1–31. In honor of one of the most versatile and underrated inventions of the human race, this month is dedicated to the purchase of, use of and conversation about umbrellas. For info: Thomas Edward Knibb. E-mail: tomknibb@juno.com.

NATIONAL WOMEN'S HISTORY MONTH. Mar 1–31. A time for reexamining and celebrating the wide range of women's contributions and achievements that are too often overlooked in the telling of US history. A Presidential Proclamation is issued for this month. For info: National Women's History Project. Web: www.nwhp.org.

NEBRASKA: ADMISSION DAY: ANNIVERSARY. Mar 1. Became 37th state in 1867.

OHIO: ADMISSION DAY: ANNIVERSARY. Mar 1. Became 17th state in 1803.

PEACE CORPS FOUNDED: ANNIVERSARY. Mar 1, 1961. Official establishment of the Peace Corps by President John F. Kennedy's signing of an executive order. The Peace Corps has sent more than 153,000 volunteers to 134 countries to help people help themselves. The volunteers assist in projects such as health, education, water sanitation, agriculture, nutrition and forestry. For info: Peace Corps. Web: www.peacecorps .gov.

POISON PREVENTION AWARENESS MONTH. Mar 1–31. To educate parents, grandparents, school-children and PTAs about accidental poisoning and how to prevent it. For info: Pharmacists Planning Service. Web: www.ppsinc.org.

RED CROSS MONTH. Mar 1–31. To make the public aware of American Red Cross service in the community. There are some 1,300 Red Cross offices nationwide; each local office plans its own activities. Presidential Proclamation for Red Cross Month issued each year for March since 1943. Issued as American Red Cross Month since 1987. For info: American Red Cross National Headquarters. Web: www.red cross.org.

ROSACEA AWARENESS MONTH. Mar 1–31. Rosacea Awareness Month has been designated by the National Rosacea Society to raise understanding of this increasingly common disease. Rosacea is a facial skin condition that can cause permanent physical and psychological damage if it is not diagnosed and treated. For info: National Rosacea Society. Web: www.rosacea .org.

SAVE YOUR VISION MONTH. Mar 1–31. To remind Americans of the importance of eye health and regular exams. For info: American Optometric Association. Web: www.aoanet.org.

WORKPLACE EYE HEALTH AND SAFETY MONTH. Mar 1–31. Can you see the dangers at your workplace? Accidents at work are a major cause of preventable blindness. Find out more about Prevent Blindness America®'s workplace safety program, The Wise Owl Club, and find out how to make your work environment easier on your eyes. For info: Prevent Blindness America®. Web: www.preventblindness.org.

YELLOWSTONE NATIONAL PARK ESTABLISHED: ANNIVERSARY. Mar 1, 1872. The first area in the world to be designated a national park, most of Yellowstone is in Wyoming, with small sections in Montana and Idaho. It was established by an act of Congress. Web: www.nps.gov/yell.

YOUTH ART MONTH. Mar 1–31. To emphasize the value and importance of participation in art in the development of all children and youth. For info: Council for Art Education. Web: acminet.org/youthartmonth.

★ *Birthdays* ★

Harry Belafonte, actor (*Carmen Jones*), singer ("Mary's Boy Child," "Banana Boat Song"), born New York, NY, Mar 1, 1927.

Ron Howard, actor ("The Andy Griffith Show," "Happy Days"), director (*Cocoon, Backdraft*; Oscar for *A Beautiful Mind*), born Duncan, OK, Mar 1, 1954.

March 2

GEISEL, THEODOR "DR. SEUSS": BIRTH ANNIVERSARY. Mar 2, 1904. Theodor Seuss Geisel, the creator of *The Cat in the Hat* and *How the Grinch Stole Christmas*, was born at Springfield, MA. Known to children and parents as Dr. Seuss, his books have sold more than 200 million copies and have been translated into 20 languages. His career began with *And to Think That I Saw It on Mulberry Street*, which was turned down by 27 publishing houses before being published by Vanguard Press. His books included many messages, from environmental consciousness in *The Lorax* to the dangers of pacifism in *Horton Hatches the Egg* and *Yertle the Turtle*'s thinly veiled references to Hitler as the title character. He was awarded a Pulitzer Prize in 1984 "for his contribution over nearly half a century to the education and enjoyment of America's children and their parents." He died Sept 24, 1991, at La Jolla, CA.

HIGHWAY NUMBERS INTRODUCED: ANNIVERSARY. Mar 2, 1925. A joint board of state and federal highway officials created the first system of interstate highway numbering in the US. Standardized road signs identifying the routes were also introduced. Later the system would be improved with the use of odd and even numbers that distinguish between north-south and east-west routes respectively.

HOUSTON, SAM: BIRTH ANNIVERSARY. Mar 2, 1793. American soldier and politician, born at Rockbridge County, VA, is remembered for his role in Texas history. Houston was a congressman (1823–27) and governor (1827–29) of Tennessee. He resigned his office as governor in 1829 and rejoined the Cherokee Indians (with whom he had lived for several years as a teenage runaway), who accepted him as a member of their tribe. Houston went to Texas in 1832 and became commander of the Texan army in the War for Texan Independence, which was secured when Houston routed the much larger Mexican forces led by Santa Anna, Apr 21,

1836, at the Battle of San Jacinto. After Texas's admission to the Union, Houston served as US senator and later as governor of the state. He was deposed in 1861 when he refused to swear allegiance to the Confederacy. Houston, the only person to have been elected governor of two different states, failed to serve his full term of office in either. The city of Houston, TX, was named for him. He died July 26, 1863, at Huntsville, TX.

MOUNT RAINIER NATIONAL PARK ESTABLISHED: ANNIVERSARY. Mar 2, 1899. Located in the Cascade Mountains of Washington State, this is the fourth oldest national park. Web: www .nps.gov/mora.

READ ACROSS AMERICA DAY. Mar 2. A national reading campaign that advocates that all children read a book the evening of Mar 2. Celebrated on Dr. Seuss's birthday. For info: National Education Association. Web: www.nea .org/readacross.

SPACE MILESTONE: *PIONEER 10* (US). Mar 2, 1972. This unmanned probe began a journey on which it passed and photographed Jupiter and its moons, 620 million miles from Earth, in December 1973. It crossed the orbit of Pluto, and then in 1983 become the first known Earth object to leave our solar system. On Sept 22, 1987, *Pioneer 10* reached another space milestone at 4:19 PM, when it reached a distance 50 times farther from the sun than the sun is from Earth.

TEXAS INDEPENDENCE DAY. Mar 2, 1836. Texas adopted Declaration of Independence from Mexico.

★ *Birthdays* ★

John Cullum, actor (stage: *Shenandoah*; "Northern Exposure"), born Knoxville, TN, Mar 2, 1930.

John Irving, author (*The Cider House Rules, The World According to Garp*), born Exeter, NH, Mar 2, 1942.

March 3

BELL, ALEXANDER GRAHAM: BIRTH ANNIVERSARY. Mar 3, 1847. Inventor of the telephone, born at Edinburgh, Scotland, Bell acquired his interest in the transmission of sound from his father, Melville Bell, a teacher of the deaf. Bell's use of visual devices to teach articulation to the deaf contributed to the theory from which he derived the principle of the vibrating membrane used in the telephone. On Mar 10, 1876, Bell spoke the first electrically transmitted sentence to his assistant in the next room: "Mr Watson, come here, I want you." Bell's other accomplishments include a refinement of Edison's phonograph, the first successful phonograph record and the audiometer, and he continued exploring the nature and causes of deafness. He died near Baddeck, NS, Canada, Aug 2, 1922.

BONZA BOTTLER DAY™. Mar 3. To celebrate when the number of the day is the same as the number of the month. Bonza Bottler Day™ is an excuse to have a party at least once a month. For info: Gail M. Berger. E-mail: gberger5@aol .com.

FLORIDA: ADMISSION DAY: ANNIVERSARY. Mar 3. Became 27th state in 1845.

MISSOURI COMPROMISE: ANNIVERSARY. Mar 3, 1820. In February of 1819, a bill was introduced into Congress that would admit Missouri to the Union as a state that prohibited slavery. At the time there were 11 free states and ten slave states. Southern congressmen feared this would upset the balance of power between North and South. As a compromise, on this date Missouri was admitted as a slave state but slavery was forever prohibited in the northern part of the Louisiana Purchase. In 1854, this act was repealed when Kansas and Nebraska were allowed to decide on slave or free status by popular vote.

NATIONAL ANTHEM DAY: ANNIVERSARY. Mar 3, 1931. The bill designating "The Star-Spangled Banner" as our national anthem was adopted by the US Senate and went to President Herbert Hoover for signature. The president signed it the same day.

***TIME* MAGAZINE FIRST PUBLISHED: ANNIVERSARY.** Mar 3, 1923. The first issue of *Time* bore this date. The magazine was founded by Henry Luce and Briton Hadden.

WHAT IF CATS AND DOGS HAD OPPOSABLE THUMBS DAY. Mar 3. We are grateful today that the infinite wisdom of the universe has not allowed cats and dogs to have thumbs. Imagine the cat able to operate the can opener! Imagine the dog able to open the refrigerator door! [©2001 by WH.] For info: Wellcat Holidays. Web: www.well cat.com.

★ *Birthdays* ★

Brian Leetch, hockey player, born Corpus Christi, TX, Mar 3, 1968.
Miranda Richardson, actress (*The Crying Game, Enchanted April*), born Lancashire, England, Mar 3, 1958.

March 4

GROVER CLEVELAND'S SECOND PRESIDENTIAL INAUGURATION: ANNIVERSARY. Mar 4, 1893. Grover Cleveland was inaugurated for a second but nonconsecutive term as president. In 1885 he had become the 22nd president of the US and in 1893 the 24th. Originally a source of some controversy, the Congressional Directory for some time listed him only as the 22nd president. The directory now lists him as both the 22nd and 24th presidents though some historians continue to argue that one person cannot be both. Benjamin Harrison served during the intervening term, defeating Cleveland in electoral votes, though not in the popular vote.

OLD INAUGURATION DAY. Mar 4. Anniversary of the date set for beginning the US presidential term of office, 1789–1933. Although the Continental Congress had set the first Wednesday of March 1789 as the date for the new government to convene, a quorum was not present to count the electoral votes until Apr 6. Though George Washington's term of office began on Mar 4, he did not take the oath of office until Apr 30, 1789. All subsequent presidential terms (except successions following the death of an incumbent), until Franklin D. Roosevelt's second term, began Mar 4. The 20th Amendment (ratified Jan 23, 1933) provided that "the terms of the President and Vice President shall end at noon on the 20th day of January . . . and the terms of their successors shall then begin."

PEOPLE MAGAZINE: ANNIVERSARY. Mar 4, 1974. The popular magazine highlighting celebrities was officially launched with the Mar 4, 1974, issue featuring a cover photo of Mia Farrow.

PULASKI, CASIMIR: BIRTH ANNIVERSARY. Mar 4, 1747. American Revolutionary hero, General Kazimierz (Casimir) Pulaski, born at Winiary, Mazovia, Poland, the son of a count. He was a patriot and military leader in Poland's fight against Russia of 1770–71 and went into exile at the partition of Poland in 1772. He came to America in 1777 to join the Revolution, fighting with General Washington at Brandywine and also serving at Germantown and Valley Forge. He organized the Pulaski Legion to wage guerrilla warfare against the British. Mortally wounded in a heroic charge at the siege of Savannah, GA, he died aboard the warship *Wasp* Oct 11, 1779. Pulaski Day is celebrated on the first Monday of March in Illinois.

TELEVISION ACADEMY HALL OF FAME: FIRST INDUCTEES ANNOUNCED: ANNIVERSARY. Mar 4, 1984. The Television Academy of Arts and Sciences announced the formation of the Television Academy Hall of Fame at Burbank, CA.

The first inductees were Lucille Ball, Milton Berle, Paddy Chayefsky, Norman Lear, Edward R. Murrow, William S. Paley and David Sarnoff.

VERMONT: ADMISSION DAY: ANNIVERSARY. Mar 4. Became 14th state in 1791.

★ Birthdays ★

Patricia Heaton, actress ("Everybody Loves Raymond"), born Bay Village, OH, Mar 4, 1959.

Steven Weber, actor (*Leaving Las Vegas*, "Wings," "Once and Again"), born Queens, NY, Mar 4, 1961.

March 5

BOSTON MASSACRE: ANNIVERSARY. Mar 5, 1770. A skirmish between British troops and a crowd at Boston, MA, became widely publicized and contributed to the unpopularity of the British regime in America before the American Revolution. Five men were killed and six more were injured by British troops. One of the dead was Crispus Attucks, possibly a runaway slave.

"IRON CURTAIN" SPEECH: ANNIVERSARY. Mar 5, 1946. Winston Churchill, speaking at Westminster College, Fulton, MO, established the cold war boundary with these words: "From Stettin in the Baltic to Trieste in the Adriatic an iron curtain has descended across the continent." Though Churchill was not the first to use the phrase *iron curtain*, his speech gave it a new currency and its usage persisted.

MERCATOR, GERHARDUS: BIRTH ANNIVERSARY. Mar 5, 1512. Cartographer-geographer Mercator was born at Rupelmonde, Belgium. His Mercator projection for maps provided an accurate ratio of latitude to longitude and is still used today. He also introduced the term "atlas" for a collection of maps. He died at Duisberg, Germany, Dec 2, 1594.

US BANK HOLIDAY: ANNIVERSARY. Mar 5, 1933. On his first full day in office (Sunday, Mar 5, 1933), President Franklin Roosevelt proclaimed a national "Bank Holiday" to help save the nation's faltering banking system. Most banks were able to reopen after the ten-day "holiday" (Mar 4–14), but in the meantime, "scrip" had temporarily replaced money in many American households.

★ Birthdays ★

Penn Jillette, magician with his partner Teller, born Greenfield, MA, Mar 5, 1955.

Marsha Warfield, actress ("Night Court," "Empty Nest"), born Chicago, IL, Mar 5, 1954.

March 6

DRED SCOTT DECISION: ANNIVERSARY. Mar 6, 1857. The Supreme Court ruled that Dred Scott, a slave, was not a citizen and could not sue in the federal courts. Chief Justice Roger Taney wrote that blacks could not be citizens and that Congress had no power to restrict slavery in the territories. The most famous court case in the long slavery controversy.

FALL OF THE ALAMO: ANNIVERSARY. Mar 6, 1836. Anniversary of the fall of the Texan fort, the Alamo. The siege, led by Mexican general Santa Anna, began Feb 23 and reached its climax Mar 6, when the last of the defenders was slain. Texans, under General Sam Houston, rallied with the war cry "Remember the Alamo" and, at the Battle of San Jacinto, Apr 21, defeated and captured Santa Anna, who signed a treaty recognizing Texas's independence.

GHANA: INDEPENDENCE DAY. Mar 6. National holiday. Commemorates independence from Great Britain in 1957.

MICHELANGELO: BIRTH ANNIVERSARY. Mar 6, 1475. Anniversary of the birth, at Caprese, Italy, of Michelangelo di Lodovico Buonarroti Simoni, a prolific Renaissance painter, sculptor, architect and poet who had a profound impact on Western art. Michelangelo's fresco painting on the ceiling of the Sistine Chapel at the Vatican at Rome, Italy, is often considered the pinnacle of his achievement in painting, as well as the highest achievement of the Renaissance. Also among his works were the sculptures *David* and *The Pieta*. Appointed architect of St. Peter's in 1542, a post he held until his death Feb 18, 1564, at Rome.

NATIONAL PROCRASTINATION WEEK. Mar 6–12. To promote the benefits of relaxing through putting off until tomorrow everything that needn't be done today. For info: Procrastinators' Club of America. E-mail: tardyguys@aol.com.

★ Birthdays ★

Alan Greenspan, economist, chairman of the Federal Reserve Board, born New York, NY, Mar 6, 1926.
Shaquille O'Neal, basketball player, born Newark, NJ, Mar 6, 1972.
Rob Reiner, actor ("All in the Family"), director (*When Harry Met Sally . . ., This Is Spinal Tap*), born New York, NY, Mar 6, 1945 (some sources say 1947).

March 7

BURBANK, LUTHER: BIRTH ANNIVERSARY. Mar 7, 1849. Anniversary of birth of American naturalist and author, creator and developer of many new varieties of flowers, fruits, vegetables and trees. Luther Burbank's birthday is observed in California as Bird and Arbor Day. Born at Lancaster, MA, he died at Santa Rosa, CA, Apr 11, 1926.

MONOPOLY INVENTED: ANNIVERSARY. Mar 7, 1933. While unemployed during the Depression, Charles Darrow devised this game and sold it himself for two years. Monopoly was mass-marketed by Parker Brothers beginning in 1935. Darrow died a millionaire in 1967.

★ Birthdays ★

Franco Harris, Hall of Fame football player, born Fort Dix, NJ, Mar 7, 1950.

Willard Herman Scott, weatherman ("Today"), friend of centenarians, born Alexandria, VA, Mar 7, 1934.

March 8

UNITED NATIONS: DAY FOR WOMEN'S RIGHTS AND INTERNATIONAL PEACE. Mar 8. An international day observed by the organizations of the United Nations system. Previously known as International Women's Day. Web: www.un.org.

★ Birthdays ★

Camryn Manheim, actress ("The Practice"), born Caldwell, NJ, Mar 8, 1961.

Aidan Quinn, actor (*Desperately Seeking Susan*; stage: *A Streetcar Named Desire*), born Chicago, IL, Mar 8, 1959.

March 9

BARBIE DEBUTS: ANNIVERSARY. Mar 9, 1959. The popular girls' doll debuted in stores. More than 800 million dolls have been sold.

PANIC DAY. Mar 9. Run around all day in a panic, telling others you can't handle it anymore. [©2001 by WH.] For info: Wellcat Holidays. Web: www.wellcat.com.

VESPUCCI, AMERIGO: BIRTH ANNIVERSARY. Mar 9, 1451. Italian navigator, merchant and explorer for whom the Americas were named. Born at Florence, Italy. He participated in at least two expeditions between 1499 and 1502 that took him to the coast of South America, where he discovered the Amazon and Plata Rivers.

Vespucci's expeditions were of great importance because he believed that he had discovered a new continent, not just a new route to the Orient. Neither Vespucci nor his exploits achieved the fame of Columbus, but the New World was to be named for Amerigo Vespucci by an obscure German geographer and mapmaker, Martin Waldseemuller. Ironically, in his work as an outfitter of ships, Vespucci had been personally acquainted with Christopher Columbus. Vespucci died at Seville, Spain, Feb 22, 1512.

★ Birthdays ★

Juliette Binoche, actress (*The English Patient, Chocolat*), born Paris, France, Mar 9, 1964.
Linda Fiorentino, actress (*Men in Black*), born Philadelphia, PA, Mar 9, 1960.

March 10

TUBMAN, HARRIET: DEATH ANNIVERSARY. Mar 10, 1913. American abolitionist, Underground Railroad leader, born a slave at Bucktown, Dorchester County, MD, about 1820 or 1821. She escaped from a Maryland plantation in 1849 and later helped more than 300 slaves reach freedom. Died at Auburn, NY.

US PAPER MONEY ISSUED: ANNIVERSARY. Mar 10, 1862. The first paper money was issued in the US on this date. The denominations were $5 (Hamilton), $10 (Lincoln) and $20 (Liberty).

They became legal tender by an act of Congress Mar 17, 1862.

★ Birthdays ★

Chuck Norris, actor (*Missing in Action*, "Walker, Texas Ranger"), born Ryan, OK, Mar 10, 1940.
Sharon Stone, actress (*Basic Instinct, The Specialist, Casino*), born Meadville, PA, Mar 10, 1958.

March 11

BUREAU OF INDIAN AFFAIRS ESTABLISHED: ANNIVERSARY. Mar 11, 1824. The US War Department created the Bureau of Indian Affairs.

CAMPBELL, MALCOLM: BIRTH ANNIVERSARY. Mar 11, 1885. Record-making British auto racer, the first man to travel five miles a minute (300 MPH) in an automobile. Born at Chislehurst, Kent, England. Died at his home at Surrey, England, Dec 31, 1948.

PANDEMIC OF 1918 HITS US: ANNIVERSARY. Mar 11, 1918. The first cases of the "Spanish" influenza were reported in the US when 107 soldiers became sick at Fort Riley, KS. By the end of 1920 nearly 25 percent of the US population had had it. As many as 500,000 civilians died from the virus, exceeding the number of US troops killed abroad in World War I. Worldwide, more than 1 percent of the global population, or 22 million people, had died by 1920. The origin of the virus was never determined absolutely, though it was probably somewhere in Asia. The name "Spanish" influenza came from the relatively high number of cases in that country early in the epidemic. Due to the panic, cancellation of public events was common and many public service workers wore masks on the job. Emergency tent hospitals were set up in some locations due to overcrowding.

★ *Birthdays* ★

Sam Donaldson, journalist, born El Paso, TX, Mar 11, 1934.

Alex Kingston, actress ("ER"), born London, England, Mar 11, 1963.

Antonin Scalia, associate justice of the US Supreme Court, born Trenton, NJ, Mar 11, 1936.

March 12

AUSTRIA INVADED BY NAZI GERMANY: ANNIVERSARY. Mar 12, 1938. As a test of its own war readiness and of the response of the other major powers, Germany occupied Austria. A year later Germany invaded Czechoslovakia and, in September 1939, Poland, beginning World War II.

BOYCOTT, CHARLES CUNNINGHAM: BIRTH ANNIVERSARY. Mar 12, 1832. Charles Cunningham Boycott, born at Norfolk, England, has been immortalized by having his name become part of the English language. In County Mayo, Ireland, the Tenants' Land League in 1880 asked Boycott, an estate agent, to reduce rents (because of poor harvest and dire economic conditions). Boycott responded by serving eviction notices on the tenants, who retaliated by refusing to have any dealings with him. Charles Stewart Parnell, then president of the National Land League and agrarian agitator, retaliated against Boycott by implementing the method of economic and social ostracism that came to be called a "boycott." Boycott died at Suffolk, England, June 19, 1897.

FDR'S FIRST FIRESIDE CHAT: ANNIVERSARY. Mar 12, 1933. President Franklin Delano Roosevelt made the first of his Sunday evening "fireside chats" to the American people. Speaking by radio from the White House, he reported rather informally on the economic problems of the nation and on his actions to deal with them.

GIRL SCOUTS OF THE USA FOUNDING: ANNIVERSARY. Mar 12, 1912. Juliet Low founded the Girl Scouts of the USA at Savannah, GA.

KEROUAC, JACK: BIRTH ANNIVERSARY. Mar 12, 1922. American poet and novelist Jack (Jean-Louis) Kerouac, leader and spokesman for the Beat movement, was born at Lowell, MA. Kerouac is best known for his novel *On the Road*, published in 1957, which celebrates the Beat ideal of nonconformity. Kerouac published *The Dharma Bums* in 1958, followed by *The Subterraneans* the same year, *Big Sur* in 1962 and *Desolation Angels* in 1965. Kerouac died at St. Petersburg, FL, at age 47, Oct 21, 1969.

★ *Birthdays* ★

Edward Albee, playwright, born Washington, DC, Mar 12, 1928.
Liza Minnelli, singer, actress (Oscar for *Cabaret; The Sterile Cuckoo, Arthur*), born Los Angeles, CA, Mar 12, 1946.

March 13

DEAF HISTORY MONTH. Mar 13–Apr 15. Observance of three of the most important anniversaries for deaf Americans: Apr 15, 1817, establishment of the first public school for the deaf in America, later known as The American School for the Deaf; Apr 8, 1864, charter signed by President Lincoln authorizing the Board of Directors of the Columbia Institution (now Gallaudet University) to grant college degrees to deaf students; Mar 13, 1988, the victory of the Deaf President Now movement at Gallaudet. For info: Library for Deaf Action. Web: www.LibraryDeaf.com.

EARMUFFS PATENTED: ANNIVERSARY. Mar 13, 1887. Chester Greenwood of Maine received a patent for earmuffs.

"THE LARRY KING SHOW" TV PREMIERE: ANNIVERSARY. Mar 13, 1983. Radio talk-show host Larry King brought his topical interview program to syndicated TV in 1983. Using a telephone hookup, viewers called in to speak to particular guests. King has been appearing on CNN since 1985 interviewing a variety of newsmakers and celebrities.

PLANET URANUS DISCOVERY: ANNIVERSARY. Mar 13, 1781. German-born English astronomer Sir William Herschel discovered the seventh planet from the sun, Uranus.

PRIESTLY, JOSEPH: BIRTH ANNIVERSARY. Mar 13, 1733 (OS). English clergyman and scientist, discoverer of oxygen, born at Fieldhead, England. He and his family narrowly escaped an angry mob attacking their home because of his religious and political views. They moved to the US in 1794. Died at Northumberland, PA, Feb 6, 1804.

SAINT AUBIN, HELEN "CALLAGHAN" CANDAELE: BIRTH ANNIVERSARY. Mar 13, 1929. Helen Candaele Saint Aubin, known as Helen Callaghan during her baseball days, was born at Vancouver, BC, Canada. Saint Aubin and her sister, Margaret Maxwell, were recruited for the All-American Girls Professional Baseball League, which flourished in the 1940s when many major league players were off fighting World War II.

She first played at age 15 for the Minneapolis Millerettes, an expansion team that moved to Indiana and became the Fort Wayne Daisies. For the 1945 season the left-handed outfielder led the league with a .299 average and 24 extra base hits. In 1946 she stole 114 bases in 111 games. Her son Kelly Candaele's documentary on the women's baseball league inspired the film *A League of Their Own*. Saint Aubin, who was known as the "Ted Williams of women's baseball," died Dec 8, 1992, at Santa Barbara, CA.

★ Birthdays ★

William H. Macy, actor (*Fargo, Magnolia*, "ER"), born Miami, FL, Mar 13, 1950.
Neil Sedaka, singer, songwriter ("Breaking Up Is Hard to Do" with Howard Greenfield), born Brooklyn, NY, Mar 13, 1939.

March 14

EINSTEIN, ALBERT: BIRTH ANNIVERSARY. Mar 14, 1879. Theoretical physicist best known for his theory of relativity. Born at Ulm, Germany, he won the Nobel Prize in 1921. Died at Princeton, NJ, Apr 18, 1955.

JONES, CASEY: BIRTH ANNIVERSARY. Mar 14, 1864. Railroad engineer and hero of a ballad, whose real name was John Luther Jones. Born near Cayce, KY, he died in a railroad wreck near Vaughn, MS, Apr 30, 1900.

"TEN MOST WANTED" LIST DEBUTS: ANNIVERSARY. Mar 14, 1950. The Federal Bureau of Investigation instituted the "Ten Most Wanted Fugitives" list in an effort to publicize particularly dangerous criminals who were at large. From 1950 to 1998, 454 fugitives appeared on the list; 130 were captured. Generally, the only way to get off the list is to die or be captured. The FBI cooperates with the producers of TV's "America's Most Wanted" to further publicize these fugitives.

★ Birthdays ★

Michael Caine, actor (*Alfie, The Ipcress File, Sleuth*), born Maurice Joseph Micklewhite at London, England, Mar 14, 1933.
Billy Crystal, actor ("Soap," *When Harry Met Sally . . ., City Slickers*), born Long Beach, NY, Mar 14, 1947.
Quincy Jones, composer, producer ("We Are the World"), born Chicago, IL, Mar 14, 1933.

March 15

IDES OF MARCH. Mar 15. In the Roman calendar the days of the month were not numbered sequentially. Instead, each month had three division days: kalends, nones and ides. Days were numbered from these divisions: e.g., IV Nones or III Ides. The ides occurred on the 15th of the month (or on the 13th in months that had fewer than 31 days). Julius Caesar was assassinated on this day in 44 BC. This system was used in Europe well into the Renaissance. When Shakespeare wrote "Beware the ides of March" in *Julius Caesar* his audience knew what he meant.

JACKSON, ANDREW: BIRTH ANNIVERSARY. Mar 15, 1767. Seventh president of the US (Mar 4, 1829–Mar 3, 1837) was born in a log cabin at Waxhaw, SC. Jackson was the first president since George Washington who had not attended college. He was a military hero in the War of 1812. His presidency reflected his democratic and egalitarian values. Died at Nashville, TN, June 8, 1845. His birthday is observed as a holiday in Tennessee.

MAINE: ADMISSION DAY: ANNIVERSARY. Mar 15. Became 23rd state in 1820. Prior to this date, Maine had been part of Massachusetts.

NATIONAL BRUTUS DAY. Mar 15. No matter where you work, you must admit there's as much intrigue, plotting and backstabbing as was found in ancient Rome or is found today inside the Beltway. [©2001 by WH.] For info: Wellcat Holidays. Web: www.wellcat.com.

"THREE'S COMPANY" TV PREMIERE: ANNIVERSARY. Mar 15, 1977. This half-hour comedy featured two girls and a guy sharing an apartment. In order for the landlord to go along with the living arrangements, Jack Tripper, played by John Ritter, had to pretend he was gay. Cast included Joyce DeWitt, Suzanne Somers, Norman Fell, Audra Lindley, Richard Kline, Don Knotts and Priscilla Barnes. The last telecast aired on Sept 18, 1984.

"THE WONDER YEARS" TV PREMIERE: ANNIVERSARY. Mar 15, 1988. A coming-of-age tale set in suburbia in the 1960s and '70s. This drama/comedy starred Fred Savage as Kevin Arnold, Josh Saviano as his best friend Paul and Danica McKellar as girlfriend Winnie. Kevin's dad was played by Dan Lauria, his homemaker mom by Alley Mills, his hippie sister by Olivia d'Abo and his bully brother by Jason Hervey. Narrator Daniel Stern was the voice of the grown-up Kevin. The last episode ran Sept 1, 1993, but the show remains popular in syndication.

★ Birthdays ★

Ruth Bader Ginsburg, associate justice of the US Supreme Court, born Brooklyn, NY, Mar 15, 1933.
Judd Hirsch, actor (Emmy for "Taxi"; *Ordinary People*), born New York, NY, Mar 15, 1935.

March 16

BLACK PRESS DAY: ANNIVERSARY OF THE FIRST BLACK NEWSPAPER. Mar 16, 1827. Anniversary of the founding of the first black newspaper in the US, *Freedom's Journal*, on Varick Street at New York, NY.

FREEDOM OF INFORMATION DAY. Mar 16. On the birthday of James Madison, the American Library Association urges libraries and librarians to join in celebrating the public's "right to know" by sponsoring activities to educate their communities about the importance of promoting and protecting freedom of information. Sponsored by the Freedom Forum and the American Library Association. For info: American Library Association Washington Office. Web: www.ala.org.

MADISON, JAMES: BIRTH ANNIVERSARY. Mar 16, 1751. Fourth president of the US (Mar 4, 1809–Mar 3, 1817), born at Port Conway, VA. He was president when British forces invaded Washington, DC, requiring Madison and other high officials to flee while the British burned the Capitol, the president's residence and most other public buildings (Aug 24–25, 1814). Died at Montpelier, VA, June 28, 1836.

MY LAI MASSACRE: ANNIVERSARY. Mar 16, 1968. Most-publicized atrocity of Vietnam War. According to findings of US Army's investigating team, approximately 300 noncombatant Vietnamese villagers (at My Lai and Mykhe, near the South China Sea) were killed by infantrymen of the American Division.

US MILITARY ACADEMY FOUNDED: ANNIVERSARY. Mar 16, 1802. President Thomas Jefferson signed legislation establishing the United States Military Academy to train officers for the army. The college is located at West Point, NY, on the site of the oldest continuously occupied military post in America. Women were admitted to West Point in 1976. The Academy's motto is "Duty, Honor, Country." Web: www.usma.edu.

★ Birthdays ★

Lauren Graham, actress (*One True Thing*, "The Gilmore Girls"), born Honolulu, HI, Mar 16, 1967.
Jerry Lewis, comedian, actor (*My Friend Irma*); director (*The Bellboy*), born Newark, NJ, Mar 16, 1925.

March 17

COLE, NAT "KING" (NATHANIEL ADAMS COLE): BIRTH ANNIVERSARY. Mar 17, 1919. Nat "King" Cole was born at Montgomery, AL, and began his musical career at an early age, playing the piano at age four. He was the first black entertainer to host a national television show. His many songs included "The Christmas Song," "Nature Boy," "Mona Lisa," "Ramblin' Rose" and "Unforgettable." Although he was dogged by racial discrimination throughout his career, including the cancellation of his television show because opposition from Southern white viewers decreased advertising revenue, Cole was criticized by prominent black newspapers for not joining other black entertainers in the civil rights struggle. Cole contributed more than $50,000 to civil rights organizations in response to the criticism. Nat "King" Cole died Feb 25, 1965, at Santa Monica, CA.

JONES, BOBBY: BIRTH ANNIVERSARY. Mar 17, 1902. Golfing great Robert Tyre Jones, Jr, first golfer to win the grand slam (the four major British and American tournaments in one year). Born at Atlanta, GA, he died there Dec 18, 1971.

SAINT PATRICK'S DAY. Mar 17. Commemorates the patron saint of Ireland, Bishop Patrick (AD 389–461), who, about AD 432, left his home in the Severn Valley, England, and introduced Christianity into Ireland. Feast Day in the Roman Catholic Church. A national holiday in Ireland and Northern Ireland.

SOUTH AFRICAN WHITES VOTE TO END MINORITY RULE: ANNIVERSARY. Mar 17, 1992. A referendum proposing ending white minority rule through negotiations was supported by a whites-only ballot. The vote of 1,924,186 (68.6 percent) whites in support of President F.W. de Klerk's reform policies was greater than expected.

★ Birthdays ★

Rob Lowe, actor (*St. Elmo's Fire, About Last Night*, "The West Wing"), born Charlottesville, VA, Mar 17, 1964.
Gary Sinise, stage and screen actor (*Forrest Gump, Apollo 13*), born Chicago, IL, Mar 17, 1955.

March 18

CLEVELAND, GROVER: BIRTH ANNIVERSARY. Mar 18, 1837. The 22nd and 24th president of the US was born Stephen Grover Cleveland at Caldwell, NJ. Terms of office as president: Mar 4, 1885–Mar 3, 1889, and Mar 4, 1893–Mar 3, 1897. He ran for president for the intervening term and received a plurality of votes cast but failed to win electoral college victory. Only president to serve two nonconsecutive terms.

Also the only president to be married in the White House. He married 21-year-old Frances Folsom, his ward. Their daughter, Esther, was the first child of a president to be born in the White House. Died at Princeton, NJ, June 24, 1908.

JORDAN'S BACK!: ANNIVERSARY. Mar 18, 1995. Michael Jordan, considered one of the NBA's greatest all-time players, made history again when he announced that he was returning to professional play after a 17-month break. The 32-year-old star had retired just before the start of the 1993–94 season, following the murder of his father, James Jordan. Jordan, who averaged 32.3 points a game during regular season play, had led the Chicago Bulls to three successive NBA titles. While retired, he tried a baseball career, playing for the Chicago White Sox minor league team. On his return to the Bulls, he led them to three more NBA titles in 1996, 1997 and 1998. He announced his retirement again Jan 13, 1999, after the six-month NBA lockout was resolved. In 2001, Jordan took to the court again, playing for the Washington Wizards.

SPACE MILESTONE: *VOSKHOD 2* (USSR). Mar 18, 1965. Colonel Leonov stepped out of the capsule for 20 minutes in a special space suit, the first man to leave a spaceship. It was two months prior to the first US space walk. See also: "Space Milestone: *Gemini 4* (US)" (June 3).

★ *Birthdays* ★

Queen Latifah, rap artist, actress (*Jungle Fever*, "Living Single"), born Dana Owens at East Orange, NJ, Mar 18, 1970.

Vanessa Williams, singer, actress (*Bye, Bye Birdie; Kiss of the Spider Woman*), born New York, NY, Mar 18, 1963.

March 19

BRYAN, WILLIAM JENNINGS: BIRTH ANNIVERSARY. Mar 19, 1860. American political leader, member of Congress, Democratic presidential nominee (1896), "free silver" advocate, assisted in prosecution at Scopes trial, known as "the Silver-Tongued Orator." Born at Salem, IL, he died at Dayton, TN, July 26, 1925.

EARP, WYATT: BIRTH ANNIVERSARY. Mar 19, 1848. Born at Monmouth, IL, and died Jan 13, 1929, at Los Angeles, CA. A legendary figure of the

Old West, Earp worked as a railroad hand, saloonkeeper, gambler, lawman, gunslinger, miner and real estate investor at various times. Best known for the gunfight at the OK Corral Oct 26, 1881, at Tombstone, AZ.

"THE MARY TYLER MOORE SHOW": THE FINAL EPISODE: ANNIVERSARY. Mar 19, 1977. "Mary Tyler Moore" was the first of a new wave of sitcoms to make it big in the early '70s. It combined good writing, an effective supporting cast and contemporary attitudes. The show centered around the two most important places in Mary Richards's (Mary Tyler Moore) life—the WJM-TV newsroom and her apartment at Minneapolis. At home she shared the ups and downs of life with her friend Rhoda Morgenstern (Valerie Harper) and the manager of her apartment building, Phyllis Lindstrom (Cloris Leachman). At work, as the associate producer (later producer) of "The Six O'Clock News," Mary struggled to function in a man's world. Figuring in her professional life were her irascible boss Lou Grant (Ed Asner), levelheaded and softhearted news writer Murray Slaughter (Gavin MacLeod) and narcissistic anchorman Ted Baxter (Ted Knight). In the last episode the unthinkable happened—everyone in the WJM newsroom except the inept Ted was fired. (Pre-miered Sept 19, 1970, and ran for 168 episodes.)

SWALLOWS RETURN TO SAN JUAN CAPISTRANO. Mar 19. Traditional date (St. Joseph's Day), since 1776, for swallows to return to the old mission at San Juan Capistrano, CA.

US STANDARD TIME ACT: ANNIVERSARY. Mar 19, 1918. Anniversary of passage by the Congress of the Standard Time Act, which authorized the Interstate Commerce Commission to establish standard time zones for the US. The Act also established "Daylight Saving Time," to save fuel and to promote other economies in a country at war. Daylight Saving Time first went into operation on Easter Sunday, Mar 31, 1918. The Uniform Time Act of 1966, as amended in 1986, by Public Law 99–359, now governs standard time in the US. Daylight Saving Time begins on the first Sunday in April and ends on the last Sunday in October (except in Hawaii, Arizona and parts of Indiana).

★ Birthdays ★

Glenn Close, actress (*The Big Chill, Fatal Attraction*; stage: *Sunset Boulevard*), born Greenwich, CT, Mar 19, 1947.
Bruce Willis, actor ("Moonlighting," *The Sixth Sense, Die Hard*), born Idar-Oberstein, West Germany, Mar 19, 1955.

March 20

NERVE-GAS ATTACK ON JAPANESE SUBWAY: ANNIVERSARY. Mar 20, 1995. Twelve people were killed and 5,000 injured in a nerve-gas attack on the Tokyo subway system during rush hour. Suspected in the attack was the Japanese religious sect Aum Shinrikyo, founded and led by Shoko Asahara (real name Chizuo Matsumoto). The group, which professes belief in a hybrid of Buddhist-Hindu teachings, predicts an apocalypse. In a raid conducted against the sect's main compound in Kamikuishiki on Mar 25, police seized literature that predicted 90 percent of the people in the world would be killed by poison gas. Also seized were two tons of chemicals for making sarin, the poison used in the Mar 20 attack. This cache was reported to contain enough material to kill 5 million people. In a second raid, Asahara was arrested.

TUNISIA: INDEPENDENCE DAY. Mar 20. Commemorates treaty in 1956 by which France recognized Tunisian autonomy.

★ Birthdays ★

Holly Hunter, actress (Oscar for *The Piano; Broadcast News, The Firm*), born Conyers, GA, Mar 20, 1958.
William Hurt, actor (*The Accidental Tourist, Broadcast News*), born Washington, DC, Mar 20, 1950.
Spike Lee, actor (*She's Gotta Have It, Do the Right Thing, Malcolm X*), director (*Mo' Better Blues, Jungle Fever*), producer, writer, born Atlanta, GA, Mar 20, 1957.
Fred Rogers, producer, TV personality ("Mr Rogers' Neighborhood"), born Latrobe, PA, Mar 20, 1928.

March 21

ARIES, THE RAM. Mar 21–Apr 19. In the astronomical/astrological zodiac, which divides the sun's apparent orbit into 12 segments, the period Mar 21–Apr 19 is identified, traditionally, as the sun sign of Aries, the Ram. The ruling planet is Mars.

BACH, JOHANN SEBASTIAN: BIRTH ANNIVERSARY. Mar 21, 1685. Organist and composer, one of the most influential composers in musical history. Born at Eisenach, Germany; he died at Leipzig, Germany, July 28, 1750.

FIRST ROUND-THE-WORLD BALLOON FLIGHT: ANNIVERSARY. Mar 21, 1999. Swiss psychiatrist Bertrand Piccard and British copilot Brian Jones landed in the Egyptian desert on this date, having flown 29,056 miles nonstop around the world in a hot-air balloon. Beginning at Chateau d'Oex in the Swiss Alps on Mar 1, the trip took 19 days, 21 hours and 55 minutes. Piccard is the grandson of balloonist Auguste Piccard, who was the first to ascend into the stratosphere in a balloon.

IRANIAN NEW YEAR: NORUZ. Mar 21. National celebration for all Iranians, this is the traditional Persian New Year. It is a celebration of nature's rebirth. Every household spreads a special cover with symbols for the seven good angels on it. These symbols are sprouts, wheat germ, apples, hyacinth, fruit of the jujube, garlic and sumac heralding life, rebirth, health, happiness, prosperity, joy and beauty. A fishbowl is also customary, representing the end of the astrological year, and wild rue is burnt to drive away evil and bring about a happy New Year. This pre-Islamic holiday, a legacy of Zoroastrianism, is also celebrated as Navruz, Nau-Roz or Noo Roz in Afghanistan, Albania, Azerbaijan, Kazakhstan, Kyrgyzstan, Tajikistan, Turkmenistan and Uzbekistan.

POCAHONTAS (REBECCA ROLFE): DEATH ANNIVERSARY. Mar 21, 1617. Pocahontas, daughter of Powhatan, born about 1595, near Jamestown, VA, leader of the Indian union of Algonkin nations, helped to foster goodwill between the colonists of the Jamestown settlement and her people. Pocahontas converted to Christianity, was baptized with the name Rebecca and married John Rolfe Apr 5, 1614. In 1616, she accompanied Rolfe on a trip to his native England, where she was regarded as an overseas "ambassador." Pocahontas's stay in England drew so much attention to the Virginia Company's Jamestown settlement that lotteries were held to help support the colony. Shortly before she was scheduled to return to Jamestown, Pocahontas died at Gravesend, Kent, England, of either smallpox or pneumonia.

SELMA CIVIL RIGHTS MARCH: ANNIVERSARY. Mar 21, 1965. More than 3,000 civil rights demonstrators led by Dr. Martin Luther King, Jr, began a four-day march from Selma, AL, to Montgomery, AL, to demand federal protection of voting rights. There were violent attempts by local police, using fire hoses and dogs, to suppress the march. A march two weeks before on Mar 7, 1965, was called "Bloody Sunday" because of the use of night sticks, chains and electric cattle prods against the marchers by the police.

UNITED NATIONS: INTERNATIONAL DAY FOR THE ELIMINATION OF RACIAL DISCRIMINATION. Mar 21. Initiated by the United Nations General Assembly in 1966 to be observed annually Mar 21, the anniversary of the killing of 69 African demonstrators at Sharpeville, South Africa, in 1960, as a day to remember "the victims of Sharpeville and those countless others in different parts of the world who have fallen victim to racial injustice" and to promote efforts to eradicate racial discrimination worldwide. Web: www.un.org.

★ *Birthdays* ★

Matthew Broderick, actor (*War Games, The Freshman, Family Business*; stage: *The Producers*), born New York, NY, Mar 21, 1962.
Rosie O'Donnell, actress (*A League of Their Own*), host ("The Rosie O'Donnell Show"), born Commack, NY, Mar 21, 1962.

March 22

AS YOUNG AS YOU FEEL DAY. Mar 22. Now more than ever you are as young as you feel. So stop acting your chronological age and get out there and start feeling peppy! [©2001 by WH.] For info: Wellcat Holidays. Web: www.wellcat.com.

EQUAL RIGHTS AMENDMENT SENT TO STATES FOR RATIFICATION: ANNIVERSARY. Mar 22, 1972. The Senate passed the 27th Amendment, prohibiting discrimination on the basis of sex, sending it to the states for ratification. Hawaii led the way as the first state to ratify, and by the end of the year 22 states had ratified it. On Oct 6, 1978, the deadline for ratification was extended to June 30, 1982, by Congress. The amendment still lacked three of the required 38 states for ratification. This was the first extension granted since Congress set seven years as the limit for ratification. The amendment failed to achieve ratification as the deadline came and passed and no additional states ratified the measure.

LASER PATENTED: ANNIVERSARY. Mar 22, 1960. The first patent for a laser (light amplification by stimulated emission of radiation) granted to Arthur Schawlow and Charles Townes.

SPACE MILESTONE: RECORD TIME IN SPACE. Mar 22, 1995. A Russian cosmonaut returned to Earth after setting a record of 439 days in space aboard *Mir*. Previous records include three Soviet cosmonauts who spent 237 days in space at *Salyut 7* space station in 1984, a Soviet cosmonaut who spent 326 days aboard *Mir* in 1987 and two Soviets who spent 366 days aboard *Mir* in 1988. The longest stay in space by any US astronaut was Shannon Lucid's 188-day stay on *Mir* in 1996. This also set a record for women in space.

UNITED NATIONS: WORLD DAY FOR WATER. Mar 22. The General Assembly declared this observance (Resolution 47/193) to promote public awareness of how water resource development contributes to economic productivity and social well-being. For info: United Nations. Web: www.un.org.

★ Birthdays ★

Robert Quinlan (Bob) Costas, sportscaster, born New York, NY, Mar 22, 1952.
William Shatner, actor ("Star Trek," "T.J. Hooker"), author (*Tek* novels), born Montreal, QC, Canada, Mar 22, 1931.
Reese Witherspoon, actress (*Legally Blonde, Fear, Twilight*), born Nashville, TN, Mar 22, 1976.

March 23

LIBERTY DAY: ANNIVERSARY. Mar 23, 1775. Anniversary of Patrick Henry's speech for arming the Virginia militia at St. Johns Church, Richmond, VA. "I know not what course others may take, but as for me, give me liberty or give me death."

NEAR MISS DAY. Mar 23, 1989. A mountain-sized asteroid passed within 500,000 miles of Earth, a very close call according to NASA. Impact would have equaled the strength of 40,000 hydrogen bombs, created a crater the size of the District of Columbia and devastated everything for 100 miles in all directions.

UNITED NATIONS: WORLD METEOROLOGICAL DAY. Mar 23. An international day observed by meteorological services throughout the world and by the organizations of the UN system. For info: United Nations. Web: www.un.org.

★ Birthdays ★

Moses Malone, Hall of Fame basketball player, born Petersburg, VA, Mar 23, 1954.
Keri Russell, actress ("Felicity"), born Fountain Valley, CA, Mar 23, 1976.

March 24

EXXON VALDEZ OIL SPILL: ANNIVERSARY. Mar 24, 1989. The tanker *Exxon Valdez* ran aground at Prince William Sound, leaking 11 million gallons of oil into one of nature's richest habitats.

HOUDINI, HARRY: BIRTH ANNIVERSARY. Mar 24, 1874. Magician and escape artist. Born at Budapest, Hungary, died at Detroit, MI, Oct 31, 1926. Lecturer, athlete, author, expert on history of magic, exposer of fraudulent mediums and motion picture actor. Was best known for his ability to escape from locked restraints (handcuffs, straitjackets, coffins, boxes and milk cans). Anniversary of his death (Halloween) has been the occasion for meetings of magicians and attempts at communication by mediums.

PHILIPPINE INDEPENDENCE: ANNIVERSARY. Mar 24, 1934. President Franklin Roosevelt signed a bill granting independence to the Philippines. The bill, which took effect July 4, 1946, brought to a close almost half a century of US control of the islands.

UNITED NATIONS: WORLD TUBERCULOSIS DAY. Mar 24. Commemorates the day in 1882 when the tuberculosis bacillus was discovered by German scientist Robert Koch. For info: United Nations. Web: www.un.org.

★ Birthdays ★

Lara Flynn Boyle, actress ("Twin Peaks," "The Practice," *Dead Poets Society*), born Davenport, IA, Mar 24, 1970.

March 25

"CAGNEY & LACEY" TV PREMIERE: ANNIVERSARY. Mar 25, 1982. "Cagney & Lacey" broke new ground as the first TV crime show in which the central characters were both female. The series was based on a made-for-TV movie that aired Oct 8, 1981, starring Loretta Swit and Tyne Daly. Meg Foster played Swit's character, Chris Cagney, but after one season she was replaced by Sharon Gless. Daly and Gless won six Emmys together for their roles. The last telecast aired on Aug 25, 1988.

GREECE: INDEPENDENCE DAY. Mar 25. National holiday. Celebrates the beginning of the Greek revolt for independence from the Ottoman Empire, Mar 25, 1821. Greece attained independence in 1829.

OLD NEW YEAR'S DAY. Mar 25. In Great Britain and its North American colonies this was the beginning of the new year up through 1751, when with the adoption of the Gregorian calendar the beginning of the year was changed to Jan 1.

TRIANGLE SHIRTWAIST FIRE: ANNIVERSARY. Mar 25, 1911. At about 4:30 PM, fire broke out at the Triangle Shirtwaist Company at New York, NY, minutes before the seamstresses were to go home. Some workers were fatally burned while others leaped to their deaths from the windows of the ten-story building. The fire lasted only 18 minutes but left 146 workers dead, most of them young immigrant women. Some of the deaths were a direct result of workers being trapped on the ninth floor by a locked door. Labor law forbade locking factory doors while employees were at work, and owners of the company were indicted on charges of first- and second-degree manslaughter. The tragic fire became a turning point in labor history, bringing about reforms in health and safety laws.

★ Birthdays ★

Bonnie Bedelia, actress (*My Sweet Charlie, Die Hard, Die Hard 2*), born New York, NY, Mar 25, 1946 (some sources say 1952).
Aretha Franklin, singer ("Respect," "Think"), born Memphis, TN, Mar 25, 1942.
Elton John, musician, singer, songwriter, AIDS activist, born Reginald Kenneth Dwight at Pinner, England, Mar 25, 1947.
Sarah Jessica Parker, actress (*LA Story, Honeymoon in Vegas*, "Sex and the City"), born Nelsonville, OH, Mar 25, 1965.

March 26

BANGLADESH: INDEPENDENCE DAY. Mar 26. Commemorates East Pakistan's independence in 1971 as the state of Bangladesh. Celebrated with parades, youth festivals and symposia.

CAMP DAVID ACCORD SIGNED: ANNIVERSARY. Mar 26, 1979. Israeli prime minister Menachem Begin and Egyptian president Anwar Sadat signed the Camp David peace treaty, ending 30 years of war between their two countries. The agreement was fostered by President Jimmy Carter.

FROST, ROBERT LEE: BIRTH ANNIVERSARY. Mar 26, 1874. American poet who tried his hand at farming, teaching, shoemaking and editing before winning acclaim as a poet. Pulitzer Prize winner. Born at San Francisco, CA, he died at Boston, MA, Jan 29, 1963.

MAKE UP YOUR OWN HOLIDAY DAY. Mar 26. This day is a day you may name for whatever you wish. Reach for the stars! Make up a holiday! [©2001 by WH.] For info: Wellcat Holidays. Web: www.wellcat.com.

PRINCE JONAH KUHIO KALANIANOLE DAY. Mar 26. Hawaii. Commemorates the man who, as Hawaii's delegate to the US Congress, introduced the first bill for statehood in 1919. Not until 1959 did Hawaii become a state.

SOVIET COSMONAUT RETURNS TO NEW COUNTRY: ANNIVERSARY. Mar 26, 1992. After spending 313 days in space in the Soviet *Mir* space station, cosmonaut Serge Krikalev returned to Earth and to what was for him a new country. He left Earth May 18, 1991, a citizen of the Soviet Union, but during his stay aboard the space station, the Soviet Union crumbled and became the Commonwealth of Independent States. Originally scheduled to return in October 1991, Krikalev's return was delayed by five months due to his country's disintegration and the ensuing monetary problems.

WILLIAMS, TENNESSEE: BIRTH ANNIVERSARY. Mar 26, 1911. Tennessee Williams was born at Columbus, MS. He was one of America's most prolific playwrights, producing such works as *The Glass Menagerie; A Streetcar Named Desire,* which won a Pulitzer Prize; *Cat on a Hot Tin Roof,* which won a second Pulitzer; *Night of the Iguana; Summer and Smoke; The Rose Tattoo; Sweet Bird of Youth;* and others. Williams died at New York, NY, Feb 25, 1983.

"THE YOUNG AND THE RESTLESS" TV PREMIERE: ANNIVERSARY. Mar 26, 1973. This daytime serial is generally thought of as TV's most artistic soap and has won numerous Emmys for outstanding daytime drama series. The serial's very large and changing cast has included now-famous actors David Hasselhoff, Tom Selleck,

Wings Hauser, Deidre Hall and Michael Damian. In 1980, "Y&R" expanded from a half-hour to an hour. Its theme music is well known as "Nadia's Theme," as it was played during Nadia Comaneci's routine at the 1976 Olympics.

★ Birthdays ★

Alan Arkin, actor (*Catch-22*, "100 Centre Street"), director (*Little Murders*), born New York, NY, Mar 26, 1934.

James Caan, actor (*Rabbit Run, The Godfather*), director, born New York, NY, Mar 26, 1940.

Sandra Day O'Connor, associate justice of the US Supreme Court, first female justice, born El Paso, TX, Mar 26, 1930.

Martin Short, actor (*The Three Amigos, Inner Space*), comedian ("SCTV Network 90," "Saturday Night Live"), born Hamilton, ON, Canada, Mar 26, 1950.

March 27

CANARY ISLANDS PLANE DISASTER: ANNIVERSARY. Mar 27, 1977. The worst accident in the history of civil aviation. Two Boeing 747s collided on the ground; 570 people lost their lives—249 on the KLM Airlines plane and 321 on the Pan Am plane.

EARTHQUAKE STRIKES ALASKA: ANNIVERSARY. Mar 27, 1964. The strongest earthquake in North American history (8.4 on the Richter scale) struck Alaska, east of Anchorage; 117 people were killed. This was the world's second worst earthquake of the 20th century in terms of magnitude.

★ Birthdays ★

Mariah Carey, singer ("Vision of Love," "I'll Be There"), born Long Island, NY, Mar 27, 1970.

Quentin Tarantino, actor, director (*Pulp Fiction, Jackie Brown*), born Knoxville, TN, Mar 27, 1963.

March 28

"GREATEST SHOW ON EARTH" FORMED: ANNIVERSARY. Mar 28, 1881. P.T. Barnum and James A. Bailey merged their circuses to form the "Greatest Show on Earth."

HAIR BROADWAY OPENING: ANNIVERSARY. Mar 28, 1968. The controversial rock musical *Hair*, produced by Michael Butler, opened at the Biltmore Theatre at New York City, after playing off-Broadway. For those who opposed the Vietnam War and the "Establishment," this was a defining piece of work—as evidenced by some of its songs, such as "Aquarius," "Hair" and "Let the Sunshine In."

THREE MILE ISLAND NUCLEAR POWER PLANT ACCIDENT: ANNIVERSARY. Mar 28, 1979. A series of accidents beginning at 4 AM, EST, at Three Mile Island on the Susquehanna River about ten miles southeast of Harrisburg, PA, was responsible for extensive reevaluation of the safety of existing nuclear power–generating operations. Equipment and other failures reportedly brought Three Mile Island close to a meltdown of the uranium core, threatening extensive radiation contamination.

★ Birthdays ★

Ken Howard, actor ("The White Shadow," "Crossing Jordan"), born El Centro, CA, Mar 28, 1944.
Reba McEntire, singer, actress (stage: *Annie Get Your Gun*), born Chockie, OK, Mar 28, 1954.
Dianne Wiest, actress (Oscars for *Hannah and Her Sisters* and *Bullets Over Broadway*; "Law & Order"), born Kansas City, MO, Mar 28, 1948.

March 29

CANADA: BRITISH NORTH AMERICA ACT: ANNIVERSARY. Mar 29, 1867. This act of the British Parliament established the Dominion of Canada, uniting Ontario, Quebec, Nova Scotia and New Brunswick. The remaining colonies in Canada were still ruled directly by Great Britain until Manitoba joined the Dominion in 1870, British Columbia in 1871, Prince Edward Island in 1873, Alberta and Saskatchewan in 1905 and Newfoundland in 1949. Union was proclaimed July 1, 1867. See also: "Canada: Canada Day" (July 1).

DOW-JONES TOPS 10,000: ANNIVERSARY. Mar 29, 1999. The Dow-Jones Index of 30 major industrial stocks topped the 10,000 mark for the first time.

TWENTY-THIRD AMENDMENT TO US CONSTITUTION RATIFIED: ANNIVERSARY. Mar 29, 1961. District of Columbia residents were given the right to vote in presidential elections under the 23rd Amendment.

TYLER, JOHN: BIRTH ANNIVERSARY. Mar 29, 1790. Tenth president of the US (Apr 6, 1841–Mar 3, 1845). Born at Charles City County, VA, Tyler succeeded to the presidency upon the death of William Henry Harrison. Tyler's first wife died while he was president, and he remarried before the end of his term in office, becoming the first president to marry while in office. Fifteen children were born of the two marriages. In 1861 he was elected to the Congress of the Confederate States but died at Richmond, VA, Jan 18, 1862, before being seated. His death received no official tribute from the US government.

YOUNG, DENTON TRUE (CY): BIRTH ANNIVERSARY. Mar 29, 1867. Baseball Hall of Fame pitcher, born at Gilmore, OH. Young is baseball's all-time winningest pitcher, having accumulated 511 victories in his 22-year career. The Cy Young Award is given each year in his honor to each major league's best pitcher. Inducted into the Hall of Fame in 1937. Died at Peoli, OH, Nov 4, 1955.

★ *Birthdays* ★

Earl Christian Campbell, Hall of Fame football player, born Tyler, TX, Mar 29, 1955.
Jennifer Capriati, tennis player, born New York, NY, Mar 29, 1976.

March 30

ANESTHETIC FIRST USED IN SURGERY: ANNIVERSARY. Mar 30, 1842. Dr. Crawford W. Long, having seen the use of nitrous oxide and sulfuric ether at "laughing gas" parties, observed that individuals under their influence felt no pain. On this date, he removed a tumor from the neck of a man who was under the influence of ether.

"JEOPARDY!" TV PREMIERE: ANNIVERSARY. Mar 30, 1964. The "thinking person's" game show, "Jeopardy!" has a reputation as an intelligent and classy program. Art Fleming was the original host of the show, in which three contestants won cash by attempting to give the correct question to an answer in six different categories. Contestants go through two rounds and "final jeopardy," where they can wager up to all their earnings on one question. The series returned in 1984 with Alex Trebek as the popular host. The cable channel VH1 now hosts "Rock & Roll Jeopardy!"

NATIONAL KITE MONTH. Mar 30–May 5. Celebrates kiting through several hundred events throughout the country including kite festivals, kite-making classes for kids and adults, kite-making classes in schools, kite displays in museums and public libraries and "fun flys" at local parks and beaches. For info: Kite Trade Association. Web: www.KiteTrade.org/NationalKite Month.

PENCIL PATENTED: ANNIVERSARY. Mar 30, 1858. First pencil with the eraser top was patented by Hyman Lipman.

REAGAN, RONALD: ASSASSINATION ATTEMPT: ANNIVERSARY. Mar 30, 1981. President Ronald Reagan was shot in the chest by a 25-year-old gunman at Washington, DC. Three other persons were wounded. John W. Hinckley, Jr, the accused attacker, was arrested at the scene. On June 21, 1982, a federal jury in the District of Columbia found Hinckley not guilty by reason of insanity and he was committed to St. Elizabeth's Hospital at Washington, DC, for an indefinite time.

SEWARD'S DAY: ANNIVERSARY OF THE ACQUISITION OF ALASKA. Mar 30. The treaty of purchase was signed between Russia and the US Mar 30, 1867, and ratified by the Senate May 28, 1867. The territory was formally transferred Oct 18, 1867.

VAN GOGH, VINCENT: BIRTH ANNIVERSARY. Mar 30, 1853. Dutch post-Impressionist painter, especially known for his bold and powerful use of color. Born at Groot Zundert, Holland, he died at Auvers-sur-Oise, France, July 29, 1890.

★ *Birthdays* ★

Warren Beatty, actor (*Bonnie and Clyde*); director (*Reds, Dick Tracy*), producer, born Richmond, VA, Mar 30, 1938.

Eric Clapton, musician, singer (with The Yardbirds, Cream), songwriter ("Layla," with Jim Gordon), born Ripley, England, Mar 30, 1945. **Paul Reiser**, actor (*Diner*, "Mad About You"), born New York, NY, Mar 30, 1957.

March 31

BUNSEN BURNER DAY. Mar 31. A day to honor the inventor of the Bunsen burner, Robert Wilhelm Eberhard von Bunsen, who provided chemists and chemistry students with one of their most indispensable instruments. The Bunsen burner allows the user to regulate the proportions of flammable gas and air to create the most efficient flame. Bunsen was born at Gottingen, Germany, Mar 31, 1811, and was a professor of chemistry at the universities at Kassel, Marburg, Breslau and Heidelberg. He died at Heidelberg, Germany, Aug 16, 1899.

DALAI LAMA FLEES TIBET: ANNIVERSARY. Mar 31, 1959. The Dalai Lama fled Chinese suppression and was granted political asylum in India. In 1950, Tibet had been invaded by China, and in 1951 an agreement was signed under which Tibet became a "national autonomous region" of China. Tibetans suffered under China's persecution of Buddhism and after years of scattered protest a full-scale revolt broke out in 1959. The Dalai Lama fled, and with the beginning of the Chinese Cultural Revolution the Chinese took brutal repressive measures against the Tibetans, with the practice of religion banned and thousands of monasteries destroyed. The ban was lifted in 1976 with the end of the Cultural Revolution. The Dalai Lama received the Nobel Peace Prize in 1989 for his commitment to the nonviolent liberation of his country.

EIFFEL TOWER: ANNIVERSARY. Mar 31, 1889. Built for the Paris International Exhibition of 1889, the tower was named for its architect, Alexandre Gustave Eiffel, and is one of the world's best-known landmarks.

★ *Birthdays* ★

Richard Chamberlain, actor ("Dr. Kildare," *Shogun*), born Los Angeles, CA, Mar 31, 1935.
Gordon (Gordie) Howe, Hockey Hall of Fame right wing, born Floral, SK, Canada, Mar 31, 1928.
Shirley Jones, singer, actress ("The Partridge Family," *Elmer Gantry, Oklahoma!*), born Smithton, PA, Mar 31, 1934.

April

April 1

ALCOHOL AWARENESS MONTH. Apr 1–30. To help raise awareness among community leaders and citizens about the problem of underage drinking. Concentrates on community grassroots activities. For info: National Council on Alcoholism and Drug Dependence. Web: www.ncadd.org.

ANIMAL CRUELTY PREVENTION MONTH. Apr 1–30. The American Society for the Prevention of Cruelty to Animals (ASPCA) sponsors this crucial month that is designed to prevent cruelty to animals by focusing on public awareness, advocacy and public education campaigns. For info: ASPCA. Web: www.aspca.org.

APRIL FOOLS' or ALL FOOLS' DAY. Apr 1. April Fools' Day seems to have begun in France in 1564. Apr 1 used to be New Year's Day but the New Year was changed to Jan 1 that year. People who insisted on celebrating the "old" New Year became known as April fools, and it became common to play jokes and tricks on them. The general concept of a feast of fools is, however, an ancient one. The Romans had such a day and medieval monasteries also had days when the abbot or bishop was replaced for a day by a common monk, who would order his superiors to do the most menial or ridiculous tasks. "The joke of the day is to deceive persons by sending them upon frivolous and nonsensical errands; to pretend they are wanted when they are not, or, in fact, any way to betray them into some supposed ludicrous situation, so as to enable you to call them 'An April Fool.'"—Brady's *Clavis Calendaria*, 1812.

CIGARETTE ADVERTISING BANNED: ANNIVERSARY. Apr 1, 1970. Radio and television ads for cigarettes were banned by legislation signed by President Nixon on this date. The ban went into effect Jan 1, 1971.

"GENERAL HOSPITAL" TV PREMIERE: ANNIVERSARY. Apr 1, 1963. "General Hospital," ABC's longest-running soap, revolves around the denizens of fictional Port Charles, NY. In the '80s, story lines became unusual with plots involving international espionage, mob activity and aliens. The wedding of supercouple Luke and Laura (Anthony Geary and Genie Francis) was a ratings topper. By the '90s, stories moved away from high-powered action to more conventional romance. Many actors received their big break on the show, including Demi Moore, Janine Turner, Jack Wagner, Richard Dean Anderson, Rick Springfield, John Stamos, Emma Samms, Mark Hamill, Finola Hughes, Ricky Martin and Tia Carrere.

HARVEY, WILLIAM: BIRTH ANNIVERSARY. Apr 1, 1578. Physician, born at Folkestone, England. The first to discover the mechanics of the circulation of the blood. Died at Roehampton, England, June 3, 1657.

KEEP AMERICA BEAUTIFUL MONTH. Apr 1–30. To educate Americans about their personal responsibility for litter prevention, proper waste disposal and environmental improvement through various community projects. For info: Keep America Beautiful. Web: www.kab.org.

LUPUS ALERT DAY. Apr 1. Don't be fooled by lupus! To call attention to the confusing characteristics of this potentially fatal autoimmune disease that mimics other, less serious illnesses. For info: Lupus Foundation of America. Web: www.lupus.org.

MATHEMATICS EDUCATION MONTH. Apr 1–30. An opportunity for students, teachers, parents and the community as a whole to focus on the importance of mathematics and the changes taking place in mathematics education. For info: National Council of Teachers of Mathematics. Web: www.nctm.org.

NATIONAL AUTISM AWARENESS MONTH. Apr 1–30. A month filled with autism awareness events such as conferences, presentations, displays and media attention. Contact the New Jersey Center for Outreach & Services for the Autism Community for information on how you can become an "Autism Awareness Ambassador." For info: COSAC. Web: www.njcosac.org.

NATIONAL CHILD ABUSE PREVENTION MONTH. Apr 1–30. Presidential Proclamation issued annually. For info: National Committee to Prevent Child Abuse. Web: www.preventchildabuse.org.

NATIONAL GRILLED CHEESE SANDWICH MONTH. Apr 1–30. Dedicated to one of America's favorite foods, the gooey, oozy, melty grilled cheese sandwich. With more than 200 varieties of domestic cheese available, the grilled cheese sandwich options are endless! For info: Dairy Management. Web: www.ilovecheese.com.

NATIONAL LAWN AND GARDEN MONTH. Apr 1–30. National celebration highlighting the benefits of landscape and lawn care in the new millennium.

For info: Associated Landscape Contractors of America. Web: www.alca.org.

NATIONAL PECAN MONTH. Apr 1–30. A celebration of the great taste, health benefits and versatility of pecans. This delicious tree nut native to North America adds unmistakable flavor, crunch and texture to just about any meal or snack. Pecans have proven cholesterol-lowering properties and contain more than 19 important vitamins and minerals. Almost 90 percent of the fats in pecans are of the heart-healthy, unsaturated variety. For info: National Pecan Shellers Association. Web: www.ilovepecans.org.

NATIONAL POETRY MONTH. Apr 1–30. Annual observance to pay tribute to the great legacy and ongoing achievement of American poets and the vital place of poetry in American culture. In a proclamation issued in honor of the first observance, President Bill Clinton called it "a welcome opportunity to celebrate not only the unsurpassed body of literature produced by our poets in the past, but also the vitality and diversity of voices reflected in the works of today's American poets. . . . Their creativity and wealth of language enrich our culture and inspire a new generation of Americans to learn the power of reading and writing at its best." For info: Academy of American Poets. Web: www.poets.org.

NATIONAL WOODWORKING MONTH™. Apr 1–30. To focus attention on the beauty and satisfaction of working with wood. To help motivate Americans to undertake woodworking projects to improve their home and general surroundings. To increase consumers' knowledge and skill in woodworking and wood-finishing endeavors. For info: Minwax Co. Web: www.minwax.com.

NATIONAL YOUTH SPORTS SAFETY MONTH. Apr 1–30. Bringing public attention to the prevalent problem of injuries in youth sports. This event promotes safety in sports activities and is supported by more than 60 national sports and medical organizations. For info: National Youth Sports Safety Foundation. Web: www.nyssf.org.

PREVENT INJURIES AMERICA! Apr 1–30. Move better, play better, live better. Learn about preventing orthopaedic injuries and conditions. Throughout the month, orthopaedic surgeons will provide injury prevention information on topics such as preventing playground and sports injuries, osteoporosis, workplace injuries, low back pain and proper shoewear tips. For info: American Academy of Orthopaedic Surgeons. Web: www.aaos.org.

US HOUSE OF REPRESENTATIVES ACHIEVES A QUORUM: ANNIVERSARY. Apr 1, 1789. First session of Congress was held Mar 4, 1789, but not enough representatives arrived to achieve a quorum until Apr 1.

WOMEN'S EYE HEALTH AND SAFETY MONTH. Apr 1–30. Women often manage family health concerns. Do you know how to protect your sight? Hormonal changes, age and even the sun can endanger sight. Information on women's and family eye-health issues will be provided. For info: Prevent Blindness America®. Web: www.preventblindness.org.

ZAM! ZOO AND AQUARIUM MONTH. Apr 1–30. A national celebration to focus public attention on the role of zoos and aquariums in wildlife education and conservation. Held at 184 American Zoo and Aquarium Association member institutions in the US and Canada. For information, contact your local zoo or aquarium. For info: American Zoo and Aquarium Association. Web: www.aza.org.

★ Birthdays ★

Annette O'Toole, actress (*Smile, 48 HRS*, "Smallville"), born Houston, TX, Apr 1, 1953.
Debbie Reynolds, actress (*Singin' in the Rain, Mother*), born El Paso, TX, Apr 1, 1932.

April 2

ANDERSEN, HANS CHRISTIAN: BIRTH ANNIVERSARY. Apr 2, 1805. Author chiefly remembered for his more than 150 fairy tales, many of which are regarded as classics of children's literature. Andersen was born at Odense, Denmark, and died at Copenhagen, Denmark, Aug 4, 1875.

"AS THE WORLD TURNS" TV PREMIERE: ANNIVERSARY. Apr 2, 1956. One of the longest-running soaps currently on the air, "ATWT" premiered on CBS. Irma Phillips was the show's creator and head writer. Some of the cast members who made it big are Meg Ryan, Julianne Moore, Michael Nader, Steven Weber and Swoosie Kurtz.

"DALLAS" TV PREMIERE: ANNIVERSARY. Apr 2, 1978. Oil tycoons battled for money, power and prestige in this prime-time CBS drama that ran for nearly 13 years. The Ewings and Barneses were Texas's modern-day Hatfields and McCoys. Larry Hagman starred as the devious, scheming womanizer J.R. Ewing. When J.R. was shot in the 1980 season-ending cliff-hanger, the revelation of the mystery shooter was the single-most-watched episode of its time (it was Kristin, J.R.'s sister-in-law, played by Mary Crosby). Cast members included Jim Davis, Barbara Bel Geddes, Donna Reed, Ted Shackelford, Joan Van Ark (who, along with Shackelford, starred in the spin-off "Knots Landing"), Patrick Duffy, Linda Gray, Charlene Tilton, David Wayne, Keenan Wynn, Ken Kercheval, Victoria Principal and Steve Kanaly.

GUINNESS, SIR ALEC: BIRTH ANNIVERSARY. Apr 2, 1914. Academy Award–winning actor for *The Bridge on the River Kwai*, born at London, England. An active performer on both stage and screen, his film roles included *Star Wars, A Passage to India* and *Kind Hearts and Coronets*. He died at West Sussex, England, Aug 5, 2000.

INTERNATIONAL CHILDREN'S BOOK DAY. Apr 2. Observes Hans Christian Andersen's birthday and commemorates the international aspects of children's literature. Sponsor: International Board on Books for Young People, Basel, Switzerland. For info: US Board on Books for Young People. Web: www.usbby.org.

NICKELODEON PREMIERE: ANNIVERSARY. Apr 2, 1979. Nickelodeon, the cable TV channel for kids owned by MTV Networks, debuted on this date.

PASCUA FLORIDA DAY. Apr 2. A legal holiday in Florida, designated as State Day. When it falls on a Saturday or Sunday, the governor may declare either the preceding Friday or the following Monday as State Day. Florida also observes Pascua Florida Week from Mar 27 to Apr 2. Commemorates the sighting of Florida by Ponce de León in 1513. He named the land Pascua Florida because of its discovery at Easter, the "Feast of the Flowers."

RECONCILIATION DAY. Apr 2. Columnist Ann Landers writes, "Since 1989, I have suggested that April 2 be set aside to write that letter or make that phone call and mend a broken relationship. Life is too short to hold grudges. To forgive can be enormously life-enhancing. . . ."

US MINT: ANNIVERSARY. Apr 2, 1792. The first US mint was established at Philadelphia, PA, as authorized by an act of Congress.

★ *Birthdays* ★

Linda Hunt, actress (Oscar for *The Year of Living Dangerously*, "The Practice"), born Morristown, NJ, Apr 2, 1945.
Christopher Meloni, actor (*Runaway Bride*, "Law & Order: Special Victims Unit"), born Washington, DC, Apr 2, 1961.

April 3

INAUGURATION OF PONY EXPRESS: ANNIVERSARY. Apr 3, 1860. The Pony Express began when the first rider left St. Joseph, MO. The following day another rider headed east from Sacramento, CA. For $5 an ounce letters were delivered within ten days. There were 190 way stations between ten and 15 miles apart, and each rider had a "run" of between 75 and 100 miles. The Pony Express lasted less than two years, ceasing operation in October 1861, when the overland telegraph was completed.

MARSHALL PLAN: ANNIVERSARY. Apr 3, 1948. Suggested by Secretary of State George C. Marshall in a speech at Harvard, June 5, 1947, the legislation for the European Recovery Program, popularly known as the Marshall Plan, was signed by President Truman on Apr 3, 1948. After distributing more than $12 billion, the program ended in 1952.

TWEED DAY: ANNIVERSARY. Apr 3, 1823. Day to consider the cost of political corruption. Birthday of William March Tweed, New York City political boss, whose "Tweed Ring" is said to have stolen $30 million to $200 million from the city. Born at New York, NY, Apr 3, 1823, he died in his cell at New York's Ludlow Street Jail, Apr 12, 1878. Cartoonist Thomas Nast deserves much credit for Tweed's arrests and convictions.

2001: A SPACE ODYSSEY PREMIERE: ANNIVERSARY. Apr 3, 1968. Directed by Stanley Kubrick, this influential film has elicited many different interpretations. Sci-fi novelist Arthur C. Clarke based the screenplay on his 1966 book, which was prescient in several ways. Written before men had landed on the moon, Clarke describes an expedition launched to Jupiter to track a mysterious signal emanating from the moon. Clarke gave the world's population as 6 billion (achieved in 1999) and described a space station (the US is currently building one with Russia). During flight, a character reads the news on his electronic newspad. The film starred Keir Dullea, William Sylvester, Gary Lockwood, Daniel Richter and HAL 9000, the creepy computer that had human emotions. The theme music was Richard Strauss's *Also Sprach Zarathrustra*.

WOMAN PRESIDES OVER US SUPREME COURT: ANNIVERSARY. Apr 3, 1995. Supreme Court Justice Sandra Day O'Connor became the first woman to preside over the US high court when she sat in for Chief Justice William H. Rehnquist and second in seniority Justice John Paul Stevens when both were out of town.

★ Birthdays ★

Doris Day, actress (*The Man Who Knew Too Much, Pillow Talk*, "The Doris Day Show"), singer ("Secret Love," "Que Sera Sera"), born Doris Von Kappelhoff at Cincinnati, OH, Apr 3, 1924.
Eddie Murphy, comedian ("Saturday Night Live"), actor (*Trading Places, 48 HRS, Beverly Hills Cop*), born Brooklyn, NY, Apr 3, 1961.
David Hyde Pierce, actor ("Frasier"), born Albany, NY, Apr 3, 1959.

April 4

BONZA BOTTLER DAY™. Apr 4. To celebrate when the number of the day is the same as the number of the month. Bonza Bottler Day™ is an excuse to have a party at least once a month. For info: Gail M. Berger. E-mail: gberger5@aol.com.

NORTH ATLANTIC TREATY RATIFIED: ANNIVERSARY. Apr 4, 1949. The North Atlantic Treaty Organization was created by this treaty, which was signed by 12 nations, including the US. (Other countries joined later.) The NATO member nations are united for common defense. The treaty went into effect Apr 24, 1949, and the first session of the North Atlantic Council was held Sept 17, 1949.

SENEGAL: INDEPENDENCE DAY. Apr 4. National holiday. Commemorates independence from France in 1960.

VITAMIN C ISOLATED: ANNIVERSARY. Apr 4, 1932. Vitamin C was first isolated by C.C. King at the University of Pittsburgh.

★ Birthdays ★

Robert Downey, Jr, actor (*Chaplin, Short Cuts, Natural Born Killers,* "Ally McBeal"), born New York, NY, Apr 4, 1965.

Craig T. Nelson, actor ("Coach," *Private Benjamin, Poltergeist, The Killing Fields*), born Spokane, WA, Apr 4, 1946.

April 5

DAVIS, BETTE: BIRTH ANNIVERSARY. Apr 5, 1908. American actress Bette Davis was born Ruth Elizabeth Davis at Lowell, MA. In addition to acting in more than 80 films, earning ten Academy Award nominations and winning the best actress Academy Award twice, for *Dangerous* (1935) and *Jezebel* (1938), Davis also claimed to have nicknamed the Academy Award "Oscar" after her first husband, Harmon Oscar Nelson, Jr. She died Oct 6, 1989, at Neuilly-sur-Seine, France.

"MARRIED . . . WITH CHILDREN" TV PREMIERE: ANNIVERSARY. Apr 5, 1987. This raunchy Fox TV show premiered as the antidote to Cosby-style family shows. Ed O'Neill starred as boorish, luckless shoe salesman Al Bundy, Katey Sagal portrayed Al's big-haired, spandex-clad, sex-starved wife Peggy, Christina Applegate played airheaded bombshell daughter Kelly and David Faustino played hormone-driven son Bud. The last episode aired Apr 20, 1997.

WASHINGTON, BOOKER TALIAFERRO: BIRTH ANNIVERSARY. Apr 5, 1856. Black educator and leader born at Franklin County, VA. "No race can prosper," he wrote in *Up from Slavery*, "till it learns that there is as much dignity in tilling a field as in writing a poem." Died at Tuskegee, AL, Nov 14, 1915.

★ *Birthdays* ★

Michael Moriarty, actor (*The Last Detail, Bang the Drum Slowly*, "Law & Order"), born Detroit, MI, Apr 5, 1942.

Colin Luther Powell, Secretary of State, retired US Army general, former chairman US Joint Chiefs of Staff, born New York, NY, Apr 5, 1937.

April 6

"BARNEY & FRIENDS" TV PREMIERE: ANNIVERSARY. Apr 6, 1992. Although most adults find it hopelessly saccharine, this PBS program is hugely popular with preschoolers. Purple dinosaur Barney, his pals, dinosaurs Baby Bop and B.J. and a multiethnic group of children sing, play games and learn simple lessons about getting along with one another. "Bedtime with Barney" was a 1994 prime-time special.

DOW-JONES TOPS 9,000: ANNIVERSARY. Apr 6, 1998. The Dow-Jones Index of 30 major industrial stocks topped the 9,000 mark for the first time.

FIRST MODERN OLYMPICS: ANNIVERSARY. Apr 6, 1896. The first modern Olympics formally opened at Athens, Greece, after a 1,500-year hiatus. Thirteen nations participated, represented by 235 male athletes.

FIRST TONY AWARDS PRESENTED: ANNIVERSARY. Apr 6, 1947. The American Theatre Wing bestowed the first annual Tony Awards for distinguished service to the theater.

NORTH POLE DISCOVERED: ANNIVERSARY. Apr 6, 1909. Robert E. Peary reached the North Pole after several failed attempts. The team consisted of Peary, leader of the expedition; Matthew A. Henson (a black man who had served with Peary since 1886 as ship's cook, carpenter and blacksmith, and then as Peary's co-explorer and valuable assistant) and four Eskimo guides—Coquesh, Ootah, Eginwah and Seegloo. They sailed July 17, 1908, on the ship *Roosevelt*, wintering on Ellesmere Island. After a grueling trek with dwindling food supplies, Henson and two of the Eskimos were first to reach the Pole. An exhausted Peary arrived 45 minutes later and confirmed their location.

TARTAN DAY. Apr 6. Groups and societies throughout North America take the anniversary of the Declaration of Arbroath (1320) as the day to celebrate their Scottish roots. Web: www.tartanday.com.

TEFLON INVENTED: ANNIVERSARY. Apr 6, 1938. Polytetrafluoroethylene resin was invented by Roy J. Plunkett while he was employed by E.I. Du Pont de Nemours & Co. Commonly known as Teflon, it revolutionized the cookware industry. This substance or something similar coated three-quarters of the pots and pans in America at the time of Plunkett's death in 1994.

TRAGEDY IN RWANDA: ANNIVERSARY. Apr 6, 1994. A plane carrying the presidents of Rwanda and Burundi was shot down near Kigali, the Rwandan capital, exacerbating a brutal ethnic war that led to the massacre of hundreds of thousands. Presidents Juvenal Habyarimana of Rwanda and Cyprien Ntaryamira of Burundi were returning from a summit in Tanzania where they discussed ways of ending the killing in their countries sparked by ethnic rivalries between the Hutu and Tutsi tribes. Following the attack on the two leaders, Rwanda descended into chaos as the two tribes began killing each other in a genocidal battle for power, leading to a mass exodus of civilians caught in the maelstrom.

US ENTERS WORLD WAR I: ANNIVERSARY. Apr 6, 1917. Congress approved a declaration of war against Germany and the US entered World War I, which had begun in 1914. The first US "doughboys" landed in France June 27, 1917.

US SENATE ACHIEVES A QUORUM: ANNIVERSARY. Apr 6, 1789. The US Senate was formally organized after achieving a quorum.

★ *Birthdays* ★

Marilu Henner, actress ("Taxi," "Evening Shade"), born Chicago, IL, Apr 6, 1952.
Paul Rudd, actor (*The Object of My Affection, Clueless*), born Passaic, NJ, Apr 6, 1969.

April 7

METRIC SYSTEM: ANNIVERSARY. Apr 7, 1795. The metric system was adopted in France, where it had been developed.

NO HOUSEWORK DAY. Apr 7. No trash. No dishes. No making of beds or washing of laundry. And no guilt. Give it a rest. [©2001 by WH.] For info: Wellcat Holidays. Web: www.wellcat.com.

UNITED NATIONS: WORLD HEALTH DAY. Apr 7. A United Nations observance commemorating the establishment of the World Health Organization in 1948. It is headquartered in Geneva, Switzerland. Among its achievements is the elimination of smallpox. For info: World Health Organization. Web: www.who.int.

WINCHELL, WALTER: BIRTH ANNIVERSARY. Apr 7, 1897. Journalist, broadcaster, reporter and gossip columnist Walter Winchell was born at New York, NY, and died at Los Angeles, CA, Feb 20, 1972. He was admired for his way with turning a phrase. His show business columns were voraciously read by millions of Americans between 1924 and 1963.

★ Birthdays ★

Jackie Chan, martial artist, actor (*Rumble in the Bronx, Rush Hour*), born Kong-sang Chan at Hong Kong, Apr 7, 1954.

Russell Crowe, actor (*LA Confidential, A Beautiful Mind*; Oscar for *Gladiator*), born Auckland, New Zealand, Apr 7, 1964.

James Garner, actor (*The Americanization of Emily*, "Maverick," "The Rockford Files"), born James Baumgardner at Norman, OK, Apr 7, 1928.

April 8

THE BUDDHA: BIRTH ANNIVERSARY. Apr 8. This is the most important Buddhist holiday. It is also known as the Day of Vesak. The founder of Buddhism had the given name Siddhartha, the family name Gautama and the clan name Shaka. He is commonly called the Buddha, meaning in Sanskrit "the enlightened one." He is thought to have lived in India from c. 563 BC to 483 BC. Some countries celebrate this holiday on the lunar calendar, so the date changes from year to year, but it always occurs in either April or May. This day is a holiday in Indonesia, Korea, Singapore and Thailand.

HOME RUN RECORD SET BY HANK AARON: ANNIVERSARY. Apr 8, 1974. Henry ("Hammerin' Hank") Aaron hit the 715th home run of his career, breaking the record set by Babe Ruth in 1935. Playing for the Atlanta Braves, Aaron broke the record at Atlanta in a game against the Los Angeles Dodgers. He finished his career in 1976 with a total of 755 home runs. This record remains unbroken. At the time of his retirement, Aaron also held records for first in RBIs, second in at-bats and runs scored and third in base hits.

SEVENTEENTH AMENDMENT TO US CONSTITUTION RATIFIED: ANNIVERSARY. Apr 8, 1913. Prior to the 17th Amendment, members of the Senate were elected by each state's respective legislature. The advent and popularity of primary elections during the last decade of the 19th century and the early 20th century and a string of senatorial scandals, most notably a scandal involving William Lorimer, an Illinois political boss, in 1909, forced the Senate to end its resistance to a constitutional amendment requiring direct popular election of senators.

★ Birthdays ★

Kofi Annan, Secretary General of the United Nations, born Kumasi, Ghana, Apr 8, 1938.

John J. Havlicek, Hall of Fame basketball player, born Lansing, OH, Apr 8, 1940.

April 9

AFRICAN METHODIST EPISCOPAL CHURCH ORGANIZED: ANNIVERSARY. Apr 9, 1816. The first all-black US religious denomination, the AME Church was organized at Philadelphia with Richard Allen, a former slave who had bought his freedom, as the first bishop.

CIVIL RIGHTS BILL OF 1866: ANNIVERSARY. Apr 9, 1866. The Civil Rights Bill of 1866, passed by Congress over the veto of President Andrew Johnson, granted blacks the rights and privileges of American citizenship and formed the basis for the 14th Amendment to the US Constitution.

CIVIL WAR ENDING: ANNIVERSARY. Apr 9, 1865. At 1:30 PM General Robert E. Lee, commander of the Army of Northern Virginia, surrendered to General Ulysses S. Grant, commander-in-chief of the Union Army, ending four years of civil war. The meeting took place in the house of Wilmer McLean at the village of Appomattox Court House, VA. Confederate soldiers were permitted to keep their horses and go free to their homes, while Confederate officers were allowed to retain their swords and side arms as well. Grant wrote the terms of surrender. Formal surrender took place at the courthouse on Apr 12. Death toll for the Civil War is estimated at 500,000 men.

MARIAN ANDERSON EASTER CONCERT: ANNIVERSARY. Apr 9, 1939. On this Easter Sunday, black American contralto Marian Anderson sang an open-air concert from the steps of the Lincoln Memorial at Washington, DC, to an audience of 75,000, after having been denied use of the Daughters of the American Revolution (DAR) Constitution Hall. The event became an American antidiscrimination cause célèbre and led First Lady Eleanor Roosevelt to resign from the DAR.

ROBESON, PAUL: BIRTH ANNIVERSARY. Apr 9, 1898. Paul Robeson, born at Princeton, NJ, was an All-American football player at Rutgers University and received his law degree from Columbia University in 1923. After being seen by Eugene O'Neill in an amateur stage production, he was offered a part in O'Neill's play *The Emperor Jones*. His performance in that play with the Provincetown Players established him as an actor. Without ever having taken a voice lesson, he also became a popular singer. His stage credits include *Show Boat, Porgy and Bess, The Hairy Ape* and *Othello*, which enjoyed the longest Broadway run of a Shakespeare play. In 1950 he was denied a passport by the US for refusing to sign an affidavit stating whether he was a member of the Communist Party. The action was overturned by the Supreme Court in 1958. His film credits include *Emperor Jones, Show Boat* and *King Solomon's Mines*. Robeson died at Philadelphia, PA, Jan 23, 1976.

★ *Birthdays* ★

Severiano (Seve) Ballesteros, golfer, born Pedrena, Spain, Apr 9, 1957.

Hugh Hefner, founder of *Playboy*, born Chicago, IL, Apr 9, 1926.

April 10

BATAAN DEATH MARCH: ANNIVERSARY. Apr 10, 1942. On this morning American and Filipino prisoners were herded together by Japanese soldiers on Mariveles Airfield on Bataan (in the Philippine Islands) and began the Death March to Camp O'Donnell, near Cabanatuan. During the six-day march they were given only one bowl of rice. More than 5,200 Americans and many more Filipinos lost their lives in the course of the march.

SAFETY PIN PATENTED: ANNIVERSARY. Apr 10, 1849. Walter Hunt of New York patented the first safety pin.

SALVATION ARMY FOUNDER'S DAY. Apr 10, 1829. Birth anniversary of William Booth, a Methodist minister who began an evangelical ministry in the East End of London in 1865 and established mission stations to feed and house the poor. In 1878 he changed the name of the organization to the Salvation Army. Booth was born at Nottingham, England; he died at London, Aug 20, 1912.

★ *Birthdays* ★

Haley Joel Osment, actor (*The Sixth Sense, AI: Artificial Intellingence*), born Los Angeles, CA, Apr 10, 1988.

Omar Sharif, actor (*Lawrence of Arabia, Dr. Zhivago*), born Michael Shalhoub, Alexandria, Egypt, Apr 10, 1932.

April 11

BARBERSHOP QUARTET DAY. Apr 11. Commemorates the gathering of some 26 persons at Tulsa, OK, Apr 11, 1938, and the founding there of the Society for the Preservation and Encouragement of Barbershop Quartet Singing in America.

CIVIL RIGHTS ACT OF 1968: ANNIVERSARY. Apr 11, 1968. Exactly one week after the assassination of Martin Luther King, Jr, the Civil Rights Act of 1968 (protecting civil rights workers, expanding the rights of Native Americans and providing antidiscrimination measures in housing) was signed into law by President Lyndon B. Johnson, who said: ". . . the proudest moments of my presidency have been times such as this when I have signed into law the promises of a century."

LIBERATION OF BUCHENWALD CONCENTRATION CAMP: ANNIVERSARY. Apr 11, 1945. Buchenwald, north of Weimar, Germany, was entered by Allied troops. It was the first of the Nazi concentration camps to be liberated. It had been established in 1937, and about 56,000 people died there.

SPACE MILESTONE: *APOLLO 13* (US). Apr 11, 1970. Astronauts Jim Lovell, Fred Haise and Jack Swigert were endangered when an oxygen tank ruptured in flight. The planned moon landing was canceled. Details of the accident were made public and the world shared concern for the crew, who splashed down successfully in the Pacific on Apr 17. A 1995 film, *Apollo 13*, starred Tom Hanks as Lovell, Bill Paxton as Haise and Kevin Bacon as Swigert.

★ Birthdays ★

Joel Grey, actor (Oscar for *Cabaret; The Seven Per Cent Solution*), born Joe Katz, Cleveland, OH, Apr 11, 1932.
Meshach Taylor, actor ("Designing Women," "Dave's World"), born Boston, MA, Apr 11, 1947.

April 12

ANNIVERSARY OF THE BIG WIND. Apr 12, 1934. The highest-velocity natural wind ever recorded occurred in the morning at the Mount Washington, NH, Observatory. Three weather observers, Wendell Stephenson, Alexander McKenzie and Salvatore Pagliuca, observed and recorded the phenomenon in which gusts reached 231 miles per hour—"the strongest natural wind ever recorded on the earth's surface." The 50th anniversary was observed at the site in 1984, with the three original observers participating in the ceremony.

ATTACK ON FORT SUMTER: ANNIVERSARY. Apr 12, 1861. After months of escalating tension, Major Robert Anderson refused to evacuate Fort Sumter at Charleston, SC. Confederate troops under the command of General P.T. Beauregard opened fire on the harbor fort at 4:30 PM and continued until Major Anderson surrendered on Apr 13. No lives were lost despite the firing of some 40,000 shells in the first major engagement of the American Civil War.

CLAY, HENRY: BIRTH ANNIVERSARY. Apr 12, 1777. Statesman, born at Hanover County, VA. Was the Speaker of the House of Representatives and later became the leader of the new Whig party. He was defeated for the presidency three times. Clay died at Washington, DC, June 29, 1852.

POLIO VACCINE: ANNIVERSARY. Apr 12, 1955. Anniversary of announcement that the polio vaccine developed by American physician Dr.

Jonas E. Salk was "safe, potent and effective." Incidence of the dreaded infantile paralysis, or poliomyelitis, declined by 95 percent following introduction of preventive vaccines. The first mass innoculations of children with the Salk vaccine had begun in Pittsburgh, Feb 23, 1954.

SPACE MILESTONE: *COLUMBIA STS-1* **(US): FIRST SHUTTLE FLIGHT.** Apr 12, 1981. First flight of shuttle *Columbia.* Two astronauts (John Young and Robert Crippen), on first manned US space mission since *Apollo-Soyuz* in July 1976, spent 54 hours in space (36 orbits of Earth) before landing at Edwards Air Force Base, CA, Apr 14.

SPACE MILESTONE: *VOSTOK I,* **FIRST MAN IN SPACE.** Apr 12, 1961. Yuri Gagarin became the first man in space when he made a 108-minute voyage, orbiting Earth in a 10,395-lb vehicle, *Vostok I,* launched by the USSR.

TRUANCY LAW: ANNIVERSARY. Apr 12, 1853. The first truancy law was enacted at New York. A $50 fine was charged against parents whose children between the ages of five and 15 were absent from school.

★ *Birthdays* ★

Andy Garcia, actor (*The Untouchables; The Godfather, Part III*), born Havana, Cuba, Apr 12, 1956.
David Letterman, comedian, TV talk-show host ("Late Show with David Letterman"), born Indianapolis, IN, Apr 12, 1947.
Ed O'Neill, actor ("Married . . . With Children," *Deliverance, Wayne's World*), born Youngstown, OH, Apr 12, 1946.

April 13

BUTTS, ALFRED M.: BIRTH ANNIVERSARY. Apr 13, 1899. Alfred Butts was a jobless architect in the Depression when he invented the board game Scrabble. The game was just a fad for Butts's friends until a Macy's executive saw the game being played at a resort in 1952, and the world's largest store began carrying it. Manufacturing of the game was turned over to Selchow & Righter when 35 workers were producing 6,000 sets a week. Butts received three cents per set for years. He said, "One-third went to taxes. I gave one-third away, and the other third enabled me to have an enjoyable life." Butts was born at Poughkeepsie, NY. He died Apr 4, 1993, at Rhinebeck, NY.

JEFFERSON, THOMAS: BIRTH ANNIVERSARY. Apr 13, 1743. Third president of the US (Mar 4, 1801–Mar 3, 1809), second vice president (1797–1801), born at Albermarle County, VA. Jefferson, who died at Charlottesville, VA, July

4, 1826, wrote his own epitaph: "Here was buried Thomas Jefferson, author of the Declaration of American Independence, of the statute of Virginia for religious freedom, and father of the University of Virginia." A holiday in Alabama and Oklahoma.

SILENT SPRING PUBLICATION: ANNIVERSARY. Apr 13, 1962. Rachel Carson's *Silent Spring* warned humankind that for the first time in history every person is subjected to contact with dangerous chemicals from conception until death. Carson painted a vivid picture of how chemicals—used in many ways but particularly in pesticides—have upset the balance of nature, undermining the survival of countless species. This enormously popular and influential book was a soft-spoken battle cry to protect our natural surroundings. Its publication signaled the beginning of the environmental movement.

★ Birthdays ★

Rick Schroeder, actor ("Silver Spoons," "NYPD Blue," *The Champ*), born Staten Island, NY, Apr 13, 1970.

Paul Sorvino, actor ("Law & Order," *Goodfellas*), born Brooklyn, NY, Apr 13, 1939.

April 14

FIRST DICTIONARY OF AMERICAN ENGLISH PUBLISHED: ANNIVERSARY. Apr 14, 1828. Noah Webster published his *American Dictionary of the English Language*.

GRAPES OF WRATH PUBLISHED: ANNIVERSARY. Apr 14, 1939. John Steinbeck's novel of the Great Depression, *Grapes of Wrath*, won the 1940 Pulitzer Prize. It chronicled the mass migration to California of dispossessed farmers from the Dust Bowl region of the Great Plains.

LINCOLN, ABRAHAM: ASSASSINATION ANNIVERSARY. Apr 14, 1865. President Abraham Lincoln was shot while watching a performance of *Our American Cousin* at Ford's Theatre, Washington, DC. He died the following day. Assassin was John Wilkes Booth, a young actor.

PAN AMERICAN DAY. Apr 14. Presidential Proclamation 1912, of May 28, 1930, covers every Apr 14 (required by Governing Board of Pan American Union). Proclamation issued each year since 1948. Commemorates the first International Conference of American States in 1890.

Sarah Michelle Gellar, actress (*I Know What You Did Last Summer*, "Buffy the Vampire Slayer"), born New York, NY, Apr 14, 1977.

April 15

ASTRONOMERS FIND NEW SOLAR SYSTEM: ANNIVERSARY. Apr 15, 1999. Astronomers from San Francisco State University working at an observatory in Arizona announced the discovery of the first multiplanet system ever found orbiting around a star other than our own. Three planets orbit the star Upsilon Andromedae, which can be seen with the naked eye. This suggests that the Milky Way probably teems with similar planetary systems.

FIRST MCDONALD'S OPENS: ANNIVERSARY. Apr 15, 1955. The first franchised McDonald's was opened at Des Plaines, IL, by Ray Kroc, who had gotten the idea from a hamburger joint at San Bernardino, CA, run by the McDonald brothers. On opening day a hamburger was 15 cents. The Big Mac was introduced in 1968 for 49 cents and the Quarter Pounder in 1971 for 53 cents. By the late 1990s, there were more than 25,000 McDonald's in 115 countries.

SINKING OF THE *TITANIC*: ANNIVERSARY. Apr 15, 1912. The "unsinkable" luxury liner *Titanic* on its maiden voyage from Southampton, England, to New York, NY, struck an iceberg just before midnight Apr 14, and sank at 2:27 AM, Apr 15. The *Titanic* had 2,224 persons aboard. Of these, more than 1,500 were lost. About 700 people were rescued from the icy waters off Newfoundland by the liner *Carpathia*, which reached the scene about two hours after the *Titanic* went down. The sunken *Titanic* was located and photographed in September 1985. In July 1986 an expedition aboard the *Atlantis II* descended to the deck of the *Titanic* in a submersible craft, *Alvin*, and guided a robot named Jason, Jr, in a search of the ship. Two memorial bronze plaques were left on the deck of the sunken ship.

Jason Sehorn, football player, born Mt Shasta, CA, Apr 15, 1971.

Emma Thompson, actress (*Howard's End, Sense and Sensibility*), born London, England, Apr 15, 1959.

April 16

CHAPLIN, CHARLES SPENCER: BIRTH ANNIVERSARY. Apr 16, 1889. Celebrated film comedian who portrayed "The Little Tramp" was born at London, England. Film debut in 1914. Knighted in 1975. Died at Vevey, Switzerland, Dec 25, 1977. In his autobiography Chaplin wrote: "There are more valid facts and details in works of art than there are in history books."

SLAVERY ABOLISHED IN THE DISTRICT OF COLUMBIA. Apr 16, 1862. Congress abolished slavery in the District of Columbia. One million dollars was appropriated to compensate owners of freed slaves, and $100,000 was set aside to pay the expenses of district slaves who wanted to emigrate to Haiti, Liberia or any other foreign country.

★ Birthdays ★

Kareem Abdul-Jabbar, Hall of Fame basketball player, born Lewis Ferdinand Alcindor, Jr, New York, NY, Apr 16, 1947.

Martin Lawrence, actor (*Bad Boys*, "Martin"), born Frankfurt, Germany, Apr 16, 1965.

April 17

BAY OF PIGS INVASION LAUNCHED: ANNIVERSARY. Apr 17, 1961. More than 1,500 Cuban exiles invaded Cuba in an ill-fated attempt to overthrow Fidel Castro.

CAMBODIA FALLS TO THE KHMER ROUGE: ANNIVERSARY. Apr 17, 1975. Cambodia fell when its capital, Phnom Penh, was captured by the Khmer Rouge. The Pol Pot regime inaugurated "Year One," and the wholesale slaughter of intellectuals, political enemies and peasants began. As many as 2 million Cambodians perished. In 1979 the Pol Pot regime fell to Cambodian rebels and Vietnamese soldiers.

DOW-JONES TOPS 3,000: ANNIVERSARY. Apr 17, 1991. The Dow-Jones Index of 30 major industrial stocks topped the 3,000 mark for the first time.

SYRIAN ARAB REPUBLIC: INDEPENDENCE DAY. Apr 17. Official holiday. Proclaimed independence from League of Nations mandate under French administration in 1946.

★ Birthdays ★

Sean Bean, actor (*Stormy Monday, The Field, Patriot Games*), born Sheffield, Yorkshire, England, Apr 17, 1958.

Lela Rochon, actress (*Waiting to Exhale, Boomerang*), born Los Angeles, CA, Apr 17, 1966.

April 18

DARROW, CLARENCE SEWARD: BIRTH ANNIVERSARY. Apr 18, 1857. American attorney often associated with unpopular causes, from the Pullman strike in 1894 to the Scottsboro case in 1932, born at Kinsman, OH. At the Scopes trial, July 13, 1925, Darrow said: "I do not consider it an insult, but rather a compliment, to be called an agnostic. I do not pretend to know where many ignorant men are sure—that is all that agnosticism means." Darrow died at Chicago, IL, Mar 13, 1938.

THE HOUSE THAT RUTH BUILT: ANNIVERSARY. Apr 18, 1923. More than 74,000 fans attended Opening Day festivities as the New York Yankees inaugurated their new stadium. Babe Ruth christened it with a game-winning three-run homer into the right-field bleachers. In his coverage of the game for the *New York Evening Telegram* sportswriter Fred Lieb described Yankee Stadium as "The House That Ruth Built," and the name stuck.

PAUL REVERE'S RIDE: ANNIVERSARY. Apr 18, 1775. The "Midnight Ride" of Paul Revere and William Dawes started at about 10 PM, to warn American patriots between Boston, MA, and Concord, MA, of the approaching British.

PET OWNERS INDEPENDENCE DAY. Apr 18. Dog and cat owners take a day off from work and the pets go to work in their place, since most pets are jobless, sleep all day and do not even take out the trash. [©2001 by WH.] For info: Wellcat Holidays. Web: www.wellcat.com.

SAN FRANCISCO 1906 EARTHQUAKE: ANNIVERSARY. Apr 18, 1906. Business section of San Francisco, some 10,000 acres, destroyed by earthquake. First quake at 5:13 AM, followed by fire. Nearly 4,000 lives lost.

"THIRD WORLD" DAY: ANNIVERSARY. Apr 18, 1955. Anniversary of the first use of the phrase "third world," which was by Indonesia's president Achmad Sukarno in his opening speech at the Bandung Conference. Representatives of nearly 30 African and Asian countries heard Sukarno praise the American war of independence, "the first successful anticolonial war in history." The phrase and the idea of a "third world" rapidly gained currency, generally signifying the aggregate of nonaligned peoples and nations—the nonwhite and underdeveloped portion of the world.

ZIMBABWE: INDEPENDENCE DAY. Apr 18. National holiday commemorates the recognition by Great Britain of Zimbabwean independence on this day in 1980. Prior to this, the country had been the British colony of Southern Rhodesia.

★ Birthdays ★

Melissa Joan Hart, actress ("Clarissa Explains It All," "Sabrina the Teenage Witch"), born Long Island, NY, Apr 18, 1976.

Jane Leeves, actress ("Murphy Brown," "Frasier"), born East Grinstead, England, Apr 18, 1961.

Conan O'Brien, host ("Late Night with Conan O'Brien"), born Brookline, MA, Apr 18, 1963.

April 19

BATTLE OF LEXINGTON AND CONCORD: ANNIVERSARY. Apr 19, 1775. Massachusetts. Start of the American Revolution as the British fired the "shot heard 'round the world."

OKLAHOMA CITY BOMBING: ANNIVERSARY. Apr 19, 1995. A car bomb exploded outside the Alfred P. Murrah Federal Building at Oklahoma City, OK, at 9:02 AM, killing 168 people, 19 of them children at a day-care center; a nurse died of head injuries sustained while helping in rescue efforts. The bomb, estimated to have weighed 5,000 pounds, had been placed in a rented truck. The blast ripped off the north face of the nine-story building, leaving a 20-foot-wide crater and debris two stories high. Structurally unsound and increasingly dangerous, the bombed building was razed May 23. Timothy J. McVeigh, a decorated Gulf War army vet who is alleged to have been angered by the Bureau of Alcohol, Tobacco and Firearms (ATF) attack on the Branch Davidian compound at Waco, TX, exactly two years before, was convicted of the bombing and was executed June 11, 2001. The ATF had offices in the OK federal building. Terry L. Nicholls, an army buddy of McVeigh, was convicted of lesser charges.

SPACE MILESTONE: *SALYUT* (USSR). Apr 19, 1971. The Soviet Union launched *Salyut*, the first manned orbiting space laboratory. It was replaced in 1986 by *Mir*, a manned space station and laboratory.

WARSAW GHETTO REVOLT: ANNIVERSARY. Apr 19, 1943. A prolonged revolt began at Warsaw, Poland, when German troops tried to resume deportation of Jewish residents of the Warsaw Ghetto to the Treblinka concentration camp. With only 17 rifles and handmade grenades, for almost a month 1,200 Jewish fighters resisted 2,100 German troops who were armed with machine guns. When the uprising ended on May 16, 300 Germans and 7,000 Jews had died and the Warsaw Ghetto lay in ruins.

★ Birthdays ★

Hayden Christiansen, actor (*Star Wars, Episodes II and III*), born Vancouver, BC, Canada, Apr 19, 1981.

Kate Hudson, actress (*Almost Famous, 200 Cigarettes*), born Los Angeles, CA, Apr 19, 1979.
Ashley Judd, actress ("Sisters," *Double Jeopardy*), born Los Angeles, CA, Apr 19, 1968.

★ *Birthdays* ★

Jessica Lange, actress (Oscars for *Tootsie* and *Blue Skies*; *Frances, Sweet Dreams*), born Cloquet, MN, Apr 20, 1949.

April 20

COLUMBINE HIGH SCHOOL KILLINGS: ANNIVERSARY. Apr 20, 1999. At this high school at Littleton, CO, students Eric Harris and Dylan Klebold killed 12 other students, a teacher and then themselves.

HITLER, ADOLF: BIRTH ANNIVERSARY. Apr 20, 1889. German dictator, frustrated artist, obsessed with superiority of the "Aryan race" and the evil of Marxism (which he saw as a Jewish plot). Hitler was born at Braunau am Inn, Austria. Turning to politics, despite a five-year prison sentence (writing *Mein Kampf* during the nine months he served), his rise was predictable and, Aug 19, 1934, a German plebiscite vested sole executive power in Führer Adolf Hitler. Facing certain defeat by the Allied Forces, he shot himself, Apr 30, 1945, while his mistress, Eva Braun, took poison in a Berlin bunker where they had been hiding for more than three months.

TAURUS, THE BULL. Apr 20–May 20. In the astronomical/astrological zodiac that divides the sun's apparent orbit into 12 segments, the period Apr 20–May 20 is identified, traditionally, as the sun sign of Taurus, the Bull. The ruling planet is Venus.

April 21

ITALY: BIRTHDAY OF ROME. Apr 21. Celebration of the founding of Rome, traditionally thought to be in 753 BC.

KINDERGARTEN DAY. Apr 21. A day to recognize the importance of play, games and "creative self-activity" in children's education and to note the history of the kindergarten. Observed on the anniversary of the birth of Friedrich Froebel, in 1782, who established the first kindergarten in 1837. German immigrants brought Froebel's ideas to the US in the 1840s. The first kindergarten in a public school in the US was started in 1873, at St. Louis, MO.

QUINN, ANTHONY: BIRTH ANNIVERSARY. Apr 21, 1915. Actor, sculptor and painter, Anthony Rudolf Oaxaca Quinn was born at Chihuahua, Mexico, and moved to the US as a child. He became a US citizen in 1947. He won Academy Awards for best supporting actor in 1952 for

Viva Zapata! and in 1956 for *Lust for Life*. His best-remembered role was that of *Zorba the Greek*, for which he was nominated for best actor in 1964. He died at Boston, MA, on June 3, 2001.

SAN JACINTO DAY. Apr 21. Texas. Commemorates Battle of San Jacinto in 1836, in which Texas won independence from Mexico. A 570-foot monument, dedicated on the 101st anniversary of the battle, marks the site on the banks of the San Jacinto River, about 20 miles from present city of Houston, TX, where General Sam Houston's Texans decisively defeated the Mexican forces led by Santa Anna in the final battle between Texas and Mexico.

★ Birthdays ★

Queen Elizabeth II, queen of the United Kingdom, born London, England, Apr 21, 1926.
Charles Grodin, actor (*Midnight Run, Beethoven*); director, host ("The Charles Grodin Show"), born Pittsburgh, PA, Apr 21, 1935.
Andie MacDowell, actress (*sex, lies, and videotape; Groundhog Day*), born Gaffney, SC, Apr 21, 1958.

April 22

BRAZIL: DISCOVERY OF BRAZIL DAY: ANNIVERSARY. Apr 22. Commemorates discovery by Pedro Alvarez Cabral in 1500.

COINS STAMPED "IN GOD WE TRUST": ANNIVERSARY. Apr 22, 1864. By act of Congress, the phrase "In God We Trust" began to be stamped on all US coins.

EARTH DAY: ANNIVERSARY. Apr 22. Earth Day, first observed Apr 22, 1970, with message "New Energy for a New Era" and attention to accelerating the transition to renewable energy worldwide. Earth Day 1990 was a global event with more than 200 million participating in 142 countries. Earth Day activities are held by many groups on various dates, often on the weekend before or after Apr 22. For info: Earth Day Network. Web: www.earthday.org.

LENIN, NIKOLAI: BIRTH ANNIVERSARY. Apr 22, 1870. Russian Socialist and revolutionary leader (real name: Vladimir Ilyich Ulyanov), ideological follower of Karl Marx, born at Simbirst, on the Volga, Russia. Leader of the Great October Socialist Revolution of 1917. Died at Gorky, near Moscow, Jan 21, 1924. His embalmed body, in a glass coffin at the Lenin Mausoleum, has been viewed by millions of visitors to Moscow's Red Square.

OKLAHOMA LAND RUSH: ANNIVERSARY. Apr 22, 1889. At noon a gunshot signaled the start of the Oklahoma land rush as thousands of settlers rushed into the territory to claim land. Under pressure from cattlemen, the federal government opened 1,900,000 acres of central Oklahoma that had been bought from the Creek and Seminole tribes.

★ Birthdays ★

Glen Campbell, singer ("Gentle on My Mind," "By the Time I Get to Phoenix"), born Billstown, AR, Apr 22, 1935.

Jack Nicholson, actor (Oscars for *One Flew Over the Cuckoo's Nest, Terms of Endearment* and *As Good as It Gets*), born Neptune, NJ, Apr 22, 1936.

April 23

"BAYWATCH" TV PREMIERE: ANNIVERSARY. Apr 23, 1989. Set on a California beach, this program starred David Hasselhoff and a changing cast of nubile young men and women as lifeguards. Later the program was moved to Hawaii; the last episode was made in 2001. The most widely viewed TV series in the world, the program aired in 142 countries with an estimated weekly audience of 1.1 billion.

BUCHANAN, JAMES: BIRTH ANNIVERSARY. Apr 23, 1791. Fifteenth president of the US, born at Cove Gap, PA, was the only president who never married. He served one term in office, Mar 4, 1857–Mar 3, 1861, and died at Lancaster, PA, June 1, 1868.

FIRST MOVIE THEATER OPENS: ANNIVERSARY. Apr 23, 1896. The first movie was shown at Koster and Bials Music Hall at New York City. Up until this time, people saw films individually by looking into a Kinetoscope, a boxlike "peep show." This was the first time in the US that an audience sat in a theater and watched a movie together.

FIRST PUBLIC SCHOOL IN AMERICA: ANNIVERSARY. Apr 23, 1635. The Boston Latin School opened—America's oldest public school.

PEARSON, LESTER: BIRTH ANNIVERSARY. Apr 23, 1897. Fourteenth prime minister of Canada, born at Toronto, Canada. He was Canada's chief delegate at the San Francisco conference where the UN charter was drawn up, and he later served as president of the General Assembly. He wrote the proposal that resulted in the formation of the North Atlantic Treaty Organization (NATO). He was awarded the Nobel Peace Prize. Died at Rockcliffe, Canada, Dec 27, 1972.

SHAKESPEARE, WILLIAM: BIRTH AND DEATH ANNIVERSARY. Apr 23. England's most famous and most revered poet and playwright. He was born at Stratford-on-Avon, England, Apr 23, 1564 (OS), baptized there three days later and died there on his birthday, Apr 23, 1616 (OS). Author of at least 36 plays and 154 sonnets, Shakespeare created the most influential and lasting body of work in the English language, an extraordinary exploration of human nature.

UNITED NATIONS: WORLD BOOK AND COPYRIGHT DAY. Apr 23. Observed throughout the United Nations system. For info: United Nations. Web: www.un.org.

★ *Birthdays* ★

Judy Davis, actress (*A Passage to India, Deconstructing Harry*), born Perth, Australia, Apr 23, 1955.
Melina Kanakaredes, actress ("Providence," "Guiding Light"), born Akron, OH, Apr 23, 1967.

April 24

IRELAND: EASTER RISING: ANNIVERSARY. Apr 24, 1916. Irish nationalists seized key buildings in Dublin and proclaimed an Irish republic. The rebellion collapsed, however, and it wasn't until 1922 that the Irish Free State, the predecessor of the Republic of Ireland, was established.

LIBRARY OF CONGRESS: ANNIVERSARY. Apr 24, 1800. Congress approved an act providing "for the purchase of such books as may be necessary for the use of Congress . . . and for fitting up a

suitable apartment for containing them." Thus began one of the world's greatest libraries.

★ *Birthdays* ★

Eric Bogosian, actor (*Under Siege 2*), playwright, performance artist, born Boston, MA, Apr 24, 1953.
Shirley MacLaine, author, actress (Oscar for *Terms of Endearment; The Turning Point, Being There*), born Richmond, VA, Apr 24, 1934.
Barbra Streisand, actress (Oscar for *Funny Girl; The Way We Were, Yentl*), director (*Prince of Tides*), singer, born Brooklyn, NY, Apr 24, 1942.

April 25

EAST MEETS WEST: ANNIVERSARY. Apr 25, 1945. During World War II US Army lieutenant Albert Kotzebue encountered a single Soviet soldier near the German village of Lechwitz, 75 miles south of Berlin. Patrols of General Leonard Gerow's V Corps saluted the advance guard of Marshall Ivan Konev's Soviet 58th Guards Division. Soldiers of both nations embraced and exchanged toasts. The Allied armies of East and West had finally met.

FIRST LICENSE PLATES: ANNIVERSARY. Apr 25, 1901. New York began requiring license plates on automobiles, the first state to do so.

MARCONI, GUGLIELMO: BIRTH ANNIVERSARY. Apr 25, 1874. Inventor of wireless telegraphy

(1895), born at Bologna, Italy. Died at Rome, Italy, July 20, 1937.

SPACE MILESTONE: HUBBLE SPACE TELESCOPE DEPLOYED (US). Apr 25, 1990. Deployed by *Discovery* (launched Apr 12, 1990, from Kennedy Space Center, FL), the telescope is the largest in-orbit observatory to date and is capable of imaging objects up to 14 billion light-years away. The resolution of images was expected to be seven to ten times greater than images from Earth-based telescopes, since the Hubble Space Telescope is not hampered by Earth's atmospheric distortion. Unfortunately, the telescope's lenses were defective, so the anticipated high quality of imaging was not possible. In 1993, however, the world watched as a shuttle crew successfully retrieved the Hubble from orbit, executed the needed repair and replacement work and released it into orbit once more. In December 1999 the space shuttle *Discovery* was launched to do extensive repairs on the telescope.

★ Birthdays ★

Hank Azaria, actor (*The Birdcage*, many voices on "The Simpsons"), born Forest Hills, NY, Apr 25, 1964.

Al Pacino, actor (Oscar for *Scent of a Woman; Dog Day Afternoon, Godfather* movies), born New York, NY, Apr 25, 1940.

Renee Zellweger, actress (*Jerry Maguire, Nurse Betty, Bridget Jones's Diary*), born Katy, TX, Apr 25, 1969.

April 26

AUDUBON, JOHN JAMES: BIRTH ANNIVERSARY. Apr 26, 1785. American artist and naturalist, best known for his *Birds of America*, born at Haiti. Died Jan 27, 1851, at New York, NY.

CHERNOBYL NUCLEAR REACTOR DISASTER: ANNIVERSARY. Apr 26, 1986. At 1:23 AM, local time, an explosion occurred at the Chernobyl atomic power station at Pripyat in the Ukraine. The resulting fire burned for days, sending radioactive material into the atmosphere. More than 100,000 persons were evacuated from a 300-square-mile area around the plant. Three months later 31 people were reported to have died and thousands were exposed to dangerous levels of radiation. Estimates projected an additional 1,000 cancer cases in nations downwind of the radioactive discharge. The plant was encased in a concrete tomb in an effort to prevent the still-hot reactor from overheating again and to minimize further release of radiation.

GUERNICA MASSACRE: ANNIVERSARY. Apr 26, 1937. Late in the afternoon, the ancient Basque town of Guernica, in northern Spain, was attacked without warning by German-made airplanes. Three hours of intensive bombing left the town in flames, and citizens who fled to the fields and ditches around Guernica were machine-gunned from the air. This atrocity inspired Pablo Picasso's mural *Guernica*. Responsibility for the bombing was never officially established, but the suffering and anger of the victims and their survivors are still evident at anniversary demonstrations. Intervention by Nazi Germany in the Spanish Civil War has been described as practice for World War II.

OLMSTED, FREDERICK LAW: BIRTH ANNIVERSARY. Apr 26, 1822. Known as the "father of landscape architecture in America," Olmsted participated in the designing of Yosemite National Park, New York City's Central Park and parks for Boston, Hartford and Louisville. Born at Hartford, CT, died at Waverly, MA, Aug 28, 1903. Olmsted's home and studio, Fairsted Estate in Brookline, MA, is now preserved as a National Historic Site and is open to the public.

RICHTER SCALE DAY. Apr 26. A day to recognize the importance of Charles Francis Richter's research and his work on development of the earthquake magnitude scale that is known as the Richter scale. Richter, an American author, physicist and seismologist, was born Apr 26, 1900, near Hamilton, OH. An Earthquake Awareness Week was observed in recognition of his work. Richter died at Pasadena, CA, Sept 30, 1985.

SOUTH AFRICAN MULTIRACIAL ELECTIONS: ANNIVERSARY. Apr 26–29, 1994. For the first time in the history of South Africa, the nation's approximately 18 million blacks voted in multiparty elections. This event marked the definitive end of apartheid, the system of racial separation that had kept blacks and other minorities out of the political process. The election resulted in Nelson Mandela of the African National Congress being elected president and F.W. de Klerk (incumbent president) of the National Party vice president.

★ *Birthdays* ★

Carol Burnett, actress ("Garry Moore Show," "Carol Burnett Show," *The Four Seasons*), born San Antonio, TX, Apr 26, 1936.
Joan Chen, actress ("Twin Peaks," "Golden Gates"), born Shanghai, China, Apr 26, 1961.

April 27

BABE RUTH DAY: ANNIVERSARY. Apr 27, 1947. Babe Ruth Day was celebrated in every ballpark in organized baseball in the US as well as Japan. Mortally ill with throat cancer, Ruth appeared at Yankee Stadium to thank his former club for the honor.

GRANT, ULYSSES S.: BIRTH ANNIVERSARY. Apr 27, 1822. Eighteenth president of the US (Mar 4, 1869–Mar 3, 1877), born Hiram Ulysses Grant at Point Pleasant, OH. He graduated from the US Military Academy in 1843. President Lincoln promoted Grant to lieutenant general in command of all the Union armies Mar 9, 1864. On Apr 9, 1865, Grant received General Robert E. Lee's surrender, at Appomattox Court House, VA, which he announced to the secretary of war as follows: "General Lee surrendered the Army of Northern Virginia this afternoon on terms proposed by myself. The accompanying additional correspondence will show the conditions fully." Nicknamed "Unconditional Surrender Grant," he died at Mount McGregor, NY, July 23, 1885, just four days after completing his memoirs. He was buried at Riverside Park, New York, NY, where Grant's Tomb was dedicated in 1897.

MAGELLAN, FERDINAND: DEATH ANNIVERSARY. Apr 27, 1521. Portuguese explorer Ferdinand Magellan was probably born near Oporto, Portugal, about 1480, but neither the place nor the date is certain. Usually thought of as the first man to circumnavigate Earth, he died before completing the voyage; thus his coleader, Basque navigator Juan Sebastian de Elcano, became the world's first circumnavigator. The westward 'round-the-world expedition began Sept 20, 1519, with five ships and about 250 men. Magellan was killed by natives of the Philippine island of Mactan.

SIERRA LEONE: INDEPENDENCE DAY. Apr 27. National Day. Commemorates independence from Britain in 1961.

TOGO: INDEPENDENCE DAY. Apr 27. National holiday. In 1960 Togo gained its independence from French administration under a United Nations trusteeship.

★ Birthdays ★

Coretta Scott King, lecturer, widow of Dr. Martin Luther King, Jr, born Marion, AL, Apr 27, 1927.

Jack Klugman, actor ("The Odd Couple," "Quincy, ME"), born Philadelphia, PA, Apr 27, 1922.

April 28

BIOLOGICAL CLOCK GENE DISCOVERED: ANNIVERSARY. Apr 28, 1994. Researchers at Northwestern University announced that the so-called biological clock, that gene governing the daily cycle of waking and sleeping called the circadian rhythm, had been found in mice. Never before pinpointed in a mammal, the biological clock gene was found on mouse chromosome #5.

MARYLAND CONSTITUTION RATIFIED: ANNIVERSARY. Apr 28, 1788. Maryland became the seventh state to ratify the Constitution, by a vote of 63 to 11.

MONROE, JAMES: BIRTH ANNIVERSARY. Apr 28, 1758. Fifth president of the US was born at Westmoreland County, VA, and served two terms in that office (Mar 4, 1817–Mar 3, 1825). Monrovia, the capital city of Liberia, is named after him, as is the Monroe Doctrine, which he enunciated at Washington, DC, Dec 2, 1823. Last of three presidents to die on US Independence Day, Monroe died at New York, NY, July 4, 1831.

MUTINY ON THE *BOUNTY*: ANNIVERSARY. Apr 28, 1789. The most famous of all naval mutinies occurred on board HMS *Bounty*. Captain of the *Bounty* was Lieutenant William Bligh, an able seaman and a mean-tempered disciplinarian. The ship, with a load of breadfruit tree plants from Tahiti, was bound for Jamaica. Fletcher Christian, leader of the mutiny, put Bligh and 18 of his loyal followers adrift in a 23-foot open boat. Miraculously Bligh and all of his supporters survived a 47-day voyage of more than 3,600 miles, before landing on the island of Timor, June 14, 1789. In the meantime, Christian had put all of the remaining crew (excepting eight men and himself) ashore at Tahiti where he picked up 18 Tahitians (six men and 12 women) and set sail again. Landing at Pitcairn Island in 1790 (probably uninhabited at the time), they burned the *Bounty* and remained undiscovered for 18 years, when an American whaler, the *Topaz*, called at the island (in 1808) and found only one member of the mutinous crew surviving. However, the little colony had actually thrived and, when counted by the British in 1856, numbered 194 persons.

SPACE MILESTONE: FIRST TOURIST IN SPACE. Apr 28, 2001. Millionaire US businessman Dennis Tito reportedly paid the Russian space agency $20 million to accompany *Soyuz TM* to the International Space Station (ISS). The rocket with Tito and two Russian cosmonauts was launched this day from the Baikonur launch in Kazakhstan and arrived at the ISS on Apr 30, 2001. The crew returned to Earth in a week. NASA initially objected to the inclusion of the 60-year-old tycoon on the mission but dropped its opposition.

★ Birthdays ★

Ann-Margret, actress (*Carnal Knowledge, Tommy*), born Ann-Margret Olsson, Stockholm, Sweden, Apr 28, 1941.

Jay Leno, TV talk-show host ("The Tonight Show"), comedian, born New Rochelle, NY, Apr 28, 1950.

April 29

ELLINGTON, (EDWARD KENNEDY) "DUKE": BIRTH ANNIVERSARY. Apr 29, 1899. "Duke" Ellington, one of the most influential individuals in jazz history, was born at Washington, DC. Ellington's professional career began when he was 17, and by 1923 he was leading a small group of musicians at the Kentucky Club at New York City who became the core of his big band.

Ellington is credited with being one of the founders of big band jazz. He used his band as an instrument for composition and orchestration to create big band pieces, film scores, operas, ballets, Broadway shows and religious music. Ellington was responsible for more than 1,000 musical pieces. He drew together instruments from different sections of the orchestra to develop unique and haunting sounds such as that of his famous "Mood Indigo." "Duke" Ellington died May 24, 1974, at New York City.

LOS ANGELES RIOTS: ANNIVERSARY. Apr 29, 1992. A jury in Simi Valley, CA, failed to convict four Los Angeles police officers accused in the videotaped beating of Rodney King, providing the spark that set off rioting, looting and burning at South Central Los Angeles, CA, and other areas across the country. The anger unleashed during and after the violence was attributed to widespread racism, lack of job opportunities and the resulting hopelessness of inner-city poverty.

ZIPPER PATENTED: ANNIVERSARY. Apr 29, 1913. Gideon Sundbach of Hoboken, NJ, received a patent for the zipper.

★ Birthdays ★

Michelle Pfeiffer, actress (*Batman Returns, Dangerous Liaisons, The Fabulous Baker Boys*), born Santa Ana, CA, Apr 29, 1958.

Jerry Seinfeld, comedian, actor ("Seinfeld"), born Brooklyn, NY, Apr 29, 1954.

Uma Thurman, actress (*Henry and June, Pulp Fiction*), born Boston, MA, Apr 29, 1970.

April 30

FIRST PRESIDENTIAL TELECAST: ANNIVERSARY. Apr 30, 1939. Franklin D. Roosevelt became the first president to appear on television when he was televised at the New York World's Fair. However, the appearance was beamed to only 200 TV sets in a 40-mile radius. See also: "First Scheduled Television Broadcast: Anniv" (July 1).

LOUISIANA: ADMISSION DAY: ANNIVERSARY. Apr 30. Became 18th state in 1812.

SOUTH VIETNAM FALLS TO VIETCONG: ANNIVERSARY. Apr 30, 1975. The president of South Vietnam announced the country's unconditional surrender to the Vietcong. Communist troops moved into Saigon and 1,000 Americans in the city were hastily evacuated. Thousands of South Vietnamese also tried to flee. The surrender announcement came 21 years after the 1954 Geneva agreements divided Vietnam into North and South. The last American troops had left South Vietnam in March 1973.

WASHINGTON, GEORGE: PRESIDENTIAL INAUGURATION ANNIVERSARY. Apr 30, 1789. George Washington was inaugurated as the first president of the US under the new Constitution at New York, NY. Robert R. Livingston administered the oath of office to Washington on the balcony of Federal Hall, at the corner of Wall and Broad Streets.

★ Birthdays ★

Cloris Leachman, actress (Oscar for *The Last Picture Show*; "Phyllis"), born Des Moines, IA, Apr 30, 1930.
Isiah Thomas, Hall of Fame basketball player, born Chicago, IL, Apr 30, 1961.

May

May 1

AMTRAK: ANNIVERSARY. May 1, 1971. Amtrak, the national rail service that combined the operations of 18 passenger railroads, went into service.

ASIAN PACIFIC AMERICAN HERITAGE MONTH. May 1–31. Presidential Proclamation issued honoring Asian Pacific Americans each year since 1979. Public Law 102-450 of Oct 28, 1992, designated the observance for the month of May each year.

BETTER HEARING AND SPEECH MONTH. May 1–31. A nationwide public information campaign held each May to inform the 41 million Americans with hearing and speech problems that help is available. For info: American Speech–Language–Hearing Association. Web: www.professional.asha.org.

BREATHE EASY MONTH. May 1–31. A public awareness campaign to educate the public on the American Lung Association's mission to prevent lung disease and promote lung health. Areas of public concern include the dangers of secondhand smoke, air pollution—both indoors and outdoors—and how asthma can be controlled with proper education. For info: American Lung Association. Web: www.lungusa.org.

CLEAN AIR MONTH. May 1–31. More than 141 million Americans live in areas that receive a failing grade for smog. This is a call for enforcement of the Clean Air Act. For info: American Lung Association. Web: www.lungusa.org.

FIRST SKYSCRAPER: ANNIVERSARY. May 1, 1884. Construction was begun on the Home Insurance Company building on this date in Chicago. The ten-story building was completed in 1885. Designed by William Le Baron Jenney, it had a steel frame that carried the weight of the building. The walls provided no support but hung like curtains on the metal frame. This method of construction revolutionized American architecture and allowed architects to build taller and taller buildings.

FREQUENT FLYER PROGRAM DEBUTS: ANNIVERSARY. May 1, 1981. American Airlines began the first frequent flyer program on this date. Now most airlines offer a frequent flyer program, but American is still the industry leader with 45 million members. Today 40 percent of all miles are earned on the ground with affiliated businesses that pay the airlines for the miles, such as hotels, car rental companies, credit card companies, phone companies and retailers.

GET CAUGHT READING MONTH. May 1–31. Celebrities appear in ads appealing to people of all ages to remind them of the joys of reading. Events will be held throughout the country to celebrate reading. For info: Association of American Publishers. Web: www.publishers.org or www.getcaughtreading.org.

GREAT BRITAIN FORMED: ANNIVERSARY. May 1, 1707. A union between England and Scotland resulted in the formation of Great Britain. (Wales had been part of England since the 1500s.) Today's United Kingdom consists of Great Britain and Northern Ireland.

HUNTINGTON'S DISEASE AWARENESS MONTH. May 1–31. For info: Huntington's Disease Society of America. Web: www.hdsa.org.

LAW DAY. May 1. Presidential Proclamation issued each year for May 1 since 1958 at request. (Public Law 87–20 of Apr 7, 1961.)

LOYALTY DAY. May 1. Presidential Proclamation issued annually for May 1 since 1959 at request. (Public Law 85–529 of July 18, 1958.) Note that an earlier proclamation was issued in 1955.

MAY DAY. May 1. The first day of May has been observed as a holiday since ancient times. Spring festivals, maypoles and maying are still common, but the political importance of May Day has grown since the 1880s, when it became a workers' day. Now widely observed in countries as a workers' holiday or as Labor Day. (The US and Canada observe Labor Day in September.) In most European countries, when May Day falls on Saturday or Sunday, the Monday following is observed as a holiday, with bank and store closings, parades and other festivities.

MELANOMA/SKIN CANCER DETECTION AND PREVENTION MONTH. May 1–31. For info: American Academy of Dermatology. Web: www.aad.org.

NATIONAL ARTHRITIS MONTH. May 1–31. Increases awareness of the more than 100 diseases known as arthritis and increases support for the 40 million Americans with arthritis. For info: Arthritis Foundation. Web: www.arthritis .org.

NATIONAL BARBECUE MONTH. May 1–31. To encourage people to start enjoying barbecuing early in the season when Daylight Saving Time lengthens the day. For info: Barbecue Industry Association. Web: www.bbqind.org.

NATIONAL BIKE MONTH. May 1–31. Annual celebration of bicycling for recreation and transportation. Local activities sponsored by bicycling organizations, environmental groups, PTAs, police departments, health organizations and civic groups. About 5 million participants nationwide. For info: League of American Bicyclists. Web: www.bikeleague.org.

NATIONAL BOOK MONTH. May 1–31. When the world demands more and more of our time, National Book Month invites everyone in America to take time out to treat themselves to a unique pleasure: reading a good book. Readers participate in National Book Month annually through literary events held at schools, bookstores, libraries, community centers and arts organizations. The organization also sponsors the annual National Book Awards. For info:

National Book Foundation. Web: www.national book.org.

NATIONAL CORRECT POSTURE MONTH. May 1–31. For info: American Chiropractic Association. Web: www.acatoday.com.

NATIONAL EGG MONTH. May 1–31. Dedicated to the versatility, convenience, economy and good nutrition of the incredible edible egg™. For info: American Egg Board. Web: www.aeb.org.

NATIONAL HAMBURGER MONTH. May 1–31. Sponsored by White Castle, the original fast-food hamburger chain, founded in 1921, to pay tribute to one of America's favorite foods. With or without condiments, on or off a bun or bread, hamburgers have grown in popularity since the early 1920s and are now an American meal mainstay. For info: White Castle Management Co. Web: www.whitecastle.com.

NATIONAL HEPATITIS AWARENESS MONTH. May 1–31. For info: Hepatitis Foundation International. Web: www.hepfi.org.

NATIONAL MENTAL HEALTH MONTH. May 1–31. For info: National Mental Health Association. E-mail: infoctr@nmha.org. Web: www.nmha .org.

NATIONAL MOVING MONTH. May 1–31. Kicking off the busiest moving season of the year. Each year more than 21 million Americans move between Memorial Day and Labor Day, with the average American moving every seven years. During this month moving experts will be educating Americans on how to plan a successful move, pack efficiently and handle the uncertainties and questions that moving children may have. For info: Allied Van Lines. Web: www.alliedvan.com.

NATIONAL OSTEOPOROSIS PREVENTION MONTH. May 1–31. Osteoporosis is not a natural part of aging but is a preventable disease for most people. For info: National Osteoporosis Foundation. Web: www.nof.org.

NATIONAL PHYSICAL FITNESS AND SPORTS MONTH. May 1–31. Encourages individuals and organizations to promote fitness activities and programs. For info: President's Council on Physical Fitness and Sports. Web: www.fitness.gov.

NATIONAL PROM GRADUATION SAFETY MONTH. May 1–31. Comprehensive public awareness campaign providing information to high school students as well as parents, educators and other influencers of high school–aged children about the dangers of drinking and driving and the importance of making responsible decisions. For info: The Century Council. Web: www.centurycouncil.org.

NATIONAL SIGHT-SAVING MONTH. May 1–31. Prevent Blindness America® annually devotes this observance to a different topic in the fields of vision health or vision safety. Each topic reflects the latest developments in the specific area of focus. For info: Prevent Blindness America. Web: www.preventblindness.org.

NATIONAL STROKE AWARENESS MONTH. May 1–31. For info: National Stroke Association. Web: www.stroke.org.

OLDER AMERICANS MONTH. May 1–31. Presidential Proclamation; from 1963 through 1973 this was called "Senior Citizens Month." In May 1974 it became Older Americans Month.

SIGHT-SAVING ULTRAVIOLET AWARENESS MONTH. May 1–31. While the damage ultraviolet (UV) causes to skin is obvious, the damage it can do to eyes may not be. Not enough attention is paid to the damage UV can do to the eyes. Exposure to UV can burn delicate eye tissue and raise the risk of developing cataracts and cancers of the eye. For info: Prevent Blindness America®. Web: www.preventblindness.org.

U-2 INCIDENT: ANNIVERSARY. May 1, 1960. On the eve of a summit meeting between US president Dwight D. Eisenhower and Soviet Premier Nikita Khrushchev, a U-2 espionage plane flying at about 60,000 feet was shot down over Sverdlovsk, in central USSR. The pilot, CIA agent Francis Gary Powers, survived the crash, as did large parts of the aircraft, a suicide kit and sophisticated surveillance equipment. The sensational event, which US officials described as a weather reconnaissance flight gone astray, resulted in cancellation of the summit meeting. Powers was tried, convicted and sentenced to ten years in prison by a Moscow court. In 1962 he was returned to the US in exchange for an imprisoned Soviet spy. He died in a helicopter crash in 1977.

★ Birthdays ★

Judy Collins, singer ("Both Sides Now," "Chelsea Morning"), born Seattle, WA, May 1, 1939.
Tim McGraw, country singer, born Delhi, LA, May 1, 1967.

May 2

KING JAMES BIBLE PUBLISHED: ANNIVERSARY. May 2, 1611. King James I had appointed a committee of learned men to produce a new translation of the Bible in English. This version, popularly called the King James Version, is known in England as the Authorized Version.

LEONARDO DA VINCI: DEATH ANNIVERSARY. May 2, 1519. Italian artist, scientist and inventor. Painter of the famed *Last Supper*, perhaps the first painting of the High Renaissance, and of the *Mona Lisa*. Inventor of the first parachute. Born at Vinci, Italy, in 1452 (exact date unknown), he died at Amboise, France.

ROBERT'S RULES DAY. May 2, 1837. Anniversary of the birth of Henry M. Robert (General, US Army), author of *Robert's Rules of Order*, a standard parliamentary guide. Born at Robertville, SC. Died at Hornell, NY, May 11, 1923.

SPOCK, BENJAMIN: BIRTH ANNIVERSARY. May 2, 1903. Pediatrician and author, born at New Haven, CT. His book on childrearing, *Common Sense Book of Baby and Child Care*, later called *Baby and Child Care*, has sold more than 30 million copies. In 1955 he became professor of child development at Western Reserve University at Cleveland, OH. He resigned from this position in 1967 to devote his time to the pacifist movement. Spock died at San Diego, CA, Mar 15, 1998.

★ Birthdays ★

Christine Baranski, actress ("Cybill"), born Buffalo, NY, May 2, 1952.
Sarah Hughes, Olympic figure skater, born Manhasset, NY, May 2, 1985.

May 3

"CBS EVENING NEWS" TV PREMIERE: ANNIVERSARY. May 3, 1948. The news program began as a 15-minute telecast with Douglas Edwards as anchor. Walter Cronkite succeeded him in 1962 and expanded the show to 30 minutes; Eric Sevareid served as commentator. Dan Rather anchored the newscasts upon Cronkite's retirement in 1981. At one point, to boost sagging ratings, Connie Chung was added to the newscast as Rather's coanchor, but she left in 1995 in a well-publicized dispute. Rather remains solo, and, as Cronkite would say, ". . . that's the way it is."

CROSBY, HARRY LILLIS ("BING"): BIRTH ANNIVERSARY. May 3, 1903. Singer, composer and actor (*White Christmas, High Society*, various *Road* movies), born at Tacoma, WA (some sources say

May 4, 1904). Died while playing golf near Madrid, Spain, Oct 14, 1977.

DOW-JONES TOPS 11,000: ANNIVERSARY. May 3, 1999. The Dow-Jones Index of 30 major industrial stocks topped the 11,000 mark for the first time.

NATIONAL PUBLIC RADIO FIRST BROADCAST: ANNIVERSARY. May 3, 1971. National noncommercial radio network, financed by Corporation for Public Broadcasting, began programming.

ROBINSON, SUGAR RAY: BIRTH ANNIVERSARY. May 3, 1921. Ray ("Sugar Ray") Robinson, boxer, born Walker Smith, Jr, at Detroit, MI. Generally considered "pound for pound the greatest boxer of all time," Robinson was a welterweight and middleweight champion who won 175 professional fights and lost only 19. A smooth and precise boxer, he fought until he was 45, dabbled in show business and established the Sugar Ray Robinson Youth Foundation to counter juvenile delinquency. Died at Los Angeles, CA, Apr 12, 1989.

TAX FREEDOM DAY. May 3. According to the Tax Freedom Foundation, the average American had to work until this day in 2000 to pay federal, state and local taxes. Because state and local taxes vary, this date can vary by almost a whole month depending on the state you live in, ranging from April 23 (Alabama, Alaska, Kentucky, Mississippi, Oklahoma, Tennessee) to May 18 (Connecticut). Web: www.taxfoundation.org.

UNITED NATIONS: WORLD PRESS FREEDOM DAY. May 3. A day to recognize that a free, pluralistic and independent press is an essential component of any democratic society and to promote press freedom in the world. For info: United Nations. Web: www.un.org.

★ *Birthdays* ★

James Brown, singer, songwriter ("Papa's Got a Brand New Bag"), born Augusta, GA, May 3, 1933.

Greg Gumbel, TV sportscaster, born New Orleans, LA, May 3, 1946.

May 4

FREEDOM RIDERS: ANNIVERSARY. May 4, 1961. Militant students joined James Farmer of the Congress of Racial Equality (CORE) to conduct "freedom rides" on public transportation from Washington, DC, across the deep South to New Orleans. The trips were intended to test Supreme Court decisions and Interstate Commerce Commission regulations prohibiting discrimination in interstate travel. In several places riders were brutally beaten by local people and policemen. On May 14, members of the Ku Klux Klan attacked the Freedom Riders in Birmingham, AL, while local police watched. In Mississippi Freedom Riders were jailed. They never made it to New Orleans. The rides were patterned after a similar challenge to segregation, the 1947 Journey of Reconciliation, which tested the US Supreme Court's June 3, 1946, ban against segregation in interstate bus travel.

HAYMARKET SQUARE RIOT: ANNIVERSARY. May 4, 1886. Labor union unrest at Chicago led to violence when a crowd of unemployed men tried to enter the McCormick Reaper Works, where a strike was under way. Although no one was killed, anarchist groups called a mass meeting in Haymarket Square to avenge the "massacre." When the police advanced on the demonstrators, a bomb was thrown and several policemen were killed. Four leaders of the demonstration were hanged and another committed suicide in jail. Three others were given jail terms. The case aroused considerable controversy around the world.

KENT STATE STUDENTS' MEMORIAL DAY: ANNIVERSARY. May 4, 1970. Four students (Allison Krause, 19; Sandra Lee Scheuer, 20; Jeffrey Glenn Miller, 20 and William K. Schroeder, 19) were killed by the National Guard during demonstrations against the Vietnam War at Kent (Ohio) State University.

★ Birthdays ★

Ben Grieve, baseball player, born Arlington, TX, May 4, 1976.

Randy Travis, country singer ("Forever and Ever, Amen"), born Marshville, NC, May 4, 1959.

★ Birthdays ★

Richard E. Grant, actor (*LA Story, The Age of Innocence*), born Mbabane, Swaziland, May 5, 1957.

Michael Palin, actor, comedian ("Monty Python's Flying Circus," *Life of Brian*), born Sheffield, Yorkshire, England, May 5, 1943.

May 5

BASEBALL'S FIRST PERFECT GAME: ANNIVERSARY. May 5, 1904. Denton T. "Cy" Young pitched baseball's first perfect game, not allowing a single opposing player to reach first base. Young's outstanding performance led the Boston Americans in a 3–0 victory over Philadelphia in the American League. The Cy Young Award for pitching was named in his honor.

BONZA BOTTLER DAY™. May 5. To celebrate when the number of the day is the same as the number of the month. Bonza Bottler Day™ is an excuse to have a party at least once a month. For info: Gail M. Berger. E-mail: gberger5@aol.com.

MEXICO: CINCO DE MAYO. May 5. Mexican national holiday recognizing the anniversary of the Battle of Puebla in 1862, in which Mexican troops under General Ignacio Zaragoza, outnumbered three to one, defeated invading French forces of Napoleon III. Anniversary is observed by Mexicans everywhere with parades, festivals, dances and speeches.

May 6

BANNISTER BREAKS FOUR-MINUTE MILE: ANNIVERSARY. May 6, 1954. Running for the British Amateur Athletic Association in a meet at Oxford University, Roger Bannister broke the four-minute barrier with a time of 3:59.4. Four minutes for a mile at the time was considered not only a physical barrier but also a psychological one.

FREUD, SIGMUND: BIRTH ANNIVERSARY. May 6, 1856. Austrian physician, born at Freiberg, Moravia. Founder of psychoanalysis. Freud died at London, England, Sept 23, 1939.

HINDENBURG DISASTER: ANNIVERSARY. May 6, 1937. At 7:20 PM, the dirigible *Hindenburg* exploded as it approached the mooring mast at

Lakehurst, NJ, after a transatlantic voyage. Of its 97 passengers and crew, 36 died in the accident, which ended the dream of mass transportation via dirigible.

NATIONAL NURSES DAY AND WEEK. May 6–12. A week to honor the outstanding efforts of nurses everywhere to strengthen the health of the nation. Annually, beginning May 6, National Nurses Day, and ending May 12, Florence Nightingale's birthday. For info: American Nurses Association. Web: www.nursingworld .org.

WELLES, ORSON: BIRTH ANNIVERSARY. May 6, 1915. Actor and director born at Kenosha, WI. *Citizen Kane*, which he directed and in which he played the title role, is one of the most influential films ever made. Other films in which he had a role include *The Third Man* and *The Magnificent Ambersons*. Welles died at Los Angeles, CA, Oct 10, 1985.

★ *Birthdays* ★

George Clooney, actor ("ER," *Batman and Robin, One Fine Day*), born Lexington, KY, May 6, 1961.
Roma Downey, actress ("Touched by an Angel"), born Derry, Northern Ireland, May 6, 1964.

Willie Howard Mays, Hall of Fame baseball player, born Westfield, AL, May 6, 1931.

May 7

BEAUFORT SCALE DAY (FRANCIS BEAUFORT BIRTH ANNIVERSARY). May 7, 1774. A day to honor the British naval officer, Sir Francis Beaufort, who devised in 1805 a scale of wind force from 0 (calm) to 12 (hurricane) that was based on observation, not requiring any special instruments. The scale was adopted for international use in 1874 and has since been enlarged and refined. Beaufort was born at Flower Hill, Meath, Ireland, and died at Brighton, England, Dec 17, 1857.

COOPER, GARY: BIRTH ANNIVERSARY. May 7, 1901. Frank James Cooper was born at Helena, MT. He changed his name to Gary at the start of his movie career. He is best known by baseball fans for his portrayal of Lou Gehrig in *The Pride of the Yankees*. Other films included *Wings, The Virginian, The Plainsman, Beau Geste, Sergeant York* (for which he won his first Academy Award), *High Noon* (winning his second Oscar for best actor), *The Court Martial of Billy Mitchell* and *Friendly Persuasion*. He died May 13, 1961, at Hollywood, CA.

DIEN BIEN PHU FALLS: ANNIVERSARY. May 7, 1954. Vietnam's victory over France at Dien Bien Phu ended the Indochina War. This battle is considered one of the greatest victories won by a former colony over a colonial power.

GERMANY'S FIRST SURRENDER: ANNIVERSARY. May 7, 1945. Russian, American, British and French ranking officers crowded into a second-floor recreation room of a small redbrick schoolhouse (which served as US General Dwight D. Eisenhower's headquarters) at Reims, Germany. Representing Germany, Field Marshall Alfred Jodl signed an unconditional surrender of all German fighting forces. After a signing that took almost 40 minutes, Jodl was ushered into Eisenhower's presence. The American general asked the German if he fully understood what he had signed and informed Jodl that he would be held personally responsible for any deviation from the terms of the surrender, including the requirement that German commanders sign a formal surrender to the USSR at a time and place determined by that government.

***LUSITANIA* SINKING: ANNIVERSARY.** May 7, 1915. British passenger liner *Lusitania*, on its return trip from New York to Liverpool, carrying nearly 2,000 passengers, was torpedoed by a German submarine off the coast of Ireland, sinking within minutes; 1,198 lives were lost. President Woodrow Wilson sent note of protest to Berlin on May 13, but Germany, which had issued warning in advance, pointed to *Lusitania*'s cargo of ammunition for Britain. US maintained neutrality for the time being.

TCHAIKOVSKY, PETER ILICH: BIRTH ANNIVERSARY. May 7, 1840. Ranked among the outstanding composers of all time, Peter Ilich Tchaikovsky was born at Vatkinsk, Russia. His musical talent was not encouraged, and he embarked upon a career in jurisprudence, not studying music seriously until 1861. Among his famous works are the three-act ballet *Sleeping Beauty*, two-act ballet *The Nutcracker* and the symphony *Pathetique*. Mystery surrounds Tchaikovsky's death. It was believed he had caught cholera from contaminated water, but 20th-century scholars believe he probably committed suicide to avoid his homosexuality being revealed. He died at St. Petersburg, Nov 6, 1893.

TWENTY-SEVENTH AMENDMENT RATIFIED: ANNIVERSARY. May 7, 1992. The 27th amendment to the Constitution was ratified, prohibiting Congress from giving itself midterm pay raises.

★ *Birthdays* ★

Tim Russert, TV news talk-show moderator ("Meet the Press"), born Buffalo, NY, May 7, 1950.

John Constantine (Johnny) Unitas, Hall of Fame football player, born Pittsburgh, PA, May 7, 1933.

May 8

BEATLES'S LAST ALBUM RELEASED: ANNIVERSARY. May 8, 1970. The Beatles's 13th album, *Let It Be*, was released in the United Kingdom on this date. The album zoomed to number one on the record charts. It was the last album the Beatles made together.

GERMANY'S SECOND SURRENDER: ANNIVERSARY. May 8, 1945. Stalin refused to recognize the document of unconditional surrender signed at Reims the previous day, so a second signing was held near Berlin. The event was turned into an elaborate formal ceremony by the Soviets, who had lost some 20 million lives during the war. As in the Reims document, the end of hostilities was set for 12:01 AM local time on May 9.

LAVOISIER, ANTOINE LAURENT: EXECUTION ANNIVERSARY. May 8, 1794. French chemist and the "father of modern chemistry." Especially noted for having first explained the real nature of combustion and for showing that matter is not destroyed in chemical reactions. Born at Paris, France, Aug 26, 1743, Lavoisier was guillotined at the Place de la Revolution for his former position as a tax collector. The Revolutionary Tribunal is reported to have responded to a plea to spare his life with the statement: "We need no more scientists in France."

NO SOCKS DAY. May 8. If we give up wearing socks for one day, it will mean a little less laundry, thereby contributing to the betterment of the environment. Besides, we will all feel a bit freer, at least for one day. [©2001 by WH.] For info: Wellcat Holidays. Web: www.wellcat.com.

TRUMAN, HARRY S.: BIRTH ANNIVERSARY. May 8, 1884. The 33rd president of the US, succeeded to that office upon the death of Franklin D. Roosevelt, Apr 12, 1945, and served until Jan 20, 1953. Born at Lamar, MO, Truman was the last of the nine US presidents who did not attend college. Affectionately nicknamed "Give 'em Hell Harry" by admirers. Truman died at Kansas City, MO, Dec 26, 1972. His birthday is a holiday in Missouri.

V-E DAY: ANNIVERSARY. May 8, 1945. Victory in Europe Day commemorates unconditional surrender of Germany to Allied Forces. The surrender document was signed by German representatives at General Dwight D. Eisenhower's headquarters at Reims to become effective, and hostilities to end, at one minute past midnight May 9, 1945, which was 9:01 PM, EDT, on May 8 in the US. President Harry S. Truman on May 8 declared May 9, 1945, to be "V-E Day," but it later came to be observed on May 8. A separate German surrender to the USSR was signed at Karlshorst, near Berlin, May 8.

★ Birthdays ★

David Attenborough, author, naturalist (*Life on Earth, Trials of Life*), born London, England, May 8, 1926.

Ronald Mandel (Ronnie) Lott, Hall of Fame football player, born Albuquerque, NM, May 8, 1959.

May 9

EUROPEAN UNION: ANNIVERSARY OBSERVANCE. May 9, 1950. Member countries of the European Union commemorate the announcement by French statesman Robert Schuman of the "Schuman Plan" for establishing a single authority for production of coal, iron and steel in France and Germany. The European Coal and Steel Community was founded in 1952. This organization was a forerunner of the European Economic Community, founded in 1958, which later became the European Union. At the European Summit at Milan in 1985, this day was proclaimed the Day of Europe.

"VAST WASTELAND" SPEECH: ANNIVERSARY. May 9, 1961. Speaking before the bigwigs of network TV at the annual convention of the National Association of Broadcasters, Newton Minow, the new chairman of the Federal Communications Commission, exhorted those executives to sit through an entire day of their own programming. He suggested that they "will observe a vast wasteland." Further, he urged them to try for "imagination in programming, not sterility; creativity, not imitation; experimentation, not conformity; excellence, not mediocrity."

★ Birthdays ★

John D. Ashcroft, US Attorney General, born Chicago, IL, May 9, 1942.

Candice Bergen, actress (*Starting Over, The Group*, "Murphy Brown"), daughter of ventriloquist Edgar Bergen, born Beverly Hills, CA, May 9, 1946.

Albert Finney, actor (*Tom Jones, Shoot the Moon, Annie, The Dresser*), born Salford, England, May 9, 1936.

Billy Joel, singer, composer ("It's Still Rock and Roll to Me," "Just the Way You Are"), born Hicksville, NY, May 9, 1949.

May 10

ASTAIRE, FRED: BIRTH ANNIVERSARY. May 10, 1899. Actor, dancer and choreographer, born at Omaha, NE. Astaire began dancing with his sister Adele and in the mid-1930s began dancing with Ginger Rogers. His resume said, "Can't act. Slightly bald. Can dance a little." Despite this, Astaire starred in more than 40 films including *Holiday Inn, The Gay Divorcee, Silk Stockings* and *Easter Parade*. Died at Los Angeles, CA, June 22, 1987.

GOLDEN SPIKE DRIVING: ANNIVERSARY. May 10, 1869. Anniversary of the meeting of Union Pacific and Central Pacific railways, at Promontory Point, UT. On that day a golden spike was driven by Leland Stanford, president of the Central Pacific, to celebrate the linkage. The golden spike was promptly removed for preservation. Long called the final link in the ocean-to-ocean railroad, this event cannot be accurately described as completing the transcontinental railroad, but it did complete continuous rail tracks between Omaha and Sacramento. The final link in the route reaching from the Atlantic to the Pacific Ocean was made Aug 15, 1870.

★ Birthdays ★

Bono, singer (U2), born Paul David Hewson, Dublin, Ireland, May 10, 1960.

Ara Parseghian, former football coach, born Akron, OH, May 10, 1923.

May 11

BERLIN, IRVING: BIRTH ANNIVERSARY. May 11, 1888. Songwriter born Israel Isidore Baline at Tyumen, Russia. Irving Berlin moved to New York, NY, with his family when he was four years old. After the death of his father, he began singing in saloons and on street corners in order to help his family and worked as a singing waiter as a teenager. Berlin became one of America's most prolific songwriters, authoring such songs as "Alexander's Ragtime Band," "White Christmas," "God Bless America," "There's No Business Like Show Business," "Doin' What Comes Naturally," "Puttin' On the Ritz," "Blue Skies" and "Oh! How I Hate to Get Up in the Morning" among others. He could neither read nor write musical notation. Berlin died Sept 22, 1989, at New York, NY.

EAT WHAT YOU WANT DAY. May 11. Here's a day you may actually enjoy yourself. Ignore all those on-again/off-again warnings. [©2001 by WH.] For info: Wellcat Holidays. E-mail: wellcat@supernet.com. Web: www.wellcat.com.

GLACIER NATIONAL PARK ESTABLISHED: ANNIVERSARY. May 11, 1910. Located in northwest Montana on the Canadian border. In 1932 Glacier and Waterton Lakes National Park in Alberta were joined together by the governments of the US and Canada as Waterton-

Glacier International Peace Park. Web: www.nps.gov/glac.

MINNESOTA: ADMISSION DAY: ANNIVERSARY. May 11. Became 32nd state in 1858.

★ *Birthdays* ★

Jonathan Jackson, actor (*The Deep End of the Ocean*, "General Hospital"), born Orlando, FL, May 11, 1982.

Natasha Richardson, actress (*The Handmaid's Tale, Nell*), born London, England, May 11, 1963.

May 12

LIMERICK DAY. May 12. Observed on the birthday of one of its champions, Edward Lear. The limerick, which dates from the early 18th century, has been described as the "only fixed verse form indigenous to the English language." It gained its greatest popularity following the publication of Edward Lear's *Book of Nonsense* (and its sequels). Write a limerick today! Example: There was a young poet named Lear/Who said, it is just as I fear/Five lines are enough/For this kind of stuff/Make a limerick each day of the year.

NIGHTINGALE, FLORENCE: BIRTH ANNIVERSARY. May 12, 1820. English nurse and public health activist who, through her unselfish devotion to nursing, contributed perhaps more than any other single person to the development of modern nursing procedures and dignity of nursing as a profession. Founder of the Nightingale training school for nurses. Author of *Notes on Nursing*. Born at Florence, Italy. Died at London, England, Aug 13, 1910.

ODOMETER INVENTED: ANNIVERSARY. May 12, 1847. Anniversary of the invention of the first odometer, invented by Mormon pioneer William Clayton while crossing the plains in a covered wagon. Previous to this, mileage was calculated by counting the revolutions of a rag tied to a spoke of a wagon wheel.

PORTUGAL: PILGRIMAGE TO FATIMA: ANNIVERSARY. May 12–13. Commemorates first appearance of the Virgin of the Rosary to little shepherd children May 13, 1917. Pilgrims come to Cova da Iria, religious center, for a candlelit procession, Mass of the Sick.

★ *Birthdays* ★

Lawrence Peter "Yogi" Berra, Hall of Fame baseball player, former baseball coach and manager, born St. Louis, MO, May 12, 1925.

Emilio Estevez, actor (*The Breakfast Club, The Mighty Ducks*), born New York, NY, May 12, 1962.

Ving Rhames, actor (*Pulp Fiction*), born New York, NY, May 12, 1961.

May 13

LOUIS, JOE: BIRTH ANNIVERSARY. May 13, 1914. World heavyweight boxing champion, 1937–49, nicknamed the "Brown Bomber," Joseph Louis Barrow was born near Lafayette, AL. He died Apr 12, 1981, at Las Vegas, NV, and was buried at Arlington National Cemetery. (Louis's burial there, by presidential waiver, was the 39th exception ever to the eligibility rules for burial in Arlington National Cemetery.)

★ Birthdays ★

Beatrice Arthur, actress (*Mame*, "Maude," "Golden Girls"), born Bernice Frankel, New York, NY, May 13, 1926.

Harvey Keitel, actor (*Mean Streets, Blue Collar, Bugsy, The Piano*), born Brooklyn, NY, May 13, 1939.

Stevie Wonder, singer, musician (16 Grammy Awards; "I Just Called to Say I Love You"), born Steveland Morris Hardaway, Saginaw, MI, May 13, 1950.

May 14

FAHRENHEIT, GABRIEL DANIEL: BIRTH ANNIVERSARY. May 14, 1686. German physicist whose name is attached to one of the major temperature measurement scales. He introduced the use of mercury in thermometers and greatly improved their accuracy. Born at Danzig, Germany, he died at Amsterdam, Holland, Sept 16, 1736.

JAMESTOWN, VIRGINIA: FOUNDING ANNIVERSARY. May 14, 1607 (OS). The first permanent English settlement in what is now the US took place at Jamestown, VA (named for England's King James I), on this date. Captains John Smith and Christopher Newport were among the leaders of the group of royally chartered Virginia Company settlers who had traveled from Plymouth, England, in three small ships: *Susan Constant, Godspeed* and *Discovery*.

LEWIS AND CLARK EXPEDITION: ANNIVERSARY. May 14, 1804. Charged by President Thomas Jefferson with finding a route to the Pacific, Meriwether Lewis and Captain William Clark left St. Louis. They arrived at the Pacific coast of Oregon in November 1805 and returned to St. Louis, Sept 23, 1806.

MILLION MOM MARCH: ANNIVERSARY. May 14, 2000. Women rallied in Washington, DC, and 60 other US cities to urge Congress to "get serious about common sense gun legislation." For info: Million Mom March. Web: www.million mommarch.com.

SMALLPOX VACCINE DISCOVERED: ANNIVERSARY. May 14, 1796. In the 18th century, smallpox was a widespread and often fatal disease. Edward Jenner, a physician in rural England, heard reports of dairy farmers who apparently became immune to smallpox as a result of exposure to cowpox, a related but milder disease. After two decades of studying the phenomenon, Jenner injected cowpox into a healthy eight-year-old boy, who subsequently developed cowpox. Six weeks later, Jenner inoculated the boy with smallpox. He remained healthy. Jenner called this new procedure *vaccination*, from *vaccinia*, another term for cowpox. Within 18 months, 12,000 people in England had been vaccinated and the number of smallpox deaths dropped by two-thirds.

★ Birthdays ★

Cate Blanchett, actress (*Elizabeth, The Lord of the Rings*), born Melbourne, Australia, May 14, 1969.

George Lucas, filmmaker (*Star Wars* trilogy), director (*American Graffiti*), born Modesto, CA, May 14, 1944.

May 15

BAUM, L. FRANK: BIRTH ANNIVERSARY. May 15, 1856. American newspaperman who wrote the Wizard of Oz stories was born at Chittenango, NY. Although *The Wonderful Wizard of Oz* is the most famous, Baum also wrote many other books for children, including more than a dozen about Oz. He died at Hollywood, CA, May 6, 1919.

FIRST FLIGHT ATTENDANT: ANNIVERSARY. May 15, 1930. Ellen Church became the first airline stewardess (today's flight attendant), flying on a United Airlines flight from San Francisco to Cheyenne, WY.

NYLON STOCKINGS: ANNIVERSARY. May 15, 1940. Nylon hose went on sale at stores throughout the country. W.H. Carothers of DuPont developed nylon, called "Polymer 66," in 1935. It was the first totally man-made fiber and over time substituted for other materials and came to have widespread application.

PARAGUAY: INDEPENDENCE DAY. May 15. Commemorates independence from Spain, attained in 1811.

UNITED NATIONS: INTERNATIONAL DAY OF FAMILIES. May 15. The general assembly (Resolution 47/237) Sept 20, 1993, voted this as an annual observance beginning in 1994. For info: United Nations. Web: www.un.org.

★ Birthdays ★

Giselle Fernandez, TV host ("Access Hollywood"), born Mexico City, Mexico, May 15, 1961.

Chazz Palminteri, actor (*Bullets Over Broadway*), born the Bronx, NY, May 15, 1951.

May 16

FIRST ACADEMY AWARDS: ANNIVERSARY. May 16, 1929. About 270 people attended a dinner at the Hollywood Roosevelt Hotel at which the first Academy Awards were given in 12 categories. The silent film *Wings* won the award for best picture. A committee of only 20 members selected the winners that year. By the third year, the entire membership of the Academy voted. The Academy Awards were first televised in 1953.

FONDA, HENRY: BIRTH ANNIVERSARY. May 16, 1905. Stage, TV and screen actor (*The Grapes of Wrath, Mister Roberts*), Academy Award winner, born Henry Jaynes Fonda at Grand Island, NE. Began his acting career at the Omaha (NE) Playhouse. Fonda died at Los Angeles, CA, Aug 12, 1982.

★ Birthdays ★

David Boreanaz, actor ("Buffy the Vampire Slayer"), born Philadelphia, PA, May 16, 1971.

Pierce Brosnan, actor ("Remington Steele," James Bond in *GoldenEye*), born County Meath, Ireland, May 16, 1952.

May 17

BELL, JAMES ("COOL PAPA"): BIRTH ANNIVERSARY. May 17, 1903. Negro League baseball player James "Cool Papa" Bell was born at Starkville, MS. He played 25 seasons from 1922 to 1946 (one year before Jackie Robinson broke the "color barrier" in major league baseball) with a career average of .338. Regarded as the fastest man ever to play the game—he could round the bases in 13 seconds—he was inducted into the Baseball Hall of Fame in 1974. Bell died Mar 7, 1991, at St. Louis, MO.

***BROWN v BOARD OF EDUCATION* DECISION: ANNIVERSARY.** May 17, 1954. The US Supreme Court ruled unanimously that segregation of public schools "solely on the basis of race" denied black children "equal educational opportunity" even though "physical facilities and other 'tangible' factors may have been equal. Separate educational facilities are inherently unequal." The case was argued before the Court by Thurgood Marshall, who would go on to become the first black appointed to the Supreme Court.

FIRST KENTUCKY DERBY: ANNIVERSARY. May 17, 1875. The first running of the Kentucky Derby took place at Churchill Downs, Louisville, KY. Jockey Oliver Lewis rode the horse Aristides to a winning time of 2:37.25.

NEW YORK STOCK EXCHANGE ESTABLISHED: ANNIVERSARY. May 17, 1792. Some two dozen merchants and brokers agreed to establish what is now known as the New York Stock Exchange. In fair weather they operated under a buttonwood tree on Wall Street, at New York, NY. In bad weather they moved to the shelter of a coffeehouse to conduct their business.

NORWAY: CONSTITUTION DAY OR INDEPENDENCE DAY. May 17. National holiday. Constitution signed and Norway separated from Denmark in 1814.

UNITED NATIONS: WORLD TELECOMMUNICATION DAY. May 17. A day to draw attention to the necessity and importance of further development of telecommunications in the global community. For info: United Nations. Web: www .un.org.

★ Birthdays ★

Mia Hamm, soccer player (US National Soccer Team), born Selma, AL, May 17, 1972.
Dennis Hopper, actor (*Easy Rider, Giant, Rebel Without a Cause*), born Dodge City, KS, May 17, 1936.
Bill Paxton, actor (*Aliens, One False Move, Twister*), born Fort Worth, TX, May 17, 1955.

Debra Winger, actress (*Terms of Endearment, Shadowlands*), born Columbus, OH, May 17, 1955.

May 18

CAPRA, FRANK: BIRTH ANNIVERSARY. May 18, 1897. The Academy Award–winning director whose movies were suffused with affectionate portrayals of the common man and the strengths and foibles of American democracy. Capra was born at Palermo, Sicily. He bluffed his way into silent movies in 1922 and, despite total ignorance of moviemaking, directed and produced a profitable one-reeler. He was the first to win three directorial Oscars—for *It Happened One Night* (1934), *Mr Deeds Goes to Town* (1936) and *You Can't Take It with You* (1938). The motion picture academy voted the first and third of these as best picture. Capra said his favorite of the films he made was *It's a Wonderful Life* (1946). He died at La Quinta, CA, Sept 3, 1991.

INTERNATIONAL MUSEUM DAY. May 18. To pay tribute to museums of the world. "Museums are an important means of cultural exchange, enrichment of cultures and development of mutual understanding, cooperation and peace among people." Sponsor: International Council of Museums, Paris, France. For info: American Association of Museums. Web: www.aam-us.org.

MOUNT SAINT HELENS ERUPTION: ANNIVERSARY. May 18, 1980. A major eruption of Mount St. Helens volcano, in southwestern Washington, blew steam and ash more than 11 miles into the sky. First major eruption of Mount St. Helens since 1857, though on Mar 26, 1980, there had been a warning eruption of smaller magnitude.

POPE JOHN PAUL II: BIRTHDAY. May 18, 1920. Karol Wojtyla, 264th pope of the Roman Catholic Church, born at Wadowice, Poland. Elected pope Oct 16, 1978. He was the first non-Italian to be elected pope in 456 years (since the election of Pope Adrian VI, in 1522) and the first Polish pope.

★ *Birthdays* ★

Reginald Martinez (Reggie) Jackson, Hall of Fame baseball player, born Wyncote, PA, May 18, 1946.
Brooks Robinson, Hall of Fame baseball player, born Little Rock, AR, May 18, 1937.

May 19

BOYS' CLUBS FOUNDED: ANNIVERSARY. May 19, 1906. The Federated Boys' Clubs, which later became the Boys' and Girls' Clubs of America, was founded.

HO CHI MINH: BIRTH ANNIVERSARY. May 19, 1890. Vietnamese leader and first president of the Democratic Republic of Vietnam, born at Kim Lien, a central Vietnamese village (Nghe An Province), probably May 19, 1890. His original name was Nguyen That Thanh. Died at Hanoi, Vietnam, Sept 3, 1969. The anniversary of his birth is a national holiday in Vietnam as is the anniversary of his death.

★ *Birthdays* ★

David Hartman, TV host (Emmy for "Good Morning America"), actor (*Hello Dolly*), born Pawtucket, RI, May 19, 1937.
James Lehrer, journalist, anchor ("The Newshour with Jim Lehrer"), born Wichita, KS, May 19, 1934.

May 20

HOMESTEAD ACT: ANNIVERSARY. May 20, 1862. President Lincoln signed the Homestead Act opening millions of acres of government-owned land in the West to settlers or "homesteaders," who had to reside on the land and cultivate it for five years.

LINDBERGH FLIGHT: ANNIVERSARY. May 20–21, 1927. Anniversary of the first solo transatlantic flight. Captain Charles Augustus Lindbergh, 25-year-old aviator, departed from rainy, muddy Roosevelt Field, Long Island, NY, alone at 7:52 AM, May 20, 1927, in a Ryan monoplane named *Spirit of St. Louis*. He landed at Le Bourget airfield, Paris, at 10:24 PM Paris time (5:24 PM, NY time), May 21, winning a $25,000 prize offered by Raymond Orteig for the first nonstop flight between New York City and Paris, France (3,600 miles). The "flying fool" as he had been dubbed by some doubters became "Lucky Lindy," an instant world hero.

MOTOR VOTER BILL SIGNED: ANNIVERSARY. May 20, 1993. The latest effort to remove barriers to voter registration resulted in the passage of the Motor Voter Bill, which was signed into law by President William Clinton. This bill requires the states to allow voter registration by mail or when a citizen applies for or renews a driver's license.

STEWART, JIMMY: BIRTH ANNIVERSARY. May 20, 1908. Film actor born James Stewart at Indiana, PA. Best known for his roles in *Mr Smith Goes to Washington* and the Christmas classic *It's a Wonderful Life*, he won an Oscar for *The Philadelphia Story*. Died July 2, 1997, at Beverly Hills, CA.

UNITED NATIONS: WORLD REFUGEE DAY. June 20. For info: United Nations. Web: www.un.org.

WEIGHTS AND MEASURES DAY: ANNIVERSARY. May 20. Anniversary of international treaty, signed May 20, 1875, providing for the establishment of an International Bureau of Weights and Measures. The bureau was founded on international territory at Sevres, France.

★ *Birthdays* ★

Cher, singer ("Half Breed"; "I've Got You, Babe" [with Sonny Bono]), actress (Oscar for *Moonstruck*), born Cherilyn Sarkisian, El Centro, CA, May 20, 1946.
Anthony Zerbe, actor (*Cool Hand Luke, Papillon*), born Long Beach, CA, May 20, 1936.

May 21

AMERICAN RED CROSS FOUNDED: ANNIVERSARY. May 21, 1881. Commemorates the founding of the American Red Cross by Clara Barton, its first president. The Red Cross had been founded in Switzerland in 1864 by representatives from 16 European nations. The organization is a not-for-profit organization governed and directed by volunteers and provides disaster relief at home and abroad; 1.1 million volunteers are involved in community services such as collecting and distributing donated blood and blood products, teaching health and safety classes and acting as a medium for emergency communication between Americans and their armed forces.

BURR, RAYMOND: BIRTH ANNIVERSARY. May 21, 1917. Stage, film and TV actor best known for the role of Perry Mason in the series of the same name. He was born at New Westminster, British Columbia, and died near Healdsburg, CA, Sept 12, 1993.

GEMINI, THE TWINS. May 21–June 20. In the astronomical/astrological zodiac, which divides the sun's apparent orbit into 12 segments, the period May 21–June 20 is traditionally identified as the sun sign of Gemini, the Twins. The ruling planet is Mercury.

★ Birthdays ★

Al Franken, comedian, writer (*Rush Limbaugh Is a Big Fat Idiot and Other Observations*), actor ("Saturday Night Live"), born New York, NY, May 21, 1951.

Judge Reinhold, actor (*Beverly Hills Cop*), born Wilmington, DE, May 21, 1957.

May 22

"MISTER ROGERS' NEIGHBORHOOD" TV PREMIERE: ANNIVERSARY. May 22, 1967. Presbyterian minister Fred Rogers hosted this long-running PBS children's program. Puppets and human characters interacted in the neighborhood of make-believe. Rogers played the voices of many of the puppets and educated young viewers on a variety of important subjects. The last episodes of the program were made in 2001. Almost 1,000 episodes were produced over the show's history.

NATIONAL MARITIME DAY. May 22. Anniversary of departure for first steamship crossing of Atlantic from Savannah, GA, to Liverpool, England, by steamship *Savannah* in 1819. A Presidential Proclamation has been issued for this day since 1933.

NIXON FIRST AMERICAN PRESIDENT TO VISIT MOSCOW: ANNIVERSARY. May 22, 1972. President Richard Nixon became the first American president to visit Moscow. Four days later on May 26, Nixon and Soviet leader Leonid Brezhnev signed a treaty on antiballistic missile systems and an interim agreement on limitation of strategic missiles.

OLIVIER, LAURENCE: BIRTH ANNIVERSARY. May 22, 1907. Actor, director and theater manager, born at Dorking, England. Honored with nine Academy Award nominations, three Oscars and five Emmy awards, his repertoire included most of the prime Shakespearean roles and roles in such films as *Rebecca, Pride and Prejudice, Marathon Man* and *Wuthering Heights*. Olivier was an innovative theater manager with London's Old Vic company and the National Theatre of Great Britain. The National Theatre's largest auditorium and Britain's equivalent of Broadway's Tony Awards carry his name. Olivier died at Ashurst, England, July 11, 1989.

"THERE WENT JOHNNY!" NIGHT: ANNIVERSARY. May 22, 1992. After almost 30 years as host of the "Tonight" show, Johnny Carson hosted his last show. On Oct 1, 1962, Carson became host of the late-night talk show, which began as a local New York program hosted by Steve Allen. Over the years Carson occasionally made headlines with such extravaganzas as the on-air marriage of Tiny Tim and Miss Vicki. Johnny received Emmys for his work four years in a row, 1976–79. Ed McMahon, his sidekick of 30 years, and Doc Severinsen, longtime bandleader, left the show with Carson. Jay Leno, the show's exclusive guest host, became the new regular host.

TRUMAN DOCTRINE: ANNIVERSARY. May 22, 1947. Congress approved the Truman Doctrine on this day. In order to contain Communism after World War II, it provided for US aid to Greece and Turkey. A corollary of this doctrine was the Marshall Plan, which began sending aid to war-torn European countries in 1948.

UNITED NATIONS: INTERNATIONAL DAY FOR BIOLOGICAL DIVERSITY. May 22. On Dec 19, 1994, the General Assembly proclaimed this observance for Dec 29, the date of entry into force of the Convention on Biological Diversity (Resolution 49/119). In 2000, the date was changed to May 22. For info: United Nations. Web: www.un.org.

WORST EARTHQUAKE OF THE 20th CENTURY: ANNIVERSARY. May 22, 1960. An earthquake of a magnitude 9.5 struck southern Chile, killing 2,000 people and leaving 2 million homeless. The earthquake also caused damage in Hawaii, Japan and the Philippines. While 20th-century earthquakes in Mexico City, Japan and Turkey resulted in far more deaths, this earthquake in Chile was of the highest magnitude.

★ *Birthdays* ★

Richard Benjamin, actor (*Goodbye Columbus, Diary of a Mad Housewife*), born New York, NY, May 22, 1938.

Paul Winfield, actor (*Sounder, Star Trek II, Presumed Innocent*), born Los Angeles, CA, May 22, 1940.

May 23

FAIRBANKS, DOUGLAS ELTON: BIRTH ANNIVERSARY.
May 23, 1883. Douglas Fairbanks was born at Denver, CO. He made his professional debut as an actor at Richmond, VA, Sept 10, 1900, in *The Duke's Jester.* His theatrical career turned to Hollywood, and he became a movie idol appearing in such films as *The Mark of Zorro, The Three Musketeers, Robin Hood, The Thief of Bagdad, The Black Pirate* and *The Gaucho.* He married "America's Sweetheart," Mary Pickford, in 1918, and in 1919 they joined with D.W. Griffith and Charlie Chaplin to form the production company United Artists. He died at Santa Monica, CA, Dec 12, 1939.

MESMER, FRIEDRICH ANTON: BIRTH ANNIVERSARY.
May 23, 1734. German physician after whom Mesmerism was named. Magnetism and hypnotism were used by him in treating disease. Born at Iznang, Swabia, Germany. Died Mar 5, 1815, at Mecrsburg, Swabia, Germany.

SOUTH CAROLINA CONSTITUTION RATIFIED: ANNIVERSARY. May 23, 1788. By a vote of 149 to 73, South Carolina became the eighth state to ratify the Constitution.

★ Birthdays ★

Drew Carey, actor ("The Drew Carey Show"), born Cleveland, OH, May 23, 1961 (some sources say 1958).
Jewel, singer, born Jewel Kilcher, Payson, UT, May 23, 1974.

May 24

BASEBALL FIRST PLAYED UNDER LIGHTS: ANNIVERSARY. May 24, 1935. The Cincinnati Reds defeated the Philadelphia Phillies by a score of 2–1, as more than 20,000 fans enjoyed the first night baseball game in the major leagues. The game was played at Crosley Field, Cincinnati, OH.

BROOKLYN BRIDGE OPENED: ANNIVERSARY. May 24, 1883. Nearly 14 years in construction, the $16 million Brooklyn Bridge over the East River opened. Designed by John A. Roebling, the steel suspension bridge has a span of 1,595 feet.

ERITREA: INDEPENDENCE DAY. May 24. National Day. Gained independence from Ethiopia in 1993 after 30-year civil war.

MORSE OPENS FIRST US TELEGRAPH LINE: ANNIVERSARY. May 24, 1844. The first US telegraph line was formally opened between Baltimore, MD, and Washington, DC. Samuel F.B. Morse sent the first officially telegraphed words "What hath God wrought?" from the Capitol building to Baltimore. Earlier messages had been sent along the historic line during testing, and one, sent May 1, contained the news that Henry Clay had been nominated for president by the Whig party, from a meeting in Baltimore. This message reached Washington one hour prior to a train carrying the same news.

★ Birthdays ★

Bob Dylan, composer, singer, born Robert Zimmerman, Duluth, MN, May 24, 1941.
Kristin Scott Thomas, actress (*The English Patient, The Horse Whisperer*), born Cornwall, England, May 24, 1960.

May 25

JORDAN: INDEPENDENCE DAY. May 25. National holiday. Commemorates treaty in 1946, proclaiming independence from Britain and establishing monarchy.

NATIONAL TAP DANCE DAY. May 25. To celebrate this unique American art form that represents a fusion of African and European cultures and to transmit tap to succeeding generations through documentation and archival and performance support. Held on the anniversary of the birth of Bill "Bojangles" Robinson in 1878 to honor his outstanding contribution to the art of tap dancing on stage and in films through the unification of diverse stylistic and racial elements.

SIKORSKY, IGOR: BIRTH ANNIVERSARY. May 25, 1889. Aeronautical engineer best remembered for his development of the first successful helicopter in 1939. Also pioneered in multiengine airplanes and large flying boats that made transoceanic air transportation possible. Born at Kiev, Russia, he died Oct 26, 1972, at Easton, CT.

SOLZHENITSYN GOES HOME: ANNIVERSARY. May 25, 1994. After 20 years living in exile, mostly in the US, Russian author Alexander Solzhenitsyn returned to his homeland. The author had been expelled from the Soviet Union in 1974 after his three-volume work exposing the Soviet prison camp system, *The Gulag Archipelago*, was published in the West. After the collapse of the Soviet Union late in 1991, he announced his intention to go back.

★ Birthdays ★

Dixie Carter, actress ("Designing Women," "Family Law"), born McLemoresville, TN, May 25, 1939.
Sir Ian McKellen, actor (stage: *Amadeus* [Tony Award]; *Six Degrees of Separation, The Lord of the Rings*), born Burnley, England, May 25, 1939.

Mike Myers, comedian, actor ("Saturday Night Live," *Wayne's World, Austin Powers: International Man of Mystery*), born Scarsborough, ON, Canada, May 25, 1963.

May 26

DUNKIRK EVACUATED: ANNIVERSARY. May 26, 1940. The British Expeditionary Force had become trapped by advancing German armies near this port on the northern coast of France. On this date, the evacuation of 200,000 British and 140,000 French and Belgian soldiers began. Sailing on every kind of transport available, including fishing boats and recreational craft, these men were safely across the English Channel by June 2.

GEORGIA: INDEPENDENCE DAY. May 26. National Day. Commemorates declaration of independence from Russia in 1918. Was absorbed by the Soviet Union in 1922.

VIETNAM AND US RESUME RELATIONS: ANNIVERSARY. May 26, 1994. Nearly 20 years after the end of the Vietnam War, the US and Vietnam agreed to resume diplomatic relations. In the early 1990s Vietnam had become one of the fastest growing economies in Asia after giving up Communist controls and allowing economic reform. Earlier in 1994 President Bill Clinton had lifted the American embargo that hindered Americans from doing business in Vietnam.

WAYNE, JOHN: BIRTH ANNIVERSARY. May 26, 1907. Motion picture actor, born Marion Michael Morrison, at Winterset, IA. He died at Los Angeles, CA, June 11, 1979. "Talk low, talk slow and don't say too much" was his advice on acting.

★ Birthdays ★

Helena Bonham Carter, actress (*A Room with a View, Howard's End*), born London, England, May 26, 1966.
Lenny Kravitz, singer ("Circus"), musician, songwriter ("Justify My Love"), born New York, NY, May 26, 1964.
Brent Musburger, sportscaster, born Portland, OR, May 26, 1939.

May 27

BLOOMER, AMELIA JENKS: BIRTH ANNIVERSARY. May 27, 1818. American social reformer and women's rights advocate, born at Homer, NY. Her name is remembered especially because of her work for more sensible dress for women and her recommendation of a costume that had been introduced about 1849 by Elizabeth Smith Miller but came to be known as the "Bloomer Costume" or "Bloomers." Amelia Bloomer died at Council Bluffs, IA, Dec 30, 1894.

CELLOPHANE TAPE PATENTED: ANNIVERSARY. May 27, 1930. Richard Gurley Drew received a patent for his adhesive tape, later manufactured by 3M as Scotch tape.

DUNCAN, ISADORA: BIRTH ANNIVERSARY. May 27, 1878. American-born interpretive dancer who revolutionized the entire concept of dance. Bare-footed, freedom-loving, liberated woman and rebel against tradition, she experienced worldwide professional success and profound personal tragedy (her two children drowned, her marriage failed and she met a bizarre death when the long scarf she was wearing caught in a wheel of the open car in which she was riding, strangling her). Born at San Francisco, CA; died at Nice, France, Sept 14, 1927.

FIRST FLIGHT INTO THE STRATOSPHERE: ANNIVERSARY. May 27, 1931. In a balloon launched from Augsburg, Germany, Paul Kipfer and Auguste Piccard became the first to reach the stratosphere. In a pressurized cabin they rose almost ten miles during their flight.

GOLDEN GATE BRIDGE OPENED: ANNIVERSARY. May 27, 1937. On its opening day, 200,000 people crossed San Francisco's Golden Gate Bridge.

★ *Birthdays* ★

Joseph Fiennes, actor (*Shakespeare In Love*), born Salisbury, England, May 27, 1970.
Louis Gossett, Jr, actor (Emmy for "Roots"; Oscar for *An Officer and a Gentleman*), born Brooklyn, NY, May 27, 1936.

May 28

DIONNE QUINTUPLETS: BIRTHDAY. May 28, 1934. Five daughters (Marie, Cecile, Yvonne, Emilie and Annette) were born to Oliva and Elzire Dionne, near Callander, ON, Canada. They were the first quints known to have lived for more than a few hours after birth. Emilie died in 1954, Marie in 1970, Yvonne in 2001. The other two sisters are still living.

GUILLOTIN, JOSEPH IGNACE: BIRTH ANNIVERSARY. May 28, 1738. French physician and member of the Constituent Assembly who urged the use of a machine that was sometimes called the "Maiden" for the execution of death sentences—a less painful, more certain way of dispatching those sentenced to death. The guillotine was first used on Apr 25, 1792, for the execution of a highwayman, Nicolas Jacques Pelletier. Other machines for decapitation had been in use in other countries since the Middle

Ages. Guillotin was born at Saintes, France, and died at Paris, Mar 26, 1814.

SIERRA CLUB FOUNDED: ANNIVERSARY. May 28, 1892. Founded by famed naturalist John Muir, the Sierra Club promotes conservation of the natural environment by influencing public policy. It has been especially important in the founding and protection of our national parks. For info: Sierra Club. Web: www.sierraclub.org.

THORPE, JIM: BIRTH ANNIVERSARY. May 28, 1888. Jim Thorpe, Pro Football Hall of Famer, distinguished Native American athlete, winner of pentathlon and decathlon events at the 1912 Olympic Games, professional baseball and football player. Born near Prague, OK, and died at Lomita, CA, Mar 28, 1953.

★ Birthdays ★

Rudolph Giuliani, former mayor of New York City, born Brooklyn, NY, May 28, 1944.
Christa Miller, actress ("The Drew Carey Show"), born New York, NY, May 28, 1964.

May 29

AMNESTY ISSUED FOR SOUTHERN REBELS: ANNIVERSARY. May 29, 1865. President Andrew Johnson issued a proclamation giving a general amnesty to all who participated in the rebellion against the US. High-ranking members of the Confederate government and military and those who owned more than $20,000 worth of property were excepted and had to apply individually to the president for a pardon. Once an oath of allegiance was taken, all former property rights, except those in slaves, were returned to the former owners.

MOUNT EVEREST SUMMIT REACHED: ANNIVERSARY. May 29, 1953. New Zealand explorer Sir Edmund Hillary and Tensing Norgay, a Sherpa guide, became the first team to reach the summit of Mount Everest, the world's highest mountain.

RHODE ISLAND: RATIFICATION DAY. May 29. The last of the 13 original states to ratify the Constitution in 1790.

WISCONSIN: ADMISSION DAY: ANNIVERSARY. May 29. Became 30th state in 1848.

★ Birthdays ★

Annette Bening, actress (*The American President, Bugsy, The Grifters*), born Topeka, KS, May 29, 1958.
Rupert Everett, actor (*My Best Friend's Wedding*), born Norfolk, England, May 29, 1959.

May 30

FIRST AMERICAN DAILY NEWSPAPER PUBLISHED: ANNIVERSARY. May 30, 1783. *The Pennsylvania Evening Post* became the first daily newspaper published in the US. The paper was published at Philadelphia, PA, by Benjamin Towne.

INDIANAPOLIS 500: ANNIVERSARY. May 30, 1911. Ray Harroun won the first Indy 500, averaging 74.6 MPH. The race was created by Carl Fisher, who in 1909 replaced the stone surface of his 2.5-mile racetrack with a brick one—hence the nickname "The Brickyard."

LINCOLN MEMORIAL DEDICATION: ANNIVERSARY. May 30, 1922. The memorial is made of marble from Colorado and Tennessee and limestone from Indiana. It stands in West Potomac Park at Washington, DC. A skylight lets light into the interiors where the compelling statue "Seated Lincoln," by sculptor Daniel Chester French, is situated.

SPACE MILESTONE: *MARINER 9* (US). May 30, 1971. Unmanned spacecraft was launched, entering Martian orbit the following Nov 13. The craft relayed temperature and gravitational field information and sent back spectacular photographs of both the surface of Mars and of her two moons. First spacecraft to orbit another planet.

★ *Birthdays* ★

Gale Eugene Sayers, Hall of Fame football player, born Wichita, KS, May 30, 1943.

May 31

COPYRIGHT LAW PASSED: ANNIVERSARY. May 31, 1790. President George Washington signed the first US copyright law. It gave protection for 14 years to books written by US citizens. In 1891 the law was extended to cover books by foreign authors as well.

JOHNSTOWN FLOOD: ANNIVERSARY. May 31, 1889. Heavy rains caused the Connemaugh River Dam to burst. At nearby Johnstown, PA, the resulting flood killed more than 2,300 people and destroyed the homes of thousands more. Nearly 800 unidentified drowning victims were buried in a common grave at Johnstown's Grandview Cemetery. So devastating was the flood and so widespread the sorrow for its victims that "Johnstown Flood" entered the language as a phrase to describe a disastrous event. The valley city of Johnstown, in the Allegheny Mountains, has been damaged repeatedly by floods. Floods in 1936 (25 deaths) and 1977 (85 deaths) were the next most destructive.

"SEINFELD" TV PREMIERE: ANNIVERSARY. May 31, 1990. "Seinfeld"—the show about nothing—premiered on NBC to wide acclaim. The show revolved around the lives and exploits of its four main leads whose story lines were intertwined for some surprising plot twists. Comedian Jerry Seinfeld used his stand-up routines as an introduction to the show; some of the programs concerned relationships, valet parking, annoying dogs and waiting for Chinese food. The cast featured Seinfeld as himself; Julia Louis-Dreyfus as his ex-girlfriend, Elaine Benes; Jason Alexander as his best friend, George Costanza; Wayne Knight as Newman and Michael Richards as his neighbor, Cosmo Kramer. The series ended with the May 14, 1998, episode.

"SURVIVOR" TV PREMIERE: ANNIVERSARY. May 31, 2000. On this immensely popular "reality TV" show, 16 people were sequestered on a deserted island in Malaysia for 39 days. They competed for the right to remain on the island, with the final survivor winning $1 million. Hosted by Jeff Probst, the show drew a total audience of 51 million people. On Jan 28, 2001, another group of "Survivor" contestants began their stay in the Australian outback; later that year another group went to Africa and the next year to the Marquesas.

UNITED NATIONS: WORLD NO-TOBACCO DAY. May 31. For info: United Nations. Web: www.un.org.

WHITMAN, WALT: BIRTH ANNIVERSARY. May 31, 1819. Poet and journalist, born at West Hills, Long Island, NY. Whitman's best-known work, *Leaves of Grass* (1855), is a classic of American poetry. His poems celebrated all of modern life, including subjects that were considered taboo at the time. Died Mar 26, 1892, at Camden, NJ.

★ *Birthdays* ★

Clint Eastwood, actor, director (Oscar for *Unforgiven*), former mayor of Carmel, CA, born San Francisco, CA, May 31, 1930.
Joseph William (Joe) Namath, Hall of Fame football player, former sportscaster, actor, born Beaver Falls, PA, May 31, 1943.
Brooke Shields, actress (*Pretty Baby, The Blue Lagoon*, "Suddenly Susan"), born New York, NY, May 31, 1965.

June

June 1

ADOPT-A-SHELTER-CAT MONTH. June 1–30. To promote the adoption of cats from local shelters, the ASPCA sponsors this important observance. For info: ASPCA. Web: www.aspca.org.

ATLANTIC, CARIBBEAN AND GULF HURRICANE SEASON. June 1–Nov 30. For info: National Oceanic and Atmospheric Administration. Web: www.nws.noaa.gov.

CNN DEBUTS: ANNIVERSARY. June 1, 1980. The Cable News Network, TV's first all-news service, went on the air.

FIREWORKS EYE SAFETY MONTH. June 1–30. An estimated 1 million people in the US suffer eye injuries each year, but 90 percent are preventable. This month is to educate people on protecting their eyes from top causes of injury, such as fireworks, sports injuries and chemical burns. For info: American Academy of Ophthalmology. Web: www.eyenet.org.

GAY AND LESBIAN PRIDE MONTH. June 1–30. Observed this month because on June 28, 1969, the clientele of a gay bar at New York City rioted after the club was raided by the police. See also: "Stonewall Riot: Anniversary" (June 28).

INTERNATIONAL MEN'S MONTH. June 1–30. This program was initiated in 1996 to increase media and local community awareness of the many unique issues that impact men's lives and that are of concern to the people who love them. In an effort to promote positive changes in male roles and relationships, a different issue is addressed each day of the month during June and information and resources on that issue are provided on the website. For info: National Men's Resource Center. Web: www.menstuff.org.

JUNE IS TURKEY LOVERS' MONTH. June 1–30. Monthlong campaign to promote awareness and increase turkey consumption at a nonholiday time. For info: National Turkey Federation. Web: www.eatturkey.com.

KENTUCKY: ADMISSION DAY: ANNIVERSARY. June 1. Became 15th state in 1792.

MONROE, MARILYN: BIRTH ANNIVERSARY. June 1, 1926. American actress and sex symbol of the '50s, born at Los Angeles, CA, as Norma Jean Mortensen or Baker. Her film career came to epitomize Hollywood glamour. In 1954 she wed Yankee legend "Jolting Joe" DiMaggio, but the marriage didn't last. Monroe remained fragile and insecure, tormented by the pressures of Hollywood life. She died from a drug overdose Aug 5, 1962, at Los Angeles. Among her films: *The Seven Year Itch, Bus Stop, Some Like It Hot* and *Gentlemen Prefer Blondes.*

NATIONAL ICED TEA MONTH. June 1–30. To celebrate one of the most widely consumed beverages in the world and one of nature's most perfect beverages, and to encourage Americans to refresh themselves with this all-natural, low-calorie, refreshing thirst-quencher. For info: The Tea Council of the USA. Web: www.tea usa.com.

NATIONAL RIVERS MONTH. June 1–30. Commemorated by local groups in many states.

NATIONAL SAFETY MONTH. June 1–30. Week one targets driver safety; week two emphasizes home, community and environmental safety; week three, emergency and disaster preparedness and week four, workplace safety. For info: National Safety Council. Web: www.nsc.org.

STAND FOR CHILDREN DAY. June 1. Stand for Children is a national organization that encourages individuals to improve children's lives. Its mission is to identify, train and connect local children's activists engaging in advocacy, service initiatives and awareness-raising as part of Children's Action Teams. On this day each year a special issue, such as safer and healthier communities, is highlighted. For info: Children's Defense Fund. Web: www.stand.org.

TENNESSEE: ADMISSION DAY: ANNIVERSARY. June 1. Became 16th state in 1796. Observed as a holiday in Tennessee.

VISION RESEARCH MONTH. June 1–30. While millions of Americans benefit from vision research, many eye diseases have no effective treatments or cures. An overview of vision research successes and the urgent need for future studies will be offered. For info: Prevent Blindness America®. Web: www.preventblindness.org.

★ *Birthdays* ★

Morgan Freeman, stage and film actor (*Driving Miss Daisy*), born Memphis, TN, June 1, 1937.
Jonathan Pryce, actor (*The Age of Innocence, Glengarry Glen Ross*; stage: Tony Awards for

Comedians and *Hamlet*), born Holywell, North Wales, June 1, 1947.

June 2

ITALY: REPUBLIC DAY. June 2. Commemorates 1946 referendum that led to republic status instead of a return to monarchy.

UNITED KINGDOM: CORONATION DAY. June 2. Commemorates the crowning of Queen Elizabeth II in 1953.

WEISSMULLER, JOHNNY: BIRTH ANNIVERSARY. June 2, 1904. Peter John (Johnny) Weissmuller, actor and Olympic gold medal swimmer, born at Windber, PA. Weissmuller won three gold medals at the 1924 Olympics and two more at the 1928 games. He set 24 world records and in 1950 was voted the best swimmer of the first half of the 20th century. After retiring from amateur competition, he appeared as Tarzan in a dozen movies and as "Jungle Jim" in movies and on television. Died at Acapulco, Mexico, Jan 20, 1984.

YELL "FUDGE" AT THE COBRAS IN NORTH AMERICA DAY. June 2. Anywhere north of the Panama Canal. In order to keep poisonous cobra snakes out of North America, all citizens are asked to go outdoors at noon, local time, and yell "Fudge." Fudge makes cobras gag and the mere mention of it makes them skedaddle. [©2001 by WH.] For info: Wellcat Holidays. Web: www.wellcat.com.

★ Birthdays ★

Dana Carvey, comedian, actor (*Wayne's World*, "Saturday Night Live"), born Missoula, MT, June 2, 1955.

Marvin Hamlisch, composer (Oscars for *The Sting, The Way We Were*; Tony for *A Chorus Line*), born New York, NY, June 2, 1944.

June 3

DAVIS, JEFFERSON: BIRTH ANNIVERSARY. June 3, 1808. Only president of the Confederate States of America. Prior to the war, Davis was a military hero, served as secretary of war under Franklin Pierce and as a US senator. He spoke widely to the dividing halves of the nation, calling for peaceful solutions. Though Davis opposed secession, he believed states had the constitutional right to leave the Union. President of the Confederate States of America 1861–1865. Davis led the Confederacy with skill and courage in a fight that seemed impossible to win. Imprisoned May 10, 1865–May 13, 1867, but never brought to trial, deprived of rights of citizenship after the Civil War. Davis was born at Todd County, KY, and died at New Orleans, LA, Dec 6, 1889. His citizenship was restored, posthumously, Oct 17, 1978, when

President Carter signed an Amnesty Bill. Davis's birth anniversary is observed in Florida, Kentucky and South Carolina on this day, in Alabama on the first Monday in June and in Mississippi on the last Monday in May. Davis's birth anniversary is observed as Confederate Memorial Day in Tennessee.

FIRST WOMAN RABBI IN US: ANNIVERSARY. June 3, 1972. Sally Jan Priesand was ordained the first woman rabbi in the US. She became assistant rabbi at the Stephen Wise Free Synagogue, New York City, Aug 1, 1972.

SPACE MILESTONE: *GEMINI 4* **(US).** June 3, 1965. James McDivitt and Edward White made 66 orbits of Earth. White took the first space walk by an American and maneuvered 20 minutes outside the capsule.

★ Birthdays ★

Tony Curtis, actor ("Vega$," *Some Like It Hot*), born Bernard Schwartz, New York, NY, June 3, 1925.

June 4

BATTLE OF MIDWAY: ANNIVERSARY. June 4–6, 1942. A Japanese task force attempted to capture Midway Island in the Central Pacific. American bombers from Midway and from two nearby aircraft carriers sent the Japanese into retreat, having lost four carriers, two large cruisers and three destroyers. Midway was one of the most decisive naval battles of World War II. Japan never regained its margin in carrier strength, and the Central Pacific was made safe for American troops.

CHINA: TIANANMEN SQUARE MASSACRE: ANNIVERSARY. June 4, 1989. After almost a month and a half of student demonstrations for democracy, the Chinese government ordered its troops to open fire on the unarmed protesters at Tiananmen Square at Beijing. The demonstrations began Apr 18 as several thousand students marched to mourn the death of Hu Yaobang, a proreform leader within the Chinese government. A ban was imposed on such demonstrations; on Apr 22, 100,000 gathered in Tiananmen Square in defiance of the ban. On May 13, 2,000 of the students began a hunger strike, and on May 20 the government imposed martial law and began to bring in troops. On June 2 the demonstrators turned back an advance of unarmed troops in the first clash with the People's Army. Under the cover of darkness, early June 4, troops opened fire on the assembled crowds, and armored personnel carriers rolled into the square crushing many of the students as they lay sleeping in their tents. Although the government claimed that few died in the attack, estimates range from several hundred to several thousand casualties. In the following months thousands of demonstrators were rounded up and jailed.

PULITZER PRIZES FIRST AWARDED: ANNIVERSARY. June 4, 1917. The first Pulitzer Prizes were awarded on this date: biography, *Julia Ward Howe* by Laura E. Richards and Maude H. Elliott assisted by Florence H. Hall; history, *With Americans of Past and Present Days* by Jean Jules Jusserand, the French ambassador to the US. Prizes were also awarded for journalistic achievement. The awards are named after American journalist and newspaper publisher Joseph Pulitzer. For info: Pulitzer Prize Board, Columbia University. Web: www.pulitzer.org.

★ Birthdays ★

Bruce Dern, actor (*Coming Home, The Burbs*), born Chicago, IL, June 4, 1936.
Angelina Jolie, actress (Oscar for *Girl, Interrupted*), daughter of Jon Voight, born Los Angeles, CA, June 4, 1975.
Noah Wyle, actor (*A Few Good Men*, "ER"), born Hollywood, CA, June 4, 1971.

June 5

AIDS FIRST NOTED: ANNIVERSARY. June 5, 1981. The Centers for Disease Control first described a new illness striking gay men in a newsletter on June 5, 1981. On July 27, 1982, Acquired Immune Deficiency Syndrome was adopted by the CDC as the official name for the new disease. The virus that causes AIDS was identified in 1983 and in May 1985 was named Human Immunodeficiency Virus (HIV) by the International Committee on the Taxonomy of Viruses. The first person killed by this disease in the developed world died in 1959. More than 420,000 Americans have died of AIDS. Worldwide, more than 22 million people have died of AIDS. About 40 million people worldwide are living with HIV/AIDS.

APPLE II COMPUTER RELEASED: ANNIVERSARY. June 5, 1977. The Apple II computer, with 4K of memory, went on sale for $1,298. Its predecessor, the Apple I, was sold largely to electronic hobbyists the previous year. Apple released the Macintosh computer Jan 24, 1984.

FIRST BALLOON FLIGHT: ANNIVERSARY. June 5, 1783. The first public demonstration of a hot-air balloon flight took place at Annonay, France, where the coinventor brothers, Joseph and Jacques Montgolfier, succeeded in launching their 33-foot-diameter *globe aerostatique*. The unmanned balloon rose an estimated 1,500 feet and traveled, windborne, about 7,500 feet before landing after a ten-minute flight—the first sustained flight of any object achieved by man.

KENNEDY, ROBERT F.: ASSASSINATION ANNIVERSARY. June 5, 1968. Senator Kennedy was shot while campaigning for the Democratic presidential nomination at Los Angeles, CA; he died the following day. Sirhan Sirhan was convicted of his murder.

UNITED NATIONS: WORLD ENVIRONMENT DAY. June 5. Observed annually June 5, the anniversary of the opening of the UN Conference on the Human Environment held in Stockholm in 1972, which led to establishment of UN Environment Programme, based in Nairobi. The General Assembly has urged marking the day with activities reaffirming concern for the preservation and enhancement of the environment. For info: United Nations. Web: www.un .org.

★ Birthdays ★

Bill Moyers, journalist ("Bill Moyers' Journal"), born Hugo, OK, June 5, 1934.

Mark Wahlberg, actor (*Boogie Nights*), also known as rapper Marky Mark (Marky Mark and the Funky Bunch, "Good Vibrations"), born Dorchester, MA, June 5, 1971.

June 6

BONZA BOTTLER DAY™. June 6. To celebrate when the number of the day is the same as the number of the month. Bonza Bottler Day™ is an excuse to have a party at least once a month. For info: Gail M. Berger. E-mail: gberger5@aol .com.

D-DAY: ANNIVERSARY. June 6, 1944. In the early morning hours Allied forces landed in Normandy on the north coast of France. In an operation that took months of planning, a fleet of 2,727 ships of every description converged from British ports from Wales to the North Sea. Operation *Overlord* involved 2 million tons of war materials, including more than 50,000 tanks, armored cars, jeeps, trucks and half-tracks. The US alone sent 1.7 million fighting men. The Germans believed the invasion would not take place under the adverse weather conditions of this early June day. But as the sun came up the village of Saint Mère Eglise was liberated by American parachutists, and by nightfall the landing of 155,000 Allies attested to the success of D-Day. The long-awaited second front had at last materialized.

FIRST DRIVE-IN MOVIE OPENS: ANNIVERSARY. June 6, 1933. Richard M. Hollingshead, Jr, opened

America's first drive-in movie theater in Camden, NJ, on this date. At the height of their popularity in 1958, there were more than 4,000 drive ins across America. In the 1990s fewer than 600 remained open.

SECURITIES AND EXCHANGE COMMISSION CREATED: ANNIVERSARY. June 6, 1934. President Franklin D. Roosevelt signed the Securities Exchange Act that established the SEC. Wall Street had operated almost unfettered since the end of the eighteenth century. However, the stock market crash of 1929 necessitated regulation of the exchanges. The SEC is composed of five members appointed by the president of the US.

SPACE MILESTONE: *SOYUZ 11* **(USSR).** June 6, 1971. Three Soviet cosmonauts died during the return landing June 30, 1971, after a 24-day space flight. *Soyuz 11* had docked at *Salyut* orbital space station June 7–29; the cosmonauts entered the space station for the first time and conducted scientific experiments. The first humans to die in space.

SWEDEN: FLAG DAY. June 6. Commemorates the day in 1523 when Gustavus I ascended the throne of Sweden.

"20/20" TV PREMIERE: ANNIVERSARY. June 6, 1978. An hourly newsmagazine developed by ABC to compete with CBS's "60 Minutes." Hosted by Hugh Downs; Barbara Walters became coanchor in 1984. The show consists of investigative and background reports. Contributors to the show have included Tom Jarriel, Sylvia Chase, Geraldo Rivera, Thomas Hoving, John Stossel, Lynn Sherr and Stone Phillips.

★ *Birthdays* ★

Bjorn Borg, former tennis player, born Sodertalje, Sweden, June 6, 1956.
Dalai Lama, Tibet's spiritual leader and Nobel Peace Prize winner, born Taktser, China, June 6, 1935.

June 7

GAUGUIN, (EUGENE HENRI) PAUL: BIRTH ANNIVERSARY. June 7, 1848. French painter born at Paris, France. Formerly a stockbroker, he became a painter in his middle age and three years later renounced his life at Paris to move to Tahiti. He is remembered best for his broad, flat tones and bold colors. Gauguin died May 8, 1903, at Atoana on the island of Hiva Oa in the Marquesas.

"THE $64,000 QUESTION" TV PREMIERE: ANNIVERSARY. June 7, 1955. This game show was a big hit and the first of prime-time's big money shows. Contestants, each an expert in one area, answered questions; each time a question was answered correctly, contestants doubled their money. The host was Hal March and questions were compiled by Dr. Bergen Evans. Some famous contestants were Dr. Joyce Brothers, Barbara Feldon and Jack Benny (as a joke). The show was dropped in 1958 amid the game show scandals.

SUPREME COURT STRIKES DOWN CONNECTICUT LAW BANNING CONTRACEPTION: ANNIVERSARY. June 7, 1965. In *Griswold v Connecticut,* the Supreme Court guaranteed the right to privacy, including the freedom from government intrusion into matters of birth control.

VCR INTRODUCED: ANNIVERSARY. June 7, 1975. The Sony Corporation released its videocassette recorder, the Betamax, which sold for $995 (more than $2,000 in today's dollars). Eventually, another VCR format, VHS, proved more successful and Sony stopped making the Betamax.

★ Birthdays ★

Allen Iverson, basketball player, born Hampton, VA, June 7, 1975.
Anna Kournikova, tennis player, born Moscow, Russia, June 7, 1981.

Liam Neeson, actor (*Excalibur, Schindler's List*), born Ballymena, Northern Ireland, June 7, 1952.

June 8

COCHISE: DEATH ANNIVERSARY. June 8, 1874. Born around 1810 in the Chiricahua Mountains of Arizona, Cochise became a fierce and courageous leader of the Apache. After his arrest in 1861, he escaped and launched the Apache Wars, which lasted for 25 years. He died 13 years later near his stronghold in southeastern Arizona.

WRIGHT, FRANK LLOYD: BIRTH ANNIVERSARY. June 8, 1867. American architect born at Richland Center, WI. In his autobiography Wright wrote: "No house should ever be *on* any hill or on anything. It should be *of* the hill, belonging to it, so hill and house could live together each the happier for the other." Wright died at Phoenix, AZ, Apr 9, 1959.

★ Birthdays ★

Kathy Baker, actress ("Picket Fences," *The Right Stuff*), born Midland, TX, June 8, 1950.
Tim Berners-Lee, inventor of the World Wide Web, born London, England, June 8, 1955.
Julianna Margulies, actress ("ER"), born Spring Valley, NY, June 8, 1966.

June 9

DONALD DUCK: BIRTHDAY. June 9, 1934. Donald Duck was "born."

PORTER, COLE: BIRTH ANNIVERSARY. June 9, 1891. Cole Porter's career as a composer and lyricist for Broadway was launched in 1928 when five of his songs were used in the musical play *Let's Do It*. His prolific contributions to the Broadway stage include *Fifty Million Frenchmen, The Gay Divorcée, Anything Goes, Du Barry Was a Lady, Kiss Me Kate, Can Can* and *Silk Stockings*. Porter was born at Peru, IN, and died at Santa Monica, CA, Oct 15, 1964.

★ Birthdays ★

Johnny Depp, actor ("21 Jump Street," *Edward Scissorhands, Ed Wood*), born Owensboro, KY, June 9, 1963.

Michael J. Fox, actor ("Family Ties," "Spin City," *Back to the Future* films), born Edmonton, AB, Canada, June 9, 1961.

June 10

ALCOHOLICS ANONYMOUS FOUNDED: ANNIVERSARY. June 10, 1935. On this day at Akron, OH, Dr. Robert Smith completed his first day of permanent sobriety. "Doctor Bob" and William G. Wilson are considered to have founded Alcoholics Anonymous on that day.

BALL-POINT PEN PATENTED: ANNIVERSARY. June 10, 1943. Hungarian Laszlo Biro patented the ball-point pen, which he had been developing since the 1930s. He was living in Argentina, where he had gone to escape the Nazis. In many languages, the word for ball-point pen is "biro."

GARLAND, JUDY: BIRTH ANNIVERSARY. June 10, 1922. American actress and singer born Frances Gumm at Grand Rapids, MN. While Garland played in many films and toured widely as a singer, she is probably most remembered for her portrayal of Dorothy Gale in the now-classic *The Wizard of Oz*. Died June 22, 1969, at London, England.

★ Birthdays ★

Elizabeth Hurley, model, actress (*Austin Powers: International Man of Mystery*), born Basingstoke, England, June 10, 1965.

Leelee Sobieski, actress (*A Soldier's Daughter Never Cries*), born New York, NY, June 10, 1982.

June 11

COUSTEAU, JACQUES: BIRTH ANNIVERSARY. June 11, 1910. French undersea explorer, writer and filmmaker born at St. Andre-de-Cubzac, France. He invented the Aqualung, which allowed him and his colleagues to produce more than 80 documentary films about undersea life, two of which won Oscars. This scientist and explorer was awarded the French Legion of Honor for his work in the Resistance in World War II. He died June 25, 1997, at Paris.

LOMBARDI, VINCE: BIRTH ANNIVERSARY. June 11, 1913. Vincent Thomas (Vince) Lombardi, Pro Football Hall of Fame coach, born at New York, NY. Lombardi played football for Fordham's famed "Seven Blocks of Granite" line in the mid-1930s. He became offensive line coach at West Point in 1949 and moved to the New York Giants in 1954. Five years later, he was named head coach of the Green Bay Packers. His Packers won five NFL titles and two Super Bowls in nine years, and Lombardi was generally regarded as the greatest coach and the finest motivator in pro football history. He retired in 1968 but was lured back to coach the Washington Redskins a year later. Inducted into the Pro Football Hall of Fame in 1971. Died at Washington, DC, Sept 3, 1970.

MOUNT PINATUBO ERUPTS IN PHILIPPINES: ANNIVERSARY. June 11, 1991. Long-dormant volcano Mount Pinatubo erupted with a violent explosion, spewing ash and gases that could be seen for more than 60 miles into the air. The surrounding areas were covered with ash and mud created by rainstorms. US military bases Clark and Subic Bay were also damaged. On July 6, 1992, Ellsworth Dutton of the National Oceanic and Atmospheric Administration's Climate Monitoring and Diagnostics Laboratory announced that a layer of sulfuric acid droplets released into Earth's atmosphere by the eruption had cooled the planet's average temperature by about 1 degree Fahrenheit. The greatest difference was noted in the Northern Hemisphere with a drop of 1.5 degrees. Although the temperature drop was temporary, the climate trend made determining the effect of greenhouse warming on Earth more difficult.

★ Birthdays ★

Joseph C. (Joe) Montana, Jr, former sportscaster and Hall of Fame football player, born New Eagle, PA, June 11, 1956.

Gene Wilder, actor (*The Producers, Willy Wonka & the Chocolate Factory, Blazing Saddles, Young Frankenstein*), director, born Milwaukee, WI, June 11, 1939 (some sources say 1935 or 1933).

June 12

NATIONAL BASEBALL HALL OF FAME: ANNIVERSARY. June 12, 1939. The National Baseball Hall of Fame and Museum, Inc, was dedicated at Cooperstown, NY. More than 200 individuals have been honored for their contributions to the game of baseball by induction into the Baseball Hall of Fame. The first players chosen for membership (1936) were Ty Cobb, Honus Wagner, Babe Ruth, Christy Mathewson and Walter Johnson. Relics and memorabilia from the history of baseball are housed at this shrine of America's national sport.

PHILIPPINES: INDEPENDENCE DAY. June 12. National holiday. Declared independence from Spain in 1898.

RUSSIA: INDEPENDENCE DAY. June 12. National holiday. Commemorates the election in 1991 of the first popularly elected leader (Yeltsin) in the 1,000-year history of the Russian state.

★ *Birthdays* ★

Timothy Busfield, actor ("thirtysomething," *Field of Dreams*), born Lansing, MI, June 12, 1957.

George Herbert Walker Bush, 41st president of the US, born Milton, MA, June 12, 1924. His son George W. Bush is the 43rd president of the US.

June 13

GRANGE, RED: BIRTH ANNIVERSARY. June 13, 1903. Harold Edward ("Red") Grange, Pro Football Hall of Fame halfback and broadcaster, born at Forskville, PA. Perhaps the most famous football player of all time, Grange had a spectacular college career at the University of Illinois, being named an All-American in 1923, 1924 and 1925. When Illinois dedicated its Memorial Stadium on Oct 18, 1924, Grange scored four touchdowns against Michigan in the game's first 12 minutes. Known as the "Galloping Ghost," Grange joined the Chicago Bears in 1925 for what amounted to a barnstorming tour, the start of a professional career dictated by Grange and his manager, Charles C. ("Cash and Carry") Pyle. He retired in 1934 following a knee injury, having put pro football on the sports map. Inducted into the Hall of Fame as a charter member in 1963. Died at Lake Wales, FL, Jan 28, 1991.

HOME OWNERS LOAN ACT: ANNIVERSARY. June 13, 1933. The Federal Savings and Loan Association was authorized with the passage of the Home Owners Loan Act. The purpose of the legislation was to provide a convenient place for investment and to lend money on first mortgages. The first association was the First Federal Savings and Loan Association of Miami, FL, which was chartered on Aug 8, 1933.

MIRANDA **DECISION: ANNIVERSARY.** June 13, 1966. The US Supreme Court rendered a 5–4 decision in the case of *Miranda v Arizona*, holding that the Fifth Amendment of the Constitution "required warnings before valid statements could be taken by police." The decision has been described as "providing basic legal protections to persons who might otherwise not be aware of their rights." Ernesto Miranda, the 23-year-old whose name became nationally known, was retried after the Miranda Decision, convicted and sent back to prison. Miranda was stabbed to death in a card game dispute at Phoenix, AZ, in 1976. A suspect in the killing was released by police after he had been read his "Miranda rights." Police procedures now routinely require the reading of a prisoner's constitutional rights ("Miranda") before questioning.

★ *Birthdays* ★

Tim Allen, comedian, actor ("Home Improvement," *Galaxy Quest*), born Denver, CO, June 13, 1953.

Ashley and Mary-Kate Olsen, actresses ("Full House," "Two of a Kind"), born Los Angeles, CA, June 13, 1986.

June 14

BARTLETT, JOHN: BIRTH ANNIVERSARY. June 14, 1820. American editor and compiler (*Bartlett's Familiar Quotations* [1855]) was born at Plymouth, MA. Though he had little formal education, he created one of the most-used reference works of the English language. No quotation of his own is among the more than 22,000 listed today, but in the preface to the first edition he wrote that the object of this work "originally made without any view of publication" was to show "the obligation our language owes to various authors for numerous phrases and familiar quotations which have become 'household words.'" Bartlett died at Cambridge, MA, Dec 3, 1905.

FIRST NONSTOP TRANSATLANTIC FLIGHT: ANNIVERSARY. June 14–15, 1919. Captain John Alcock and Lieutenant Arthur W. Brown flew a Vickers Vimy bomber 1,900 miles nonstop from St. Johns, Newfoundland, to Clifden, County Galway, Ireland. In spite of their crash landing in an Irish peat bog, their flight inspired public interest in aviation. See also: "Lindbergh Flight: Anniv" (May 20).

FLAG DAY: ANNIVERSARY OF THE STARS AND STRIPES. June 14, 1777. John Adams introduced the following resolution before the Continental Congress, meeting at Philadelphia, PA: "Resolved, That the flag of the thirteen United States shall be thirteen stripes, alternate red and white; that the union be thirteen stars, white on a blue field, representing a new constellation."

Presidential Proclamation issued each year for June 14. Has been issued annually since 1941. (Public Law 81–203 of Aug 3, 1949.) Customarily issued as "Flag Day and National Flag Week."

"THE GONG SHOW" TV PREMIERE: ANNIVERSARY. June 14, 1976. This popular show featured a panel of three celebrities judging amateur and professional acts, from the ordinary to the unusual. At any time, a judge could bang a gong to end the act; this was often done with gusto. Completed acts were then rated and the winner received a cash prize. Chuck Barris created and hosted the show with the exception of one syndicated season hosted by Gary Owens. Celebrities who frequently appeared were Jaye P. Morgan, Rex Reed, Arte Johnson, Phyllis Diller and Jamie Farr.

STOWE, HARRIET BEECHER: BIRTH ANNIVERSARY. June 14, 1811. Author of *Uncle Tom's Cabin*, an antislavery novel that provoked a storm of protest and resulted in fame for its author. Two characters in the novel attained such importance that their names became part of the English language—the Negro slave, Uncle Tom, and the villainous slave owner, Simon Legree. The reaction to *Uncle Tom's Cabin* and its profound political impact are without parallel in American literature. It is said that during the Civil War, when Harriet Beecher Stowe was introduced to President Abraham Lincoln, his words to her were, "So you're the little woman who wrote the book that made this great war." Stowe was born

at Litchfield, CT, and died at Hartford, CT, July 1, 1896.

UNIVAC COMPUTER: ANNIVERSARY. June 14, 1951. Univac 1, the world's first commercial computer, designed for the US Bureau of the Census, was unveiled, demonstrated and dedicated at Philadelphia, PA. Though this milestone of the computer age was the first commercial electronic computer, it had been preceded by ENIAC (Electronic Numeric Integrator and Computer), completed under the supervision of J. Presper Eckert, Jr, and John W. Mauchly, at the University of Pennsylvania in 1946.

WARREN G. HARDING BECOMES FIRST PRESIDENT TO BROADCAST ON RADIO: ANNIVERSARY. June 14, 1922. Warren G. Harding became the first president to broadcast a message over the radio. The event was the dedication of the Francis Scott Key Memorial at Baltimore, MD. The first official government message was broadcast Dec 6, 1923.

★ *Birthdays* ★

Yasmine Bleeth, actress ("Baywatch," "Nash Bridges"), born New York, NY, June 14, 1968.

Boy George, lead singer (Culture Club), born George Alan O'Dowd, London, England, June 14, 1961.

June 15

ARKANSAS: ADMISSION DAY: ANNIVERSARY. June 15. Became 25th state in 1836.

MAGNA CARTA DAY: ANNIVERSARY. June 15. Anniversary of King John's sealing, in 1215, of the Magna Carta "in the meadow called Ronimed between Windsor and Staines on the fifteenth day of June in the seventeenth year of our reign." This document is regarded as the first charter of English liberties and one of the most important documents in the history of political and human freedom. Four original copies of the 1215 charter survive.

NATIVE AMERICAN CITIZENSHIP DAY. June 15. Commemorates the day in 1924 when the US Congress passed legislation recognizing the citizenship of Native Americans.

TWELFTH AMENDMENT TO US CONSTITUTION RATIFIED: ANNIVERSARY. June 15, 1804. The 12th Amendment to the Constitution changed the method of electing the president and vice president after a tie in the electoral college during the election of 1800. Rather than each elector voting for two candidates with the candidate receiving the most votes elected president and the second-place candidate elected vice president, each elector was now required to designate his choice for president and vice president, respectively.

★ *Birthdays* ★

Courteney Cox Arquette, actress ("Family Ties," "Friends"), born Birmingham, AL, June 15, 1964.

Helen Hunt, actress ("Mad About You," *Twister*, Oscar for *As Good as It Gets*), born Los Angeles, CA, June 15, 1963.

June 16

BLOOMSDAY: ANNIVERSARY. June 16, 1904. Anniversary of events in Dublin recorded in James Joyce's *Ulysses*, whose central character is Leopold Bloom.

LADIES' DAY INITIATED IN BASEBALL: ANNIVERSARY. June 16, 1883. The New York Giants hosted the first Ladies' Day baseball game. Both escorted and unescorted ladies were admitted to the game free.

SPACE MILESTONE: *VOSTOK 6* (USSR): FIRST WOMAN IN SPACE. June 16, 1963. Valentina Tereshkova, 26, former cotton-mill worker, born on collective farm near Yaroslavl, USSR, became the first woman in space when her spacecraft, *Vostok 6*, took off from the Tyuratam launch site. She manually controlled *Vostok 6* during the 70.8-hour flight through 48 orbits of Earth and landed by parachute (separate from her cabin) June 19, 1963. In November 1963 she married cosmonaut Andrian Nikolayev, who had piloted *Vostok 3* through 64 Earth orbits, Aug 11–15, 1962. Their child Yelena (1964) was the first born to space-traveler parents.

★ *Birthdays* ★

Laurie Metcalf, actress (Emmy for "Roseanne"; "The Norm Show"), born Edwardsville, IL, June 16, 1955.
Kerry Wood, baseball player, born Irving, TX, June 16, 1977.

June 17

ICELAND: INDEPENDENCE DAY. June 17. National holiday. Anniversary of founding of republic and independence from Denmark in 1944.

SOUTH AFRICA REPEALS LAST APARTHEID LAW: ANNIVERSARY. June 17, 1991. The Parliament of South Africa repealed the Population Registration Act, removing the law that was the foundation of apartheid. The law, first enacted in 1950, required the classification by race of all South Africans at birth. It established four compulsory racial categories: white, mixed race, Asian and black. Although this marked the removal of the last of the apartheid laws, blacks in South Africa still could not vote.

UNITED NATIONS: WORLD DAY TO COMBAT DESERTIFICATION AND DROUGHT. June 17. Proclaimed by the General Assembly Dec 19, 1994 (Resolution 49/115). States were invited to devote the World Day to promoting public awareness of the need for international cooperation to combat desertification and the effects of drought, and of the implementation of the UN Convention to Combat Desertification. For info: United Nations. Web: www.un.org.

WATERGATE DAY: ANNIVERSARY. June 17, 1972. Anniversary of arrests at Democratic Party Headquarters (in Watergate complex, Washington, DC) that led to revelations of political espionage, threats of imminent impeachment of the president and, on Aug 9, 1974, the resignation of President Richard M. Nixon.

★ *Birthdays* ★

Greg Kinnear, actor (*Sabrina, As Good as It Gets*), born Logansport, IN, June 17, 1963.
Barry Manilow, singer ("Mandy," "I Write the Songs"), songwriter, born Brooklyn, NY, June 17, 1946.
Venus Williams, tennis player, born Lynwood, CA, June 17, 1980.

June 18

BATTLE OF WATERLOO: ANNIVERSARY. June 18, 1815. Date of the decisive defeat of Napoleon by British generals Wellington and Blucher, near Waterloo in central Belgium.

FIRST AMERICAN WOMAN IN SPACE: ANNIVERSARY. June 18, 1983. Dr. Sally Ride, 32-year-old physicist and pilot, functioned as a "mission specialist" and became the first American woman in space when she began a six-day mission aboard the space shuttle *Challenger*. The "near-perfect" mission was launched from Cape Canaveral, FL, and landed June 24, 1983, at Edwards Air Force Base, CA. See also: "Space Milestone: *Vostok 6* (USSR): First Woman in Space" (June 16).

WAR OF 1812: DECLARATION ANNIVERSARY. June 18, 1812. After much debate in Congress between "hawks" such as Henry Clay and John Calhoun and "doves" such as John Randolph, Congress issued a declaration of war on Great Britain. The action was prompted primarily by Britain's violation of America's rights on the high seas and British incitement of Indian warfare on the frontier. War was seen by some as a way to acquire Florida and Canada. The hostilities ended with the signing of the Treaty of Ghent on Dec 24, 1814, at Ghent, Belgium.

★ Birthdays ★

Roger Joseph Ebert, film critic ("Ebert and Roeper and the Movies"), born Urbana, IL, June 18, 1942.

Paul McCartney, singer, songwriter (The Beatles, Wings), born Liverpool, England, June 18, 1942.

June 19

FIRST RUNNING OF THE BELMONT STAKES: ANNIVERSARY. June 19, 1867. The first running of the Belmont Stakes took place at Jerome Park, NY. The Belmont Stakes continued at Jerome Park until 1889, then moved to Morris Park, NY, between 1890 and 1905, and in 1906 settled at Belmont Park, NY, where it has continued to the present day. The Belmont Stakes is the oldest event of horse racing's Triple Crown (with the Kentucky Derby and the Preakness).

GEHRIG, LOU: BIRTH ANNIVERSARY. June 19, 1903. Baseball great Henry Louis Gehrig (lifetime batting average of .341), who played in seven World Series, was born at New York, NY, and died there June 2, 1941, from the degenerative muscle disease amyotropic lateral sclerosis, which has become known as Lou Gehrig's disease.

JUNETEENTH. June 19. Celebrated in Texas to commemorate the day in 1865 when Union General Granger proclaimed the slaves of Texas free. Also proclaimed as Emancipation Day by the Florida legislature. Juneteenth has become an occasion for commemoration by African Americans in many parts of the US.

ROSENBERG EXECUTION: ANNIVERSARY. June 19, 1953. Anniversary of the electrocution of the only married couple ever executed together in the US. Julius (35) and Ethel (37) Rosenberg were executed for espionage at Sing Sing Prison, Ossining, NY. Time for the execution was advanced several hours to avoid conflict with the Jewish Sabbath. Their conviction has been a subject of controversy over the years.

★ Birthdays ★

Phylicia Rashad, actress ("The Cosby Show"), born Houston, TX, June 19, 1948.
Kathleen Turner, actress (*Body Heat, Peggy Sue Got Married, Romancing the Stone*), born Springfield, MO, June 19, 1954.

June 20

"THE ED SULLIVAN SHOW" ("TOAST OF THE TOWN") TV PREMIERE: ANNIVERSARY. June 20, 1948. "The Ed Sullivan Show" was officially titled "Toast of the Town" until 1955. It was the longest-running variety show (through 1971) and the most popular for decades. Ed Sullivan, the host, signed all types of acts, both well known and new, trying to have something to please everyone. Thousands of performers appeared, many making their television debut, such as Irving Berlin, Victor Borge, Hedy Lamarr, Walt Disney, Fred Astaire and Jane Powell. Two acts attracted the largest audience of the time: Elvis Presley and the Beatles.

FIRST DOCTOR OF SCIENCE DEGREE EARNED BY A WOMAN: ANNIVERSARY. June 20, 1895. Caroline Willard Baldwin became the first woman to earn a doctor of science degree at Cornell University, Ithaca, NY.

LIZZIE BORDEN VERDICT: ANNIVERSARY. June 20, 1893. Spectators at her trial cheered when the "not guilty" verdict was read by the jury foreman in the murder trial of Lizzie Borden on this date. Elizabeth Borden had been accused of and tried for the hacking to death of her father and stepmother in their Fall River, MA, home, Aug 4, 1892.

MURPHY, AUDIE: BIRTH ANNIVERSARY. June 20, 1924. Born at Kingston, TX, Murphy was the most decorated soldier in World War II and later became an actor in western and war movies. He died May 28, 1971, in a plane crash near Roanoke, VA.

WEST VIRGINIA: ADMISSION DAY: ANNIVERSARY. June 20, 1863. Became 35th state in 1863. Observed as a holiday in West Virginia. The state of West Virginia is a product of the Civil War. Originally part of Virginia, West Virginia became a separate state when Virginia seceded from the Union.

★ Birthdays ★

John Goodman, actor ("Roseanne," *The Flint-stones*), born Afton, MO, June 20, 1952.
Nicole Kidman, actress (*Eyes Wide Shut, Moulin Rouge*), born Honolulu, HI, June 20, 1967.
Brian Wilson, singer (The Beach Boys), songwriter, born Hawthorne, CA, June 20, 1942.

June 21

BATTLE OF OKINAWA: ANNIVERSARY. June 21, 1945. On Easter Sunday, Apr 1, 1945, the US Tenth Army began Operation Iceberg, the invasion of the islands of Okinawa. Ground troops numbering 180,000 plus 368,000 men in support services made a total of 548,000 troops involved—the biggest amphibious operation of the Pacific war. By the end of the battle, the American death toll reached enormous proportions by Pacific battle standards—7,613 died on land and 4,907 in the air or from kamikaze attacks. A total of 36 US warships were sunk. More than 70,000 Japanese and 80,000 civilian Okinawans died in the course of the battle.

CANCER, THE CRAB. June 21–July 22. In the astronomical/astrological zodiac, which divides the sun's apparent orbit into 12 segments, the period June 21–July 22 is identified, traditionally, as the sun sign of Cancer, the Crab. The ruling planet is the moon.

CONSTITUTION GOES INTO EFFECT: ANNIVERSARY. June 21, 1788. By a vote of 57 to 47, New Hampshire became the ninth state to ratify the Constitution. With this ratification, the Constitution became effective for all ratifying states, as the approval of nine states was required for the Constitution to go into effect.

★ Birthdays ★

Meredith Baxter, actress ("Bridget Loves Bernie," "Family," "Family Ties"), born Los Angeles, CA, June 21, 1947.
Prince William (William Arthur Philip Louis), son of Prince Charles and Princess Diana, born London, England, June 21, 1982.

June 22

JOE LOUIS v BRADDOCK/SCHMELING FIGHT ANNIVERSARIES. June 22, 1937. At Chicago's Comiskey Park Joe Louis won the World Heavyweight Championship title by knocking out James J. Braddock (eighth round). Louis retained the title until his retirement in 1949. Exactly one year after the Braddock fight, on June 22, 1938, Louis met Germany's Max Schmeling, at New York City's Yankee Stadium. Louis knocked out Schmeling in the first round.

SOVIET UNION INVADED: ANNIVERSARY. June 22, 1941. German troops invaded the Soviet Union, beginning a conflict that left 27 million Soviet citizens dead. Ceremonies are held this day in Russia, Belarus and Ukraine, the areas of the former Soviet Union that bore the brunt of the initial invasion.

US DEPARTMENT OF JUSTICE: ANNIVERSARY. June 22. Established by an act of Congress, the Department of Justice is headed by the attorney general. Prior to 1870, the attorney general (whose office had been created Sept 24, 1789) had been a member of the president's cabinet but had not been the head of a department.

★ Birthdays ★

Ed Bradley, broadcast journalist ("60 Minutes"), born Philadelphia, PA, June 22, 1941.

Amy Brenneman, actress ("Judging Amy"), born Glastonbury, CT, June 22, 1964.

Meryl Streep, actress (Oscars for *Kramer vs Kramer* and *Sophie's Choice*), born Summit, NJ, June 22, 1949.

June 23

FIRST TYPEWRITER: ANNIVERSARY. June 23, 1868. First US typewriter was patented by Luther Sholes.

LET IT GO DAY. June 23. Whatever it is that's bugging you, drop it! It's only eating away at you and providing nothing positive. [©2001 by WH.] For info: Wellcat Holidays. Web: www.wellcat.com.

RUDOLPH, WILMA: BIRTH ANNIVERSARY. June 23, 1940. Olympic gold medal sprinter, born at Bethlehem, TN. She won the 100-meter and the 200-meter races and the 400-meter relay at the 1960 Rome games, thus becoming the first woman to win three gold medals at the same Olympics. She overcame polio as a child and went on to Tennessee State University to become an athlete. Rudolph won the Sullivan Award in 1961. Died at Brentwood, TN, Nov 12, 1994.

★ Birthdays ★

Frances McDormand, actress (*Fargo, Mississippi Burning, Almost Famous*), born Chicago, IL, June 23, 1957.

Clarence Thomas, associate justice of the Supreme Court, born Pinpoint, GA, June 23, 1948.

June 24

BERLIN AIRLIFT: ANNIVERSARY. June 24, 1948. In the early days of the cold war the Soviet Union challenged the West's right of access to Berlin. The Soviets created a blockade, and an airlift to supply some 2,250,000 people resulted. The airlift lasted a total of 321 days and brought into Berlin 1,592,787 tons of supplies. Joseph Stalin finally backed down and the blockade ended May 12, 1949.

DEMPSEY, JACK: BIRTH ANNIVERSARY. June 24, 1895. William Harrison Dempsey, known as "The Manassa Mauler," was world heavyweight boxing champion from 1919 to 1926. Following his boxing career Dempsey became a successful New York restaurant operator. Born at Manassa, CO, Dempsey died May 31, 1983, at New York, NY.

★ Birthdays ★

Sherry Stringfield, actress ("NYPD Blue," "ER"), born Colorado Springs, CO, June 24, 1967.

June 25

BATTLE OF LITTLE BIGHORN: ANNIVERSARY. June 25, 1876. Lieutenant Colonel George Armstrong Custer, leading military forces of more than 200 men, attacked an encampment of Sioux Indians led by Chiefs Sitting Bull and Crazy Horse near Little Bighorn River, MT. Custer and all of the men in his immediate command were killed in the brief battle (about two hours) at Little Bighorn. One horse, named Comanche, is said to have been the only survivor among Custer's forces.

CBS SENDS FIRST COLOR TV BROADCAST OVER THE AIR: ANNIVERSARY. June 25, 1951. Columbia Broadcast System broadcast the first color television program. The four-hour program was carried by stations at New York City, Baltimore, Philadelphia, Boston and Washington, DC, although no color sets were owned by the public. At the time, CBS itself owned fewer than 40 color receivers.

KOREAN WAR BEGAN: ANNIVERSARY. June 25, 1950. Forces from northern Korea invaded southern Korea, beginning a civil war. US ground forces entered the conflict June 30. An armistice was signed at Panmunjom July 27,

1953, formally dividing the country into two—North Korea and South Korea.

SUPREME COURT BANS SCHOOL PRAYER: ANNIVERSARY. June 25, 1962. The US Supreme Court ruled that a prayer read aloud in public schools violated the First Amendment's separation of church and state. The court again struck down a law pertaining to the First Amendment when it disallowed an Alabama law that permitted a daily one-minute period of silent meditation or prayer in public schools June 1, 1985 (vote 6–3).

SUPREME COURT UPHOLDS RIGHT TO DIE: ANNIVERSARY. June 25, 1990. In the case *Cruzan v Missouri*, the Supreme Court, in a 5–4 ruling, upheld the constitutional right of a person whose wishes are clearly known to refuse life-sustaining medical treatment.

VIRGINIA: RATIFICATION DAY. June 25. Tenth state to ratify the Constitution in 1788.

★ *Birthdays* ★

Dikembe Mutombo, basketball player, born Kinshasa, Zaire, June 25, 1966.
Willis Reed, Jr, basketball executive and former coach, Hall of Fame basketball player, born Hico, LA, June 25, 1942.

June 26

BAR CODE INTRODUCED: ANNIVERSARY. June 26, 1974. A committee formed in 1970 by US grocers and food manufacturers recommended in 1973 a Universal Product Code (i.e., a bar code) for supermarket items that would allow electronic scanning of prices. On this day in 1974 a pack of Wrigley's gum was swiped across the first checkout scanner at a supermarket in Troy, OH. Today bar codes are used to keep track of everything from freight cars to cattle.

FLAG AMENDMENT DEFEATED: ANNIVERSARY. June 26, 1990. The Senate rejected a proposed constitutional amendment that would have permitted states to prosecute those who destroyed or desecrated American flags. Similar legislation continues to be introduced in Congress.

HUMAN GENOME MAPPED: ANNIVERSARY. June 26, 2000. Biologists J. Craig Venter and Francis S. Collins announced that their research groups had mapped the human genome, a strand of DNA with 3 billion parts that spells out our genetic code.

UNITED NATIONS CHARTER SIGNED: ANNIVERSARY. June 26, 1945. The UN charter was signed at San Francisco by representatives of 50 nations.

UNITED NATIONS: INTERNATIONAL DAY AGAINST DRUG ABUSE AND ILLICIT TRAFFICKING. June 26. Following a recommendation of the 1987 International Conference on Drug Abuse and Illicit Trafficking, the United Nations General Assembly (Resolution 42/112), expressed its determination to strengthen action and cooperation for an international society free of drug abuse and proclaimed June 26 as an annual observance to raise public awareness. For info: United Nations. Web: www.un.org.

ZAHARIAS, MILDRED "BABE" DIDRIKSON: BIRTH ANNIVERSARY. June 26, 1914. Born Mildred Ella Didrikson at Port Arthur, TX, the great athlete was nicknamed "Babe" after legendary baseball player Babe Ruth. She was named to the women's All-America basketball team when she was 16. At the 1932 Olympic Games, she won two gold medals and also set world records in the javelin throw and the 80-meter high hurdles; only a technicality prevented her from obtaining the gold in the high jump. Didrikson married professional wrestler George Zaharias in 1938, six years after she began playing golf casually. In 1946 Babe won the US Women's Amateur tournament, and in 1947 she was the first American winner of the British Ladies' Amateur Tournament. Turning professional in 1948, she won the US Women's Open in 1950 and 1954. Babe also excelled in softball, baseball, swimming, figure skating, billiards—even football. In a 1950 Associated Press poll she was named the woman athlete of the first half of the 20th century. She died Sept 27, 1956, at Galveston, TX.

★ Birthdays ★

Derek Jeter, baseball player, born Pequannock, NJ, June 26, 1974.

Chris O'Donnell, actor (*Scent of a Woman*), born Winnetka, IL, June 26, 1970.

June 27

HAPPY BIRTHDAY TO "HAPPY BIRTHDAY TO YOU." June 27, 1859. The melody of probably the most often sung song in the world, "Happy Birthday to You," was composed by Mildred J. Hill, a schoolteacher born at Louisville, KY, on this date. Her younger sister, Patty Smith Hill, was the author of the lyrics which were first published in 1893 as "Good Morning to All," a classroom greeting published in the book *Song Stories for the Sunday School*. The lyrics were amended in 1924 to include a stanza beginning "Happy Birthday to You." Now it is sung somewhere in the world every minute of the day. Although the authors are believed to have earned very little from the song, reportedly it later generated about $1 million a year for its copyright owner. The song is expected to enter public domain upon expiration of copyright in 2010. Mildred Hill died at Chicago, IL, June 5, 1916, without knowing that her melody would become the world's most popular song.

KELLER, HELEN: BIRTH ANNIVERSARY. June 27, 1880. Born at Tuscumbia, AL, Helen Keller was left deaf and blind by a disease she contracted at 18 months of age. With the help of her teacher, Anne Sullivan, she graduated from college and had a career as an author and lecturer. She died June 1, 1968, at Westport, CT.

NATIONAL HIV TESTING DAY. June 27. A nationwide campaign encouraging education, voluntary HIV testing and counseling to people at risk for HIV. For info: National Association of People with AIDS. Web: www.nhtd.org.

★ *Birthdays* ★

Captain Kangaroo, TV personality, born Bob Keeshan, Lynbrook, NY, June 27, 1927.
Tobey Maguire, actor (*Pleasantville, The Cider House Rules*), born Santa Monica, CA, June 27, 1975.

June 28

MONDAY HOLIDAY LAW: ANNIVERSARY. June 28, 1968. President Lyndon B. Johnson approved Public Law 90–363, which amended section 6103(a) of title 5, United States Code, establishing Monday observance of Washington's Birthday, Memorial Day, Labor Day, Columbus Day and Veterans Day. The new holiday law took effect Jan 1, 1971. Veterans Day observance subsequently reverted to its former observance date, Nov 11.

STONEWALL RIOT: ANNIVERSARY. June 28, 1969. Early in the morning of June 28, 1969, the clientele of a gay bar, the Stonewall Inn at New York City, rioted after the club was raided by police. The riot was followed by several days of demonstrations. Stonewall is now recognized as the start of the gay liberation movement.

★ *Birthdays* ★

Kathy Bates, actress (Oscar for *Misery; Fried Green Tomatoes*), born Memphis, TN, June 28, 1948.
Mel Brooks, actor, director (*The Producers, Blazing Saddles*), born Melvyn Kaminsky, New York, NY, June 28, 1928.
John Cusack, actor (*Say Anything, The Grifters, Bullets over Broadway*), born Chicago, IL, June 28, 1966.

June 29

DEATH PENALTY BANNED: ANNIVERSARY. June 29, 1972. In a decision that spared the lives of 600 individuals then sitting on death row, the US Supreme Court, in a 5–4 vote, found capital punishment a violation of the Eighth Amendment, which prohibits "cruel and unusual punishment." Later overruling themselves, the court determined on July 2, 1976, that the death penalty was not cruel and unusual punishment and on Oct 4, 1976, lifted the ban on the death penalty in murder cases. On Jan 15, 1977, Gary Gilmore became the first individual executed in the US in more than ten years.

INTERSTATE HIGHWAY SYSTEM BORN: ANNIVERSARY. June 29, 1956. President Dwight Eisenhower signed a bill providing $33.5 billion for highway construction. It was the biggest public works program in history.

SPACE MILESTONE: *ATLANTIS* (US) AND *MIR* (USSR) DOCK. June 29, 1995. An American space shuttle docked with a Russian space station for the first time, resulting in the biggest craft ever assembled in space. The cooperation involved in this linkup was to serve as a stepping-stone to building the International Space Station.

★ Birthdays ★

Gary Busey, musician, actor ("The Texas Wheelers," *The Buddy Holly Story*), born Goose Creek, TX, June 29, 1944.

Harmon Killebrew, Hall of Fame baseball player, born Payette, ID, June 29, 1936.

June 30

CONGO (KINSHASA): INDEPENDENCE DAY. June 30. National holiday. The Democratic Republic of Congo was previously known as Zaire. Commemorates independence from Belgium in 1960.

LAST HURRAH FOR BRITISH HONG KONG: ANNIVERSARY. June 30, 1997. The crested flag of the British Crown Colony was officially lowered at midnight and replaced by a new flag (marked by the bauhinia flower) representing China's sovereignty and the official transfer of power. Though Britain owned Hong Kong in perpetuity, the land areas surrounding the city were leased from China and the lease expired July 1, 1997. Rather than renegotiate a new lease, Britain ceded its claim to Hong Kong.

NOW FOUNDED: ANNIVERSARY. June 30, 1966. The National Organization for Women was founded at Washington, DC, by people attending the Third National Conference on the

Commission on the Status of Women. NOW's purpose is to take action to take women into full partnership in the mainstream of American society, exercising all privileges and responsibilities in equal partnership with men. For info: National Organization for Women. Web: www.now.org.

Vincent D'Onofrio, actor (*Ed Wood, Men in Black*), born Brooklyn, NY, June 30, 1959.
Michael Gerard (Mike) Tyson, former heavyweight champion boxer, born New York, NY, June 30, 1966.

July

July 1

BATTLE OF GETTYSBURG: ANNIVERSARY. July 1, 1863. After the Southern success at Chancellorsville, VA, Confederate general Robert E. Lee led his forces on an invasion of the North, initially targeting Harrisburg, PA. As Union forces moved to counter the invasion, the battle lines were eventually formed at Gettysburg, PA, in one of the Civil War's most crucial battles. On the climactic third day of the battle (July 3), Lee ordered an attack on the center of the Union line, later to be known as Pickett's Charge. The 15,000 rebels were repulsed, ending the Battle of Gettysburg. After the defeat, Lee's forces retreated back to Virginia, listing more than one-third of the troops as casualties in the failed invasion. Union general George Meade initially failed to pursue the retreating rebels, allowing Lee's army to escape across the rain-swollen Potomac River. With more than 50,000 casualties, this was the worst battle of the Civil War.

BURUNDI: INDEPENDENCE DAY. July 1. National holiday. Anniversary of establishment of independence from Belgian administration in 1962. Had been part of Ruanda-Urundi.

CANADA: CANADA DAY. July 1. National holiday. Canada's national day, formerly known as Dominion Day. Observed on following day when July 1 is a Sunday.

COURT TV DEBUT: ANNIVERSARY. July 1, 1991. The continuing evolution of entertainment brought on by the advent of cable television added another twist on July 1, 1991, with the debut of Court TV. Trials are broadcast in their entirety, with occasional commentary from the channel's anchor desk and switching among several trials in progress. Trials with immense popular interest, such as the William Kennedy Smith rape trial, the sentencing hearing of Marlon Brando's son and the Jeffrey Dahmer and O.J. Simpson trials, are broadcast along with more low-profile cases.

DIANA, PRINCESS OF WALES: BIRTH ANNIVERSARY. July 1, 1961. Former wife of Charles, Prince of Wales, and mother of Prince William and

Prince Harry. Born Lady Diana Spencer at Sandringham, England, she died in an automobile accident at Paris, France, Aug 31, 1997.

FIRST SCHEDULED TELEVISION BROADCAST: ANNIVERSARY. July 1, 1941. The National Broadcasting Company (NBC) began broadcasting from the Empire State Building on this day. The Federal Communications Commission had granted the first commercial TV licenses to ten stations on May 2, 1941.

FIRST US POSTAGE STAMPS ISSUED: ANNIVERSARY. July 1, 1847. The first US postage stamps were issued by the US Postal Service, a 5¢ stamp picturing Benjamin Franklin and a 10¢ stamp honoring George Washington. Stamps had been issued by private postal services in the US prior to this date.

FIRST US ZOO: ANNIVERSARY. July 1, 1874. The Philadelphia Zoological Society, the first US zoo, opened. Three thousand visitors traveled by foot, horse and carriage and steamboat to visit the exhibits. Price of admission was 25¢ for adults and 10¢ for children. There were 1,000 animals in the zoo on opening day.

MAMMOTH CAVE NATIONAL PARK ESTABLISHED: ANNIVERSARY. July 1, 1941. Area of central Kentucky, originally authorized May 25, 1926, was established as a national park. For info: www.nps.gov/maca.

MEDICARE: ANNIVERSARY. July 1, 1968. Medicare, the US health insurance program for senior citizens, went into effect. The legislation authorizing the program had been signed by President Lyndon Johnson July 30, 1965. Former President Harry Truman received the first Medicare card.

NATIONAL BAKED BEAN MONTH. July 1–31. To pay tribute to one of America's favorite and most healthful and nutritious foods, baked beans, made with dry or canned beans. For info: Bean Education & Awareness Network. Web: www.americanbean.org.

NATIONAL HOT DOG MONTH. July 1–31. Celebrates one of America's favorite handheld foods with fun facts and new topping ideas. More than 16 billion hot dogs per year are sold in the US. For info: National Hot Dog & Sausage Council. Web: www.hot-dog.org.

NATIONAL JULY BELONGS TO BLUEBERRIES MONTH. July 1–31. To make the public aware that this is the peak month for fresh blueberries. For info: North American Blueberry Council. Web: www.blueberry.org.

NATIONAL RECREATION AND PARKS MONTH. July 1–31. To showcase and invite community participation in quality leisure activities for all segments of the population. For info: National Recreation and Park Association. Web: www.nrpa.org.

RWANDA: INDEPENDENCE DAY. July 1. National holiday. Commemorates independence from Belgium in 1962.

TWENTY-SIXTH AMENDMENT RATIFIED: ANNIVERSARY. July 1, 1971. The 26th Amendment to the Constitution granted the right to vote in all federal, state and local elections to all persons 18 years or older. On the date of ratification the US gained an additional 11 million voters. Up until this time, the minimum voting age was set by the states; in most states it was 21.

WALKMAN DEBUTS: ANNIVERSARY. July 1, 1979. This month Sony introduced the Walkman under the name Soundabout, selling for $200. It had been released in Japan six months earlier. More than 185 million have been sold. Now there is a Discman for playing CDs.

ZIP CODES INAUGURATED: ANNIVERSARY. July 1, 1963. The US Postal Service introduced the five-digit zip code on this day.

★ Birthdays ★

Dan Aykroyd, actor (*The Blues Brothers, Dragnet, Ghostbusters*, "Saturday Night Live"), born Ottawa, ON, Canada, July 1, 1952.
Andre Braugher, actor ("Homicide," *City of Angels*), born Chicago, IL, July 1, 1962.
Liv Tyler, actress (*That Thing You Do, The Lord of the Rings*), born Portland, ME, July 1, 1977.

July 2

CIVIL RIGHTS ACT OF 1964: ANNIVERSARY. July 2, 1964. President Lyndon Johnson signed the Voting Rights Act into law, prohibiting discrimination on the basis of race in public accomodations, in publicly owned facilities, in employment and union membership and in the registration of voters.

HALFWAY POINT OF THE YEAR. July 2. At noon, July 2, 182½ days of the year will have elapsed and 182½ will remain until the end of the year. In a leap year (2004), the halfway point is July 1 at midnight.

★ Birthdays ★

José Canseco, Jr, former baseball player, born Havana, Cuba, July 2, 1964.
Vicente Fox Quesada, president of Mexico, born Mexico City, Mexico, July 2, 1942.

July 3

BELARUS: INDEPENDENCE DAY. July 3. National holiday. Commemorates liberation of Minsk in 1944.

DOG DAYS. July 3–Aug 11. Hottest days of the year in Northern Hemisphere. Usually about 40 days, but variously reckoned at 30–54 days. Popularly believed to be an evil time "when the sea boiled, wine turned sour, dogs grew mad, and all creatures became languid." Originally the days when Sirius, the Dog Star, rose just before or at about the same time as sunrise (no longer true owing to precession of the equinoxes). Ancients sacrificed a brown dog at beginning of Dog Days to appease the rage of Sirius, believing that the star was the cause of the hot, sultry weather.

IDAHO: ADMISSION DAY: ANNIVERSARY. July 3. Became 43rd state in 1890.

STAY OUT OF THE SUN DAY. July 3. For health's sake, give your skin a break today. [©2001 by WH.] For info: Wellcat Holidays. Web: www .wellcat.com.

★ Birthdays ★

Tom Cruise, actor (*Eyes Wide Shut, The Color of Money, Born on the Fourth of July*), born Syracuse, NY, July 3, 1962.
Thomas Gibson, actor ("Dharma & Greg"), born Charleston, SC, July 3, 1962.

Montel Williams, talk-show host ("The Montel Williams Show"), born Baltimore, MD, July 3, 1956.

July 4

COOLIDGE, CALVIN: BIRTH ANNIVERSARY. July 4, 1872. The 30th president of the US was born John Calvin Coolidge at Plymouth, VT. He succeeded to the presidency Aug 3, 1923, following the death of Warren G. Harding. Coolidge was elected president once, in 1924, but did "not choose to run for president in 1928." Nicknamed Silent Cal, he is reported to have said, "If you don't say anything, you won't be called on to repeat it." Coolidge died at Northampton, MA, Jan 5, 1933.

DECLARATION OF INDEPENDENCE APPROVAL: ANNIVERSARY. July 4, 1776. The Declaration of Independence was approved by the Continental Congress: "Signed by Order and in Behalf of the Congress, John Hancock, President, Attest, Charles Thomson, Secretary." The official signing by the rest of the members of the Congress occurred Aug 2, 1776. This day is observed as Independence Day, a legal holiday in all states and territories.

HAWTHORNE, NATHANIEL: BIRTH ANNIVERSARY. July 4, 1804. Novelist and short story writer, born at Salem, MA. Works included *The Scarlet Letter, The House of the Seven Gables* and *The Blithedale Romance.* Hawthorne died at Plymouth, NH, May 19, 1864.

TUSKEGEE INSTITUTE OPENING: ANNIVERSARY. July 4, 1881. The famed agricultural-industrial institution started by Booker T. Washington was built from the ground up by dedicated students seeking academic and vocational training. The institute started in a shanty before Washington purchased an abandoned plantation at Tuskegee, AL. The students built the dormitories, classrooms and chapel from bricks out of their own kiln.

★ *Birthdays* ★

Neil Simon, playwright (*The Odd Couple, Barefoot in the Park*), born New York, NY, July 4, 1927.
Abigail Van Buren, advice columnist, born Pauline Esther Friedman, Sioux City, IA, July 4, 1918.

July 5

ALGERIA: INDEPENDENCE DAY. July 5. National holiday. Commemorates the day in 1962 when Algeria gained independence from France.

BARNUM, PHINEAS TAYLOR: BIRTH ANNIVERSARY. July 5, 1810. Promoter of the bizarre and unusual. Barnum's American Museum opened in 1842, promoting unusual acts including Chang and Eng (the original Siamese Twins) and General Tom Thumb. In 1850 he began his promotion of Jenny Lind, "The Swedish Nightingale," and parlayed her singing talents into a major financial success. In 1871 his circus "The Greatest Show on Earth" opened at Brooklyn, NY; Barnum merged with his rival J.A. Bailey in 1881 to form the Barnum and Bailey Circus. P.T. Barnum was born at Bethel, CT, and died at Bridgeport, CT, Apr 7, 1891.

BIKINI DEBUTED: ANNIVERSARY. July 5, 1946. The skimpy two-piece bathing suit created by Louis Reard debuted at a fashion show in Paris. It was named after an atoll in the Pacific where the hydrogen bomb was first tested.

RHODES, CECIL JOHN: BIRTH ANNIVERSARY. July 5, 1853. English-born, South African millionaire politician. Said to have controlled at one time 90 percent of the world's diamond production. His will founded the Rhodes Scholarships at Oxford University for superior scholastic achievers. Rhodesia (now Zimbabwe) was named for him. Born at Bishop's Stortford,

Hertfordshire, England, Rhodes died Mar 26, 1902, at Cape Town, South Africa.

VENEZUELA: INDEPENDENCE DAY. July 5. National holiday. Commemorates Proclamation of Independence from Spain in 1811. Independence was not achieved until 1821.

★ Birthdays ★

Katherine Helmond, actress (stage: *The House of Blue Leaves*; "Soap," "Who's the Boss?"), born Galveston, TX, July 5, 1934.
Shirley Knight, actress (stage: *Kennedy's Children* [Tony]; *The Dark at the Top of the Stairs, Sweet Bird of Youth*), born Goessell, KS, July 5, 1936.

July 6

FIRST SUCCESSFUL ANTIRABIES INOCULATION: ANNIVERSARY. July 6, 1885. Louis Pasteur gave the first successful antirabies inoculation to a boy who had been bitten by an infected dog.

MAJOR LEAGUE BASEBALL HOLDS FIRST ALL-STAR GAME: ANNIVERSARY. July 6, 1933. The first midsummer All-Star Game was held at Comiskey Park, Chicago, IL. Babe Ruth led the American League with a home run, as they defeated the National League 4–2. Prior to the summer of 1933, All-Star contests consisted of pre- and postseason exhibitions that often found teams made up of a few stars playing beside journeymen and even minor leaguers.

MALAWI: REPUBLIC DAY. July 6. National holiday. Commemorates attainment of independence from Britain in 1965 and Malawi's becoming a republic in 1966. Malawi was formerly known as Nyasaland.

REPUBLICAN PARTY FORMED: ANNIVERSARY. July 6, 1854. The Republican Party originated at a convention at Ripon, WI, on Feb 28, 1854. A state convention meeting in Michigan formally adopted the name Republican on July 6.

★ Birthdays ★

Ned Beatty, actor (*Deliverance*, "Homicide," *Hear My Song*), born Lexington, KY, July 6, 1937.
George W. Bush, 43d president of the US, former governor of Texas (R), born New Haven, CT, July 6, 1946.
Della Reese, singer ("And That Reminds Me"), actress ("Touched by an Angel"), born Deloreese Patricia Early, Detroit, MI, July 6, 1932.
Sylvester Stallone, actor (*Rocky* and *Rambo* films), director, born New York, NY, July 6, 1946.

July 7

BONZA BOTTLER DAY™. July 7. To celebrate when the number of the day is the same as the number of the month. Bonza Bottler Day™ is an excuse to have a party at least once a month. For info: Gail M. Berger. E-mail: gber ger5@aol.com.

PAIGE, LEROY (SATCHEL): BIRTH ANNIVERSARY. July 7, 1906. Baseball Hall of Fame pitcher born at Mobile, AL. Paige was the greatest attraction in the Negro Leagues and was also, at age 42, the first black pitcher in the American League. Inducted into the Hall of Fame in 1971. Died at Kansas City, MO, June 8, 1982.

★ Birthdays ★

Billy Campbell, actor ("Once and Again"), born Charlottesville, VA, July 7, 1959.
Michelle Kwan, figure skater, born Torrance, CA, July 7, 1980.
Ringo Starr, singer, musician (The Beatles), born Richard Starkey, Liverpool, England, July 7, 1940.

July 8

OLIVE BRANCH PETITION: ANNIVERSARY. July 8, 1775. Representatives of 12 of the 13 colonies signed a petition from the Second Continental Congress to King George III, a final attempt by moderates to avoid a complete break with England.

★ Birthdays ★

Kevin Bacon, actor (stage: *Forty Deuce* [Obie Award]; *A Few Good Men, Apollo 13*), born Philadelphia, PA, July 8, 1958.
Anjelica Huston, actress (Oscar for *Prizzi's Honor; The Addams Family*), born Los Angeles, CA, July 8, 1951.

July 9

ARGENTINA: INDEPENDENCE DAY. July 9. Anniversary of establishment of independent republic, with the declaration of independence from Spain in 1816.

FIRST OPEN-HEART SURGERY: ANNIVERSARY. July 9, 1893. In Provident Hospital on Chicago's south side, black surgeon Dr. Daniel Hale Williams performed the first successful open-heart surgery.

FOURTEENTH AMENDMENT TO US CONSTITUTION RATIFIED: ANNIVERSARY. July 9, 1868. The 14th Amendment defined US citizenship and provided that no state shall have the right to abridge the rights of any citizen without due process and equal protection under the law. Coming three years after the Civil War, the 14th Amendment also included provisions for barring individuals who assisted in any rebellion or insurrection against the US from holding public office, and releasing federal and state governments from any financial liability incurred in the assistance of rebellion or insurrection against the US.

★ *Birthdays* ★

Brian Dennehy, actor ("Star of the Family," *Tommy Boy*), born Bridgeport, CT, July 9, 1938.
Tom Hanks, actor (*Big, Sleepless in Seattle, Saving Private Ryan, Cast Away*; Oscars for *Philadelphia, Forrest Gump*), born Concord, CA, July 9, 1956.
Donald Rumsfeld, US secretary of defense (Ford and George W. Bush administrations), born Evanston, IL, July 9, 1932.

July 10

ASHE, ARTHUR: BIRTH ANNIVERSARY. July 10, 1943. Born at Richmond, VA, Arthur Ashe became a legend for his list of firsts as a black tennis player. Ashe won a total of 33 career titles. In 1985 he was inducted into the International Tennis Hall of Fame. He helped create inner-city tennis programs for youth and wrote the three-volume *A Hard Road to Glory: A History of the African-American Athlete*. Aware that

USA Today intended to reveal that he had AIDS, Ashe announced Apr 8, 1992, that he probably contracted HIV through a transfusion during bypass surgery. In September 1992 he began a fund-raising effort on behalf of the Arthur Ashe Foundation for the Defeat of AIDS. He died at New York, NY, Feb 6, 1993.

BAHAMAS: INDEPENDENCE DAY. July 10. Public holiday. In 1973 the Bahamas gained their independence after 250 years as a British Crown Colony.

DON'T STEP ON A BEE DAY. July 10. Wellcat Holidays reminds kids and grown-ups that now is the time of year when going barefoot can mean getting stung by a bee. If you get stung, tell Mom. [©2001 by WH.] For info: Wellcat Holidays. Web: www.wellcat.com.

WHISTLER, JAMES ABBOTT McNEILL: BIRTH ANNIVERSARY. July 10, 1834. American painter (especially known for painting of his mother) born at Lowell, MA. Died at London, England,

July 17, 1903. When a woman declared that a landscape reminded her of Whistler's paintings, he reportedly said, "Yes, madam, Nature is creeping up."

WYOMING: ADMISSION DAY: ANNIVERSARY. July 10. Became 44th state in 1890.

★ *Birthdays* ★

Ron Glass, actor ("Barney Miller," voice on "Rugrats"), born Evansville, IN, July 10, 1945.

July 11

ADAMS, JOHN QUINCY: BIRTH ANNIVERSARY. July 11, 1767. Sixth president of the US and the son of the second president, John Quincy Adams was born at Braintree, MA. After his single term as president, he served 17 years as a member of Congress from Plymouth, MA. He died Feb 23, 1848, at the House of Representatives (in the same room in which he had taken the presidential Oath of Office Mar 4, 1825). John Quincy Adams was the only president whose father had also been president of the US until George W. Bush became president in January 2001.

BOWDLER'S DAY. July 11. A day to remember the prudish medical doctor, Thomas Bowdler, born near Bath, England, on July 11, 1754. He undertook the cleansing of the works of Shakespeare by removing all the words and expressions he considered to be indecent or impious.

His *Family Shakespeare*, in ten volumes, omitted all those words "which cannot with propriety be read aloud in a family." He also "purified" Edward Gibbon's *History of the Decline and Fall of the Roman Empire* and selections from the Old Testament. His name became synonymous with self-righteous expurgation, and the word *bowdlerize* has become part of the English language. Bowdler died in South Wales, Feb 24, 1825.

SPACE MILESTONE: *SKYLAB* **(US): FALLS TO EARTH.** July 11, 1979. The 82-ton spacecraft launched May 14, 1973, reentered Earth's atmosphere. Expectation was that 20–25 tons probably would survive to hit Earth, including one piece of about 5,000 pounds. This generated intense international public interest in where it would fall. The chance that some person would be hit by a piece of *Skylab* was calculated at 1 in 152. Targets were drawn and *Skylab* parties were held but *Skylab* broke up and fell to Earth in a shower of pieces over the Indian Ocean and Australia, with no known casualties.

UNITED NATIONS: WORLD POPULATION DAY. July 11. An outgrowth of the Day of Five Billion (July 11, 1987), the day seeks to focus public attention on the urgency and importance of population issues, particularly in the context of overall development plans and programs and the need to create solutions to these problems. For info: United Nations. Web: www.un.org.

★ *Birthdays* ★

Giorgio Armani, fashion designer, born Romagna, Italy, July 11, 1936.

Sela Ward, actress ("Sisters," "Once and Again"), born Meridian, MS, July 11, 1956.

July 12

"EVENING AT POPS" TV PREMIERE: ANNIVERSARY. July 12, 1970. PBS's popular concert series premiered with conductor Arthur Fiedler heading the Boston Pops Orchestra. Conductor/composer John Williams took over the post upon Fiedler's death in 1979; Keith Lockhart is the current conductor.

FULLER, BUCKMINSTER: ANNIVERSARY. July 12, 1895. Architect, inventor, engineer and philosopher, born Richard Buckminster Fuller at Milton, MA. His geodesic dome is one of the most important structural innovations of the 20th century. He died July 1, 1983, at Los Angeles, CA.

"NORTHERN EXPOSURE" TV PREMIERE: ANNIVERSARY. July 12, 1990. CBS's comedy-drama was essentially a fish-out-of-water (or rather a New Yorker out of Manhattan) series. Dr. Joel Fleischman (Rob Morrow) was forced to practice medicine in remote Cicely, Alaska, to pay off his student loans. The show's cast featured Barry Corbin as Maurice Minnefield, a former NASA astronaut; Janine Turner as bush pilot Maggie O'Connell; Elaine Miles as Joel's assistant Marilyn Whirlwind; Darren E. Burrows as Ed Chigliak, an aspiring filmmaker; John Cullum as tavern owner Holling Vincoeur; Cynthia Geary as waitress Shelly Tambo; Peg Phillips as store proprietor Ruth-Anne Miller; and John Corbett as deejay Chris Stevens. The last epsiode aired in 1995.

NORTHERN IRELAND: ORANGEMEN'S DAY. July 12. National holiday commemorates Battle of Boyne, July 1, 1690 (OS), in which the forces of King William III of England, Prince of Orange, defeated those of James II, at Boyne River in Ireland. If July 12 is a Saturday or a Sunday the holiday observance is on the following Monday.

THOREAU, HENRY DAVID: BIRTH ANNIVERSARY. July 12, 1817. American author and philosopher, born at Concord, MA. Died there May 6, 1862.

In *Walden* he wrote, "I frequently tramped eight or ten miles through the deepest snow to keep an appointment with a beechtree, or a yellow birch, or an old acquaintance among the pines."

TURNER'S FRONTIER ADDRESS: ANNIVERSARY. July 12, 1893. Historian Frederick Jackson Turner delivered his paper, "The Significance of the Frontier in American History," at a meeting of the American Historical Association at Chicago during the Columbian Exposition. Stating that the frontier was a spawning ground for many of the traits that made Americans different from Europeans, Turner saw the end of the frontier as a major break in the psychology of the nation. Turner's formalization of this idea came in part from his reading an 1890 *Extra Census Bulletin,* which said, "Up to and including 1890 the country had a frontier of settlement, but at present the unsettled area has been so broken into by isolated bodies of settlement that there can hardly be said to be a frontier line."

★ *Birthdays* ★

Lisa Nicole Carson, actress ("Ally McBeal," "ER"), born Brooklyn, NY, July 12, 1961.
Bill Cosby, comedian, actor (Emmys for "I Spy," "The Cosby Show"), born Philadelphia, PA, July 12, 1938.

July 13

FRANCE: NIGHT WATCH or LA RETRAITE AUX FLAMBEAUX. July 13. France. Celebrates eve of the Bastille's fall. On the eve of Bastille Day, there are parades and fireworks.

JAPAN: BON FESTIVAL (FEAST OF LANTERNS). July 13–15. Religious rites throughout Japan in memory of the dead, who, according to Buddhist belief, revisit Earth during this period. Lanterns are lighted for the souls. Spectacular bonfires in the shape of the character *dai* are burned on hillsides on the last day of the Bon or O-Bon Festival, bidding farewell to the spirits of the dead.

"LIVE AID" CONCERTS: ANNIVERSARY. July 13, 1985. Concerts at Philadelphia, PA, and London, England (Kennedy and Wembley stadiums), were seen by 162,000 attendees and an estimated 1.5 billion television viewers. Organized to raise funds for African famine relief; the musicians performed without a fee, and nearly $100 million was pledged toward aid to the hungry.

NORTHWEST ORDINANCE: ANNIVERSARY. July 13, 1787. The Northwest Ordinance, providing for government of the territory north of the Ohio River, became law. The ordinance guaranteed freedom of worship and the right to trial by jury, and it prohibited slavery.

WORLD CUP INAUGURATED: ANNIVERSARY. July 13, 1930. The first World Cup soccer competition was held at Montevideo, Uruguay, with 14 countries participating. The host country had the winning team.

★ *Birthdays* ★

Cameron Crowe, writer, screenwriter (*Fast Times at Ridgemont High, Jerry Maguire*; Oscar for *Almost Famous*), born Palm Springs, CA, July 13, 1957.

Harrison Ford, actor (*American Graffiti, Star Wars* films, *Indiana Jones* films), born Chicago, IL, July 13, 1942.

Patrick Stewart, actor ("Star Trek: The Next Generation," *Excalibur, LA Story*), born Mirfield, England, July 13, 1940.

July 14

FRANCE: BASTILLE DAY OR FETE NATIONAL. July 14. Public holiday commemorating the fall of the Bastille at the beginning of the French Revolution, July 14, 1789. Also celebrated or observed in many other countries.

GUTHRIE, WOODROW WILSON "WOODY": BIRTH ANNIVERSARY. July 14, 1912. American folksinger, songwriter ("This Land Is Your Land," "Union Maid," "Hard Traveling"), born at Okemah, OK. Traveled the country by freight train, singing and listening. Died Oct 3, 1967, at New York, NY. Father of Arlo Guthrie.

★ *Birthdays* ★

Gerald Rudolph Ford, 41st vice president, 38th US president, born Leslie King at Omaha, NE, July 14, 1913. The first nonelected vice president and president.

Robin Ventura, baseball player, born Santa Maria, CA, July 14, 1967.

July 15

BATTLE OF THE MARNE: ANNIVERSARY. July 15, 1918. General Erich Ludendorff launched Germany's fifth, and last, offensive to break through the Chateau-Thierry salient. This all-out effort involved three armies branching out from Reims to cross the Marne River. The Germans were successful in crossing the Marne near Chateau-Thierry before American, British and Italian divisions stopped their progress. On July 18 General Foch, commander-in-chief of the Allied troops, launched a massive counteroffensive that resulted in a German retreat that continued for four months until they sued for peace in November.

MOORE, CLEMENT CLARKE: BIRTH ANNIVERSARY. July 15, 1779. American author and teacher, best remembered for his popular verse "A Visit from Saint Nicholas" (" 'Twas the Night Before

Christmas"), which was first published anonymously and without Moore's knowledge in a newspaper, Dec 23, 1823. Moore was born at New York, NY, and died at Newport, RI, July 10, 1863.

"ONE LIFE TO LIVE" TV PREMIERE: ANNIVERSARY. July 15, 1968. Set in a fictional Pennsylvania town, this soap opera was created by Agnes Nixon to depict the class and ethnic struggles of the town's denizens. Award-winning actress Erika Slezak heads the cast as the venerable Viki Lord Riley Buchanan Carpenter, the town's matron with five alternate personalities. Among those who have appeared on "OLTL" are Tom Berenger, Judith Light, Tommy Lee Jones, Laurence Fishburne, Jameson Parker, Phylicia Rashad, Christine Ebersole, Blair Underwood, Joe Lando, Christian Slater and Yasmine Bleeth.

REMBRANDT: BIRTH ANNIVERSARY. July 15, 1606. Dutch painter and etcher, born at Leiden, Holland. One of the undisputed giants of Western art. Known for *The Night Watch* and many portraits and self-portraits, died at Amsterdam, Holland, Oct 4, 1669.

★ Birthdays ★

Alex Karras, former football player, actor ("Webster," *Babe*, *Victor/Victoria*), born Gary, IN, July 15, 1935.
Forest Whitaker, actor (*Platoon*, *The Crying Game*), director (*Waiting to Exhale*), born Longview, TX, July 15, 1961.

July 16

ATOMIC BOMB TESTED: ANNIVERSARY. July 16, 1945. In the New Mexican desert at Alamogordo Air Base, 125 miles southeast of Albuquerque, the experimental atomic bomb was set off at 5:30 AM. Dubbed "Fat Boy" by its creator, the plutonium bomb vaporized the steel scaffolding holding it as the immense fireball rose 8,000 feet in a fraction of a second—ultimately creating a mushroom cloud to a height of 41,000 feet. At ground zero the bomb emitted heat three times the temperature of the interior of the sun. All plant and animal life for a mile around ceased to exist. When informed by President Truman at Potsdam of the successful experiment, Winston Churchill responded, "It's the Second Coming in wrath!"

COMET CRASHES INTO JUPITER: ANNIVERSARY. July 16, 1994. The first fragment of the comet Shoemaker-Levy crashed into the planet Jupiter, beginning a series of spectacular collisions, each unleashing more energy than the combined effect of an explosion of all our world's nuclear arsenal. Video imagery from earthbound telescopes as well as the Hubble telescope provided vivid records of the explosions and their after-effects. In 1993 the comet had shattered into a series of about a dozen large chunks that resembled "pearls on a string" after its orbit brought it within the gravitational effects of our solar system's largest planet.

DOW-JONES TOPS 8,000: ANNIVERSARY. July 16, 1997. The Dow-Jones Index of 30 major industrial stocks topped the 8,000 mark for the first time.

ROGERS, GINGER: BIRTH ANNIVERSARY. July 16, 1911. Ginger Rogers is best remembered as Fred Astaire's dance partner in a series of romantic musicals. She appeared in 70 films during her six-decade career, winning an Oscar for her leading role in the 1940 film *Kitty Foyle*. Rogers was born at Independence, MO, and died Apr 25, 1995, at Rancho Mirage, CA.

WELLS, IDA B.: BIRTH ANNIVERSARY. July 16, 1862. African American journalist and anti-lynching crusader Ida B. Wells was born the daughter of slaves at Holly Springs, MS, and grew up as Jim Crow and lynching were becoming prevalent. Wells argued that lynchings occurred not to defend white women but because of whites' fear of economic competition from blacks. She traveled extensively, founding antilynching societies and black women's clubs. Wells's *Red Record* (1895) was one of the first accounts of lynchings in the South. She died Mar 25, 1931, at Chicago, IL.

★ *Birthdays* ★

Ruben Blades, singer (two Grammy Awards), actor (*Crossover Dreams, The Milagro Beanfield War*), born Panama City, Panama, July 16, 1948.
Michael Flatley, dancer (*Lord of the Dance*), born Chicago, IL, July 16, 1958.

July 17

CZAR NICHOLAS II AND FAMILY EXECUTED: ANNIVERSARY. July 17, 1918. Russian Czar Nicholas II, his wife Alexandra, son and heir Alexis, and daughters Anastasia, Tatiana, Olga and Marie were executed by firing squad on this date. The murder of the last of the 300-year-old Romanov dynasty occurred at Yekaterinburg, in the Ural mountains of Siberia where Nicholas had been imprisoned since his abdication in 1917. Local Soviet officials, concerned about advancing pro-monarchist forces, executed the royal family rather than have them serve as a rallying point for the White Russians. In 1992 two of nine skeletons dug up the previous summer from a pit at Yekaterinburg were identified as the remains of the czar and czarina.

DISNEYLAND OPENED: ANNIVERSARY. July 17, 1955. Disneyland, America's first theme park, opened at Anaheim, CA.

IRAQ: NATIONAL DAY. July 17. National holiday commemorating anniversary of revolution of 1968.

KANSAS CITY HOTEL DISASTER: ANNIVERSARY. July 17, 1981. Anniversary of the collapse of aerial walkways at the Hyatt Regency Hotel at Kansas City, MO. About 1,500 people were attending the popular weekly tea dance when, at about 7 PM, two concrete and steel skywalks that were suspended from the ceiling of the hotel's atrium broke loose and fell on guests in the crowded lobby, killing 114 people. In 1986 a state board revoked the licenses of two engineers convicted of gross negligence for their part in designing the hotel.

SPACE MILESTONE: *APOLLO-SOYUZ* **TEST PROJECT (US, USSR).** July 17, 1975. After three years of planning, negotiation and preparation, the first US–USSR joint space project reached fruition with the linkup in space of *Apollo 18* and *Soyuz 19.* They were linked for 47 hours (July 17–19) while joint experiments and transfer of personnel and materials back and forth between craft took place. Launch date was July 15, 1975.

"WRONG WAY" CORRIGAN DAY. July 17, 1938. Douglas Groce Corrigan, an unemployed airplane mechanic, left Brooklyn, NY's Floyd Bennett field, ostensibly headed for Los Angeles, CA, in a 1929 Curtiss Robin monoplane. He landed 28 hours later at Dublin, Ireland, after a 3,150-mile nonstop flight without radio or special navigation equipment and in violation of American and Irish flight regulations. Corrigan received a hero's welcome home; he was nicknamed "Wrong Way" Corrigan because he claimed he accidentally followed the wrong end of his compass needle. Born at Galveston, TX, Jan 22, 1907, he died at New York, NY, Dec 9, 1995.

★ *Birthdays* ★

David Hasselhoff, actor ("Knight Rider," "Baywatch"), born Baltimore, MD, July 17, 1952.
Donald Sutherland, actor (*M*A*S*H, Klute, Backdraft*), born St. John, NB, Canada, July 17, 1935.

July 18

MANDELA, NELSON: BIRTHDAY. July 18, 1918. Former South African president Nelson Rolihlahla Mandela was born the son of a Tembu tribal chieftain at Qunu, near Umtata, in the Transkei territory of South Africa. Giving up his hereditary rights, Mandela chose to become a lawyer and earned his degree at the University of South Africa. He joined the African National Congress

(ANC) in 1944, eventually becoming deputy national president in 1952. His activities in the struggle against apartheid resulted in his conviction for sabotage in 1964. During his 28 years in jail, Mandela remained a symbol of hope to South Africa's nonwhite majority, the demand for his release a rallying cry for civil rights activists. That release finally came Feb 11, 1990, as millions watched via satellite television. In 1994 Mandela was elected president of South Africa in the first all-race election there. See also: "Mandela, Nelson: Prison Release: Anniv" (Feb 11).

SPAIN: CIVIL WAR BEGINS: ANNIVERSARY. July 18, 1936. General Francisco Franco led an uprising of army troops based in North Africa against the elected government of the Spanish Republic. Spain was quickly divided into a Nationalist and a Republican zone. Franco's Nationalists drew support from Fascist Italy and Nazi Germany. On Apr 1, 1939, the Nationalists won a complete victory when they entered Madrid. Franco ruled as dictator in Spain until his death in 1975.

★ *Birthdays* ★

James Brolin, actor (Emmy for "Marcus Welby, MD"; "Hotel"), born Los Angeles, CA, July 18, 1941.
John Glenn, astronaut, first American to orbit Earth, former US senator (D, Ohio), born Cambridge, OH, July 18, 1921.
Anfernee "Penny" Hardaway, basketball player, born Memphis, TN, July 18, 1972.

July 19

DEGAS, EDGAR: BIRTH ANNIVERSARY. July 19, 1834. French Impressionist painter, especially noted for his paintings of dancers in motion, was born at Paris, France, and died there Sept 26, 1917.

FIRST WOMAN VICE PRESIDENTIAL CANDIDATE: ANNIVERSARY. July 19, 1984. Congresswoman Geraldine Ferraro was nominated to run with presidential candidate Walter Mondale on the Democratic ticket. They were defeated by the Republican ticket headed by Ronald Reagan.

WOMEN'S RIGHTS CONVENTION AT SENECA FALLS: ANNIVERSARY. July 19, 1848. A convention concerning the rights of women, called by Lucretia Mott and Elizabeth Cady Stanton, was held at Seneca Falls, NY, July 19–20, 1848. The issues discussed included voting, property rights and divorce. The convention drafted a "Declaration of Sentiments" that paraphrased the Declaration of Independence, addressing man instead of King George, and called for women's "immediate admission to all the rights and privileges which belong to them as citizens of the United States." This convention was the beginning of an organized women's rights movement in the US. The most controversial issue was Stanton's demand for women's right to vote.

★ Birthdays ★

Anthony Edwards, actor ("ER," *Fast Times at Ridgemont High, Top Gun*), born Santa Barbara, CA, July 19, 1962.

July 20

COLOMBIA: INDEPENDENCE DAY. July 20. National holiday. Commemorates the beginning of the independence movement with an uprising against Spanish officials in 1810 at Bogota. Colombia gained independence from Spain in 1819 when Simon Bolivar decisively defeated the Spanish.

RIOT ACT: ANNIVERSARY. July 20. To "read the riot act" now usually means admonishing someone, but in 18th-century England this was a more serious matter. On July 20, 1715, the Riot Act took effect. If 12 or more persons were unlawfully assembled an authority was required to read the Riot Act proclamation: "Our sovereign lord the king chargeth and commandeth all persons, being assembled, immediately to disperse themselves, and peaceably to depart to their habitations, or to their lawful business, upon the pains contained in the act made in the first year of King George, for preventing tumults and riotous assemblies." Any persons who failed to obey within one hour were to be seized, apprehended and carried before a justice of the peace.

SPACE MILESTONE: MOON DAY. July 20, 1969. Anniversary of man's first landing on moon.

Two US astronauts (Neil Alden Armstrong and Edwin Eugene Aldrin, Jr) landed lunar module *Eagle* at 4:17 PM, EDT, and remained on lunar surface 21 hours, 36 minutes and 16 seconds. The landing was made from the *Apollo XI*'s orbiting command and service module, code named *Columbia*, whose pilot, Michael Collins, remained aboard. Armstrong was first to set foot on the moon. Armstrong and Aldrin were outside the spacecraft, walking on the moon's surface, approximately 2¼ hours. The astronauts returned to Earth July 24, bringing photographs and rock samples.

SPECIAL OLYMPICS DAY. July 20. Official anniversary of the first ever International Special Olympics Competition, held in 1968 at Soldier Field, Chicago, IL. Special Olympics is an international year-round program of sports training and competition for individuals with mental retardation. More than 1 million athletes in over 160 countries train and compete in 26 Olympic-style summer and winter sports. Founded in 1968 by Eunice Kennedy Shriver, Special Olympics provides people with mental retardation continuing opportunities to develop fitness, demonstrate courage and experience joy as they participate in the sharing of gifts and friendship with other athletes, their families and the community. For info: Special Olympics. Web: www.specialolympics.org.

★ *Birthdays* ★

Diana Rigg, actress (Tony for *Medea*; "The Avengers"), born Doncaster, Yorkshire, England, July 20, 1938.

Carlos Santana, musician, born Autlan, Mexico, July 20, 1947.

July 21

BELGIUM: NATIONAL HOLIDAY. July 21. Marks accession of first Belgian king, Leopold I in 1831, after independence from Netherlands.

HEMINGWAY, ERNEST: BIRTH ANNIVERSARY. July 21, 1899. American short story writer and novelist born at Oak Park, IL. Made his name with such works as *The Sun Also Rises* (1926), *A Farewell to Arms* (1929), *For Whom the Bell Tolls* (1940) and *The Old Man and the Sea* (1952). He was awarded the Nobel Prize in 1954 and wrote little thereafter; he shot himself July 2, 1961, at Ketchum, ID, having been seriously ill for some time.

★ *Birthdays* ★

Josh Hartnett, actor (*40 Days and 40 Nights*), born San Francisco, CA, July 21, 1978.

Jon Lovitz, actor (*A League of Their Own*, "NewsRadio"), born Tarzana, CA, July 21, 1957.

Robin Williams, actor ("Mork and Mindy," *Mrs Doubtfire*, *Dead Poets Society*; Oscar for *Good Will Hunting*), born Chicago, IL, July 21, 1952.

July 22

DILLINGER, JOHN: DEATH ANNIVERSARY. July 22, 1934. Bank robber, murderer, prison escapee and the first person to receive the FBI's appellation "Public Enemy No. 1" (July 1934). After nine years in prison (1924–33), Dillinger traveled through the Midwest, leaving a path of violent crimes. Reportedly betrayed by the "Lady in Red," he was killed by FBI agents as he left Chicago's Biograph movie theater (where he had watched *Manhattan Melodrama*, starring Clark Gable and Myrna Loy), July 22, 1934. He was born at Indianapolis, IN, June 28, 1902.

SPOONER'S DAY *(WILLIAM SPOONER BIRTH ANNIVERSARY)*. July 22. A day named for the Reverend William Archibald Spooner (born at London, England, July 22, 1844, warden of New College, Oxford, 1903–24, died at Oxford, England, Aug 29, 1930), whose frequent slips of the tongue led to coinage of the term *spoonerism* to describe them. His accidental transpositions gave us "blushing crow" (for crushing blow), "tons of soil" (for sons of toil), "queer old dean" (for dear old queen), "swell foop" (for fell swoop) and "half-warmed fish" (for half-formed wish).

★ Birthdays ★

Willem Dafoe, actor (*Platoon, Mississippi Burning*), born Appleton, WI, July 22, 1955.
Danny Glover, actor ("Chiefs," *Lethal Weapon, The Color Purple*), born San Francisco, CA, July 22, 1947.
David Spade, actor ("Saturday Night Live," "Just Shoot Me," *Black Sheep*), born Birmingham, MI, July 22, 1965.
Alex Trebek, game-show host ("Concentration," "Jeopardy!"), born Sudbury, ON, Canada, July 22, 1940.

July 23

HOT ENOUGH FOR YA DAY. July 23. We are permitted today to utter the words that suffice when nothing of intelligence comes to mind. "Is it hot enough for ya?" [©2001 by WH.] For info: Wellcat Holidays. Web: www.wellcat.com.

LEO, THE LION. July 23–Aug 22. In the astronomical/astrological zodiac, which divides the sun's apparent orbit into 12 segments, the period July 23–Aug 22 is identified, traditionally, as the sun sign of Leo, the Lion. The ruling celestial body is the sun.

SPACE MILESTONE: FIRST FEMALE COMMANDER: *COLUMBIA* (US). July 23, 1999. Colonel Eileen Collins led a shuttle mission to deploy a $1.5 billion X-ray telescope, the Chandra observatory, into space. It is a sister satellite to the Hubble Space Telescope. The observatory is named after Nobel Prize winner Subrahamyar Chandrasekhar.

★ Birthdays ★

Woody Harrelson, actor (Emmy for "Cheers"; *White Men Can't Jump, Natural Born Killers*), born Midland, TX, July 23, 1961.
Anthony M. Kennedy, associate justice of the Supreme Court, born Sacramento, CA, July 23, 1936.
Eriq La Salle, actor ("ER," *Coming to America*), born Hartford, CT, July 23, 1962.

July 24

BOLIVAR, SIMON: BIRTH ANNIVERSARY. July 24, 1783. "The Liberator," born at Caracas, Venezuela. Commemorated in Venezuela and other Latin American countries. Died Dec 17, 1830, at Santa Marta, Colombia. Bolivia is named after him.

COUSINS DAY. July 24. A day to celebrate, honor and appreciate our cousins. For info: Claudia A. Evart. E-mail: siblingsday@earthlink.net.

EARHART, AMELIA: BIRTH ANNIVERSARY. July 24, 1897. American aviatrix lost on flight from New Guinea to Howland Island, in the Pacific Ocean, July 2, 1937. First woman to cross the Atlantic solo and fly solo across the Pacific from Hawaii to California. Born at Atchison, KS.

PIONEER DAY: ANNIVERSARY. July 24. Utah. State holiday. Commemorates the day in 1847 when Brigham Young and his followers entered the Salt Lake Valley.

★ *Birthdays* ★

Barry Bonds, baseball player, seven-time All-Star, three-time National League MVP, born Riverside, CA, July 24, 1964.
Jennifer Lopez, singer, actress (*Selena, Blood and Wine*), born the Bronx, NY, July 24, 1970.
Karl Malone, basketball player, born Summerfield, LA, July 24, 1963.

July 25

SPAIN: SAINT JAMES DAY. July 25. Holy day of the patron saint of Spain. When this day falls on a Sunday it is a holy year and pilgrims make the pilgrimage to Santiago de Compostela, the site of the saint's tomb.

TEST-TUBE BABY: BIRTHDAY. July 25, 1978. Anniversary of the birth of Louise Brown at Oldham, England. First documented birth of a baby conceived outside the body of a woman. Parents: Gilbert John and Lesley Brown, of Bristol, England. Physicians: Patrick Christopher Steptoe and Robert Geoffrey Edwards.

★ *Birthdays* ★

Illeana Douglas, actress (*Message in a Bottle, Can't Stop Dancing*), born Boston, MA, July 25, 1965.
Matt LeBlanc, actor ("Friends"), born Newton, MA, July 25, 1967.

July 26

AMERICANS WITH DISABILITIES ACT SIGNED: ANNIVERSARY. July 26, 1990. President George H.W. Bush signed the Americans with Disabilities Act, which went into effect two years later. It required that public facilities be made accessible to the disabled.

ARMED FORCES UNIFIED: ANNIVERSARY. July 26, 1947. President Truman signed legislation unifying the two branches of the armed forces into the Department of Defense. The branches merged were the War Department (Army) and the Navy. The Air Force was separated from the Army at the same time and made an independent force. Truman nominated James Forrestal to be the first secretary of defense. The legislation also provided for the National Security Council, the Central Intelligence Agency and the Joint Chiefs of Staff.

CUBA: NATIONAL DAY: ANNIVERSARY OF REVOLUTION. July 26. Anniversary of 1953 beginning of Fidel Castro's revolutionary "26th of July Movement."

LIBERIA: INDEPENDENCE DAY. July 26. National holiday. Became republic in 1847, under aegis of the US societies for repatriating former slaves in Africa.

NEW YORK RATIFICATION DAY. July 26, 1788. Eleventh state to ratify Constitution in 1788.

SHAW, GEORGE BERNARD: BIRTH ANNIVERSARY. July 26, 1856. Irish playwright, essayist, vegetarian, socialist, antivivisectionist and, he said, ". . . one of the hundred best playwrights in the world." Born at Dublin, Ireland. Died at Ayot St. Lawrence, England, Nov 2, 1950.

US ARMY FIRST DESEGREGATION: ANNIVERSARY. July 26, 1944. During World War II the US Army ordered desegregation of its training camp facilities. Later the same year black platoons were assigned to white companies in a tentative step toward integration of the battlefield. However, it was not until after the war—July 26, 1948—that President Harry Truman signed an order officially integrating the armed forces.

★ Birthdays ★

Kate Beckinsale, actress (*Cold Comfort Farm, Pearl Harbor*), born in England, July 26, 1973.
Sandra Bullock, actress (*Speed, While You Were Sleeping*), born Arlington, VA, July 26, 1964.
Mick Jagger, musician, lead singer (Rolling Stones), born Dartford, England, July 26, 1943.
Kevin Spacey, actor (Oscar for *American Beauty; The Usual Suspects, Working Girl*; stage: *Lost in Yonkers*), born South Orange, NJ, July 26, 1959.

July 27

INSULIN FIRST ISOLATED: ANNIVERSARY. July 27, 1921. Dr. Frederick Banting and his assistant at the University of Toronto Medical School, Charles Best, gave insulin to a dog whose pancreas had been removed. In 1922 insulin was first administered to a diabetic, a 14-year-old boy.

KOREAN WAR ARMISTICE: ANNIVERSARY. July 27, 1953. Ending the war that had lasted three years and 32 days, an armistice agreement was signed at Panmunjom, Korea (July 26, US time), by US and North Korean delegates. Both sides claimed victory at conclusion of two years, 17 days of truce negotiations. The president of the US proclaims this annually as National Korean War Veterans Day.

US DEPARTMENT OF STATE FOUNDED: ANNIVERSARY. July 27, 1789. The first presidential cabinet department, called the Department of Foreign Affairs, was established by the Congress. Later the name was changed to Department of State.

★ Birthdays ★

Peggy Fleming, Olympic figure skater, born San Jose, CA, July 27, 1948.

Alex Rodriguez, baseball player, born New York, NY, July 27, 1975.

July 28

ONASSIS, JACQUELINE LEE BOUVIER KENNEDY: BIRTH ANNIVERSARY. July 28, 1929. Editor, widow of John Fitzgerald Kennedy (35th president of the US), born at Southampton, NY. Later married (Oct 20, 1968) Greek shipping magnate Aristotle Socrates Onassis, who died Mar 15, 1975. The widely admired and respected former First Lady died May 19, 1994, at New York City.

PERU: INDEPENDENCE DAY. July 28. San Martin declared independence from Spain on this day in 1821. After the final defeat of Spanish troops by Simon Bolivar in 1824, Spanish rule ended.

SINGING TELEGRAM: ANNIVERSARY. July 28, 1933. Anniversary of the first singing telegram, said to have been delivered to singer Rudy Vallee on his 32nd birthday. Early singing telegrams often were delivered in person by uniformed messengers on bicycle. Later they were usually sung over the telephone.

WORLD WAR I BEGINS: ANNIVERSARY. July 28, 1914. Archduke Francis Ferdinand of Austria-Hungary and his wife were assassinated at Sarajevo, Bosnia, by a Serbian nationalist June 28, 1914, touching off the conflict that became World War I. Austria-Hungary declared war on Serbia July 28, the formal beginning of the war.

Within weeks, Germany entered the war on the side of Austria-Hungary and Russia, France and Great Britain on the side of Serbia.

★ Birthdays ★

Bill Bradley, Hall of Fame basketball player, former US senator, born Crystal City, MO, July 28, 1943.

Jim Davis, cartoonist ("Garfield"), born Marion, IN, July 28, 1945.

July 29

INDIANAPOLIS SUNK: ANNIVERSARY. July 29, 1945. After delivering the atomic bomb to Tinian Island, the American cruiser *Indianapolis* was headed for Okinawa to train for the invasion of Japan when it was torpedoed by a Japanese submarine. Of 1,196 crew members, more than 350 were immediately killed in the explosion or went down with the ship. There were no rescue ships nearby, and survivors endured the next 84 hours in ocean waters. By the time they were spotted by air on Aug 2, only 318 sailors remained alive, the others either having drowned or been eaten by sharks. This is the US Navy's worst loss at sea.

NASA ESTABLISHED: ANNIVERSARY. July 29, 1958. President Eisenhower signed a bill creating the National Aeronautics and Space Administration to direct US space policy.

★ Birthdays ★

Ken Burns, documentary filmmaker ("Civil War," "Jazz" series), born New York, NY, July 29, 1953.

Peter Jennings, journalist (anchorman for "ABC Evening News"), born Toronto, ON, Canada, July 29, 1938.

July 30

FORD, HENRY: BIRTH ANNIVERSARY. July 30, 1863. Industrialist Henry Ford, whose assembly-line method of automobile production revolutionized the industry, was born at Wayne County, MI, on the family farm. His Model T made up half of the world's output of cars during its years of production. Ford built racing cars until in 1903 he and his partners formed the Ford Motor Company. In 1908 the company presented the Model T, which was produced until 1927, and in 1913 Ford introduced the assembly line and mass production. This innovation reduced the time it took to build each car from 12½ hours to only 1½. This enabled Ford to sell cars for $500, making automobile ownership a possibility for an unprecedented percentage of the population. He is also remembered for introducing a $5-a-day wage for automotive workers and for his statement: "History is bunk." Died Apr 7, 1947, at age 83 at Dearborn, MI, where his manufacturing complex was located.

HOFFA, JAMES: DISAPPEARANCE ANNIVERSARY. July 30, 1975. Former Teamsters Union leader, 62-year-old James Riddle Hoffa was last seen on this date outside a restaurant in Bloomfield Township, near Detroit, MI. His 13-year federal prison sentence had been commuted by former president Richard M. Nixon in 1971. On Dec 8, 1982, seven years and 131 days after his disappearance, an Oakland County judge declared Hoffa officially dead as of July 30, 1982.

PAPERBACK BOOKS INTRODUCED: ANNIVERSARY. July 30, 1935. Although books bound in soft covers were first introduced in 1841 at Leipzig, Germany, by Christian Bernhard Tauchnitz, the modern paperback revolution dates to the publication of the first Penguin paperback by Sir Allen Lane at London in 1935. Penguin No. 1 was *Ariel*, a life of Shelley by André Maurois.

STENGEL, CHARLES DILLON (CASEY): BIRTH ANNIVERSARY. July 30, 1890. Baseball Hall of Fame outfielder and manager born at Kansas City, MO. His success as manager of the New York Yankees (ten pennants and seven World Series titles in 12 years) made him one of the game's enduring stars. Inducted into the Hall of Fame in 1966. Died at Glendale, CA, Sept 29, 1975.

★ *Birthdays* ★

Laurence Fishburne, actor (*Boyz N the Hood, What's Love Got to Do with It, Higher Learning*; stage: *Two Trains Running* [Tony Award]), born Augusta, GA, July 30, 1961.

Lisa Kudrow, actress ("Friends," *Romy and Michele's High School Reunion*), born Encino, CA, July 30, 1963.

Arnold Schwarzenegger, bodybuilder, actor (*The Terminator, Twins, True Lies*), born Graz, Austria, July 30, 1947.

Hilary Swank, actress (Oscar for *Boys Don't Cry*), born Lincoln, NE, July 30, 1974.

July 31

KENNEDY INTERNATIONAL AIRPORT DEDICATION: ANNIVERSARY. July 31, 1948. New York's International Airport at Idlewild Field was dedicated by President Harry S. Truman. It was later renamed John F. Kennedy International Airport.

US PATENT OFFICE OPENS: ANNIVERSARY. July 31, 1790. The first US Patent Office opened its doors and the first US patent was issued to Samuel Hopkins of Vermont for a new method of making pearlash and potash. The patent was signed by George Washington and Thomas Jefferson.

★ *Birthdays* ★

J.K. Rowling, author (the Harry Potter series), born Joanne Rowling, Bristol, England, July 31, 1965.

Wesley Snipes, actor (*Jungle Fever, White Men Can't Jump, Rising Sun*), born Orlando, FL, July 31, 1962.

August

August 1

BENIN: INDEPENDENCE DAY. Aug 1. Public holiday. Commemorates independence from France in 1960. Benin at that time was known as Dahomey.

CATARACT AWARENESS MONTH. Aug 1–31. Cataracts are a common cause of poor vision, particularly for the elderly, but they are treatable. More than 1.4 million people have their vision restored with cataract surgery each year in the US. During the month of August, the American Academy of Ophthalmology, the Eye MD Association, makes a special effort to increase the public's understanding of the causes of cataracts and ways to keep your vision clear. For info: American Academy of Ophthalmology. Web: www.eyenet.org.

CHILDREN'S VISION AND LEARNING MONTH. Aug 1–31. A monthlong campaign encouraging parents to have their children's vision examined by an eye-care professional prior to the start of the new school year. For info: American Foundation for Vision Awareness. Web: www.afva.org.

COLORADO: ADMISSION DAY: ANNIVERSARY. Aug 1, 1876. Colorado admitted to the Union as the 38th state. The first Monday in August is celebrated as Colorado Day.

***DIARY OF ANNE FRANK*: THE LAST ENTRY: ANNIVERSARY.** Aug 1, 1944. To escape deportation to concentration camps, the Jewish family of Otto Frank hid for two years in the warehouse of his business at Amsterdam. Thirteen-year-old Anne Frank, who kept a journal during the time of their hiding, penned her last entry in the diary Aug 1, 1944: "[I] keep on trying to find a way of becoming what I would like to be, and what I could be, if . . . there weren't any other people living in the world." Three days later (Aug 4, 1944) Grüne Polizei raided the "Secret Annex" where the Frank family was hidden. Anne and her sister were sent to Bergen-Belsen concentration camp where Anne died at age 15, two months before the liberation of Holland.

Young Anne's diary, later found in the family's hiding place, has been translated into 30 languages and has become a symbol of the indomitable strength of the human spirit.

FIRST US CENSUS: ANNIVERSARY. Aug 1, 1790. The first census revealed that there were 3,939,326 citizens in the 16 states and the Ohio Territory. The US has taken a census every ten years since 1790. The next one will be in 2010.

GARCIA, JERRY: BIRTH ANNIVERSARY. Aug 1, 1942. Jerome John Garcia was born at San Francisco, CA. Country, bluegrass and folk musician, a guitar player of remarkable ability, Garcia was the leading force behind the legendary Grateful Dead, the band that sustained a veritable industry for its legion of followers. He died Aug 9, 1995, at Forest Knolls, CA, ending a musical career that spanned more than three decades.

MELVILLE, HERMAN: BIRTH ANNIVERSARY. Aug 1, 1819. American author, best known for his novel *Moby-Dick*, born at New York, NY, and died there Sept 28, 1891.

MTV PREMIERE: ANNIVERSARY. Aug 1, 1981. The all-music-video channel debuted on this date. VH1, another music channel owned by MTV

Networks that is aimed at older pop music fans, premiered in 1985.

NATIONAL INVENTORS' MONTH. Aug 1–31. To educate the American public about the value of creativity and inventiveness and the importance of inventions and inventors to the quality of our lives. This will be accomplished by specially designed displays for libraries, an interactive website and media stories about living inventors in most of the top national, local and trade publications. Sponsored by the United Inventors Association of the USA (UIA-USA), the Academy of Applied Science and *Inventors' Digest*. For info: Inventors' Digest. Web: www.inventorsdigest.com.

SWITZERLAND: CONFEDERATION DAY. Aug 1. National holiday. Anniversary of the founding of the Swiss Confederation. Commemorates a pact made in 1291. Observed since 600th anniversary of Swiss Confederation was celebrated in 1891.

WORLD WIDE WEB: ANNIVERSARY. Aug 1, 1990. The creation of what would become the World Wide Web was suggested this month in 1990 by Tim Berners-Lee and Robert Cailliau at CERN, the European Laboratory for Particle Physics at Switzerland. By October, they had designed a prototype Web browser. They also introduced HTML (Hypertext Markup Language) and the URL (Universal Resource Locator). Mosaic, the first graphical Web browser, was designed by Marc Andreessen and released in 1993. By early 1993, there were 50 Web servers worldwide.

★ *Birthdays* ★

Yves Saint Laurent, former fashion designer, born Oran, Algeria, Aug 1, 1936.

August 2

BALDWIN, JAMES: BIRTH ANNIVERSARY. Aug 2, 1924. Black American author noted for descriptions of black life in the US. Born at New York, NY. His best-known work, *Go Tell It on the Mountain*, was published in 1953. Died at Saint Paul-de-Vence, France, Nov 30, 1987.

DECLARATION OF INDEPENDENCE: OFFICIAL SIGNING: ANNIVERSARY. Aug 2, 1776. Contrary to widespread misconceptions, the 56 signers of the Declaration did not sign it on July 4, 1776. John Hancock and Charles Thomson signed only draft copies that day, the official day the Declaration was adopted by Congress. The signing of the official Declaration occurred Aug 2, 1776, when 50 men probably took part. Later that year, 5 more apparently signed separately and one added his name in a subsequent year. See also: "Declaration of Independence Approval: Anniv" (July 4).

MACEDONIA: NATIONAL DAY. Aug 2. Known as St. Elias Day or *Illenden*, the most sacred, honored and celebrated day of the Macedonian people.

Commemorates the nationalist uprising against the Ottoman Empire in 1903.

US VIRGIN ISLANDS NATIONAL PARK ESTABLISHED: ANNIVERSARY. Aug 2, 1956. The US Virgin Islands, including areas on St. John and St. Thomas, were established as a national park and preserve. On Oct 5, 1962, the Virgin Islands National Park was enlarged to include offshore areas, including coral reefs, shorelines and sea grass beds. For info: National Parks Service. Web: www.nps.gov/viis.

★ *Birthdays* ★

Edward Furlong, actor (*Before and After, Terminator 2*), born Glendale, CA, Aug 2, 1977.
Peter O'Toole, actor (*Lawrence of Arabia, Becket*), born Connemara, Ireland, Aug 2, 1933.

August 3

COLUMBUS SAILS FOR THE NEW WORLD: ANNIVERSARY. Aug 3, 1492. Christopher Columbus, "Admiral of the Ocean Sea," set sail half an hour before sunrise from Palos, Spain, Aug 3, 1492. With three ships, *Niña*, *Pinta* and *Santa Maria*, and a crew of 90, he sailed "for Cathay" but found instead a New World of the Americas, first landing at Guanahani (San Salvador Island in the Bahamas) Oct 12. See also: "Columbus Day (Traditional)" (Oct 12).

NIGER: INDEPENDENCE DAY. Aug 3. Niger gained its independence from France on this day in 1960.

PYLE, ERNEST TAYLOR: BIRTH ANNIVERSARY. Aug 3, 1900. Ernie Pyle was born at Dana, IN, and began his career in journalism in 1923. After serving as managing editor of the Washington *Daily News*, he returned to his first journalistic love of working as a roving reporter in 1935. His column was syndicated by nearly 200 newspapers and often focused on figures behind the news. His reports of the bombing of London in 1940 and subsequent reports from Africa, Sicily, Italy and France earned him a Pulitzer Prize in 1944. He was killed by machine-gun fire at the Pacific island of Ie Shima, Apr 18, 1945.

SCOPES, JOHN T.: BIRTH ANNIVERSARY. Aug 3, 1900. Central figure in a cause célèbre (the "Scopes Trial" or the "Monkey Trial"), John Thomas Scopes was born at Paducah, KY. An obscure 24-year-old schoolteacher at the Dayton, TN, high school in 1925, he became the focus of world attention. Scopes never uttered a word at his trial, which was a contest between two of America's best-known lawyers, William Jennings Bryan and Clarence Darrow. The trial, July 10–21, 1925, resulted in Scopes's conviction. He was fined $100 "for teaching evolution" in Tennessee. The verdict was upset on a technicality and the statute he was accused of breaching was repealed in 1967. Scopes died at Shreveport, LA, Oct 21, 1970.

★ *Birthdays* ★

Tony Bennett, singer ("I Left My Heart in San Francisco"), born Anthony Dominick Benedetto, New York, NY, Aug 3, 1926.
Martin Sheen, actor (*Apocalypse Now*, "The West Wing"), born Ramon Estevez, Dayton, OH, Aug 3, 1940.
Martha Stewart, lifestyle consultant, TV personality, writer, born Nutley, NJ, Aug 3, 1941.

August 4

ARMSTRONG, LOUIS: BIRTH ANNIVERSARY. Aug 4, 1900 (some sources say 1901). Jazz musician extraordinaire born at New Orleans, LA. Died at New York, NY, July 6, 1971. Asked to define jazz, Armstrong reportedly replied, "Man, if you gotta ask, you'll never know." The trumpet player was also known as Satchmo. He appeared in many films. Popular singles included "What a Wonderful World" and "Hello, Dolly" (with Barbra Streisand).

CIVIL RIGHTS WORKERS FOUND SLAIN: ANNIVERSARY. Aug 4, 1964. After disappearing on June 21, three civil rights workers were found murdered and buried in an earthen dam outside Philadelphia, MS. The three young men were workers on the Mississippi Summer Project organized by the Student Nonviolent Coordinating Committee (SNCC) to increase black voter registration. Prior to their disappearance, James Chaney, Andrew Goodman and Michael Schwerner were detained by Neshoba County police on charges of speeding. When their car was found, burned, on June 23, President Johnson ordered an FBI search for the men.

★ Birthdays ★

Richard Belzer, comedian, actor (*Mad Dog and Glory*, "Homicide: Life on the Street"), born Bridgeport, CT, Aug 4, 1944.

Billy Bob Thornton, actor (*The Man Who Wasn't There, Monster's Ball*), born Hot Springs, AR, Aug 4, 1955.

August 5

"AMERICAN BANDSTAND" TV PREMIERE: ANNIVERSARY. Aug 5, 1957. "American Bandstand" and Dick Clark are synonyomous; he hosted the show for more than 30 years. "AB" started out as a local show at Philadelphia in 1952. Clark, then a disc jockey, took over as host at the age of 26. The format was simple: teens dancing, performers doing their latest hits, Clark introducing songs and listing the top ten songs each week. This hour-long show was not only TV's longest-running musical series but also the first one devoted exclusively to rock and roll. The show was canceled six months after Clark turned over the hosting duties to David Hirsch in 1989.

WALLENBERG, RAOUL: BIRTH ANNIVERSARY. Aug 5, 1912. Swedish architect Raoul Gustaf Wallenberg was born at Stockholm, Sweden. He was the second person in history (Winston Churchill was the first) to be voted honorary American citizenship (US House of Representatives 396–2, Sept 22, 1981). He is credited with saving 100,000 Jews from almost certain death at the hands of the Nazis during WWII. Wallenberg was arrested by Soviet troops at Budapest, Hungary, Jan 17, 1945, and, according to the official Soviet press agency Tass, died in prison at Moscow, July 17, 1947.

★ Birthdays ★

Neil Alden Armstrong, former astronaut (first man to walk on the moon), born Wapakoneta, OH, Aug 5, 1930.

Patrick Aloysius Ewing, basketball player, born Kingston, Jamaica, Aug 5, 1962.

August 6

ATOMIC BOMB DROPPED ON HIROSHIMA: ANNIVERSARY. Aug 6, 1945. At 8:15 AM, local time, an American B-29 bomber, the *Enola Gay*, dropped an atomic bomb named "Little Boy" over the center of the city of Hiroshima, Japan. The bomb exploded about 1,800 feet above the ground, killing more than 105,000 civilians and destroying the city. It is estimated that another 100,000 persons were injured and died subsequently as a direct result of the bomb and the radiation it produced. This was the first time in history that such a devastating weapon had been used by any nation.

BOLIVIA: INDEPENDENCE DAY. Aug 6. National holiday. Gained freedom from Spain in 1825. Named after Simon Bolivar.

ELECTROCUTION FIRST USED TO CARRY OUT DEATH PENALTY: ANNIVERSARY. Aug 6, 1890. At Auburn Prison, Auburn, NY, William Kemmler of Buffalo, NY, became the first man to be executed by electrocution. He had been convicted of the hatchet murder of his common-law wife, Matilde Ziegler, on Mar 28, 1889. This first attempt at using electrocution to carry out the death penalty was a botched affair. As reported by George Westinghouse, Jr, "It has been a brutal affair. They could have done better with an axe."

FLEMING, ALEXANDER: BIRTH ANNIVERSARY. Aug 6, 1881. Sir Alexander Fleming, Scottish bacteriologist, discoverer of penicillin and 1954 Nobel Prize recipient, was born at Lochfield, Scotland. He died at London, England, Mar 11, 1955.

JAMAICA: INDEPENDENCE DAY. Aug 6. National holiday observing achievement of Jamaican independence from Britain Aug 6, 1962. Commemorated on the first Monday in August.

VOTING RIGHTS ACT OF 1965 SIGNED: ANNIVERSARY. Aug 6, 1965. Signed into law by President Lyndon Johnson, the Voting Rights Act of 1965 was designed to thwart attempts to discriminate against minorities at the polls. The act suspended literacy and other disqualifying tests, authorized appointment of federal voting examiners and provided for judicial relief on the federal level to bar discriminatory poll taxes. Congress voted to extend the Act in 1975, 1984 and 1991.

★ Birthdays ★

David Robinson, basketball player, born Key West, FL, Aug 6, 1965.

August 7

CÔTE D'IVOIRE: NATIONAL DAY. Aug 7. Commemorates the independence of the Ivory Coast from France in 1960.

DESERT SHIELD: ANNIVERSARY. Aug 7, 1990. Five days after the Iraqi invasion of Kuwait, US President George Bush ordered the military buildup that would become known as Desert Shield to prevent further Iraqi advances.

FIRST PICTURE OF EARTH FROM SPACE: ANNIVERSARY. Aug 7, 1959. US satellite *Explorer VI* transmitted the first picture of Earth from space. For the first time we had a likeness of our planet based on more than projections and conjectures.

PARTICULARLY PREPOSTEROUS PACKAGING DAY. Aug 7. Buy anything lately? Did you succeed in getting the durn thing open? What do older people do when even mainstream society can't open a simple bottle of aspirin, let alone a milk carton? [©2001 by WH.] For info: Wellcat Holidays. Web: www.wellcat.com.

★ Birthdays ★

David Duchovny, actor ("The X-Files"), born New York, NY, Aug 7, 1960.
Garrison Keillor, humorist, producer (host "The Prairie Home Companion"), writer (*Lake Wobegon Days*), born Anoka, MN, Aug 7, 1942.

Charlize Theron, actress (*The Cider House Rules, The Legend of Bagger Vance*), born Benoni, South Africa, Aug 7, 1975.

August 8

BONZA BOTTLER DAY™. Aug 8. To celebrate when the number of the day is the same as the number of the month. Bonza Bottler Day™ is an excuse to have a party at least once a month. For info: Gail M. Berger. E-mail: gberger5@aol.com.

HENSON, MATTHEW A.: BIRTH ANNIVERSARY. Aug 8, 1866. American black explorer, born at Charles County, MD. He accompanied Robert E. Peary on his seven Arctic expeditions. During the successful 1908–09 expedition to the North Pole, Henson and two of the four Eskimo guides reached their destination Apr 6, 1909. Peary arrived minutes later and verified the location. Henson's account of the expedition, *A Negro Explorer at the North Pole*, was published in 1912. In addition to the Congressional medal awarded all members of the North Pole expedition, Henson received the Gold Medal of the Geographical Society of Chicago and, at 81, was made an honorary member of the Explorers Club at New York, NY. Died Mar 9, 1955, at New York, NY.

SNEAK SOME ZUCCHINI ONTO YOUR NEIGHBORS' PORCH NIGHT. Aug 8. Due to overzealous planting of zucchini, citizens are asked to drop off baskets of the squash on neighbors' doorsteps. [©2001 by WH.] For info: Wellcat Holidays. Web: www.wellcat.com.

★ *Birthdays* ★

Keith Carradine, actor (*Nashville, Will Rogers Follies*), singer, born San Mateo, CA, Aug 8, 1950.

Dustin Hoffman, actor (Oscars for *Rain Man* and *Kramer vs. Kramer; The Graduate, Midnight Cowboy, Outbreak*), born Los Angeles, CA, Aug 8, 1937.

August 9

ATOMIC BOMB DROPPED ON NAGASAKI: ANNIVERSARY. Aug 9, 1945. Three days after the atomic bombing of Hiroshima, an American B-29 bomber named *Bock's Car* left its base on Tinian Island carrying a plutonium bomb nicknamed "Fat Man." Its target was the Japanese city of Kokura, but because of clouds and poor visibility the bomber headed for a secondary target, Nagasaki, where at 11:02 AM, local time, it dropped the bomb, killing an estimated 70,000 persons and destroying about half the city. Memorial services are held annually at Nagasaki and also at Kokura, where those who were spared because of the bad weather also grieve for those at Nagasaki who suffered in their stead.

NIXON RESIGNS: ANNIVERSARY. Aug 9, 1974. The resignation from the presidency of the US by Richard Milhous Nixon, which had been announced in a speech to the American people the night before, became effective at noon. Nixon, under threat of impeachment as a result of the Watergate scandal, became the first US president to resign. Vice President Gerald Ford became president. This was the first time the new constitutional provisions for presidential succession took effect.

PERSEID METEOR SHOWERS. Aug 9–13. Among the best-known and most spectacular meteor showers are the Perseids, peaking about Aug 10–12. As many as 50–100 may be seen in a single night. Wish upon a "falling star"!

SINGAPORE: NATIONAL DAY. Aug 9, 1965. Most festivals in Singapore are Chinese, Indian or Malay, but celebration of national day is shared by all to commemorate the withdrawal of Singapore from Malaysia and its becoming an independent state in 1965. Music, parades, dancing.

★ *Birthdays* ★

Gillian Anderson, actress ("The X-Files"), born Chicago, IL, Aug 9, 1968.

Melanie Griffith, actress (*Working Girl, Something Wild, Milk Money*), born New York, NY, Aug 9, 1957.

Whitney Houston, singer ("And I Will Always Love You"), actress (*Waiting to Exhale*), born Newark, NJ, Aug 9, 1963.

August 10

"CANDID CAMERA" TV PREMIERE: ANNIVERSARY. Aug 10, 1948. This show—which appeared at various times on the big three networks and in syndication—was created and hosted by Allen Funt. The show's modus operandi was to catch people unawares on camera—either as part of a practical joke or just being themselves. It spawned numerous imitators such as "Totally Hidden Video," "People Do the Craziest Things" and "America's Funniest Home Videos."

ECUADOR: INDEPENDENCE DAY. Aug 10. National holiday. Celebrates declaration of independence in 1809. Freedom from Spain was attained May 24, 1822.

HOOVER, HERBERT CLARK: BIRTH ANNIVERSARY. Aug 10, 1874. The 31st president of the US (1929–33) was born at West Branch, IA. Hoover was the first president born west of the Mississippi River and the first to have a telephone on his desk (installed Mar 27, 1929). "Older men declare war. But it is youth that must fight and die," he said at Chicago, IL, at the Republican National Convention, June 27,

1944. Hoover died at New York, NY, Oct 20, 1964. The Sunday nearest Aug 10 is observed in Iowa as Herbert Hoover Day.

MISSOURI: ADMISSION DAY: ANNIVERSARY. Aug 10. Became 24th state in 1821.

★ Birthdays ★

Antonio Banderas, actor (*Too Much, Four Rooms*), born Malaga, Spain, Aug 10, 1960.

Angie Harmon, actress ("Law & Order," "Baywatch Nights"), born Dallas, TX, Aug 10, 1972.

August 11

CHAD: INDEPENDENCE DAY. Aug 11. National holiday. Commemorates independence from France in 1960.

HALEY, ALEX PALMER: BIRTH ANNIVERSARY. Aug 11, 1921. Born at Ithaca, NY, Alex Palmer Haley was raised by his grandmother at Henning, TN. In 1939 he entered the US Coast Guard and served as a cook, but eventually he became a writer and college professor. His interview with Malcolm X for *Playboy* led to his first book, *The Autobiography of Malcolm X*, which sold 6 million copies and was translated into eight languages. *Roots*, his Pulitzer Prize–winning novel published in 1976, sold millions, was translated into 37 languages and was made into an eight-part TV miniseries in 1977. The story generated an enormous interest in family ancestry. Haley died at Seattle, WA, Feb 13, 1992.

PRESIDENTIAL JOKE DAY: ANNIVERSARY. Aug 11, 1984. Anniversary of President Ronald Reagan's voice-test joke. In preparation for a radio broadcast, during a thought-to-be-off-the-record voice-level test, instead of counting "one, two, three . . ." the president said: "My fellow Americans, I am pleased to tell you I just signed legislation which outlaws Russia forever. The bombing begins in five minutes." The statement was picked up by live television cameras and was heard by millions worldwide. The incident provoked national and international reactions, including a news network proposal of new ground rules concerning the use of "off-the-record" remarks.

★ *Birthdays* ★

Hulk Hogan, wrestler, actor, born Terry Gene Bollea, Augusta, GA, Aug 11, 1953.

August 12

De MILLE, CECIL B.: BIRTH ANNIVERSARY. Aug 12, 1881. Film pioneer, born at Ashfield, MA. Cecil Blount De Mille was a film showman extraordinaire known for lavish screen spectacles. He produced more than 70 major films, which were noted more for their large scale than for their subtle artistry. He produced one of the earliest four-reel films, *The Squaw Man*, in 1913, which boasted the first use of indoor lighting on an actor and was the first film to publicize the names of its stars. His other innovations included the sneak preview and the idea of producing different versions of a popular film. His films include *King of Kings, Cleopatra* and *The Ten Commandments*, which was first made in 1923 and followed by a new version in 1956. De Mille was awarded an Oscar for *The Greatest Show on Earth* in 1953. He died Jan 21, 1959, at Hollywood, CA.

IBM PERSONAL COMPUTER INTRODUCED: ANNIVERSARY. Aug 12, 1981. IBM's first personal computer was released. The computer cost the equivalent of $3,000 in today's currency. Although IBM was one of the pioneers in making mainframe and other large computers, this was the company's first foray into the desktop computer market. Eventually, more IBM-compatible computers were manufactured by IBM's competitors than by IBM itself.

SEWING MACHINE INVENTED: ANNIVERSARY. Aug 12, 1851. Isaac Singer developed the sewing machine for use in homes.

UNITED NATIONS: INTERNATIONAL YOUTH DAY. Aug 12. For info: United Nations. Web: www.un.org.

★ *Birthdays* ★

George Hamilton, actor (*Love at First Bite*, *Act One*, "The Survivors"), born Memphis, TN, Aug 12, 1939.

Pete Sampras, tennis player, born Washington, DC, Aug 12, 1971.

August 13

BERLIN WALL ERECTED: ANNIVERSARY. Aug 13, 1961. Early in the morning, the East German government closed the border between east and west sectors of Berlin with barbed wire fence to discourage further population movement to the west. Telephone and postal services were interrupted, and, later in the week, a concrete wall was built to strengthen the barrier between official crossing points. The dismantling of the wall began Nov 9, 1989. See also: "Berlin Wall Opened: Anniv" (Nov 9).

CENTRAL AFRICAN REPUBLIC: INDEPENDENCE DAY. Aug 13. Commemorates proclamation of independence from France in 1960.

OAKLEY, ANNIE: BIRTH ANNIVERSARY. Aug 13, 1860. Annie Oakley was born at Darke County, OH. She developed an eye as a markswoman as a child, becoming so proficient that she was able to pay off the mortgage on her family farm by selling the game she killed. A few years after defeating vaudeville marksman Frank Butler in a shooting match, she married him and they toured as a team until joining Buffalo Bill's Wild West Show in 1885. She was one of the star attractions for 17 years. She died Nov 3, 1926, at Greenville, OH.

SPACE MILESTONE: *HELIOS* SOLAR WING. Aug 13, 2001. The solar-powered plane *Helios* broke the altitude records for propeller-driven aircraft and nonrocket planes, soaring as high as 96,500 feet. The plane was launched this day on the Hawaiian island of Kauai. The plane has a wingspan longer than a Boeing 747 and uses solar-powered motors to power 14 propellers, flying at speeds as high as 170 MPH. NASA plans to develop similar craft for unmanned flights on Mars.

★ *Birthdays* ★

Danny Bonaduce, radio personality, actor ("The Partridge Family"), born Broomall, PA, Aug 13, 1959.

August 14

PAKISTAN: INDEPENDENCE DAY. Aug 14, 1947. Gained independence from Britain (as part of India) in 1947.

SOCIAL SECURITY ACT: ANNIVERSARY. Aug 14, 1935. President Franklin D. Roosevelt signed the Social Security Act, which contained provisions for the establishment of a Social Security Board to administer federal old-age and survivors' insurance in the US. By signing the bill into law, Roosevelt was fulfilling a 1932 campaign promise.

V-J DAY (ANNOUNCEMENT). Aug 14, 1945. Anniversary of President Truman's announcement that Japan had surrendered to the Allies, setting off celebrations across the nation. Official ratification of surrender occurred aboard the USS *Missouri* at Tokyo Bay, Sept 2 (Far Eastern time).

★ Birthdays ★

Halle Berry, actress (Oscar for *Monster's Ball*), born Cleveland, OH, Aug 14, 1968.
Marcia Gay Harden, actress (Oscar for *Pollock; Space Cowboys*), born La Jolla, CA, Aug 14, 1959.
Earvin "Magic" Johnson, Jr, former basketball player, born Lansing, MI, Aug 14, 1959.
Steve Martin, comedian, actor ("Saturday Night Live," *LA Story, Roxanne, Parenthood*), born Waco, TX, Aug 14, 1945.

August 15

ASSUMPTION OF THE VIRGIN MARY. Aug 15. Greek and Roman Catholic churches celebrate Mary's ascent to heaven. In Orthodox churches, the holiday is called the Dormition of the Theotokos and commemorated on Aug 15 or 28. A holiday in many Christian countries.

BONAPARTE, NAPOLEON: BIRTH ANNIVERSARY. Aug 15, 1769. Anniversary of birth of French emperor Napoleon Bonaparte on the island of Corsica. He died in exile May 5, 1821, on the island of St. Helena. Public holiday at Corsica, France.

CHAUVIN DAY. Aug 15. A day named for Nicholas Chauvin, French soldier from Rochefort, France, who idolized Napoleon and who eventually became a subject of ridicule because of his blind loyalty and dedication to anything French. Originally referring to bellicose patriotism, chauvinism has come to mean blind or absurdly intense attachment to any cause. Observed on Napoleon's birth anniversary because Chauvin's birth date is unknown.

CONGO (BRAZZAVILLE): NATIONAL DAY. Aug 15. National day of the People's Republic of the Congo. Commemorates independence from France in 1960.

INDIA: INDEPENDENCE DAY. Aug 15. National holiday. Anniversary of Indian independence from Britain in 1947.

KOREA: INDEPENDENCE DAY. Aug 15. National holiday commemorates acceptance by Japan of Allied terms of surrender in 1945, thereby freeing Korea from 36 years of Japanese domination. Also marks formal proclamation of the Republic of Korea in 1948.

WOODSTOCK: ANNIVERSARY. Aug 15, 1969. The Woodstock Music and Art Fair opened on this day on an alfalfa field on or near Yasgur's Farm at Bethel, NY. The three-day rock concert featured 24 bands and drew a crowd of more than 400,000 people.

★ *Birthdays* ★

Ben Affleck, actor (*Good Will Hunting, Forces of Nature*), born Berkeley, CA, Aug 15, 1972.
Stephen G. Breyer, associate justice of the US Supreme Court, born San Francisco, CA, Aug 15, 1938.

Debra Messing, actress ("Ned and Stacey," "Will & Grace"), born Brooklyn, NY, Aug 15, 1968.

August 16

BENNINGTON BATTLE DAY: ANNIVERSARY. Aug 16, 1777. The anniversary of this battle is a legal holiday in Vermont.

LAWRENCE (OF ARABIA), T.E.: BIRTH ANNIVERSARY. Aug 16, 1888. British soldier, archaeologist and writer, born at Tremadoc, North Wales. During World War I, led the Arab revolt against the Turks and served as a spy for the British. His book, *Seven Pillars of Wisdom*, is a personal account of the Arab revolt. He was killed in a motorcycle accident at Dorset, England, May 19, 1935.

★ *Birthdays* ★

Angela Bassett, actress (*Malcolm X, What's Love Got to Do with It, Waiting to Exhale*), born New York, NY, Aug 16, 1958.
Timothy Hutton, actor (*Taps, Made in Heaven*), born Malibu, CA, Aug 16, 1960.
Madonna, singer ("Material Girl"), actress (*A League of Their Own, Evita*), born Madonna Louise Veronica Ciccone, Bay City, MI, Aug 16, 1958.

August 17

CROCKETT, DAVID "DAVY": BIRTH ANNIVERSARY. Aug 17, 1786. American frontiersman, adventurer and soldier, born at Hawkins County, TN. Died during final heroic defense of the Alamo, Mar 6, 1836, at San Antonio, TX. In his *Autobiography* (1834), Crockett wrote, "I leave this rule for others when I'm dead, Be always sure you're right—then go ahead."

INDONESIA: INDEPENDENCE DAY. Aug 17. National holiday. Republic proclaimed in 1945. It was only after several years of fighting, however, that Indonesia was formally granted its independence by the Netherlands, Dec 27, 1949.

★ *Birthdays* ★

Robert De Niro, actor (Oscars for *Raging Bull, The Godfather II; Taxi Driver*), born New York, NY, Aug 17, 1943.
Sean Penn, actor (*Fast Times at Ridgemont High, Dead Man Walking*), born Santa Monica, CA, Aug 17, 1960.

August 18

BAD POETRY DAY. Aug 18. After all the "good" poetry you were forced to study in school, here's a chance for a payback. Invite some friends over, compose some really rotten verse and send it to your old high school English teacher. [©2001 by WH.] For info: Wellcat Holidays. Web: www.wellcat.com.

BIRTH CONTROL PILLS SOLD: ANNIVERSARY. Aug 18, 1960. The first commercially produced oral contraceptives were marketed by the G.D. Searle Company of Illinois. The pill, developed by Gregory Pincus, had been undergoing clinical trials since 1954.

CLEMENTE, ROBERTO: BIRTH ANNIVERSARY. Aug 18, 1934. National League baseball player, born at Carolina, Puerto Rico. Drafted by the Pittsburgh Pirates in 1954, he played his entire major league career with them. Clemente died in a plane crash Dec 31, 1972, while on a mission of mercy to Nicaragua to deliver supplies he had collected for survivors of an earthquake. He was elected to the Baseball Hall of Fame in 1973.

MAIL-ORDER CATALOG: ANNIVERSARY. Aug 18, 1872. The first mail-order catalog was published by Montgomery Ward. It was only a single sheet of paper. By 1904 the Montgomery Ward catalog weighed four pounds. In 1985, Montgomery Ward closed its catalog operation;

in 2000, it announced the closing of its retail stores.

NINETEENTH AMENDMENT TO US CONSTITUTION RATIFIED: ANNIVERSARY. Aug 18, 1920. The 19th Amendment extended the right to vote to women.

★ Birthdays ★

Martin Mull, actor, comedian ("Sabrina, the Teenage Witch," "Roseanne"), born Chicago, IL, Aug 18, 1943.
Edward Norton, actor (*Primal Fear, American History X*), born Boston, MA, Aug 18, 1969.
Patrick Swayze, dancer, actor ("North and South," *Dirty Dancing*), born Houston, TX, Aug 18, 1954.

August 19

AFGHANISTAN: INDEPENDENCE DAY. Aug 19. National day. Gained independence from British control, Treaty of Rawalpindi in 1919.

NATIONAL AVIATION DAY. Aug 19. Presidential Proclamation 2343, of July 25, 1939, covers all succeeding years. Observed annually on anniversary of birth of Orville Wright, who piloted first self-powered flight in history, Dec 17, 1903. First proclaimed by President Franklin D. Roosevelt.

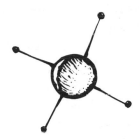

SPACE MILESTONE: *SPUTNIK 5* (USSR). Aug 19, 1960. Space menagerie satellite with dogs Belka and Strelka, mice, rats, houseflies and plants launched. These passengers became first living organisms recovered from orbit when the satellite returned safely to Earth the next day.

★ Birthdays ★

Adam Arkin, actor ("Chicago Hope," "Northern Exposure"), born Brooklyn, NY, Aug 19, 1956.
William (Bill) Clinton, 42nd president of the US (1993–2001), born Hope, AR, Aug 19, 1946.
Peter Gallagher, actor (*sex, lies and videotape; Short Cuts; The Hudsucker Proxy*), born New York, NY, Aug 19, 1955.
Gerald McRaney, actor ("Simon & Simon," "Major Dad"), born Collins, MS, Aug 19, 1948.

Matthew Perry, actor ("Friends," *Fools Rush In*), born Williamstown, MA, Aug 19, 1969.

August 20

HARRISON, BENJAMIN: BIRTH ANNIVERSARY. Aug 20, 1833. The 23rd president of the US, born at North Bend, OH. He was the grandson of William Henry Harrison, ninth president of the US. His term of office, Mar 4, 1889–Mar 3, 1893, was preceded and followed by the presidential terms of Grover Cleveland (who thus became the 22nd and 24th president of the US). Harrison died at Indianapolis, IN, Mar 13, 1901.

HUNGARY: ST. STEPHEN'S DAY. Aug 20. National holiday. Commemorates the canonization of St. Stephen, king and founder of the state, in 1083. This day was commemorated as Constitution Day when Hungary was under Communist rule.

XEROX 914 DONATED TO SMITHSONIAN: ANNIVERSARY. Aug 20, 1985. The original Xerox 914 copying machine (which had been introduced to the public 25 years earlier—in March 1960) was formally presented to the Smithsonian Institution's National Museum of American History at Washington, DC. Invented by Chester Carlson, a patent lawyer, the quick and easy copying of documents by machine revolutionized the world's offices.

★ Birthdays ★

Joan Allen, actress (*Searching for Bobby Fischer, Nixon*), born Rochelle, IL, Aug 20, 1956.
Connie Chung, journalist, born Constance Yu-Hwa, Washington, DC, Aug 20, 1946.
Al Roker, meteorologist ("Today Show"), born Brooklyn, NY, Aug 20, 1954.

August 21

CHAMBERLAIN, WILT: BIRTH ANNIVERSARY. Aug 21, 1936. Basketball Hall of Fame center, born at Philadelphia, PA. Died Oct 12, 1999, at Los Angeles, CA.

HAWAII: ADMISSION DAY: ANNIVERSARY. Aug 21, 1959. President Dwight Eisenhower signed a proclamation admitting Hawaii to the Union. The statehood bill had passed the previous March with a stipulation that statehood should be approved by a vote of Hawaiian residents. The referendum passed by a huge margin in June and Eisenhower proclaimed Hawaii the 50th state on Aug 21.

★ Birthdays ★

Steve Case, founder of America Online, born Oahu, HI, Aug 21, 1958.
Kim Cattrall, actress (*Police Academy*, "Sex & the City"), born Liverpool, England, Aug 21, 1956.

August 22

VIETNAM CONFLICT BEGINS: ANNIVERSARY. Aug 22, 1945. Less than a week after the Japanese surrender ended World War II, a team of Free French parachuted into southern Indochina in response to a successful coup by a Communist guerrilla named Ho Chi Minh in the French colony.

★ Birthdays ★

Valerie Harper, actress ("The Mary Tyler Moore Show," "Valerie"), born Suffern, NY, Aug 22, 1941.
Carl Michael Yastrzemski, Hall of Fame baseball player, born Southampton, NY, Aug 22, 1939.

August 23

FIRST MAN-POWERED FLIGHT: ANNIVERSARY. Aug 23, 1977. At Schafter, CA, Bryan Allen pedaled the 70-pound *Gossamer Condor* for a mile at a "minimal altitude of two pylons" in a flight certified by the Royal Aeronautical Society of Britain, winning a £50,000 prize offered by British industrialist Henry Kremer.

KELLY, GENE: BIRTH ANNIVERSARY. Aug 23, 1912. Actor, dancer born at Pittsburgh, PA. His movies included *Singin' in the Rain* and *An American in Paris*. Kelly died at Beverly Hills, CA, Feb 2, 1996.

SACCO-VANZETTI MEMORIAL DAY: ANNIVERSARY. Aug 23, 1927. Nicola Sacco and Bartolomeo Vanzetti were electrocuted at the Charlestown, MA, prison on this date. Convicted of a shoe factory payroll robbery during which a guard had been killed, Sacco and Vanzetti maintained their innocence to the end. Six years of appeals marked this American cause célèbre during which substantial evidence was presented to show that both men were elsewhere at the time of the crime. On the 50th anniversary of their execution, Massachusetts governor Michael S. Dukakis proclaimed Aug 23, 1977, a memorial day, noting that the 1921 trial had been "permeated by prejudice."

VIRGO, THE VIRGIN. Aug 23–Sept 22. In the astronomical/astrological zodiac, which divides the sun's apparent orbit into 12 segments, the period Aug 23–Sept 22 is identified, traditionally, as the sun sign of Virgo, the Virgin. The ruling planet is Mercury.

★ Birthdays ★

Kobe Bryant, basketball player, born Philadelphia, PA, Aug 23, 1978.
Shelley Long, actress ("Cheers," *Irreconcilable Differences*), born Fort Wayne, IN, Aug 23, 1949.

August 24

ITALY: VESUVIUS DAY. Aug 24, AD 79. Anniversary of the eruption of Vesuvius, an active volcano in southern Italy, which destroyed the cities of Pompeii, Stabiae and Herculaneum.

UKRAINE: INDEPENDENCE DAY. Aug 24. National day. Commemorates independence from the former Soviet Union in 1991.

WARNER WEATHER QUOTATION: ANNIVERSARY. Aug 24, 1897. Charles Dudley Warner, American newspaper editor for the *Hartford Courant*, published this now-famous and oft-quoted sentence, "Everybody talks about the weather, but nobody does anything about it." The quotation is often mistakenly attributed to his friend and colleague Mark Twain. Warner and Twain were part of the most notable American literary circle during the late 19th century. Warner was a journalist, essayist, novelist, biographer and author who collaborated with Mark Twain in writing *The Gilded Age* in 1873.

WASHINGTON, DC: INVASION ANNIVERSARY. Aug 24–25, 1814. During the War of 1812, British forces briefly invaded and raided Washington, DC, burning the Capitol, the president's house and most other public buildings. President James Madison and other high US government officials fled to safety until British troops (not knowing the strength of their position) departed the city two days later.

★ *Birthdays* ★

Craig Kilborn, TV host ("The Late Late Show"), born Hastings, MN, Aug 24, 1962.
Michael Richards, actor ("Seinfeld," *Trial and Error*), born Culver City, CA, Aug 24, 1950.
Calvin Edward (Cal) Ripken, Jr, former baseball player, born Havre de Grace, MD, Aug 24, 1960.

August 25

BERNSTEIN, LEONARD: BIRTH ANNIVERSARY. Aug 25, 1918. American conductor and composer Leonard Bernstein was born at Lawrence, MA. One of the greatest conductors in American music history, he first conducted the New York Philharmonic Orchestra at age 25 and was its director from 1959 to 1969. His musicals include *West Side Story* and *On the Town*, and his operas and operettas include *Candide*. He died five days after his retirement Oct 14, 1990, at New York, NY.

PARIS LIBERATED: ANNIVERSARY. Aug 25, 1944. As dawn broke, the men of the Second French Armored Division entered Paris, ending the long German occupation of the City of Light. That afternoon General Charles de Gaulle led a parade down the Champs Elysées. Though Hitler had ordered the destruction of Paris, German occupying-officer General Dietrich von Choltitz refused that order and instead surrendered to French Major General Jacques Le Clerc.

URUGUAY: INDEPENDENCE DAY. Aug 25. National holiday. Declared independence from Brazil in 1825. Independence granted in 1828.

★ Birthdays ★

Sean Connery, actor (James Bond movies; *The Man Who Would Be King*), born Edinburgh, Scotland, Aug 25, 1930.

Regis Philbin, TV show host ("Live with Regis," "Who Wants to Be a Millionaire?"), born New York, NY, Aug 25, 1933.

Tom Skerritt, actor ("Picket Fences," *Steel Magnolias*), born Detroit, MI, Aug 25, 1933.

August 26

De FOREST, LEE: BIRTH ANNIVERSARY. Aug 26, 1873. American inventor of the electron tube, radio knife for surgery and the photoelectric cell and a pioneer in the creation of talking pictures and television. Born at Council Bluffs, IA, De Forest was holder of hundreds of patents but perhaps best remembered by the moniker he gave himself in the title of his autobiography, *Father of Radio*, published in 1950. So unbelievable was the idea of wireless radio broadcasting that De Forest was accused of fraud and arrested for selling stock to underwrite the invention that later was to become an essential part of daily life. De Forest died at Hollywood, CA, June 30, 1961.

FIRST BASEBALL GAMES TELEVISED: ANNIVERSARY. Aug 26, 1939. WXBS television, at New York City, aired the first broadcast of major league baseball games—a doubleheader between the Cincinnati Reds and the Brooklyn Dodgers at Ebbets Field. Announcer Red Barber interviewed Leo Durocher, manager of the Dodgers, and William McKechnie, manager of the Reds, between games.

KRAKATOA ERUPTION: ANNIVERSARY. Aug 26, 1883. Anniversary of the biggest explosion in historic times. The eruption of the Indonesian volcanic island, Krakatoa (Krakatau) was heard 3,000 miles away, created tidal waves 120 feet high (killing 36,000 persons), hurled five cubic miles of earth fragments into the air (some to a height of 50 miles) and affected the oceans and the atmosphere for years.

WOMEN'S EQUALITY DAY. Aug 26. Anniversary of certification as part of US Constitution, in 1920, of the 19th Amendment, prohibiting discrimination on the basis of sex with regard to voting. Congresswoman Bella Abzug's bill to designate Aug 26 of each year as "Women's Equality Day" in August 1974 became Public Law 93–382.

★ Birthdays ★

Branford Marsalis, musician, born New Orleans, LA, Aug 26, 1960.
Thomas J. Ridge, director, Office of Homeland Security, former governor of Pennsylvania, born Munhall, PA, Aug 26, 1945.

August 27

FIRST COMMERCIAL OIL WELL: ANNIVERSARY. Aug 27, 1859. W.A. "Uncle Billy" Smith discovered oil in a shaft being sunk by Colonel E.L. Drake at Titusville, in western Pennsylvania. Drilling had reached 69 feet, six inches when Smith saw a dark film floating on the water below the derrick floor. Soon 20 barrels of crude were being pumped each day. The first oil was refined to make kerosene for lighting, replacing whale oil. Later it was refined to make gasoline for cars. The first gas station opened in 1907.

FIRST PLAY PRESENTED IN NORTH AMERICAN COLONIES: ANNIVERSARY. Aug 27, 1655. Acomac, VA, was the site of the first play presented in the North American colonies. The play was *Ye Bare and Ye Cubb*, by Phillip Alexander Bruce. Three local residents were arrested and fined for acting in the play. At the time, most colonies had laws prohibiting public performances; Virginia, however, had no such ordinance.

JOHNSON, LYNDON BAINES: BIRTH ANNIVERSARY. Aug 27, 1908. The 36th president of the US succeeded to the presidency following the assassination of John F. Kennedy. Johnson's term of office: Nov 22, 1963–Jan 20, 1969. In 1964, he said: "The challenge of the next half-century is whether we have the wisdom to use [our] wealth to enrich and elevate our national life—and to advance the quality of American civilization." Johnson was born near Stonewall, TX, and died at San Antonio, TX, Jan 22, 1973. His birthday is observed as a holiday in Texas.

MOLDOVA: INDEPENDENCE DAY. Aug 27. Republic of Moldova. Moldova declared its independence from the Soviet Union in 1991.

★ *Birthdays* ★

Paul Reubens (Pee-wee Herman), actor ("Pee-wee's Playhouse," *Pee-wee's Big Adventure*), born Peekskill, NY, Aug 27, 1952.

August 28

MARCH ON WASHINGTON: ANNIVERSARY. Aug 28, 1963. More than 250,000 people attended this civil rights rally at Washington, DC, at which Reverend Dr. Martin Luther King, Jr, made his famous "I have a dream" speech.

RADIO COMMERCIALS: ANNIVERSARY. Aug 28, 1922. Broadcasters realized radio could earn profits from the sale of advertising time. WEAF in New York ran a commercial "spot," which was sponsored by the Queensboro Realty Corporation of Jackson Heights to promote Hawthorne Court, a group of apartment buildings at Queens. The commercial rate was $100 for ten minutes.

★ *Birthdays* ★

Ben Gazzara, actor (*Anatomy of a Murder,* "Run for Your Life"), born New York, NY, Aug 28, 1930.
LeAnn Rimes, country singer, born Jackson, MS, Aug 28, 1982.
Shania Twain, country singer, born Eileen Twain, Windsor, ON, Canada, Aug 28, 1965.

August 29

"ACCORDING TO HOYLE" DAY (EDMOND HOYLE DEATH ANNIVERSARY). Aug 29, 1769. A day to remember Edmond Hoyle and a day for fun and games *according to the rules.* He is believed to have studied law. For many years he lived at London, England, and gave instructions in the playing of games. His "Short Treatise" on the game of whist (published in 1742) became a model guide to the rules of the game. Hoyle's name became synonymous with the idea of correct play according to the rules, and the phrase "according to Hoyle" became a part of the English language. Hoyle was born at London about 1672 and died there.

***AMISTAD* SEIZED: ANNIVERSARY.** Aug 29, 1839. In January 1839, 53 Africans were seized near modern-day Sierra Leone, taken to Cuba and sold as slaves. While being transferred to another part of the island on the ship *Amistad*, they seized control of the ship, telling the crew to take them back to Africa, under the leadership of an African named Cinque. However, the crew secretly changed course and the ship landed at Long Island, NY, where it and its "cargo" were seized as salvage. The *Amistad* was towed to New Haven, CT, where the Africans were imprisoned and a lengthy legal battle began to determine if they were property to be returned to Cuba or free men. John Quincy Adams took their case all the way to the Supreme Court, where on Mar 9, 1841, it was determined that they were free and could return to Africa.

BERGMAN, INGRID: BIRTH ANNIVERSARY. Aug 29, 1915. One of cinema's greatest actresses. Bergman was born at Stockholm, Sweden, and died at London, England, on her 67th birthday, Aug 29, 1982. Three-time Academy Award winner for *Gaslight, Anastasia* and *Murder on the Orient Express*. Controversy over her personal life made her and her films unpopular to American audiences during an interval of several years between periods of awards and adulation.

PARKER, CHARLIE: BIRTH ANNIVERSARY. Aug 29, 1920. Jazz saxophonist Charlie Parker was born at Kansas City, KS. He earned the nickname "Yardbird" (later "Bird") from his habit of sitting in the backyard of speakeasies, fingering his saxophone. His career as a jazz saxophonist took him from jam sessions in Kansas City to New York, where he met Dizzy Gillespie and others who were creating a style of music that would become known as bop or bebop. Although his musical genius was unquestioned, Parker's addiction to heroin haunted his life. He died at Rochester, NY, Mar 12, 1955, at the age of 34.

★ Birthdays ★

Richard Gere, actor (*An Officer and a Gentleman, Pretty Woman*), born Philadelphia, PA, Aug 29, 1949.

Michael Jackson, singer, songwriter ("We Are the World," "Bad," "Thriller," "Beat It"), born Gary, IN, Aug 29, 1958.

August 30

FIRST WHITE HOUSE PRESIDENTIAL BABY: BIRTH ANNIVERSARY. Aug 30, 1893. Frances Folsom Cleveland (Mrs Grover Cleveland) was the first presidential wife to have a baby at the White House when she gave birth to a baby girl (Esther). The first child ever born in the White House was a granddaughter to Thomas Jefferson in 1806.

MacMURRAY, FRED: BIRTH ANNIVERSARY. Aug 30, 1908. Fred MacMurray was born at Kankakee, IL. His film and television career included a wide variety of roles, ranging from comedy (*The Absent-Minded Professor, Son of Flubber, The Shaggy Dog, The Happiest Millionaire*) to serious drama (*The Caine Mutiny, Fair Wind to Java, Double Indemnity*). During 1960–72 he portrayed the father on "My Three Sons," which was second only to "Ozzie and Harriet" as network TV's longest running family sitcom. He died Nov 5, 1991, at Santa Monica, CA.

SAINT ROSE OF LIMA DAY. Aug 30. Saint Rose of Lima was the first saint of the Western Hemisphere. She lived at the time of the colonization by Spain in the 16th century. Patron saint of the Americas and the Philippines; public holiday in Peru.

★ *Birthdays* ★

Cameron Diaz, actress (*My Best Friend's Wedding, There's Something About Mary*), born San Diego, CA, Aug 30, 1972.

Michael Michele, actress ("Homicide: Life on the Street," "ER"), born Evansville, IN, Aug 30, 1966.

August 31

KYRGYZSTAN: INDEPENDENCE DAY. Aug 31. National holiday. Commemorates independence from the former Soviet Union in 1991.

MALAYSIA: FREEDOM DAY. Aug 31. National holiday. Commemorates independence from Britain in 1957.

POLAND: SOLIDARITY FOUNDED: ANNIVERSARY. Aug 31, 1980. The Polish trade union Solidarity was formed at the Baltic Sea port of Gdansk, Poland. Outlawed by the government, many of its leaders were arrested. Led by Lech Walesa, Solidarity persisted in its opposition to the Communist-controlled government, and Aug 19, 1989, Polish president Wojcieck Jaruzelski astonished the world by nominating for the post of prime minister Tadeusz Mazowiecki, editor-in-chief of Solidarity's weekly newspaper, bringing to an end 42 years of Communist Party domination.

★ *Birthdays* ★

James Coburn, actor (*Our Man Flint, The President's Analyst*), born Laurel, NE, Aug 31, 1928.
Hideo Nomo, baseball player, born Osaka, Japan, Aug 31, 1968.

September

September 1

BRAZIL: INDEPENDENCE WEEK. Sept 1–7. The independence of Brazil from Portugal in 1822 is commemorated with civic and cultural ceremonies promoted by federal, state and municipal authorities. On Sept 7, a grand military parade takes place and the National Defense League organizes the Running Race in Honor of the Symbolic Torch of the Brazilian Nation.

CHILE: NATIONAL MONTH. Sept 1–30. A month of special significance in Chile: arrival of spring, a Day of Unity on the first Monday in September, Independence of Chile anniversary (proclaimed Sept 18, 1810) and celebration of the 1980 Constitution and Army Day, Sept 19.

CHRISTMAS SEAL CAMPAIGN®. Sept 1–Dec 31. An American tradition dating back to 1907 when the first Christmas Seals® were made available in the US, the annual campaign is a major supporter of American Lung Association programs dedicated to fighting lung diseases such as asthma, emphysema, tuberculosis and lung cancer, as well as their causes. For info: American Lung Association. Web: www.lung usa.org.

COLLEGE SAVINGS MONTH. Sept 1–30. Encourages families to plan ahead for the cost of college attendance. College savings programs make it easy and affordable for the average family to save and are available in most states. The programs offer affordable, flexible and tax-advantaged savings options that deliver the dream of education to our most precious resources—the children of America. Sponsored by the College Savings Plan Network of the National Association of State Treasurers. For info: College Savings Plan Network. Web: www.collegesavings.org.

EMMA M. NUTT DAY. Sept 1. A day to honor the first woman telephone operator, Emma M. Nutt, who reportedly began her professional career at Boston, MA, Sept 1, 1878, and continued working as a telephone operator for some 33 years.

GERMANY: CAPITAL RETURNS TO BERLIN: ANNIVERSARY. Sept 1, 1999. In July the monthlong process of moving the German government from Bonn to Berlin began, eight years after Parliament had voted to return to its prewar seat. Berlin officially became the capital of Germany on Sept 1, 1999, and Parliament reconvened at the newly restored Reichstag on Sept 7, 1999.

LIBRARY CARD SIGN-UP MONTH. Sept 1–30. National effort to sign up every child for a library card. For info: American Library Association. Web: www.ala.org.

MARCIANO, ROCKY: BIRTH ANNIVERSARY. Sept 1, 1923. Rocky Marciano, boxer born Rocco Francis Marchegiano at Brockton, MA. Marciano used superb conditioning to fashion an impressive record that propelled him to fight against Jersey Joe Walcott for the heavyweight title on Sept 23, 1952. Marciano knocked Walcott out, and in 1956 he retired as the only undefeated heavyweight champion. Died in a plane crash at Newton, IA, Aug 31, 1969. The film *Somebody Up There Likes Me* recounts his life story.

NATIONAL CHICKEN MONTH. Sept 1–30. Focuses consumer attention on chicken as the most nutritious, convenient, economical and versatile food available; in short, "America's favorite." For info: National Chicken Council. Web: www.eatchicken.com.

NATIONAL COUPON MONTH. Sept 1–30. The Coupon Council of the Promotional Marketing Association celebrates the nearly $4 billion savings American consumers receive each year by redeeming coupons for their favorite brands. Contests and fun activities are planned on a national level to raise the awareness of coupons and their redemption value. For info: Coupon Council. Web: www.couponmonth.com.

NATIONAL HONEY MONTH. Sept 1–30. To honor the US's 211,600 beekeepers and 2.63 million colonies of honeybees, which produce more than 220 million pounds of honey each year. For info: National Honey Board. Web: www.honey.com.

NATIONAL PEDICULOSIS PREVENTION MONTH. Sept 1–30. To promote awareness of how to prevent pediculosis (lice). For info: National Pediculosis Association. Web: www.headlice.org.

NATIONAL PIANO MONTH. Sept 1–30. Recognizes America's most popular instrument and its more than 20 million players; also encourages piano study by people of all ages. For info: National Piano Foundation. Web: www.pianonet.com.

NATIONAL RICE MONTH. Sept 1–30. To focus attention on the importance of rice to the American diet and to salute the US rice industry. For info: USA Rice Federation. Web: www.usa rice.com.

NATIONAL SEWING MONTH. Sept 1–30. Celebrates the art, craft and hobby of sewing. The month-long celebration includes special sales, promotions and education programs directed at increased awareness for sewing. For info: Home Sewing Association. Web: www.sewing.org.

SEPTEMBER IS CHILDHOOD CANCER MONTH. Sept 1–30. Public awareness of infants, children and teens with cancer and the need to make research into a higher national priority are stressed each year in September. For info: National Childhood Cancer Foundation. Web: www.child hoodcancermonth.org.

SEPTEMBER IS HEALTHY AGING® MONTH. Sept 1–30. An annual health observance designed to focus national attention on the positive aspects of growing older. The month is part of the Healthy Aging® Campaign, a national, ongoing health promotion designed to broaden awareness of the positive aspects of aging and to provide inspiration for adults, ages 50-plus, to improve their physical, mental, social and financial health. For info: The Healthy Aging® Campaign. Web: www.healthyaging.net.

SLOVAKIA: CONSTITUTION DAY. Sept 1. Anniversary of the adoption of the Constitution of the Slovak Republic in 1992.

UZBEKISTAN: INDEPENDENCE DAY. Sept 1. National holiday. Commemorates independence upon the dissolution of the Soviet Union in 1991.

★ *Birthdays* ★

Gloria Estefan, singer (Miami Sound Machine, "Don't Want to Lose You"), born Havana, Cuba, Sept 1, 1957.
Timothy Duane (Tim) Hardaway, basketball player, born Chicago, IL, Sept 1, 1966.
Lily Tomlin, actress ("Laugh-In," *The Search for Signs of Intelligent Life in the Universe*), comedienne, born Detroit, MI, Sept 1, 1939.

September 2

CALENDAR ADJUSTMENT DAY: ANNIVERSARY. Sept 2. Pursuant to the British Calendar Act of 1751, Britain (and the American colonies) made the "Gregorian Correction" in 1752. The Act proclaimed that the day following Wednesday, Sept 2, should become Thursday, Sept 14, 1752. There was rioting in the streets by those who felt cheated and who demanded the 11 days back. The Act also provided that New Year's Day (and the change of year number) should fall Jan 1 (instead of Mar 25) in 1752 and every year thereafter. As a result, 1751 had only 282 days. See also: "Gregorian Calendar Adjustment: Anniv" (Oct 4).

DAYS OF MARATHON: ANNIVERSARY. Sept 2–9, 490 BC. Anniversary of the event during the

Persian Wars from which the marathon race is derived. Phidippides, "an Athenian and by profession and practice a trained runner," according to Herodotus, was dispatched from Marathon to Sparta (26 miles) Sept 2 to seek help in repelling the invading Persian army. Help being unavailable by religious law until after the next full moon, Phidippides ran the 26 miles back to Marathon Sept 4. Without Spartan aid, the Athenians defeated the Persians at the Battle of Marathon Sept 9. According to legend Phidippides carried the news of the battle to Athens and died as he spoke the words, "Rejoice, we are victorious." The marathon race was revived at the 1896 Olympic Games at Athens. Course distance, since 1924, is 26 miles, 385 yards.

V-J DAY (RATIFICATION). Sept 2, 1945. Official ratification of Japanese surrender to the Allies occurred aboard the USS *Missouri* at Tokyo Bay Sept 2 (Far Eastern time) in 1945, thus prompting President Truman's declaration of this day as Victory-over-Japan Day. Japan's initial, informal agreement of surrender was announced by Truman and celebrated in the US Aug 14.

VIETNAM: INDEPENDENCE DAY. Sept 2. Ho Chi Minh formally proclaimed the independence of Vietnam from France and the establishment of the Democratic Republic of Vietnam on this day in 1945. National holiday.

★ Birthdays ★

Terry Paxton Bradshaw, sportscaster, Pro Football Hall of Fame quarterback, born Shreveport, LA, Sept 2, 1948.
Salma Hayek, actress (*Fools Rush In, Frida*), born Veracruz, Mexico, Sept 2, 1966.
Keanu Reeves, actor (*Bill and Ted's Excellent Adventure, My Own Private Idaho, Speed*), born Beirut, Lebanon, Sept 2, 1964.

September 3

TREATY OF PARIS ENDS AMERICAN REVOLUTION: ANNIVERSARY. Sept 3, 1783. Treaty between Britain and the US, ending the Revolutionary War, signed at Paris, France. American signatories: John Adams, Benjamin Franklin and John Jay.

★ Birthdays ★

Eileen Brennan, actress (*The Last Picture Show, Private Benjamin*), born Los Angeles, CA, Sept 3, 1937.
Charlie Sheen, actor (*Platoon, Hot Shots!*), born Carlos Irwin Estevez, New York, NY, Sept 3, 1965.

September 4

FIRST ELECTRIC LIGHTING: ANNIVERSARY. Sept 4, 1882. Four hundred electric lights came on in offices on Spruce, Wall, Nassau and Pearl streets in lower Manhattan as Thomas Edison hooked up lightbulbs to an underground cable carrying direct current electrical power. Edison had demonstrated his first incandescent lightbulb in 1879. See also: "Incandescent Lamp Demonstrated: Anniv" (Oct 21).

LITTLE ROCK NINE: ANNIVERSARY. Sept 4, 1957. Governor Oval Faubus called out the Arkansas National Guard to turn away nine black students who had been trying to attend Central High School in Little Rock. President Eisenhower sent in troops to enforce the law allowing the students to integrate the school.

NEWSPAPER CARRIER DAY. Sept 4. Anniversary of the hiring of the first "newsboy" in the US, ten-year-old Barney Flaherty, who is said to have answered the following classified advertisement that appeared in *The New York Sun* in 1833: "To the Unemployed—a number of steady men can find employment by vending this paper. A liberal discount is allowed to those who buy to sell again."

WRIGHT, RICHARD: BIRTH ANNIVERSARY. Sept 4, 1908. Novelist and short-story writer whose works included *Native Son* and *Black Boy,* born at Natchez, MS. Wright died at Paris, France, Nov 28, 1960.

★ Birthdays ★

Judith Ivey, actress (*Compromising Positions, Brighton Beach Memoirs*; stage: *Steaming*), born El Paso, TX, Sept 4, 1951.

Michael Joseph (Mike) Piazza, baseball player, born Norristown, PA, Sept 4, 1968.

September 5

BE LATE FOR SOMETHING DAY. Sept 5. To create a release from the stresses and strains resulting from a consistent need to be on time. For info: Procrastinators' Club of America. E-mail: tardyguys@yahoo.com.

ISRAELI OLYMPIAD MASSACRE: ANNIVERSARY. Sept 5–6, 1972. Eleven members of the Israeli Olympic Team were killed in an attack on the Olympic Village at Munich and attempted kidnapping of team members. Four of seven guerrillas, members of the Black September faction of the Palestinian Liberation Army, were also killed. In retaliation, Israeli jets bombed Palestinian positions at Lebanon and Syria Sept 8, 1972.

JAMES, JESSE: BIRTH ANNIVERSARY. Sept 5, 1847. Western legend and bandit Jesse Woodson

James was born at Centerville (now Kearney), MO. His criminal exploits were glorified and romanticized by writers for eastern readers looking for stories of western adventure and heroism. After the Civil War, James and his brother, Frank, formed a group of eight outlaws who robbed banks, stagecoaches and stores. In 1873 the James gang began holding up trains. The original James gang was put out of business Sept 7, 1876, while attempting to rob a bank at Northfield, MN. Every member of the gang except for the James brothers was killed or captured. The brothers formed a new gang and resumed their criminal careers in 1879. Two years later, the governor of Missouri offered a $10,000 reward for their capture, dead or alive. On Apr 3, 1882 at St. Joseph, MO, Robert Ford, a member of the gang, shot 34-year-old Jesse in the back of the head and claimed the reward.

SPACE MILESTONE: *VOYAGER 1* (US). Sept 5, 1977. Twin of *Voyager 2* that was launched Aug 20. On Feb 18, 1998, *Voyager 1* set a new distance record when after more than 20 years in space it reached 6.5 billion miles from Earth.

★ Birthdays ★

Cathy Lee Guisewite, cartoonist (*Cathy*), born Dayton, OH, Sept 5, 1950.

Bob Newhart, comedian ("The Bob Newhart Show," "Newhart"), born Chicago, IL, Sept 5, 1929.

September 6

ADDAMS, JANE: BIRTH ANNIVERSARY. Sept 6, 1860. American worker for peace, social welfare, rights of women; founder of Hull House (Chicago); cowinner of Nobel Prize, 1931. Born at Cedarville, IL, she died May 21, 1935, at Chicago, IL.

LAFAYETTE, MARQUIS DE: BIRTH ANNIVERSARY. Sept 6, 1757. French general and aristocrat who came to America to assist in the revolutionary cause and served without compensation. He was awarded a major-generalship and began a lasting friendship with George Washington. After an alliance was signed with France, he returned to his native country and persuaded Louis XVI to send a 6,000-man force to assist the Americans. On his return, he was given command of an army at Virginia and was instrumental in forcing the surrender of Lord Cornwallis at Yorktown, leading to the end of the war and American independence. He was hailed as "The Hero of Two Worlds" and was appointed a brigadier general on his return to France in 1782. He became a leader of the liberal aristocrats during the early days of the French Revolution, presenting to the National Assembly his draft of "A Declaration of the Rights of Man and of the Citizen." Born at Chavaniac, France, he died at Paris, May 20, 1834.

SAINT PETERSBURG NAME RESTORED. ANNIVERSARY. Sept 6, 1991. Russian legislators voted to restore the name Saint Petersburg to the nation's second largest city. The city had been known as Leningrad for 67 years in honor of the Soviet Union's founder, Vladimir I. Lenin. The city, founded in 1703 by Peter the Great, has had three names in the 20th century, with Russian leaders changing its German-sounding name to Petrograd at the beginning of World War I in 1914, and Soviet Communist leaders changing its name to Leningrad in 1924 following their leader's death.

SWAZILAND: INDEPENDENCE DAY. Sept 6. National holiday. Commemorates attainment of independence from Britain in 1968. Also called Somhlolo Day in honor of the great 19th-century Swazi leader.

★ *Birthdays* ★

Jane Curtin, actress ("Saturday Night Live," "3rd Rock from the Sun"), comedienne, born Cambridge, MA, Sept 6, 1947.

Swoosie Kurtz, actress ("Sisters," *The World According to Garp*; Tony for *The House of Blue Leaves*), born Omaha, NE, Sept 6, 1944.

September 7

"THE FLYING NUN" TV PREMIERE: ANNIVERSARY. Sept 7, 1967. This sitcom about a nun at a convent in Puerto Rico who discovered that she could fly starred Sally Field as Elsie Ethrington (Sister Bertrille). In 2002 Field returned to network television as a supreme court judge in "The Court."

NEITHER SNOW NOR RAIN DAY. Sept 7. Anniversary of the opening to the public on Labor Day 1914 of the New York Post Office Building at Eighth Avenue between 31st and 33rd Streets. On the front of this building an inscription, a free translation from Herodotus, reads: "Neither snow nor rain nor heat nor gloom of night stays these couriers from the swift completion of their appointed rounds." This has long been believed to be the motto of the US Postal Service. They have, in fact, no motto . . . but the legend remains.

★ *Birthdays* ★

Corbin Bernsen, actor ("LA Law," "Ryan's Hope," *Major League*), born North Hollywood, CA, Sept 7, 1954.
Michael Feinstein, singer, pianist, born Columbus, OH, Sept 7, 1956.

September 8

FIRST MISS AMERICA CROWNED: ANNIVERSARY. Sept 8, 1921. Margaret Gorman of Washington, DC, was crowned the first Miss America at the end of a two-day pageant at Atlantic City, NJ.

GALVESTON HURRICANE: ANNIVERSARY. Sept 8, 1900. The worst national disaster in US history in terms of lives lost. More than 6,000 people were killed when a hurricane struck Galveston, TX, with winds of more than 120 MPH, followed by a huge tidal wave. More than 2,500 buildings were destroyed.

McGWIRE BREAKS HOME RUN RECORD: ANNIVERSARY. Sept 8, 1998. Mark McGwire of the St. Louis Cardinals hit his 62nd home run, breaking Roger Maris's 1961 record for the most home runs in a single season. McGwire hit his homer at Busch Stadium at St. Louis against pitcher Steve Trachsel of the Chicago Cubs as the Cardinals won, 6–3. McGwire finished the season with 70 home runs. On Oct 5, 2001, Barry Bonds hit his 71st home run, breaking McGwire's record. Bonds finished the season with 73 homers.

NIXON PARDON DAY: ANNIVERSARY. Sept 8, 1974. Anniversary of the "full, free, and absolute pardon unto Richard Nixon, for all offenses against the United States which he, Richard Nixon, has committed or may have committed or taken part in during the period from January 20, 1969, through August 9, 1974." (Presidential Proclamation 4311, Sept 8, 1974, by Gerald R. Ford.)

"THE OPRAH WINFREY SHOW" TV PREMIERE: ANNIVERSARY. Sept 8, 1986. This daytime talk show was the top-rated talk show for years and also has the distinction of being the first talk show hosted by a black woman, Oprah Winfrey. Her show is taped in front of a studio audience who are solicited for their questions and feedback. In the mid-1990s, fed up with the plethora of trashy talk shows that had sprung up everywhere, Winfrey decided to upgrade the quality of topics that her show presented.

"STAR TREK" TV PREMIERE: ANNIVERSARY. Sept 8, 1966. The first of 79 episodes of the TV series "Star Trek" was aired on the NBC network. Although the science fiction show set in the future lasted only a few seasons, it has remained enormously popular through syndication reruns. It has been given new life through six motion pictures, a cartoon TV series and the very popular TV series "Star Trek: The Next Generation" and "Star Trek: Deep Space Nine." It has consistently ranked among the biggest titles in the motion picture, television, home video and licensing divisions of Paramount Pictures.

UNITED NATIONS: INTERNATIONAL LITERACY DAY. Sept 8. An international day observed by the organizations of the United Nations system. For info: United Nations. Web: www.un.org.

★ *Birthdays* ★

Latrell Sprewell, basketball player, born Milwaukee, WI, Sept 8, 1970.

September 9

BONZA BOTTLER DAY™. Sept 9. To celebrate when the number of the day is the same as the number of the month. Bonza Bottler Day™ is an excuse to have a party at least once a month. For info: Gail M. Berger. E-mail: gberger5@aol.com.

CALIFORNIA: ADMISSION DAY: ANNIVERSARY. Sept 9. Became 31st state in 1850.

TAJIKISTAN: INDEPENDENCE DAY. Sept 9. National holiday commemorating independence from the Soviet Union in 1991.

"WELCOME BACK, KOTTER" TV PREMIERE: ANNIVERSARY. Sept 9, 1975. In this half-hour sitcom, Gabe Kotter (Gabe Kaplan) returned to James Buchanan High School, his alma mater, to teach the "sweathogs," a group of hopeless underachievers. Other cast members included Marcia Strassman, John Travolta, Robert Hegyes, Ron Palillo, Lawrence Hilton-Jacobs and John Sylvester White. The theme song, "Welcome Back," was sung by John Sebastian. The last telecast was Aug 10, 1979.

★ *Birthdays* ★

Hugh Grant, actor (*Impromptu, Sense and Sensibility, Four Weddings and a Funeral*), born London, England, Sept 9, 1960.

Adam Sandler, actor, comedian ("Saturday Night Live," *The Wedding Singer*), born Brooklyn, NY, Sept 9, 1966.

Joseph Robert (Joe) Theisman, sportscaster, Pro Football Hall of Fame quarterback, born New Brunswick, NJ, Sept 9, 1949.

September 10

"GUNSMOKE" TV PREMIERE: ANNIVERSARY. Sept 10, 1955. "Gunsmoke" was TV's longest-running Western, moving from radio to TV. John Wayne turned down the role of Marshall Matt Dillon but recommended James Arness, who got the role. Other regulars included Amanda Blake as Kitty Russell, saloon-owner; Dennis Weaver as Chester B. Goode, Dillon's deputy and Milburn Stone as Doc Adams. In 1962 a fifth character was added—the "rugged male." Burt Reynolds played Quint Asper, followed by Roger Ewing as Thad Greenwood, and Buck Taylor as Newly O'Brien. In 1964 Ken Curtis was added as funnyman Festus Haggen, the new deputy. "Gunsmoke" was the number one rated series for four seasons, and a top ten hit for six seasons. The last telecast was Sept 1, 1975.

"THE ROAD RUNNER SHOW" TV PREMIERE: ANNIVERSARY. Sept 10, 1966. Meep! Meep! The Road Runner, a clever bird who always outwitted Wile E. Coyote and his Acme schemes, had his own cartoon series for three seasons. Other times, this character was on a show with Bugs Bunny called "The Bugs Bunny/Road Runner Hour."

★ Birthdays ★

Colin Firth, actor (*Shakespeare in Love, Valmont,* "Pride and Prejudice"), born Grayshott, Hampshire, England, Sept 10, 1960.

Amy Irving, actress (*Carrie, Honeysuckle Rose*; singing voice of Jessica Rabbit in *Who Framed Roger Rabbit*), born Palo Alto, CA, Sept 10, 1953.

Arnold Palmer, golfer, born Latrobe, PA, Sept 10, 1929.

September 11

ATTACK ON AMERICA: ANNIVERSARY. Sept 11, 2001. Terrorists hijacked four planes, piloting two of them into the World Trade Center's twin towers in New York City and one into the Pentagon in Washington. Passengers on the fourth plane appear to have attempted to overcome the hijackers, causing the plane to crash in western Pennsylvania instead of reaching its target in Washington. The twin towers at the WTC collapsed about an hour after being hit. More than 3,000 people died as a result of the attack. The terrorists were thought to be agents of Islamic extremist Osama bin Laden, who was headquartered in Afghanistan. The US began bombing Afghanistan, trying to get the ruling Taliban to turn over bin Laden. By the end of the year, the Taliban were defeated and a new government was being established in Afghanistan, but bin Laden remained at large.

"THE CAROL BURNETT SHOW" TV PREMIERE: ANNIVERSARY. Sept 11, 1967. This popular comedy/variety show starred comedienne Carol Burnett, who started the show by taking questions from the audience and ended with an ear tug. Sketches and spoofs included recurring characters like "The Family" (later to be spun off as "Mama's Family") and "As the Stomach Turns." Regular cast members included Harvey Korman, Lyle Waggoner and Vicki Lawrence. Later, Tim Conway joined the cast. Dick Van Dyke briefly joined after Korman left in 1977.

FOOD STAMPS AUTHORIZED: ANNIVERSARY. Sept 11, 1959. Congress passed a bill authorizing food stamps for low-income Americans.

"LITTLE HOUSE ON THE PRAIRIE" TV PREMIERE: ANNIVERSARY. Sept 11, 1974. This hour-long family drama was based on books by Laura Ingalls Wilder. It focused on the Ingalls family and their neighbors living at Walnut Grove, MN: Michael Landon as Charles (Pa), Karen Grassle as Caroline (Ma), Melissa Sue Anderson as daughter Mary and Melissa Gilbert as daughter Laura, from whose point of view the stories were told. The series spent one season at Winoka, Dakota. In its last season (1982), the show's name was changed to "Little House: A New Beginning." Landon appeared less often and the show centered around Laura and her husband.

SPACE MILESTONE: *MARS GLOBAL SURVEYOR* **(US).** Sept 11, 1997. Launched Nov 7, 1996, this unmanned vehicle was put into orbit around Mars. It was designed to compile global maps of Mars by taking high-resolution photos. This mission inaugurated a new series of Mars expeditions in which NASA launched pairs of orbiters and landers to Mars. *Mars Global Surveyor* was paired with the lander *Mars Pathfinder.*

Amy Madigan, actress (*Places in the Heart, Field of Dreams, Uncle Buck*), born Chicago, IL, Sept 11, 1951.

September 12

"LASSIE" TV PREMIERE: ANNIVERSARY. Sept 12, 1954. This long-running series was originally about a boy and his courageous and intelligent dog, Lassie (played by more than six different dogs, all male). For the first few seasons, Lassie lived on the Miller farm. The family included Jeff (Tommy Rettig), his widowed mother Ellen (Jan Clayton) and George Cleveland as Gramps. Throughout the years there were many format and cast changes, as Lassie was exchanged from one family to another in order to have a variety of new perils and escapades. Other featured performers included Cloris Leachman, June Lockhart and Larry Wilcox.

"THE MONKEES" TV PREMIERE: ANNIVERSARY. Sept 12, 1966. Based on a rock-and-roll group that was supposed to be an American version of the Beatles, this half-hour show featured a blend of comedy and music. Four young actors were chosen from more than 400 to play the group members: Micky Dolenz, Davy Jones, Mike Nesmith and Peter Tork. Dolenz and Jones had previous acting experience and Tork and Nesmith had previous musical experience. Their music proved to be an enormous success, and later the Monkees insisted on writing and performing their own music. In 1986, the Monkees, except for Nesmith, were reunited for a 20th-anniversary tour and the show was broadcast in reruns on MTV. The Monkees sans Nesmith also toured in 1996 for the 30th-reunion celebration.

OWENS, JESSE: BIRTH ANNIVERSARY. Sept 12, 1913. James Cleveland (Jesse) Owens, American athlete, winner of four gold medals at the 1936 Olympic Games at Berlin, Germany, was born at Oakville, AL. Owens set 11 world records in track and field. During one track meet, at Ann Arbor, MI, May 23, 1935, Owens, representing Ohio State University, broke five world records and tied a sixth in the space of 45 minutes. Died at Tucson, AZ, Mar 31, 1980.

★ Birthdays ★

Ian Holm, actor (Oscar for *Chariots of Fire*; *The Lord of the Rings*), born Goodmayes, England, Sept 12, 1931.
Joe Pantoliano, actor (*Risky Business, The Fugitive*, "The Sopranos"), born Jersey City, NJ, Sept 12, 1954.

September 13

"LAW & ORDER" TV PREMIERE: ANNIVERSARY. Sept 13, 1990. This hour-long series is filmed on location at New York City. Each episode shows the interaction between the police and the district attorney's office in dealing with a crime. Almost the entire cast has changed over the life of this program; Steven Hill as District Attorney Adam Schiff was the only constant until 2000 when he was replaced by Dianne Wiest. Michael Moriarty as Assistant District Attorney Benjamin Stone was followed by Sam Waterston as ADA Jack McCoy. Richard Brooks as ADA Paul Robinette was replaced by Jill Hennessy as ADA Claire Kincaid, who was replaced by Carey Lowell as ADA Jamie Ross, followed by Angie Harmon as ADA Abbie Carmichael, who was replaced by Elisabeth Rohm. The police have been represented by George Dzundza as Detective Max Greevey, followed by Paul Sorvino as Detective Phil Cerreta, followed by Jerry Orbach as Detective Lennie Briscoe. Christopher Noth playing Detective Mike Logan was replaced by Benjamin Bratt as Detective Reynaldo Curtis followed by Jesse L. Martin as Detective Edward Green. Dann Florek as Captain Donald Cragen was followed by S. Epatha Merkerson as Lieutenant Anita Van Buren.

"THE MUPPET SHOW" TV PREMIERE: ANNIVERSARY. Sept 13, 1976. This comedy variety show was hosted by Kermit the Frog of "Sesame Street." The new Jim Henson puppet characters included Miss Piggy, Fozzie Bear and The Great

Gonzo. Many celebrities appeared as guests on the show, which was broadcast in more than 100 countries. The show ran until 1981. "Muppet Babies" was a Saturday morning cartoon that ran from 1984 until 1992. *The Muppet Movie* (1979) was the first of five films based on "The Muppet Show." In 1996 a new show, "Muppets Tonight!" was created.

"STAR-SPANGLED BANNER" INSPIRED: ANNIVERSARY. Sept 13–14, 1814. On the night of Sept 13, Francis Scott Key was aboard a ship that was delayed in Baltimore harbor by the British attack there on Fort McHenry. Key had no choice but to anxiously watch the battle. That experience and seeing the American flag still flying over the fort the next morning inspired him to pen the verses that, coupled with the tune of a popular drinking song, became our official national anthem in 1931, 117 years after the words were written.

★ Birthdays ★

Nell Carter, actress (Tony for *Ain't Misbehavin'*; "Gimme a Break"), born Birmingham, AL, Sept 13, 1948.
Jean Smart, actress ("Designing Women," "Frasier"), born Seattle, WA, Sept 13, 1959.

September 14

"THE GOLDEN GIRLS" TV PREMIERE: ANNIVERSARY. Sept 14, 1985. This comedy starred Bea Arthur, Betty White, Rue McClanahan and Estelle Getty as four divorced/widowed women sharing a house in Florida during their golden years. It was unique in that all four main characters were women. The last episode aired Sept 14, 1992, but the show remains popular in syndication.

NATIONAL DAY OF PRAYER AND REMEMBRANCE. Sept 14. Declared by President Goerge W. Bush to memorialize the victims of the terrorist attacks of Sept 11, 2001.

"THE WALTONS" TV PREMIERE: ANNIVERSARY. Sept 14, 1972. This epitome of the family drama spawned nearly a dozen knockoffs during its nine-year run on CBS. The drama was based on creator/writer Earl Hamner, Jr's experiences growing up during the Depression in rural Virginia. It began as the TV movie *The Homecoming*, which was turned into a weekly series covering the years 1933–43. The cast went through numerous changes through the years; the principals were Michael Learned as Olivia Walton, mother of the clan; Ralph Waite as John Walton, father; and Richard Thomas as

John-Boy, the eldest son. The Walton grand-parents were played by Ellen Corby and Will Geer. The last telecast aired Aug 20, 1981.

★ Birthdays ★

Dan Cortese, actor ("Veronica's Closet"), born Sewickley, PA, Sept 14, 1967.
Sam Neill, actor (*My Brilliant Career, Jurassic Park, The Piano*), born Northern Ireland, Sept 14, 1947.

September 15

CENTRAL AMERICAN NATIONS: INDEPENDENCE DAY. Sept 15. Costa Rica, El Salvador, Guatemala, Honduras and Nicaragua gained independence from Spain on this day in 1821.

CHRISTIE, AGATHA: BIRTH ANNIVERSARY. Sept 15, 1890. English author of nearly a hundred books (mysteries, drama, poetry and nonfiction), born at Torquay, England. Died at Wallingford, England, Jan 12, 1976. "Every murderer," she wrote, in *The Mysterious Affair at Styles*, "is prob-ably somebody's old friend."

"I SPY" TV PREMIERE: ANNIVERSARY. Sept 15, 1965. Bill Cosby made television history as the first African American actor starring in a major dramatic role in this spy series. Cosby played Alexander "Scotty" Scott, an intellectual spy with a cover as a tennis trainer. Robert Culp played Kelly Robinson, the "tennis pro" and Scotty's partner in espionage. The series was notable for filming worldwide.

NATIONAL HISPANIC HERITAGE MONTH. Sept 15–Oct 15. Presidential Proclamation. Begin-ning in 1989, always issued for Sept 15–Oct 15 of each year (Public Law 100–402 of Aug 17, 1988). Previously issued each year for the week including Sept 15 and 16.

SOMEDAY. Sept 15. You know all those things you're going to do "someday"—lose weight, start a business, learn another language, skydive, whatever. Well, someday is here! This is the day to tackle new challenges and experience the joy of accomplishment. For info: Special Interests Publishing. Web: www.idealady.com.

TAFT, WILLIAM HOWARD: BIRTH ANNIVERSARY. Sept 15, 1857. The 27th president of the US was born at Cincinnati, OH. His term of office was Mar 4, 1909–Mar 3, 1913. He was appointed chief justice of the US Supreme Court in 1921. Died at Washington, DC, Mar 8, 1930, and was buried at Arlington National Cemetery.

UNITED KINGDOM: BATTLE OF BRITAIN DAY. Sept 15. Commemorates end of biggest daylight bomb-ing raid of Britain by German Luftwaffe, in 1940. Said to have been the turning point against Hitler's siege of Britain in World War II.

★ Birthdays ★

Tommy Lee Jones, actor (Oscar for *The Fugitive; Coal Miner's Daughter*), born San Saba, TX, Sept 15, 1946.

Merlin Jay Olsen, Hall of Fame football player, sportscaster, actor ("Little House on the Prairie"), born Logan, UT, Sept 15, 1940.

Gaylord Jackson Perry, Hall of Fame baseball player, born Williamston, NC, Sept 15, 1938.

September 16

"FRASIER" TV PREMIERE: ANNIVERSARY. Sept 16, 1993. In this spin-off of "Cheers," psychiatrist Dr. Frasier Crane (Kelsey Grammer) has moved to Seattle where he dispenses advice on the radio. He lives with his father Martin (John Mahoney) and Martin's physical therapist Daphne Moon (Jane Leeves). His brother, Dr. Niles Crane (David Hyde Pierce), frequently asks for Frasier's advice about his love life. Roz Doyle, the producer of Frasier's show, is played by Peri Gilpin.

GENERAL MOTORS FOUNDED: ANNIVERSARY. Sept 16, 1908. The giant automobile manufacturing company was founded by William Crapo "Billy" Durant, a Flint, MI, entrepreneur.

MEXICO: INDEPENDENCE DAY. Sept 16. National Day. The official celebration begins at 11 PM, Sept 15 and continues through Sept 16. On the night of the 15th, the president of Mexico steps onto the balcony of the National Palace at Mexico City and voices the same "El Grito" (Cry for Freedom) that Father Hidalgo gave on the night of Sept 15, 1810, which began Mexico's rebellion from Spain.

UNITED NATIONS: INTERNATIONAL DAY FOR THE PRESERVATION OF THE OZONE LAYER. Sept 16. On Dec 19, 1994, the General Assembly proclaimed this day to commemorate the date on which the Montreal Protocol on Substances that Deplete the Ozone Layer was signed in 1987 (Resolution 49/114). States are invited to devote the day to promote, at the national level, activities in accordance with the objectives of the protocol. The ozone layer filters sunlight and prevents the adverse effects of ultraviolet radiation from reaching Earth's surface, thereby preserving life on the planet. For info: United Nations. Web: www.un.org.

★ Birthdays ★

Lauren Bacall, actress (*Applause, Woman of the Year, Key Largo*), born Betty Joan Perske, New York, NY, Sept 16, 1924.

Elgin Gay Baylor, Hall of Fame basketball player and former coach, born Washington, DC, Sept 16, 1934.

Peter Falk, actor (*The Great Race*, "Columbo"), born New York, NY, Sept 16, 1927.

B.B. King, singer ("Rock Me Baby," "The Thrill Is Gone"), born Itta Bena, MS, Sept 16, 1925.
Jennifer Tilly, actress (*Johnny Be Good, Made in America*), born Los Angeles, CA, Sept 16, 1961.

September 17

BATTLE OF ANTIETAM: ANNIVERSARY. Sept 17, 1862. This date has been called America's bloodiest day in recognition of the high casualties suffered in the Civil War battle between General Robert E. Lee's Confederate forces and General George McClellan's Union army. Estimates vary, but more than 25,000 Union and Confederate soldiers were killed or wounded in this battle on the banks of the Potomac River at Maryland.

CITIZENSHIP DAY. Sept 17. Presidential Proclamation always issued for Sept 17; customarily issued as "Citizenship Day and Constitution Week." Replaces Constitution Day.

CONSTITUTION OF THE US: ANNIVERSARY. Sept 17, 1787. Delegations from 12 states (Rhode Island did not send a delegate) at the Constitutional Convention at Philadelphia, PA, voted unanimously to approve the Constitution. Thirty-nine of the 42 delegates present signed it on this day and the Convention adjourned, after drafting a letter of transmittal to the Congress. The Constitution stipulated that it would take effect when ratified by nine states, which occurred July 2, 1788.

"THE FUGITIVE" TV PREMIERE: ANNIVERSARY. Sept 17, 1963. A nail-biting adventure series on ABC. Dr. Richard Kimble (David Janssen) was wrongly convicted and sentenced to death for his wife's murder but escaped from his captors in a train wreck. This popular program aired for four years detailing Kimble's search for the one-armed man (Bill Raisch) who had killed his wife. In the meantime, Kimble himself was being pursued by Lieutenant Philip Gerard (Barry Morse). The final episode aired Aug 29, 1967, and featured Kimble extracting a confession from the one-armed man. That single episode was the highest-rated show ever broadcast until 1976. The TV series generated a hit movie in 1993 with Harrison Ford as Kimble and Oscar-winner Tommy Lee Jones as Gerard.

"M*A*S*H" TV PREMIERE: ANNIVERSARY. Sept 17, 1972. This popular CBS series was based on the 1970 Robert Altman movie. Set during the Korean War, the show aired for 11 years (lasting longer than the war). It followed the lives of doctors and nurses on the war front with both humor and pathos. The cast included Alan Alda as Captain Benjamin Franklin "Hawkeye" Pierce, Wayne Rogers as Captain John "Trapper John" McIntyre, McLean Stevenson as Lieutenant Colonel Henry Blake, Loretta Swit as Major Margaret "Hot Lips" Houlihan, Larry

Linville as Major Frank Burns, Gary Burghoff as Corporal Walter "Radar" O'Reilly, William Christopher as Father Francis Mulcahy, Jamie Farr as Corporal Max Klinger, Harry Morgan as Colonel Sherman Potter and Mike Farrell as Captain B.J. Hunnicut. Its final episode on Feb 28, 1983, "Goodbye, Farewell and Amen," was the highest-rated program of all time, topping the "Who shot J.R.?" revelation on "Dallas."

"MISSION: IMPOSSIBLE" TV PREMIERE: ANNIVERSARY. Sept 17, 1966. This action-adventure espionage series appeared on CBS for seven years. Each week the IMF (Impossible Missions Force) leader would receive instructions on a super-secret mission to be carried out by the crew. Steven Hill played the first IMF leader; he was replaced by Peter Graves. The crew included Martin Landau, Barbara Bain, Greg Morris, Peter Lupus, Leonard Nimoy, Lynda Day George and Barbara Anderson. The show was remade for ABC in 1988; it lasted two seasons. A more recent incarnation of "Mission: Impossible" was on the silver screen in 1996, starring Tom Cruise.

NATIONAL FOOTBALL LEAGUE FORMED: ANNIVERSARY. Sept 17, 1920. The National Football League was formed at Canton, OH.

★ Birthdays ★

Anne Bancroft, actress (Tony and Oscar for *The Miracle Worker; The Graduate, The Turning Point*), born Anna Maria Italiano, New York, NY, Sept 17, 1931.

John Ritter, actor (Emmy for "Three's Company"; *Problem Child*), born Burbank, CA, Sept 17, 1948.

David H. Souter, associate justice of the US Supreme Court, born Melrose, MA, Sept 17, 1939.

September 18

GARBO, GRETA: BIRTH ANNIVERSARY. Sept 18, 1905. International film actress Greta Garbo was born Greta Lovisa Gustafsson at Stockholm, Sweden. A famous recluse, she retired temporarily, then permanently, from films after 19 years and 27 films, which spanned the late-silent era and beginning of sound movies. Her on-screen roles were characterized by an image of a seductress involved in tragic love affairs. She died Apr 15, 1990, at New York, NY.

***THE NEW YORK TIMES* FIRST PUBLISHED: ANNIVERSARY.** Sept 18, 1851. The *Times* debuted as *The New-York Daily Times*. The name was changed to the current one in 1857.

US AIR FORCE ESTABLISHED: ANNIVERSARY. Sept 18, 1947. Although its heritage dates back to 1907 when the Army first established military aviation, the US Air Force became a separate military service on this date. Responsible for providing an air force that is capable, in conjunction with the other armed forces, of preserving the peace and security of the US, the department is separately organized under the Secretary of the Air Force and operates under the authority, direction and control of the Secretary of Defense.

"WAGON TRAIN" TV PREMIERE: ANNIVERSARY. Sept 18, 1957. "Wagon Train" was a popular Western on NBC and ABC, airing for eight years with its last telecast Sept 5, 1965. Each week travelers on a journey along the wagon trail from Missouri to California encountered new surroundings and interacted with different guest stars. Ward Bond played wagonmaster Major Seth Adams until his death in 1960. He was replaced by John McIntire as Chris Hale. Other regulars were Robert Horton as scout Flint McCullough, Frank McGrath as cook Charlie Wooster, Terry Wilson as Bill Hawks, Denny (Scott) Miller as scout Duke Shannon, Michael Burns as teen passenger Barnaby West and Robert Fuller as scout Cooper.

★ *Birthdays* ★

Lance Armstrong, cyclist, national and world champion, two-time Olympian, four-time winner of the Tour de France, born Plano, TX, Sept 18, 1971.

James Gandolfini, actor ("The Sopranos"), born Westwood, NJ, Sept 18, 1961.

Jada Pinkett Smith, actress (*The Nutty Professor, Menace II Society*), born Baltimore, MD, Sept 18, 1971.

September 19

"ER" TV PREMIERE: ANNIVERSARY. Sept 19, 1994. This medical drama takes place in the emergency room of the fictional County General Hospital in Chicago. Doctors and nurses care for life-and-death cases while experiencing their personal traumas as well. Cast has included Anthony Edwards, George Clooney, Sherry Stringfield, Noah Wyle, Laura Innes, Gloria Reuben, Eriq La Salle and Alex Kingston.

★ *Birthdays* ★

Jeremy Irons, actor (*Moonlighting, Dead Ringers*), born Cowes, Isle of Wight, England, Sept 19, 1948.

Joan Lunden, broadcast journalist (former cohost of "Good Morning America"), born Sacramento, CA, Sept 19, 1951.

September 20

BILLIE JEAN KING WINS THE "BATTLE OF THE SEXES": ANNIVERSARY. Sept 20, 1973. Billie Jean King defeated Bobby Riggs in the nationally televised "Battle of the Sexes" tennis match in three straight sets.

"THE COSBY SHOW" TV PREMIERE: ANNIVERSARY. Sept 20, 1984. This Emmy Award–winning comedy set in New York City revolved around the members of the Huxtable family. Father Dr. Heathcliff Huxtable was played by Bill Cosby; his wife Clair, an attorney, was played by Phylicia Rashad. Their four daughters were played by Sabrina LeBeauf (Sondra), Lisa Bonet (Denise), Tempestt Bledsoe (Vanessa) and Keshia Knight Pulliam (Rudy); Malcolm-Jamal Warner played son Theo. By the end of the series in 1992, the two oldest daughters had finished college and were married. "A Different World" was a spin-off set at historically black Hillman College where Denise was a student.

"LOU GRANT" TV PREMIERE: ANNIVERSARY. Sept 20, 1977. This hour-long dramatic series was a spin-off of "The Mary Tyler Moore Show." Ed Asner reprised his role as newspaper editor Lou Grant, now a city editor for the *Los Angeles Tribune*. The show tackled many serious issues, including child abuse, gun control and the plight of Vietnamese refugees. The cast included Mason Adams, Nancy Marchand, Jack Bannon, Robert Walden, Daryl Anderson, Rebecca Balding, Linda Kelsey, Allen Williams and Emilio Delgado. This series was an unusual spin-off because it was the first time a character left a sitcom to headline a drama.

"THE PHIL SILVERS SHOW" TV PREMIERE: ANNIVERSARY. Sept 20, 1955. This popular half-hour sitcom starred Phil Silvers as Sergeant Ernie Bilko, a scheming but good-natured con man whose schemes rarely worked out. Guest stars included Fred Gwynne, Margaret Hamilton, Dick Van Dyke and Alan Alda in his first major TV role. The character of Sergeant Bilko was featured in a movie of the same title in 1996 starring Steve Martin.

★ Birthdays ★

Kristen Johnston, actress ("3rd Rock from the Sun"), born Washington, DC, Sept 20, 1967.
Sophia Loren, actress (Oscar for *Two Women; Black Orchid, Marriage Italian Style,* "Brief Encounter"), born Sofia Scicoloni, Rome, Italy, Sept 20, 1934.

September 21

ARMENIA: INDEPENDENCE DAY. Sept 21. Public holiday. Commemorates independence from Soviet Union in 1991.

BELIZE: INDEPENDENCE DAY. Sept 21. National holiday. Commemorates independence of the former British Honduras from Britain in 1981.

JOSEPH, CHIEF: DEATH ANNIVERSARY. Sept 21, 1904. Admirable Nez Percé chief, whose Indian name was In-Mut-Too-Yah-Lat-Lat, was born about 1840 at Wallowa Valley, Oregon Territory, and died on the Colville Reservation at Washington. Faced with war or resettlement to a reservation, Chief Joseph led a dramatic attempt to escape to Canada. After three months and more than 1,000 miles, he and his people were surrounded 40 miles from Canada and sent to a reservation at Oklahoma. Though the few survivors were later allowed to relocate to another reservation at Washington, they never regained their ancestral lands.

"NYPD BLUE" TV PREMIERE: ANNIVERSARY. Sept 21, 1993. This gritty New York City police drama has had a large and changing cast. The central characters were partners Detective Bobby Simone, played by Jimmy Smits, and Detective Andy Sipowicz, played by Dennis Franz. Other cast members have included Kim Delaney as Detective Diane Russell, James McDaniel as Lieutenant Arthur Fancy, Gordon Clapp as Detective Gregory Medavoy, Rick Schroder as Detective Danny Sorenson and Nicholas Turturro as Detective James Martinez.

WELLS, H.G.: BIRTH ANNIVERSARY. Sept 21, 1866. English novelist and historian, born at Bromley, Kent, England. Among his books: *The Time Machine, The Invisible Man, The War of the Worlds* and *The Outline of History.* H.G. Wells died at London, Aug 13, 1946. "Human history," he wrote, "becomes more and more a race between education and catastrophe."

★ Birthdays ★

David James Elliott, actor ("JAG"), born Toronto, ON, Canada, Sept 21, 1960.
Faith Hill, country singer, born Jackson, MS, Sept 21, 1967.
Stephen King, author (*Christine, Pet Sematary, The Shining, Misery, The Stand*), born Portland, ME, Sept 21, 1947.
Rob Morrow, actor ("Northern Exposure," *Quiz Show*), born New Rochelle, NY, Sept 21, 1962.

September 22

AMERICAN BUSINESS WOMEN'S DAY. Sept 22. A day on which all Americans can recognize the important contributions more than 57 million American working women have made and are continuing to make to this nation. For info: American Business Women's Association. Web: www.abwa.org.

"CHARLIE'S ANGELS" TV PREMIERE: ANNIVERSARY. Sept 22, 1976. This extremely popular show of the '70s featured three attractive women solving crimes. Sabrina Duncan (Kate Jackson), Jill Munroe (Farrah Fawcett-Majors) and Kelly Garrett (Jaclyn Smith) signed on with a detective agency. Their boss was never seen, only heard (the voice of John Forsythe); messages were communicated to the women by his associate John Bosley (David Doyle). During the course of the series, Cheryl Ladd replaced Fawcett; Shelley Hack and Tanya Roberts succeeded Kate Jackson. The show went off the air in 1981 but a feature film version was made in 2000 starring Drew Barrymore, Cameron Diaz and Lucy Liu.

EMANCIPATION PROCLAMATION: ANNIVERSARY. Sept 22, 1862. One of the most important presidential proclamations of American history is that of Sept 22, 1862, in which Abraham Lincoln, by executive proclamation, freed the slaves in the rebelling states. "That on . . . [Jan 1, 1863] . . . all persons held as slaves within any state or designated part of a state, the people whereof shall then be in rebellion against the United States, shall be then, thenceforward, and forever, free. . . ."

"FAMILY TIES" TV PREMIERE: ANNIVERSARY. Sept 22, 1982. This popular '80s sitcom was set at Columbus, OH, and focused on the Keaton family: ex-hippies Elyse (Meredith Baxter-Birney), an architect, and Steven (Michael Gross), a station manager of the local public TV station; Alex (Michael J. Fox), their smart, conservative and financially driven son; Mallory (Justine Bateman), their materialistic, ditzy daughter and Jennifer (Tina Yothers), their tomboy youngest daughter. Later in the series Elyse gave birth to Andrew (Brian Bonsall). Marc Price played Irwin "Skippy" Handleman, the nerdy next-door neighbor who adored the Keatons, and Mallory in particular. The last episode aired Sept 17, 1989.

"FRIENDS" TV PREMIERE: ANNIVERSARY. Sept 22, 1994. This NBC comedy brings together six single friends and the issues in their personal lives, ranging from their jobs to their love lives. Cast includes Courteney Cox Arquette, Lisa Kudrow, Jennifer Aniston, Matthew Perry, David Schwimmer and Matt Le Blanc.

ICE CREAM CONE: BIRTHDAY. Sept 22, 1903. Italo Marchiony emigrated from Italy in the late 1800s and soon thereafter went into business at

New York, NY, with a pushcart dispensing lemon ice. Success soon led to a small fleet of pushcarts, and the inventive Marchiony was inspired to develop a cone, first made of paper, later of pastry, to hold the tasty delicacy. On Sept 22, 1903, his application for a patent for his new mold was filed, and US Patent No 746971 was issued to him Dec 15, 1903.

LONG COUNT DAY: ANNIVERSARY. Sept 22, 1927. Anniversary of world championship boxing match between Jack Dempsey and Gene Tunney, at Soldier Field, Chicago, IL. It was the largest fight purse ($990,446) in the history of boxing to that time. Nearly half the population of the US is believed to have listened to the radio broadcast of this fight. In the seventh round of the ten-round fight, Tunney was knocked down. Following the rules, Referee Dave Barry interrupted the count when Dempsey failed to go to the farthest corner. The count was resumed and Tunney got to his feet at the count of nine. Stopwatch records of those present claimed the total elapsed time from the beginning of the count until Tunney got to his feet was 12–15 seconds. Tunney, awarded seven of the ten rounds, won the fight and claimed the world championship. Dempsey's appeal was denied and he never fought again. Tunney retired the following year after one more (successful) fight.

MALI: INDEPENDENCE DAY. Sept 22. National holiday commemorating independence from France in 1960. Mali, in West Africa, was known as the French Sudan while a colony.

★ Birthdays ★

Scott Baio, actor ("Happy Days," "Diagnosis Murder," "Charles in Charge"), born Brooklyn, NY, Sept 22, 1961.
Thomas Charles (Tommy) Lasorda, Hall of Fame baseball manager and former player, born Norristown, PA, Sept 22, 1927.

September 23

CHECKERS DAY: ANNIVERSARY. Sept 23. Anniversary of the nationally televised "Checkers Speech" by then vice presidential candidate Richard M. Nixon, on Sept 23, 1952. Nixon was found "clean as a hound's tooth" in connection with a private fund for political expenses, and he declared he would never give back the cocker spaniel dog, Checkers, which had been a gift to his daughters. Other dogs prominent in American politics: Abraham Lincoln's dog, Fido; Franklin D. Roosevelt's much-traveled terrier, Fala; Harry S. Truman's dogs, Mike and Feller; Dwight D. Eisenhower's dog, Heidi; Lyndon Johnson's beagles, Him and Her; Ronald Reagan's dogs, Lucky and Rex; and George H.W. Bush's dog, Millie.

LIBRA, THE BALANCE. Sept 23–Oct 22. In the astronomical/astrological zodiac that divides the sun's apparent orbit into 12 segments, the period Sept 23–Oct 22 is identified traditionally as the sun sign of Libra, the Balance. The ruling planet is Venus.

PLANET NEPTUNE DISCOVERY: ANNIVERSARY. Sept 23, 1846. Neptune is 2,796,700,000 miles from the sun (about 30 times as far from the sun as Earth). Eighth planet from the sun, Neptune takes 164.8 years to revolve around the sun. Diameter is about 31,000 miles compared to Earth at 7,927 miles. Discovered by German astronomer Johann Galle.

★ Birthdays ★

Jason Alexander, actor ("Seinfeld," *Pretty Woman; Bye, Bye, Birdy*; stage: *Jerome Robbins' Broadway*), born Newark, NJ, Sept 23, 1959.
Ray Charles, singer ("Georgia on My Mind," "What'd I Say"), composer, born Ray Charles Robinson, Albany, GA, Sept 23, 1930.

September 24

FITZGERALD, F. SCOTT: BIRTH ANNIVERSARY. Sept 24, 1896. American short story writer and novelist; author of *This Side of Paradise, The Great Gatsby* and *Tender Is the Night*. Born Francis Scott Key Fitzgerald, at St. Paul, MN, he died at Hollywood, CA, Dec 21, 1940.

HENSON, JIM: BIRTH ANNIVERSARY. Sept 24, 1936. Puppeteer, born at Greenville, MS. Jim Henson created a unique family of puppets known as the Muppets. Kermit the Frog, Big Bird, Bert and Ernie, Gonzo, Animal, Miss Piggy and Oscar the Grouch are a few of the puppets that captured the hearts of children and adults alike in television and film productions including "Sesame Street," "The Jimmy Dean Show," "The Muppet Show," *The Muppet Movie, The Muppets Take Manhattan, The Great Muppet Caper* and *The Dark Crystal*. Henson introduced the Muppets in 1956. His creativity was rewarded with 18 Emmy Awards, seven Grammy Awards, four Peabody Awards and five Cable ACE Awards. Henson died May 16, 1990, at New York, NY.

"THE LOVE BOAT" TV PREMIERE: ANNIVERSARY. Sept 24, 1977. This one-hour comedy-drama featured guest stars aboard a cruise ship, the *Pacific Princess*. All stories had to do with finding or losing love. The ship's crew were the only regulars (though there were occasional recurring roles, such as Charo as April): Gavin MacLeod as Captain Merrill Stubing, Jill Whelan as his daughter Vicki, Bernie Kopell as Doctor Adam Bricker, Fred Grandy as assistant purser Burl "Gopher" Smith, Ted Lange as bartender Isaac Washington and Lauren Tewes as cruise director Julie McCoy. The series ended with the last telecast on Sept 5, 1986, but three two-hour specials were broadcast the next year. MacLeod, Lange, Kopell and Whelan were reunited in a Love Boat special in 1990.

MARSHALL, JOHN: BIRTH ANNIVERSARY. Sept 24, 1755. Fourth chief justice of Supreme Court, born at Germantown, VA. Served in House of Representatives and as secretary of state under John Adams. Appointed by President Adams to the position of chief justice in January 1801, he became known as "The Great Chief Justice." Marshall's court was largely responsible for defining the role of the Supreme Court and basic organizing principles of government in the early years after adoption of the Constitution in such cases as *Marbury v Madison, McCulloch v Maryland, Cohens v Virginia* and *Gibbons v Ogden.* He died at Philadelphia, PA, July 6, 1835.

"60 MINUTES" TV PREMIERE: ANNIVERSARY. Sept 24, 1968. TV's longest-running prime-time program was originally hosted by Harry Reasoner and Mike Wallace. Dan Rather and Diane Sawyer were also reporters on TV's first news-magazine. Today the show's correspondents include Ed Bradley, Steve Kroft, Lesley Stahl, Morley Safer, Andy Rooney and Mike Wallace.

★ Birthdays ★

Gordon Clapp, actor ("NYPD Blue"), born North Conway, NH, Sept 24, 1948.
Rafael Palmiero, baseball player, born Havana, Cuba, Sept 24, 1964.

September 25

FAULKNER, WILLIAM CUTHBERT: BIRTH ANNIVERSARY. Sept 25, 1897. American novelist and short story writer William Faulkner (born Falkner) was born at New Albany, MS. A Nobel Prize winner who changed the style and structure of the American novel, he died at Byhalia, MS, on July 6, 1962. Faulkner's first novel, *Soldiers' Pay*, was published in 1926. His best-known book, *The Sound and the Fury*, appeared in 1929. Shunning literary circles, Faulkner moved to a pre–Civil War house on the outskirts of Oxford, MS, in 1930. From 1930 until the onset of World War II he published an incredible body of work. In June 1962, Faulkner published his last novel, *The Reivers*.

FIRST WOMAN SUPREME COURT JUSTICE: ANNIVERSARY. Sept 25, 1981. Sandra Day O'Connor was sworn in as the first woman associate justice on the US Supreme Court on this date. She had been nominated by President Ronald Reagan in July 1981.

SMITH, WALTER WESLEY "RED": BIRTH ANNIVERSARY. Sept 25, 1905. Pulitzer Prize–winning sports columnist and newspaperman for 54 years, Walter Wesley "Red" Smith was born at Green Bay, WI, and was called the "nation's most respected sportswriter." Smith's columns appeared in some 500 newspapers. He died at Stamford, CT, Jan 15, 1982.

★ Birthdays ★

Michael Douglas, actor ("The Streets of San Francisco," *Fatal Attraction, Basic Instinct*), director, born New York, NY, Sept 25, 1944.

Will Smith, actor (*Independence Day, Ali*, "The Fresh Prince of Bel-Air"), singer, born Philadelphia, PA, Sept 25, 1968.

Barbara Walters, journalist, interviewer, TV host ("20/20"), born Boston, MA, Sept 25, 1931.

Catherine Zeta-Jones, actress (*The Mask of Zorro*), born Swansea, Glamorgan, Wales, Sept 25, 1969.

September 26

APPLESEED, JOHNNY: BIRTH ANNIVERSARY. Sept 26, 1774. John Chapman, better known as Johnny Appleseed, believed to have been born at Leominster, MA. Died at Allen County, IN, Mar 11, 1845. Planter of orchards and friend of wild animals, he was regarded as a great medicine man by the Indians.

"THE BRADY BUNCH" TV PREMIERE: ANNIVERSARY. Sept 26, 1969. This popular sitcom starred Robert Reed as widower Mike Brady, who has three sons and is married to Carol (played by Florence Henderson), who has three daughters. Housekeeper Alice was played by Ann B. Davis.

Sons Greg (Barry Williams), Peter (Christopher Knight) and Bobby (Mike Lookinland) and daughters Marcia (Maureen McCormick), Jan (Eve Plumb) and Cindy (Susan Olsen) experienced the typical crises of youth. The program steered clear of social issues and portrayed childhood as a time of innocence. The last episode was telecast on Aug 30, 1974. The program continues to be popular in reruns in the after-school time slot. There were also many spin-offs: "The Brady Kids" (1972–74), a Saturday morning cartoon; "The Brady Bunch Hour" (1976–77), a variety series; "The Brady Brides" (1981), a sitcom about the two older daughters adjusting to marriage and "The Bradys" (1990), a short-lived dramatic series. *A Very Brady Christmas* (1988) was CBS's highest-rated special for the season. In 1995, *The Brady Bunch Movie* appealed to fans who had watched the program 25 years before.

FIRST TELEVISED PRESIDENTIAL DEBATE: ANNIVERSARY. Sept 26, 1960. The debate between presidential candidates John F. Kennedy and Richard Nixon was televised from a Chicago TV studio.

GERSHWIN, GEORGE: BIRTH ANNIVERSARY. Sept 26, 1898. American composer remembered for his many enduring songs and melodies, including "The Man I Love," "Strike Up the Band," "Funny Face," "I Got Rhythm" and the opera *Porgy and Bess*. Many of his works were in collaboration with his brother, Ira. Born at Brooklyn, NY, he died of a brain tumor at Beverly

Hills, CA, July 11, 1937. See also: "Gershwin, Ira: Birth Anniversary" (Dec 6).

"GILLIGAN'S ISLAND" TV PREMIERE: ANNIVERSARY. Sept 26, 1964. Seven people set sail aboard the *Minnow* for a three-hour tour and became stranded on an island. They used the resources on the island for food, shelter and entertainment. The cast included Bob Denver as Gilligan, Alan Hale, Jr, as the Skipper, Jim Backus as Thurston Howell, III, Natalie Schafer as Mrs "Lovey" Howell, Russell Johnson as the Professor, Dawn Wells as Mary Ann and Tina Louise as Ginger Grant, the movie star. The last telecast aired on Sept 4, 1967.

★ Birthdays ★

Olivia Newton-John, singer ("Physical"), actress (*Grease*), born Cambridge, England, Sept 26, 1948.
Serena Williams, tennis player, born Saginaw, MI, Sept 26, 1981.

September 27

SPACE MILESTONE: *SOYUZ 12* (USSR). Sept 27, 1973. Because of the death of the crew of *Soyuz 11* upon reentry, it was decided that cosmonauts must wear pressurized space suits on takeoff and landing. Thus there was no longer room for three cosmonauts on a flight. Two Soviet cosmonauts made the two-day flight launched on this date.

"THE TONIGHT SHOW" TV PREMIERE: ANNIVERSARY. Sept 27, 1954. "The Tonight Show" has gone through numerous changes over the years, yet it has remained a top-rated show that set the standards for all variety/talk shows to come. Steve Allen served as host from 1954 to 1957. He introduced the format of the show with an opening monologue, games or segments for the studio audience, and then the interview on a simple desk and couch set. Jack Paar hosted from 1957 to 1962 and Johnny Carson reigned as the king of comedy from 1962 to 1992. Comedian Jay Leno serves as its current host.

WARREN COMMISSION REPORT: ANNIVERSARY. Sept 27, 1964. On this day, the Warren Commission issued a report stating that Lee Harvey Oswald acted alone in the assassination of President John F. Kennedy on Nov 22, 1963. Congress reopened the investigation and in 1979 the House Select Committee on Assassinations issued a report stating a conspiracy was most likely involved.

WORLD TOURISM DAY. Sept 27. Observed on the anniversary of the adoption of the World Tourism Organization Statutes in 1970. For info: World Tourism Organization. Web: www.world-tourism.org.

★ Birthdays ★

Meat Loaf, singer, actor (*The Rocky Horror Picture Show*), born Marvin Lee Aday, Dallas, TX, Sept 27, 1947.

Michael Jack (Mike) Schmidt, Hall of Fame baseball player, born Dayton, OH, Sept 27, 1949.

September 28

CAPP, AL: BIRTH ANNIVERSARY. Sept 28, 1909. The creator of the fictitious village of Dogpatch, KY, Al Capp was born Alfred Gerald Caplin at New Haven, CT. The comic strip "Li'l Abner" appeared in daily newspapers from 1934 until its final episode was published Nov 13, 1977. Along with the misadventures of Abner Yokum, Capp lampooned famous public figures. The minor American institution of "Sadie Hawkins Day" made its debut in "Li'l Abner." Al Capp died Nov 5, 1979, at Cambridge, MA.

SULLIVAN, ED: BIRTH ANNIVERSARY. Sept 28, 1901. Known as the "King of TV Variety," born at New York, NY. Sullivan started his media career in 1932 as a sportswriter for the *Daily News* in New York. His popular variety show, "The Ed Sullivan Show" ("Toast of the Town"), ran from 1948 until 1971. It included such sensational acts as Elvis Presley and the Beatles. He died at New York, NY, Oct 13, 1974.

★ Birthdays ★

Se Ri Pak, golfer, born Daejeon, South Korea, Sept 28, 1977.

Gwyneth Paltrow, actress (*Emma*; Oscar for *Shakespeare in Love*), born Los Angeles, CA, Sept 28, 1973.

September 29

ENGLAND: SCOTLAND YARD: FIRST APPEARANCE: ANNIVERSARY. Sept 29, 1829. The first public appearance of Greater London's Metropolitan Police occurred amid jeering and abuse from disapproving political opponents. Public sentiment turned to confidence and respect in the ensuing years. The Metropolitan Police had been established by an act of Parliament in June 1829, at the request of home secretary Sir Robert Peel, after whom the London police officers became more affectionately known as "bobbies." Scotland Yard, the site of their first headquarters near Charing Cross, soon became the official name of the force.

FERMI, ENRICO: BIRTH ANNIVERSARY. Sept 29, 1901. Nuclear physicist, born at Rome, Italy. Played a prominent role in the splitting of the atom and the construction of the first American nuclear reactor. Died at Chicago, IL, Nov 28, 1954.

★ *Birthdays* ★

Bryant Gumbel, TV host ("Today," "The Public Eye," "CBS This Morning"), sportscaster, born New Orleans, LA, Sept 29, 1948.

Emily Lloyd, actress (*A River Runs Through It, In Country*), born North London, England, Sept 29, 1970.

September 30

BABE SETS HOME RUN RECORD: ANNIVERSARY. Sept 30, 1927. George Herman "Babe" Ruth hit his 60th home run of the season off Tom Zachary of the Washington Senators. Ruth's record for the most homers in a single season stood for 34 years—until Roger Maris hit 61 in 1961. Maris's record was broken in 1998 by Mark McGwire with a total of 70 home runs. Barry Bonds broke McGwire's record on Oct 5, 2001, with a total of 73.

BOTSWANA: INDEPENDENCE DAY. Sept 30. National holiday. The former Bechuanaland Protectorate (British Colony) became the independent Republic of Botswana in 1966.

"CHEERS" TV PREMIERE: ANNIVERSARY. Sept 30, 1982. NBC sitcom revolving around the owner, employees and patrons of a Beacon Street bar at Boston. Original cast: Ted Danson as owner Sam Malone, Shelley Long and Rhea Perlman as waitresses Diane Chambers and Carla Tortelli, Nicholas Colasanto as bartender Ernie "Coach" Pantusso, John Ratzenberger as mailman Cliff Clavin and George Wendt as accountant Norm Peterson. Later cast members: Woody Harrelson as bartender Woody Boyd, Kelsey Grammer as Dr. Frasier Crane, Kirstie Alley as Rebecca Howe and Bebe Neuwirth as Dr. Lilith Sternin Crane. The theme song "Where Everybody Knows Your Name" was sung by Gary Portnoy. The last episode aired Aug 19, 1993.

"THE FLINTSTONES" TV PREMIERE: ANNIVERSARY. Sept 30, 1960. This Hanna Barbera cartoon comedy was set in prehistoric times. Characters included two Stone Age families, Fred and Wilma Flintstone and neighbors Barney and Betty Rubble. In 1994 *The Flintstones* movie was released, starring John Goodman, Rick Moranis and Rosie O'Donnell.

GUTENBERG BIBLE PUBLISHED: ANNIVERSARY. Sept 30, 1452. The first section of the Gutenberg Bible, the first book printed from movable type, was published at Mainz, Germany. Johann Gutenberg was the printer. The book was completed by 1456.

MEREDITH ENROLLS AT OLE MISS: ANNIVERSARY.
Sept 30, 1962. Rioting broke out when James
Meredith became the first black to enroll in the
all-white University of Mississippi. President
Kennedy sent US troops to the area to force
compliance with the law. Three people died in
the fighting and 50 were injured. On June 6,
1966, Meredith was shot while participating in
a civil rights march at Mississippi. On June 25
Meredith, barely recovered, rejoined the
marchers near Jackson, MS.

**"MURDER, SHE WROTE" TV PREMIERE: ANNIVER-
SARY.** Sept 30, 1984. Angela Lansbury starred
as crime novelist Jessica Fletcher from Cabot
Cove, ME, who traveled the country solving
murders. This top-rated detective show was
unusual in having an older female star, since
young men are usually preferred in leading roles
on TV. Also appearing were Tom Bosley as
Sheriff Amos Tupper and William Windom as
Dr. Seth Hazlett. The program aired for 12
years and is still in syndication.

★ Birthdays ★

Fran Drescher, actress ("The Nanny," *Jack*),
born Flushing, NY, Sept 30, 1957.
Jenna Elfman, actress ("Dharma & Greg,"
"Townies"), born Los Angeles, CA, Sept 30,
1971.
Martina Hingis, tennis player, born Kosice, Slovakia, Sept 30, 1980.

October

October 1

ADOPT-A-SHELTER-DOG MONTH. Oct 1–31. To promote the adoption of dogs from local shelters, the ASPCA sponsors this important observance. For info: ASPCA. Web: www.aspca.org.

CD PLAYER DEBUTS: ANNIVERSARY. Oct 1, 1982. The first compact disc player, developed jointly by Sony, Philips and Polygram, went on sale. It cost $625 (more than $1,000 in current dollars).

CHINA, PEOPLE'S REPUBLIC OF: NATIONAL DAY. Oct 1. Commemorates the founding of the People's Republic of China in 1949.

DISNEY WORLD OPENED: ANNIVERSARY. Oct 1, 1971. Disney's second theme park opened at Orlando, FL. See also "Disneyland Opened: Anniv" (July 17).

GAY AND LESBIAN HISTORY MONTH. Oct 1–31. October was selected to commemorate the first two lesbian and gay marches on Washington in October 1979 and 1987.

GO NUTS OVER TEXAS PEANUTS MONTH. Oct 1–31. Everything's big in Texas, including the pride in its peanut industry! Texas is the nation's second largest peanut-producing state and is one of only two states that grow all four US peanut varieties: Runner, Spanish, Virginia and Valencia. "Go Nuts Over Texas Peanuts Month" celebrates America's favorite nut. For info: Texas Peanut Producers Board. Web: www.texaspeanutboard.com.

LEVITTOWN OPENS: ANNIVERSARY. Oct 1, 1947. On this day the first residents moved into what would become Levittown at Long Island, NY. The community developed by William Levitt and his brother Alfred with their father Abraham started as affordable rental houses built for returning World War II veterans. In 1948 the Levitts began to sell the 800-square-foot homes for less than $8,000. By 1951, when this first community was finished, the Levitts had built

17,447 mass-produced Cape Cod and ranch homes. In 1952, they started construction on a new Levittown in Bucks County, PA, where they built another 17,000 houses, and beginning in 1958, they built another 12,000 homes in Willingboro, NJ.

LUPUS AWARENESS MONTH. Oct 1–31. To promote public awareness of lupus symptoms to aid in early diagnosis and treatment of this disease. For info: Lupus Foundation of America. Web: www.lupus.org.

MARIS BREAKS HOME RUN RECORD: ANNIVERSARY. Oct 1, 1961. Roger Maris of the New York Yankees hit his 61st home run, breaking Babe Ruth's record for the most home runs in a season. Maris hit his homer against pitcher Tracy Stallard of the Boston Red Sox as the Yankees won, 1–0. Controversy over the record arose because the American League had adopted a 162-game schedule in 1961, and Maris played in 161 games. In 1927, when Ruth set his record, the schedule called for 154 games, and Ruth played in 151. On Sept 8, 1998, Mark McGwire of the St. Louis Cardinals hit his 62nd home run, breaking Maris's record. On Oct 5, 2001, Barry Bonds of the San Francisco Giants broke McGwire's record.

MODEL T INTRODUCED: ANNIVERSARY. Oct 1, 1908. Ford introduced the Model T at a price of $850 but by 1924 the basic model sold for as little as $260. Between 1908 and 1927 Ford sold 15,007,033 Model Ts in the US. Although the first Model Ts were not built on an assembly line, the demand for the cars was so high that Ford developed a system where workers remained at their stations and cars came to them. This enabled Ford to turn out a Model T every ten seconds.

NATIONAL BREAST CANCER AWARENESS MONTH. Oct 1–31. Entering its second decade of public and professional education and awareness. This month is promoted by 17 major national nonprofit cancer organizations to ensure that the media and communities everywhere focus a spotlight on the problem of breast cancer. This month is proclaimed annually by the president of the US. For info: National Breast Cancer Awareness Month Program. Phone (toll-free): (877) 88-NBCAM. Web: www.cancer.org.

NATIONAL CAR CARE MONTH. Oct 1–31. To educate motorists about the importance of maintaining their cars in an effort to improve air quality, highway safety and fuel conservation. For info: Car Care Council. Web: www.carcare council.org.

NATIONAL DENTAL HYGIENE MONTH. Oct 1–31. To increase public awareness of the importance of preventive oral health care and the dental hygienist's role as the preventive professional.

For info: American Dental Hygienists' Association. Web: www.adha.org.

NATIONAL DISABILITY EMPLOYMENT AWARENESS MONTH. Oct 1–31. To foster the full integration of people with disabilities into the workforce. Presidential Proclamation issued for the month of October (Public Law 100–630, Title III, Sec 301a of Nov 7, 1988). Previously issued as "National Employ the Handicapped Week" for a week beginning during the first week in October since 1945. For info: Department of Labor Office of Disability Employment Policy. Web: www.dol.gov/dol/odep.

NATIONAL DOMESTIC VIOLENCE AWARENESS MONTH. Oct 1–31. A Presidential Proclamation is issued for this month every year.

NATIONAL DOWN SYNDROME MONTH. Oct 1–31. To promote better understanding of Down Syndrome. For info: National Down Syndrome Congress. Web: www.ndsccenter.org.

NATIONAL LIVER AWARENESS MONTH. Oct 1–31. To increase understanding of the importance of liver functions, to promote healthful practices and to encourage research into the causes and cures of liver disease. For info: American Liver Foundation. Web: www.liverfoundation.org.

NATIONAL ORTHODONTIC HEALTH MONTH. Oct 1–31. A beautiful, healthy smile is only the most obvious benefit of orthodontic treatment. National Orthodontic Health Month spotlights the important role of orthodontic care in overall physical health and emotional well-being. For info: American Association of Orthodontists. Web: www.aaortho.org.

NATIONAL PHYSICAL THERAPY MONTH. Oct 1–31. To increase awareness of the role of physical therapy in health care, thousands of physical therapists nationwide celebrate by hosting special activities such as fitness clinics, open houses, hot lines, athletic events, health seminars and exhibits. For info: The American Physical Therapy Association. Web: www.apta.org.

NATIONAL POPCORN POPPIN' MONTH. Oct 1–31. To celebrate the wholesome, economical, natural food value of popcorn, America's native snack. For info: The Popcorn Board. Web: www.popcorn.org.

NATIONAL PORK MONTH. Oct 1–31. While pork promotions are conducted throughout the year, special emphasis is placed on Pork: The Other White Meat® during October. For info: National Pork Producers Council. Web: www.nppc.org.

NATIONAL ROLLER SKATING MONTH. Oct 1–31. A monthlong celebration recognizing the health benefits and recreational enjoyment of this long-loved pastime. Also includes in-line skating and an emphasis on safe skating. For info: Roller Skating Association. Web: www.roller skating.com.

NATIONAL SEAFOOD MONTH. Oct 1–31. To promote the taste, variety and nutrition of fish and shellfish. For info and recipes: National Fisheries Institute. Web: www.nfi.org.

NATIONAL SPINA BIFIDA AWARENESS MONTH. Oct 1–31. Promoting public awareness of current scientific, medical and educational issues related to spina bifida—the most frequently occurring permanently disabling birth defect. For info: National Spina Bifida Association of America. Web: www.sbaa.org.

NATIONAL STAMP COLLECTING MONTH. Oct 1–31. For info: US Postal Service. Web: www.usps .gov.

NIGERIA: INDEPENDENCE DAY. Oct 1. National holiday. Became independent of Great Britain in 1960 and a republic in 1963.

POLISH AMERICAN HERITAGE MONTH. Oct 1–31. A national celebration of Polish history, culture and pride, in cooperation with the Polish American Congress and Polonia Across America. For info: Polish American Cultural Center. Web: www.polishamericancenter.org.

UNITED NATIONS: INTERNATIONAL DAY OF OLDER PERSONS. Oct 1. On Dec 14, 1990, the General Assembly designated Oct 1 as the International Day for the Elderly. On Dec 21, 1995, the Assembly changed the name from "for the Elderly" to "of Older Persons" to conform with the 1991 UN Principles for Older Persons. For info: United Nations. Web: www.un.org.

US FEDERAL FISCAL YEAR BEGINS. Oct 1–Sept 30.

WORLD VEGETARIAN DAY. Oct 1. Celebration of vegetarianism's benefits to humans, animals and our planet. In addition to individuals, participants include libraries, schools, colleges, restaurants, food services, health-care centers, health food stores, workplaces and many more. For info: North American Vegetarian Society. Web: www.navs-online.org.

YOSEMITE NATIONAL PARK ESTABLISHED: ANNIVERSARY. Oct 1, 1890. Yosemite Valley and Mariposa Big Tree Grove, granted to the State of California June 30, 1864, were combined and established as a national park. For info: Yosemite National Park. Web: www.nps.gov/yose.

★ Birthdays ★

Julie Andrews, actress, singer (Emmy for "The Julie Andrews Hour"; Oscar for *Mary Poppins*), born Julia Wells, Walton-on-Thames, England, Oct 1, 1935.

Jimmy Carter, 39th US president, born James Earl Carter, Jr, Plains, GA, Oct 1, 1924.

Richard Harris, singer ("MacArthur Park"), actor (*Camelot, Hawaii, Harry Potter and the Sorcerer's Stone*), born Limerick, Ireland, Oct 1, 1930.

Mark McGwire, former baseball player, born Pomona, CA, Oct 1, 1963.

William Hubbs Rehnquist, chief justice of the US Supreme Court, born Milwaukee, WI, Oct 1, 1924.

October 2

"ALFRED HITCHCOCK PRESENTS" TV PREMIERE: ANNIVERSARY. Oct 2, 1955. Alfred Hitchcock was already an acclaimed director when he began hosting this mystery anthology series that aired on CBS and NBC for ten years. Each episode began with an introduction by Hitchcock, the man with the world's most recognized profile. Hitchcock directed about 22 episodes of the series; Robert Altman also directed. Among the many stars who appeared on the show are Barbara Bel Geddes, Brian Keith, Gena Rowlands, Dick York, Cloris Leachman, Joanne Woodward, Steve McQueen, Peter Lorre, Dick Van Dyke, Robert Redford and Katherine Ross.

GANDHI, MOHANDAS (MAHATMA): BIRTH ANNIVERSARY. Oct 2, 1869. Indian political and spiritual leader who achieved world honor and fame for his advocacy of nonviolent resistance as a weapon against tyranny was born at Porbandar, India. He was assassinated in the garden of his home at New Delhi, Jan 30, 1948. On the anniversary of Gandhi's birth (Gandhi Jayanti) thousands gather at the park on the Jumna River at Delhi where Gandhi's body was cremated. Hymns are sung, verses from the Gita, the Koran and the Bible are recited and cotton thread is spun on small spinning wheels (one of Gandhi's favorite activities). Other observances held at his birthplace and throughout India on this public holiday.

GUINEA: INDEPENDENCE DAY. Oct 2. National Day. Guinea gained independence from France in 1958.

MARSHALL, THURGOOD, SWORN IN TO SUPREME COURT: ANNIVERSARY. Oct 2, 1967. Thurgood Marshall was sworn in as the first black associate justice to the US Supreme Court. On June 27, 1991, he announced his resignation, effective upon the confirmation of his successor.

MARX, GROUCHO: BIRTH ANNIVERSARY. Oct 2, 1890. Born Julius Henry Marx at New York, NY. Comedian, who along with his brothers constituted the famous Marx Brothers. The Marx Brothers began as a singing group and then acted in such movies as *Duck Soup* and *Animal Crackers*. During the '40s and '50s, Groucho was the host of the television and radio show "You Bet Your Life." Died at Los Angeles, CA, Aug 19, 1977.

"PEANUTS" DEBUTS: ANNIVERSARY. Oct 2, 1950. This comic strip by Charles Schulz featured Charlie Brown, Lucy, Linus, Sally, Peppermint Patty and Charlie's dog Snoopy. The strip ran in more than 2,500 newspapers in many different countries. Several TV specials were spin-offs of the strip including "It's the Great Pumpkin, Charlie Brown" and "You're a Good Man, Charlie Brown." Schulz's last daily strip was published Jan 3, 2000, and his last Sunday strip was published Feb 13, 2000. Schulz died at Santa Rosa, CA, Feb 12, 2000.

PHILEAS FOGG'S WAGER DAY: ANNIVERSARY. Oct 2, 1872. Anniversary, from Jules Verne's *Around the World in Eighty Days*, of the famous wager upon which the book is based: "I will bet twenty thousand pounds against any one who wishes, that I will make the tour of the world in eighty days or less." Then, consulting a pocket almanac, Phileas Fogg said: "As today is Wednesday, the second of October, I shall be due in London, in this very room of the Reform Club, on Saturday, the twenty-first of December, at a quarter before nine PM; or else the twenty thousand pounds . . . will belong to you."

"THE TWILIGHT ZONE" TV PREMIERE: ANNIVERSARY. Oct 2, 1959. "The Twilight Zone" went on the air with these now-familiar words: "There is a fifth dimension, beyond that which is known to man. It is a dimension as vast as space and as timeless as infinity. It is the middle ground between light and shadow, between science and superstition, and it lies between the pit of man's fear and the summit of his knowledge. This is the dimension of imagination. It is an area which we call The Twilight Zone." The anthology program ran five seasons for 154 installments. It now is considered to have been one of the best dramas to appear on television.

It was created and hosted by Rod Serling. The last episode was telecast on Sept 31, 1965.

★ Birthdays ★

Lorraine Bracco, actress (*Goodfellas, Medicine Man*), born Brooklyn, NY, Oct 2, 1955.
Donna Karan, fashion designer, born Forest Hills, NY, Oct 2, 1948.
Sting, musician, lead singer (Police), songwriter ("Every Breath You Take"), actor (*Dune*), born Gordon Sumner, London, England, Oct 2, 1951.

October 3

"THE ANDY GRIFFITH SHOW" TV PREMIERE: ANNIVERSARY. Oct 3, 1960. Marks the airing of the first of 249 episodes. Set in rural Mayberry, NC, the show starred Griffith as Sheriff Andy Taylor, Ron Howard as his son Opie, Frances Bavier as Aunt Bee Taylor and Don Knotts as Deputy Barney Fife. The last telecast aired Sept 16, 1968.

"CAPTAIN KANGAROO" TV PREMIERE: ANNIVERSARY. Oct 3, 1955. On the air until 1985, this was the longest-running children's TV show until it was surpassed by "Sesame Street." Starring Bob Keeshan as Captain Kangaroo, it was broadcast on CBS and PBS. Other characters included Mr Green Jeans, Grandfather Clock, Bunny Rabbit, Mr Moose and Dancing Bear. Keeshan was an advocate for excellence in children's programming and even supervised which commercials would appear on the program. In 1997 "The All New Captain Kangaroo" debuted, starring John McDonough.

"THE DICK VAN DYKE SHOW" TV PREMIERE: ANNIVERSARY. Oct 3, 1961. This sitcom wasn't an immediate success but soon became a hit. It starred Dick Van Dyke as Rob Petrie, a TV show writer, and Mary Tyler Moore as his wife Laura, a former dancer. This was one of the first shows revolving around the goings-on at a TV series. Other cast members included Morey Amsterdam, Rose Marie, Richard Deacon, Carl Reiner, Jerry Paris, Ann Morgan Guilbert and Larry Matthews. The last episode aired Sept 7, 1966, but the show remains popular in reruns. Carl Reiner created the series.

GERMAN REUNIFICATION: ANNIVERSARY. Oct 3, 1990. After 45 years of division, East and West Germany reunited just four days short of East Germany's 41st founding anniversary (Oct 7, 1949). The new united Germany took the name the Federal Republic of Germany, the formal name of the former West Germany, and adopted the constitution of the former West Germany. Today is a national holiday in Germany, Tag der Deutschen Einheit (Day of German Unity).

"L.A. LAW" TV PREMIERE: ANNIVERSARY. Oct 3, 1986. Set in the Los Angeles law firm of McKenzie, Brackman, Chaney and Kuzak, this drama had a large cast. Divorce lawyer Arnie Becker was played by Corbin Bernsen, public defender Victor Sifuentes by Jimmy Smits and managing partner Douglas Brackman by Alan Rachins. Other cast members included Harry Hamlin as Michael Kuzak, Richard Dysart as Leland McKenzie, Susan Dey as Grace Van Owen, Jill Eikenberry as Ann Kelsey, Michael Tucker as Stuart Markowitz and Susan Ruttan as Roxanne Melman. The last telecast was May 19, 1994.

"MICKEY MOUSE CLUB" TV PREMIERE: ANNIVERSARY. Oct 3, 1955. This afternoon show for children was on ABC. Among its young cast members were Mouseketeers Annette Funicello and Shelley Fabares. A later version, "The New Mickey Mouse Club," starred Keri Russell, Christina Aguilera and Britney Spears.

"OZZIE AND HARRIET" TV PREMIERE: ANNIVERSARY. Oct 3, 1952. "Ozzie and Harriet" was TV's longest-running sitcom. The successful radio-turned-TV show about the Nelson family starred the real-life Nelsons—Ozzie, his wife Harriet and their sons David and Ricky. Officially titled "The Adventures of Ozzie and Harriet," this show was set in the family's home. The boys were one reason the show was successful, and Ricky used the advantage to become a pop star. The show was canceled at the end of the 1965–66 season after 435 episodes, 409 of which were in black and white and 26 in color. The last episode aired Sept 3, 1966.

"QUINCY" TV PREMIERE: ANNIVERSARY. Oct 3, 1976. This medically oriented crime show starred Jack Klugman as Dr. Raymond Quincy, a medical examiner for the Los Angeles coroner's office. Quincy's curiosity about his cases led to investigative work that often solved them. Later in the series the show focused on social issues that were unrelated to forensic medicine. In the final season, Quincy got married to Dr. W. Emily Hanover (Anita Gillette). The last telecast aired on Sept 5, 1983.

★ *Birthdays* ★

Neve Campbell, actress ("Party of Five," *Scream*), born Guelph, ON, Canada, Oct 3, 1973.

David Mark (Dave) Winfield, Hall of Fame baseball player, born St. Paul, MN, Oct 3, 1951.

October 4

GREGORIAN CALENDAR ADJUSTMENT: ANNIVERSARY. Oct 4, 1582. Pope Gregory XIII issued a bulletin that decreed that the day following Thursday, Oct 4, 1582, should be Friday, Oct 15, 1582, thus correcting the Julian calendar, then ten days out of date relative to the seasons. This reform was effective in most Catholic countries; the Julian calendar continued in use in Britain and the American colonies until 1752, in Russia until 1918 and in Greece until 1923. See also: "Calendar Adjustment Day: Anniv" (Sept 2).

HAYES, RUTHERFORD BIRCHARD: BIRTH ANNIVERSARY. Oct 4, 1822. Rutherford Birchard Hayes, 19th president of the US (Mar 4, 1877–Mar 3, 1881), was born at Delaware, OH. In his inaugural address, Hayes said: "He serves his party best who serves the country best." He died at Fremont, OH, Jan 17, 1893.

"LEAVE IT TO BEAVER" TV PREMIERE: ANNIVERSARY. Oct 4, 1957. This family sitcom was a stereotypical portrayal of American family life. It focused on Theodore "Beaver" Cleaver (Jerry Mathers) and his family: his patient, understanding and all-knowing father, Ward (Hugh Beaumont), impeccably dressed housewife and mother June (Barbara Billingsley) and Wally (Tony Dow), Beaver's good-natured, all-American brother. The "perfectness" of the Cleaver family was balanced by other, less-than-perfect characters played by Ken Osmond, Frank Bank, Richard Deacon, Diane Brewster, Sue Randall, Rusty Stevens and Madge Blake. The last episode aired Sept 12, 1963. "Leave It to Beaver" remains popular in reruns.

LESOTHO: INDEPENDENCE DAY. Oct 4. National holiday. Commemorates independence from Britain in 1966. Formerly Basutoland.

SAINT FRANCIS OF ASSISI: FEAST DAY. Oct 4. Giovanni Francesco Bernardone, religious leader, founder of the Friars Minor (Franciscan Order), born at Assisi, Umbria, Italy, in 1181. Died at Porziuncula, Oct 3, 1226. One of the best-loved saints of all time.

SPACE MILESTONE: *SPUTNIK 1* **(USSR).** Oct 4, 1957. Anniversary of launching of first successful man-made Earth satellite. *Sputnik I* ("satellite") weighing 184 pounds was fired into orbit from the USSR's Tyuratam launch site. Transmitted radio signal for 21 days; decayed Jan 4, 1958. Beginning of Space Age and man's exploration beyond Earth. This first-in-space triumph by the Soviets resulted in a stepped-up emphasis on the teaching of science in American classrooms.

STRATEMEYER, EDWARD L.: BIRTH ANNIVERSARY. Oct 4, 1862. American author of children's books, Stratemeyer was born at Elizabeth, NJ. He created numerous series of popular children's books including The Bobbsey Twins, The Hardy Boys, Nancy Drew and Tom Swift. He and his Stratemeyer Syndicate, using 60 or more pen names, produced more than 800 books. More than 4 million copies were in print in 1987. Stratemeyer died at Newark, NJ, May 10, 1930.

UNITED NATIONS: WORLD SPACE WEEK. Oct 4–10. To celebrate the contributions of space science and technology to the betterment of the human condition. The dates recall the launch, on Oct 4, 1957, of the first artificial satellite, *Sputnik 1,* and the entry into force, on Oct 10, 1967, of the Treaty on Principles Governing the Activities of States in the Exploration and Use of Outer Space. For info: United Nations. Web: www.un.org.

★ *Birthdays* ★

Armand Assante, actor (*Belizaire the Cajun, The Mambo Kings, Fatal Instinct*), born New York, NY, Oct 4, 1949.
Susan Sarandon, actress (Oscar for *Dead Man Walking; Atlantic City, Thelma and Louise, Lorenzo's Oil*), born Susan Tomaling, New York, NY, Oct 4, 1946.
Alicia Silverstone, actress (*Clueless, Batman & Robin*), born San Francisco, CA, Oct 4, 1976.

October 5

ARTHUR, CHESTER ALAN: BIRTH ANNIVERSARY. Oct 5, 1829. The 21st president of the US, Chester Alan Arthur, was born at Fairfield, VT, and succeeded to the presidency following the death of James A. Garfield. Term of office: Sept 20, 1881–Mar 3, 1885. Arthur was not successful in obtaining the Republican Party's nomination for the following term. He died at New York, NY, Nov 18, 1886.

BONDS BREAKS HOME RUN RECORD: ANNIVERSARY. Oct 5, 2001. Barry Bonds of the San Francisco Giants broke Mark McGwire's 1998 home run record when he hit his 71st homer of the season in a game against the Los Angeles Dodgers at Pacific Bell Park. Later in the game he hit another homer. The Dodgers beat the Giants, 11–10, eliminating them from the playoffs. On Oct 7 Bonds hit one more homer to finish the season with 73. He also broke Babe Ruth's slugging record of .847 with .863.

CHIEF JOSEPH SURRENDER: ANNIVERSARY. Oct 5, 1877. After a 1,700-mile retreat, Chief Joseph and the Nez Percé Indians surrendered to US Cavalry troops at Bear's Paw near Chinook, MT, Oct 5, 1877. Chief Joseph made his famous speech of surrender, "From where the sun now stands, I will fight no more forever."

TECUMSEH: DEATH ANNIVERSARY. Oct 5, 1813. Shawnee Indian chief and orator, born at Old Piqua near Springfield, OH, in March 1768. Tecumseh was one of the greatest of American Indian leaders. He came to prominence between the years 1799 and 1804 as a powerful orator, defending his people against whites. He denounced as invalid all treaties by which Indians ceded their lands and condemned the chieftains who had entered into such agreements. With his brother Tenskwatawa, the Prophet, he established a town on the Tippecanoe River near Lafayette, IN, and then embarked on a mission to organize an Indian confederation to stop white encroachment. Although he advocated peaceful methods and negotiation, he did not rule out war as a last resort as he visited tribes throughout the country. While he was away, William Henry Harrison defeated the Prophet at the Battle of Tippecanoe Nov 7, 1811, and burned the town. Tecumseh organized a large force of Indian warriors and assisted the British in the War of 1812. Tecumseh was defeated and killed at the Battle of the Thames, Oct 5, 1813.

★ Birthdays ★

Grant Hill, basketball player, born Dallas, TX, Oct 5, 1972.

Mario Lemieux, Hall of Fame hockey player, born Montreal, QC, Canada, Oct 5, 1965.

Kate Winslet, actress (*Titanic*), born Reading, England, Oct 5, 1975.

October 6

"MONTY PYTHON'S FLYING CIRCUS" TV PREMIERE (US): ANNIVERSARY. Oct 6, 1974. This series of wacky comedy skits debuted on the BBC in Great Britain in 1969 but didn't air on US TV until 1974. The cast was made up of Graham Chapman, John Cleese, Eric Idle, Terry Jones, Michael Palin and American Terry Gilliam. The troupe later went on to make three movies.

NATIONAL GERMAN-AMERICAN DAY. Oct 6. Celebration of German heritage and contributions German Americans have made to the building of the nation. A Presidential Proclamation has been issued each year since 1987.

YOM KIPPUR WAR: ANNIVERSARY. Oct 6–25, 1973. A surprise attack by Egypt and Syria pushed Israeli forces several miles behind the 1967 cease-fire lines. Israel was caught off guard, partly because the attack came on the holiest Jewish religious day. After 18 days of fighting, hostilities were halted by the United Nations Oct 25. Israel partially recovered from the initial setback but failed to regain all the land lost in the fighting.

★ *Birthdays* ★

Rebecca Lobo, basketball player, born Southwick, MA, Oct 6, 1973.

Elisabeth Shue, actress (*Adventures in Babysitting, Leaving Las Vegas*), born Wilmington, DE, Oct 6, 1963.

October 7

***CATS* PREMIERE: ANNIVERSARY.** Oct 7, 1982. The longest-running production in Broadway history opened this day. *Cats* was based on a book of poetry by T.S. Eliot and had a score by Andrew Lloyd Webber. More than 10 million theatergoers saw the New York City production, which closed Sept 10, 2000, after 7,485 performances. *Cats* was also produced in 30 other countries.

DOW-JONES INDUSTRIAL AVERAGE: ANNIVERSARY. Oct 7, 1896. Dow Jones began reporting an average of the prices of 12 industrial stocks in the *Wall Street Journal* on this day. In the early years, these were largely railroad stocks. In 1928 Mr Dow expanded the number of stocks to 30, where it remains today. Today, the large, frequently traded stocks in the DJIA represent about a fifth of the market value of all US stocks.

★ *Birthdays* ★

Yo-Yo Ma, cellist, born Paris, France, Oct 7, 1955.

October 8

GREAT CHICAGO FIRE: ANNIVERSARY. Oct 8, 1871. Great fire of Chicago began, according to legend, when Mrs O'Leary's cow kicked over the lantern in her barn on DeKoven Street. The fire leveled 3½ square miles, destroying 17,450 buildings and leaving 98,500 people homeless and about 250 people dead. Financially, the loss was $200 million.

PESHTIGO FOREST FIRE: ANNIVERSARY. Oct 8, 1871. One of the most disastrous forest fires in history began at Peshtigo, WI, the same day the Great Chicago Fire began. The Wisconsin fire burned across six counties, killing more than 1,100 people.

★ *Birthdays* ★

Matt Damon, actor (*Good Will Hunting, The Rainmaker*), born Cambridge, MA, Oct 8, 1970.

Jesse Jackson, clergyman, civil rights leader ("I am somebody," "Keep hope alive"), born Greenville, NC, Oct 8, 1941.

Sigourney Weaver, actress (*Ghostbusters, Gorillas in the Mist, Aliens*), born Susan Weaver, New York, NY, Oct 8, 1949.

Scott Bakula, actor ("Quantum Leap," "Murphy Brown"), born St. Louis, MO, Oct 9, 1955.

Michael (Mike) Singletary, Hall of Fame football player, born Houston, TX, Oct 9, 1958.

October 9

LEIF ERIKSON DAY. Oct 9. Presidential Proclamation always issued for Oct 9 since 1964 (Public Law 88–566 of Sept 2, 1964) at request.

LENNON, JOHN: BIRTH ANNIVERSARY. Oct 9, 1940. John Winston Lennon, English composer, musician, member of The Beatles, a sensationally popular group of musical performers who captivated audiences first in England and Germany, and later throughout the world. Born at Liverpool, England, Lennon was murdered at New York City, Dec 8, 1980.

UGANDA: INDEPENDENCE DAY. Oct 9. National holiday commemorating achievement of autonomy from Britain in 1962.

UNITED NATIONS: WORLD POST DAY. Oct 9. An annual special observance of Postal Administrations of the Universal Postal Union (UPU). For info: United Nations. Web: www.un.org.

October 10

BONZA BOTTLER DAY™. Oct 10. To celebrate when the number of the day is the same as the number of the month. Bonza Bottler Day™ is an excuse to have a party at least once a month. For info: Gail M. Berger. E-mail: gberger5@aol.com.

TUXEDO CREATED: ANNIVERSARY. Oct 10, 1886. Griswold Lorillard of Tuxedo Park, NY, fashioned the first tuxedo for men by cutting the tails off a tailcoat.

UNITED NATIONS: WORLD MENTAL HEALTH DAY. Oct 10. For info: United Nations. Web: www .un.org.

"UPSTAIRS, DOWNSTAIRS" TV PREMIERE: ANNIVERSARY. Oct 10, 1971. The 52 episodes of this Masterpiece Theatre series covered the years 1903 to 1930 in the life of a wealthy London family ("Upstairs") and their many servants ("Downstairs"). Produced by London Weekend

Television, cast members included Angela Baddeley, Pauline Collins, Gordon Jackson and Jean Marsh. Won a Golden Globe Award for best drama in 1975 and an Emmy for outstanding limited series in 1976. The last episode aired May 1, 1977, though the series has been rerun several times on PBS.

US NAVAL ACADEMY FOUNDED: ANNIVERSARY. Oct 10, 1845. A college to train officers for the navy was established at Annapolis, MD. Women were admitted in 1976. The Academy's motto is "Honor, Courage, Commitment." For info: US Naval Academy. Web: www.usna.edu.

VERDI, GIUSEPPI: BIRTH ANNIVERSARY. Oct 10, 1813. Italian composer, born at Le Roncole, Italy. His 26 operas include *Rigoletto*, *Il Trovatore*, *La Traviata* and *Aida*, and are among the most popular of all operatic music today. Died at Milan, Italy, Jan 27, 1901.

★ *Birthdays* ★

Brett Favre, football player, born Gulfport, MS, Oct 10, 1969.
Ben Vereen, actor, singer, dancer (Tony for *Pippin; Roots, All That Jazz,* "Webster"), born Miami, FL, Oct 10, 1946.

October 11

GENERAL PULASKI MEMORIAL DAY. Oct 11. Presidential Proclamation always issued for Oct 11 since 1929. Proclamation 4869, of Oct 5, 1981, covers all succeeding years.

NATIONAL COMING OUT DAY. Oct 11. A project of the Human Rights Campaign. An international day of visibility for the lesbian and gay community since 1988. Local community groups sponsor activities and events that in the past have included "coming out" dances, rallies and demonstrations, educational films, fairs and workshops, literature drops, fund-raisers, and religious blessings of lesbian and gay couples and families. For info: National Coming Out Project. Web: www.hrc.org.

ROOSEVELT, (ANNA) ELEANOR: BIRTH ANNIVERSARY. Oct 11, 1884. Wife of Franklin Delano Roosevelt, 32nd president of the US, was born at New York, NY. She led an active and independent life and was the first wife of a president to give her own news conference in the White House (1933). Widely known throughout the world, she was affectionately called "the first lady of the world." She served as US delegate to the United Nations General Assembly for a number of years before her death at New York, NY, Nov 7, 1962. A prolific writer, she wrote in *This Is My Story*, "No one can make you feel inferior without your consent."

"SATURDAY NIGHT LIVE" TV PREMIERE: ANNIVERSARY. Oct 11, 1975. Through the years this show has been through numerous cast, writing, producing and musical staff changes. However, its format has remained the same: skits, commercial parodies, recurring characters and news parodies, with a different guest host and musical guest performing every week—live. It was originally titled "NBC's Saturday Night," with its first host being comedian George Carlin. Notable cast members have included Chevy Chase, Dan Aykroyd, John Belushi, Jane Curtin, Garrett Morris, Laraine Newman, Gilda Radner, Bill Murray, Joe Piscopo, Eddie Murphy, Tim Kazurinsky, Julia Louis-Dreyfus, Jim Belushi, Billy Crystal, Martin Short, Christopher Guest, Joan Cusack, Robert Downey, Jr, Nora Dunn, Jon Lovitz, Dana Carvey, Phil Hartman, Jan Hooks, Victoria Jackson, Dennis Miller, Chris Farley and Kevin Nealon.

SPACE MILESTONE: *DISCOVERY STS-92*: **100th SHUTTLE FLIGHT.** Oct 11, 2000. *Discovery* was launched on its 28th flight. This marked the shuttle program's 100th mission. On this flight, *Discovery* was headed to the International Space Station, where it docked on Oct 13. On earlier flights, the shuttles *Columbia, Challenger, Endeavour, Atlantis* and *Discovery* had launched the Hubble Space Telescope and Chandra X-Ray Observatory, docked with the *Mir* space station and supported scientific research. The first shuttle flight took place in 1981. Since the first mission, space shuttles have carried 261 individuals and nearly 3 million pounds of payload and logged an estimated 350 million miles. See: "Space Milestone: *Columbia STS-1* (US): First Shuttle Flight" (Apr 12).

VATICAN COUNCIL II: ANNIVERSARY. Oct 11, 1962. The 21st ecumenical council of the Roman Catholic Church was convened by Pope John XXIII. It met in four annual sessions, concluding Dec 8, 1965. It dealt with the renewal of the Church and introduced sweeping changes, such as the use of the vernacular rather than Latin in the Mass.

★ *Birthdays* ★

Joan Cusack, actress (*Working Girl, Sixteen Candles*), born Evanston, IL, Oct 11, 1962.
Orlando Hernandez, baseball player, known as "El Duque," born Villa Clara, Cuba, Oct 11, 1969.
Ron Leibman, actor (*Norma Rae*; stage: *We Bombed in New Haven, Angels in America* [Tony Award]), born New York, NY, Oct 11, 1937.

October 12

COLUMBUS DAY (TRADITIONAL). Oct 12. Public holiday in most countries in the Americas and in most Spanish-speaking countries. Observed under different names (Dia de la Raza or Day of the Race) and on different dates (most often, as in the US, on the second Monday in October). Anniversary of Christopher Columbus's arrival, Oct 12, 1492, after a dangerous voyage across "shoreless Seas," at the Bahamas, which he claimed in the name of the Spanish crown. In his *Journal*, he wrote: "As I saw that they (the natives) were friendly to us, and perceived that they could be much more easily converted to our holy faith by gentle means than by force, I presented them with some red caps, and strings of beads to wear upon the neck, and many other trifles of small value, wherewith they were much delighted, and became wonderfully attached to us."

DAY OF THE 6 BILLION: ANNIVERSARY. Oct 12, 1999. According to the United Nations, the population of the world reached 6 billion on this date. More than one-third of the world's people live in China and India. It wasn't until 1804 that the world's population reached 1 billion; now a billion people are added to the population about every 12 years. The world's population reached 5 billion on July 11, 1987.

INTERNATIONAL MOMENT OF FRUSTRATION SCREAM DAY. Oct 12. To share any or all of our frustrations, all citizens of the world will go outdoors at 12 hundred hours Greenwich time and scream for 30 seconds. We will all feel better or Earth will go off its orbit. [©2001 by WH.] For info: Wellcat Holidays. Web: www.wellcat.com.

MEXICO: DIA DE LA RAZA. Oct 12. Columbus Day is observed as the "Day of the Race," a fiesta time to commemorate the discovery of America as well as the common interests and cultural heritage of the Spanish and Indian peoples and the Hispanic nations.

"SNEAK PREVIEWS" TV PREMIERE: ANNIVERSARY. Oct 12, 1978. This show with film critics Gene Siskel and Roger Ebert got its start on public television in Chicago in 1975. In 1978 it went national on PBS. In 1981 the program moved to network TV and the name was changed to "At the Movies." After Siskel's death in 1999, a rotating panel of critics joined Ebert and the show's title was changed to "Roger Ebert & the Movies." In 2000 journalist Richard Roeper joined the show and the title was changed to "Ebert & Roeper and the Movies."

SPAIN: NATIONAL HOLIDAY. Oct 12. Called Hispanity Day or Day of Spanish Consciousness. Honors Christopher Columbus and the Spanish conquerors of Latin America.

★ Birthdays ★

Hugh Jackman, actor (*Kate & Leopold, Swordfish*), born Sydney, Australia, Oct 12, 1968.

Luciano Pavarotti, opera singer, one of the "Three Tenors," born Modena, Italy, Oct 12, 1935.

★ Birthdays ★

Kelly Preston, actress (*Jerry Maguire, Twins*), born Honolulu, HI, Oct 13, 1962.

Paul Simon, singer, songwriter (with Art Garfunkel: "The Sounds of Silence," "Mrs Robinson"; solo album: *Graceland*), born Newark, NJ, Oct 13, 1941.

October 13

US NAVY: AUTHORIZATION ANNIVERSARY. Oct 13, 1775. Commemorates legislation passed by Second Continental Congress authorizing the acquisition of ships and establishment of a navy.

WHITE HOUSE CORNERSTONE LAID: ANNIVERSARY. Oct 13, 1792. The presidential residence at 1600 Pennsylvania Ave NW, Washington, DC, designed by James Hoban, observes its birthday Oct 13. The first presidential family to occupy it was that of John Adams, in November 1800. With three stories and more than 100 rooms, the White House is the oldest building at Washington. First described as the "presidential palace," it acquired the name "White House" about ten years after construction was completed. Burned by British troops in 1814, it was reconstructed, refurbished and reoccupied by 1817.

October 14

BE BALD AND BE FREE DAY. Oct 14. For those who are bald and who either do wear or do not wear a wig or toupee, this is the day to go "shiny" and be proud. [©2001 by WH.] For info: Wellcat Holidays. Web: www.wellcat.com.

DOW-JONES TOPS 6,000: ANNIVERSARY. Oct 14, 1996. The Dow-Jones Index of 30 major industrial stocks topped the 6,000 mark for the first time.

EISENHOWER, DWIGHT DAVID: BIRTH ANNIVERSARY. Oct 14, 1890. The 34th president of the US, Dwight David Eisenhower, was born at Denison, TX. Serving two terms as president, Jan 20, 1953–Jan 20, 1961, Eisenhower was the first president to be baptized after taking office (Sunday, Feb 1, 1953). Nicknamed "Ike," he held the rank of five-star general of the army. He served as supreme commander of the Allied forces in western Europe during World War II. In his Farewell Address (Jan 17, 1961), speaking about the "conjunction of an immense military establishment and a large arms industry," he warned: "In the councils of government, we must guard against the acquisition of unwarranted influence, whether sought or unsought, by the military-industrial complex. The potential of the disastrous rise of misplaced power exists and will persist." An American hero, Eisenhower died at Washington, DC, Mar 28, 1969.

KING AWARDED NOBEL PEACE PRIZE: ANNIVERSARY. Oct 14, 1964. Martin Luther King, Jr, became the youngest recipient of the Nobel Peace Prize when awarded the honor. Dr. King donated the entire $54,000 prize money to furthering the causes of the civil rights movement.

SOUND BARRIER BROKEN: ANNIVERSARY. Oct 14, 1947. Flying a Bell X-1 at Muroc Dry Lake Bed, CA, US Air Force pilot Chuck Yeager broke the sound barrier, ushering in the era of supersonic flight.

★ *Birthdays* ★

Harry Anderson, actor ("Night Court," "Dave's World"), born Newport, RI, Oct 14, 1952.
Ralph Lauren, designer, born the Bronx, NY, Oct 14, 1939.

October 15

FIRST MANNED FLIGHT: ANNIVERSARY. Oct 15, 1783. Jean Francois Pilatre de Rozier and Francois Laurent, Marquis d'Arlandes, became the first people to fly when they ascended in a Montgolfier hot-air balloon at Paris, France, only four months after the first public balloon flight demonstration (June 5, 1783), and only a year after the first experiments with small paper and fabric balloons by the Montgolfier brothers, Joseph and Jacques, in November 1782. The first manned free flight lasted about four minutes and carried the passengers to a height of about 84 feet. On Nov 21, 1783, they soared 3,000 feet over Paris for 25 minutes.

"I LOVE LUCY" TV PREMIERE: ANNIVERSARY. Oct 15, 1951. This enormously popular sitcom, TV's first smash hit, starred the real-life husband and wife team of Cuban actor/bandleader Desi Arnaz and talented redheaded actress/comedienne Lucille Ball. They played Ricky and Lucy Ricardo, a New York bandleader and his aspiring actress/homemaker wife who was always scheming to get on stage. Costarring were William Frawley and Vivian Vance as Fred and Ethel Mertz, the Ricardos' landlords and good friends who participated in the escapades and dealt with the consequences of Lucy's often well intentioned plans. Famous actors guest-starred on the show, including Harpo Marx, Rock Hudson, William Holden, Hedda Hopper and John Wayne. This was the first sitcom to be filmed live before a studio audience, and it did extremely well in the ratings both the first time around and in reruns. The last telecast ran Sept 24, 1961.

SPACE MILESTONE: *CASSINI* (US). Oct 15, 1997. The plutonium-powered spacecraft launched Oct 15, 1997, is to arrive at Saturn in July 2004. It will orbit the planet, take pictures of its 18 known moons and dispatch a probe to Titan, the largest of these moons.

WHITE CANE SAFETY DAY. Oct 15. Presidential Proclamation always issued for Oct 15 since 1964 (Public Law 88–628 of Oct 6, 1964).

★ *Birthdays* ★

Linda Lavin, actress (Tony for *Broadway Bound*; "Alice"), born Portland, ME, Oct 15, 1939.
James Alvin (Jim) Palmer, sportscaster, Baseball Hall of Fame pitcher, born New York, NY, Oct 15, 1945.

October 16

DICTIONARY DAY. Oct 16. The birthday of Noah Webster, American teacher and lexicographer, is occasion to encourage every person to acquire at least one dictionary—and to use it regularly. Webster's name became synonymous with the word "dictionary" after his compilations of the earliest American dictionaries of the English language. Born at West Hartford, CT, he died at New Haven, CT, May 28, 1843.

JOHN BROWN'S RAID: ANNIVERSARY. Oct 16, 1859. White abolitionist John Brown, with a band of about 20 men, seized the US Arsenal at Harpers Ferry, WV. Brown was captured and the insurrection put down by Oct 19. Brown was hanged at Charles Town, WV, Dec 2, 1859.

MILLION MAN MARCH: ANNIVERSARY. Oct 16, 1995. Hundreds of thousands of black men met at Washington, DC, for a "holy day of atonement and reconciliation" organized by Louis Farrakhan, leader of the Nation of Islam. Marchers pledged to take responsibility for themselves, their families and their communities.

UNITED NATIONS: WORLD FOOD DAY. Oct 16. Annual observance to heighten public awareness of the world food problem and to strengthen

solidarity in the struggle against hunger, malnutrition and poverty. Date of observance is anniversary of founding of Food and Agriculture Organization (FAO), Oct 16, 1945, at Quebec, Canada. For info: United Nations. Web: www.un.org.

WILDE, OSCAR: BIRTH ANNIVERSARY. Oct 16, 1854. Irish poet and playwright Oscar (Fingal O'Flahertie Wills) Wilde was born at Dublin, Ireland. At the height of his career he was imprisoned for two years on a morals offense, during which time he wrote "A Ballad of Reading Gaol." Best known of his plays is *The Importance of Being Earnest.* "There is only one thing in the world worse than being talked about," he wrote in his *Picture of Dorian Gray,* "and that is not being talked about." Wilde died at Paris, France, Nov 30, 1900. His dying words are said to have been: "This wallpaper is killing me; one of us has got to go."

★ Birthdays ★

Angela Lansbury, actress ("Murder She Wrote," *National Velvet*; Tony for *Sweeney Todd*), born London, England, Oct 16, 1925.
Kellie Martin, actress ("Life Goes On," "ER"), born Riverside, CA, Oct 16, 1975.
Tim Robbins, actor (*Top Gun, Shawshank Redemption*), born West Covina, CA, Oct 16, 1958.

October 17

HAMMON, JUPITER: BIRTH ANNIVERSARY. Oct 17, 1711. America's first published black poet, whose birth anniversary is celebrated annually as Black Poetry Day, was born into slavery, probably at Long Island, NY. He was taught to read, however, and as a trusted servant was allowed to use his master's library. With the publication on Christmas Day, 1760, of the 88-line broadside poem 'An Evening Thought,' Jupiter Hammon, then 49, became the first black in America to publish poetry. Hammon died in 1790. The exact date and place of his death are unknown.

"THE HOLLYWOOD SQUARES" TV PREMIERE: ANNIVERSARY. Oct 17, 1966. On this game show, nine celebrities sat in a giant grid. Two contestants played tic-tac-toe by determining if an answer given by a celebrity was correct. Peter Marshall hosted the show for many years with panelists Paul Lynde, Rose Marie, Cliff Arquette, Wally Cox, John Davidson and George Gobel among others. John Davidson took over as host in 1986 for a new version of the game show with Joan Rivers and, later, Shadoe Stevens at center square. In 1998 "Hollywood Squares" appeared again with Tom Bergeron as host and Whoopi Goldberg as the center square.

SAN FRANCISCO 1989 EARTHQUAKE: ANNIVERSARY. Oct 17, 1989. The San Francisco Bay area was rocked by an earthquake registering 7.1 on the Richter scale at 5:04 PM, PDT, just as the nation's baseball fans settled in to watch the 1989 World Series. A large audience was tuned in to the pregame coverage when the quake hit and knocked the broadcast off the air. The quake caused damage estimated at $10 billion and killed 67 people, many of whom were caught in the collapse of the double-decked Interstate 80, at Oakland, CA.

UNITED NATIONS: INTERNATIONAL DAY FOR THE ERADICATION OF POVERTY. Oct 17. The General Assembly proclaimed this observance (Resolution 47/196) to promote public awareness of the need to eradicate poverty and destitution in all countries, particularly the developing nations. For info: United Nations. Web: www.un.org.

★ Birthdays ★

Ernie Els, golfer, born Johannesburg, South Africa, Oct 17, 1969.

Norm Macdonald, comedian, actor ("Saturday Night Live," "The Norm Show"), born at Quebec City, QC, Canada, Oct 17, 1963.

October 18

ALASKA DAY. Oct 18, 1867. Alaska. Anniversary of transfer of Alaska from Russia to the US, which became official on Sitka's Castle Hill. This is a holiday in Alaska; when it falls on a weekend it is observed on the following Monday.

AZERBAIJAN: INDEPENDENCE DAY. Oct 18. National holiday. Commemorates declaration of independence from the Soviet Union in 1991.

"ROSEANNE" TV PREMIERE: ANNIVERSARY. Oct 18, 1988. This comedy showed the blue-collar Conner family trying to make ends meet. Rosanne Barr played wise-cracking Roseanne Conner, John Goodman played her husband Dan and Laurie Metcalf played her sister Jackie. The Conner children were played by Sara Gilbert (Darlene), Alicia Goranson and Sarah Chalke (Becky) and Michael Fishman (D.J.). The last episode aired Nov 14, 1997, but it remains popular in reruns.

SAINT LUKE: FEAST DAY. Oct 18. Patron saint of doctors and artists, himself a physician and painter, authorship of the third Gospel and Acts of the Apostles is attributed to him. Died about AD 68. Legend says that he painted portraits of Mary and Jesus.

★ Birthdays ★

Peter Boyle, actor (*Medium Cool, The Dream Team,* "Everybody Loves Raymond"), born Philadelphia, PA, Oct 18, 1933.
Wynton Marsalis, jazz musician, born New Orleans, LA, Oct 18, 1961.

October 19

DOW-JONES BIGGEST DROP: ANNIVERSARY. Oct 19, 1987. The Dow-Jones Industrial Average plunged 508 points, or 22.6 percent, the largest percentage drop on one day in history. On Oct 27, 1997, the Dow fell 554 points, its biggest single-day point drop. However, as the index had grown dramatically, this was only a 7.2 percent drop in overall value.

★ Birthdays ★

Evander Holyfield, boxer, born Atlanta, GA, Oct 19, 1962.
John Le Carre, author (*The Russia House*), born David John Moore Cornwell, Poole, England, Oct 19, 1931.
John Lithgow, actor (*Twilight Zone: The Movie, I'm Dancing as Fast as I Can,* "3rd Rock from the Sun"), born Rochester, NY, Oct 19, 1945.

October 20

MacARTHUR RETURNS: US LANDINGS ON LEYTE, PHILIPPINES: ANNIVERSARY. Oct 20, 1944. In mid-September of 1944 American military leaders made the decision to begin the invasion of the Philippines on Leyte, a small island north of the Surigao Strait. With General Douglas MacArthur in overall command, US aircraft dropped hundreds of tons of bombs in the area of Dulag. Four divisions were landed on the east coast, and after a few hours General MacArthur set foot on Philippine soil for the first time since he was ordered to Australia Mar 11, 1942, thus fulfilling his promise, "I shall return."

MANTLE, MICKEY: BIRTH ANNIVERSARY. Oct 20, 1931. Baseball Hall of Famer, born at Spavinaw, OK. Died Aug 13, 1995, at Dallas, TX.

"THE SIX MILLION DOLLAR MAN" TV PREMIERE: ANNIVERSARY. Oct 20, 1973. This action-adventure series based on the novel *Cyborg* was a monthly feature on "The ABC Suspense Movie" before becoming a regular series in 1974. Lee Majors starred as astronaut Steve Austin, who, after an accident, was "rebuilt" with bionic legs, arms and an eye. He worked for the Office of Strategic Information (OSI) carrying out sensitive missions. Also in the cast were Richard Anderson, Alan Oppenheimer and Martin E. Brooks. "The Bionic Woman," starring Lindsay Wagner, was a spin-off from this show, and the two main characters were paired for several made-for-TV sequels.

★ Birthdays ★

Art Buchwald, columnist, author (*While Reagan Slept*), born Mount Vernon, NY, Oct 20, 1925.
Jerry Orbach, actor ("Law & Order," *Crimes and Misdemeanors, Dirty Dancing*; stage: *The Fantasticks*; Tony for *Promises, Promises*), born the Bronx, NY, Oct 20, 1935.

October 21

INCANDESCENT LAMP DEMONSTRATED: ANNIVERSARY. Oct 21, 1879. Thomas A. Edison demonstrated the first incandescent lamp that could be used economically for domestic purposes. This prototype, developed at his Menlo Park, NJ, laboratory, could burn for 13½ hours.

VIETNAM WAR PROTESTORS STORM PENTAGON: ANNIVERSARY. Oct 21, 1967. Some 250 protestors were arrested when thousands of the 50,000 participants in a rally against the Vietnam War at Washington, DC, crossed the Potomac River and stormed the Pentagon. No shots were fired, but many demonstrators were struck with nightsticks and rifle butts.

★ Birthdays ★

Carrie Fisher, actress (*Star Wars, Shampoo*), author (*Postcards from the Edge*), born Beverly Hills, CA, Oct 21, 1956.
Edward Charles "Whitey" Ford, Hall of Fame baseball player, born New York, NY, Oct 21, 1928.

October 22

CUBAN MISSILE CRISIS: ANNIVERSARY. Oct 22, 1962. President John F. Kennedy, in a nationwide television address Oct 22, 1962, demanded the removal from Cuba of Soviet missiles, launched equipment and bombers, and imposed a naval "quarantine" to prevent further weaponry from reaching Cuba. On Oct 28, the USSR announced it would remove the weapons in question. In return, the US removed missiles from Turkey that were aimed at the USSR.

INTERNATIONAL STUTTERING AWARENESS DAY. Oct 22. For info: National Stuttering Association. Web: www.nsastutter.org or www.stuttering homepage.com.

★ Birthdays ★

Jeff Goldblum, actor (*The Big Chill, The Fly, Jurassic Park*), born Pittsburgh, PA, Oct 22, 1952.

Derek Jacobi, actor ("I, Claudius," *The Day of the Jackal*), born London, England, Oct 22, 1938.

Ichiro Suzuki, baseball player, born Kasugai, Japan, Oct 22, 1973.

October 23

BEIRUT TERRORIST ATTACK: ANNIVERSARY. Oct 23, 1983. A suicidal terrorist attack on American forces at Beirut, Lebanon, killed 240 US personnel when a truck loaded with TNT was driven into and exploded at US headquarters there. A similar attack on French forces killed scores more.

HUNGARY: ANNIVERSARY OF 1956 REVOLUTION. Oct 23. National holiday. Also called Uprising Day of Remembrance. Commemorates revolt against Soviet domination which was crushed on Nov 4, 1956. Thirty-three years later, Hungary declared itself an independent republic on this day.

SCORPIO, THE SCORPION. Oct 23–Nov 22. In the astronomical/astrological zodiac that divides the sun's apparent orbit into 12 segments, the period Oct 23–Nov 22 is identified, traditionally, as the sun sign of Scorpio, the Scorpion. The ruling planet is Pluto or Mars.

★ Birthdays ★

Johnny Carson, former TV talk-show host ("The Tonight Show"), born Corning, IA, Oct 23, 1925.

Michael Crichton, writer (*Jurassic Park, Rising Sun*), born Chicago, IL, Oct 23, 1942.

October 24

UNITED NATIONS DAY: ANNIVERSARY OF FOUNDING. Oct 24, 1945. Official United Nations holiday commemorates founding of the United Nations and effective date of the United Nations Charter. In 1971 the General Assembly recommended this day be observed as a public holiday by UN Member States (Resolution 2782/xxvi). A Presidential Proclamation is issued in the US every year on this date. For info: United Nations. Web: www.un.org.

UNITED NATIONS: DISARMAMENT WEEK. Oct 24–30. In 1978, the General Assembly called on member states to highlight the danger of the arms race, propogate the need for its cessation and increase public understanding of the urgent task of disarmament. Observed annually, beginning on the anniversary of the founding of the UN. For info: United Nations. Web: www.un.org.

★ Birthdays ★

Kevin Kline, actor (Oscar for *A Fish Called Wanda*, *Silverado*), born St. Louis, MO, Oct 24, 1947.

Yelberton Abraham (Y.A.) Tittle, Jr, Hall of Fame football player, born Marshall, TX, Oct 24, 1926.

October 25

KAZAKHSTAN: INDEPENDENCE DAY. Oct 25. National Day. Commemorates independence from the Soviet Union in 1991.

"NEWHART" TV PREMIERE: ANNIVERSARY. Oct 25, 1982. Bob Newhart starred in this sitcom as Dick Loudon, an author of how-to books who moved with his wife, Joanna (Mary Frann), to Vermont to take over the Stratford Inn. Regulars included Tom Poston, Steven Kampmann, Jennifer Holmes and Julia Duffy. The last telecast was Sept 8, 1990. Newhart had previously hosted "The Bob Newhart Show," which premiered Oct 10, 1962. This half-hour variety series was critically acclaimed, winning both an Emmy and a Peabody in its short time on the air. Newhart later starred in "The Bob Newhart Show," which aired 1972–78, a situation comedy in which he played a psychologist.

PICASSO, PABLO RUIZ: BIRTH ANNIVERSARY. Oct 25, 1881. Called by many the greatest artist of the 20th century, Pablo Picasso excelled as a painter, sculptor and engraver. He is said to have commented once: "I am only a public entertainer who has understood his time." Born at Malaga, Spain, he died Apr 9, 1973, at Mougins, France.

★ Birthdays ★

Bobby Knight, college basketball coach and former player, born Orrville, OH, Oct 25, 1940.

Pedro Martinez, baseball player, born Manoguayabo, Dominican Republic, Oct 25, 1971.

October 26

AUSTRIA: NATIONAL DAY. Oct 26. National holiday. Commemorates the withdrawal of Soviet troops in 1955.

ERIE CANAL: ANNIVERSARY. Oct 26, 1825. The Erie Canal, first US major man-made waterway, was opened, providing a water route from Lake Erie to the Hudson River. Construction started July 4, 1817, and the canal cost $7,602,000. Cannons fired and celebrations were held all along the route for the opening.

"ST. ELSEWHERE" TV PREMIERE: ANNIVERSARY. Oct 26, 1982. A popular one-hour medical drama set in St. Eligius Hospital at Boston. Among its large and changing cast were Ed Flanders, William Daniels, Ed Begley, Jr, David Morse, Howie Mandel, Christina Pickles, Denzel Washington, Norman Lloyd, David Birney, G.W. Bailey, Kavi Raz, Stephen Furst, Mark Harmon and Alfre Woodard. The last episode of the series, aired on Aug 10, 1988, cast doubt on the reality of the whole series, suggesting that a child's imagination had dreamed it up.

★ Birthdays ★

Tom Cavanagh, actor ("Ed"), born Ottawa, ON, Canada, Oct 26, 1968.
Bob Hoskins, actor (*Mona Lisa, Who Framed Roger Rabbit*), born Bury St. Edmonds, Suffolk, England, Oct 26, 1942.
Dylan McDermott, actor ("The Practice"), born Waterbury, CT, Oct 26, 1962.

October 27

COOK, JAMES: BIRTH ANNIVERSARY. Oct 27, 1728 (OS). English sea captain of the ship *Endeavour* and explorer who brought Australia and New Zealand into the British Empire. Born at Marton-in-Cleveland, Yorkshire, England, he was killed Feb 14, 1779, at the Hawaiian Islands, which he discovered.

FEDERALIST PAPERS: ANNIVERSARY. Oct 27, 1787. The first of the 85 "Federalist" papers appeared in print in a New York City newspaper, Oct 27, 1787. These essays, written by Alexander Hamilton, James Madison and John Jay, argued in favor of adoption of the new Constitution and the new form of federal government. The last of the essays was completed Apr 4, 1788.

NEW YORK CITY SUBWAY: ANNIVERSARY. Oct 27, 1904. Running from City Hall to West 145th Street, the New York City subway began operation. It was privately operated by the Interborough Rapid Transit Company and later became part of the system operated by the New York City Transit Authority.

ROOSEVELT, THEODORE: BIRTH ANNIVERSARY. Oct 27, 1858. Twenty-sixth president of the US, succeeded to the presidency on the death of William McKinley. His term of office: Sept 14, 1901–Mar 3, 1909. Roosevelt was the first president to ride in an automobile (1902), to submerge in a submarine (1905) and to fly in an airplane (1910). Although his best-remembered quote was perhaps, "Speak softly and carry a big stick," he also said: "The first requisite of a good citizen in this Republic of ours is that he shall be able and willing to pull his weight." Born at New York, NY, Roosevelt died at Oyster Bay, NY, Jan 6, 1919. His last words: "Put out the light."

TURKMENISTAN: INDEPENDENCE DAY. Oct 27. National holiday. Commemorates independence from the Soviet Union in 1991.

"WALT DISNEY" TV PREMIERE: ANNIVERSARY. Oct 27, 1954. This highly successful and long-running show appeared on different networks under different names but was essentially the same program. It was the first prime-time anthology series for kids. It was originally titled "Disneyland" to promote the park and upcoming Disney releases. Later the title was changed to "Walt Disney Presents." Later titles included "Walt Disney's Wonderful World of Color" (to highlight its being broadcast in color), "The Wonderful World of Disney," "The Disney Sunday Movie" and "The Magical World of Disney." Presentations included edited versions of previously released Disney films and original productions (including natural history documentaries and dramatic shows, including the popular Davy Crockett segments that were the first TV miniseries). The show went off the air in December 1980 after 25 years, making it the longest-running series in prime-time TV history.

★ *Birthdays* ★

John Cleese, writer, actor ("Monty Python's Flying Circus," *A Fish Called Wanda*), born Weston-Super-Mare, England, Oct 27, 1939. **Ruby Dee**, actress (*Do the Right Thing, Jungle Fever*), born Cleveland, OH, Oct 27, 1924.

October 28

CZECH REPUBLIC: INDEPENDENCE DAY. Oct 28. National Day, anniversary of the bloodless revolution at Prague in 1918 resulting in independence from the Austro-Hungarian Empire, after which the Czechs and Slovaks united to form Czechoslovakia (a union they dissolved without bloodshed in 1993).

DONNER PARTY FAMINE: ANNIVERSARY. Oct 28, 1846–Apr 21, 1847. The pioneering Donner Party, a group of 90 people consisting of immigrants, families and businessmen led by George and Jacob Donner and James F. Reed, headed toward California in 1846 from Springfield, IL, in hopes of beginning a new life. They experienced the normal travails of caravan travel until their trip took several sensational twists. Indian attacks and winter weather that forced them to interrupt their journey led to famine and outright cannibalism, which took their toll on members of the party whose numbers dwindled to 48 by journey's end.

HARVARD UNIVERSITY FOUNDED: ANNIVERSARY. Oct 28, 1636. Harvard University founded at Cambridge, MA, when the Massachusetts General Court voted to provide £400 for a "schoale or colledge." Harvard is the oldest institution of higher education in the US.

SALK, JONAS: BIRTH ANNIVERSARY. Oct 28, 1914. Dr. Jonas Salk, developer of the Salk polio vaccine, was born at New York, NY. Salk announced his development of a successful vaccine in 1953, the year after a polio epidemic claimed some 3,300 lives in the US. Polio deaths were reduced by 95 percent after the introduction of the vaccine. Salk spent the last ten years of his life doing AIDS research. He died June 23, 1995, at La Jolla, CA.

STATUE OF LIBERTY: DEDICATION ANNIVERSARY. Oct 28, 1886. Frederic Auguste Bartholdi's famous sculpture, the statue of *Liberty Enlightening the World*, on Bedloe's Island in New York Harbor, was dedicated. Ground breaking for the structure was in April 1883. A sonnet by Emma Lazarus, inside the pedestal of the statue, contains the words: "Give me your tired, your poor, your huddled masses yearning to breathe free, the wretched refuse of your teeming shore. Send these, the homeless, tempest-tost to me, I lift my lamp beside the golden door!"

★ *Birthdays* ★

Dennis Franz, actor ("Hill Street Blues," "NYPD Blue"), born Maywood, IL, Oct 28, 1944.
Bill Gates, computer software executive (Microsoft), born Seattle, WA, Oct 28, 1955.
Julia Roberts, actress (*Steel Magnolias, Pretty Woman, My Best Friend's Wedding*), born Smyrna, GA, Oct 28, 1967.

October 29

INTERNET CREATED: ANNIVERSARY. Oct 29, 1969. The first connection on what would become the Internet was made on this day when bits of data flowed between computers at UCLA and the Stanford Research Institute. This was the beginning of ARPANET, the precurser to the Internet developed by the Department of Defense. By the end of 1969, four sites were connected: UCLA, the Stanford Research Institute, the University of California at Santa Barbara and the University of Utah. By the next year there were ten sites and soon there were applications like e-mail and file transfer utilities. The @ symbol was adopted in 1972 and a year later 75 percent of ARPANET traffic was e-mail. ARPANET was decommissioned in 1990 and the National Science Foundation's NSFnet took over the role of backbone of the Internet.

SPACE MILESTONE: OLDEST MAN IN SPACE: *DISCOVERY* (US). Oct 29, 1998. Former astronaut and senator John Glenn became the oldest man in space when he traveled on the space shuttle *Discovery* at the age of 77. In 1962 on *Friendship 7* Glenn had been the first American to orbit Earth. See "Space Milestone: *Friendship 7* (US): First American to Orbit Earth" (Feb 20).

STOCK MARKET CRASH: ANNIVERSARY. Oct 29, 1929. Prices on the New York Stock Exchange plummeted and virtually collapsed four days after President Herbert Hoover had declared "The fundamental business of the country . . . is on a sound and prosperous basis." More than 16 million shares were dumped and billions of dollars were lost. The boom was over and the nation faced nearly a decade of depression. Some analysts had warned that the buying spree, with prices 15 to 150 times above earnings, had to stop at some point. Frightened investors ordered their brokers to sell at whatever price. The resulting Great Depression, which lasted until about 1939, involved North America, Europe and other industrialized countries. In 1932 one out of four US workers was unemployed.

TURKEY: REPUBLIC DAY. Oct 29. Anniversary of the founding of the republic in 1923.

★ *Birthdays* ★

Richard Dreyfuss, actor (*American Graffiti, Jaws*; Oscar for *The Goodbye Girl*), born Brooklyn, NY, Oct 29, 1947.
Kate Jackson, actress ("Charlie's Angels," "Scarecrow and Mrs King"), born Birmingham, AL, Oct 29, 1948.

Winona Ryder, actress (*Beetlejuice, Edward Scissorhands, Little Women*), born Winona, MN, Oct 29, 1971.

October 30

ADAMS, JOHN: BIRTH ANNIVERSARY. Oct 30, 1735. Second president of the US (term of office: Mar 4, 1797–Mar 3, 1801), who was George Washington's vice president and the father of John Quincy Adams (sixth president of the US). Born at Braintree, MA, he once wrote in a letter to Thomas Jefferson: "You and I ought not to die before we have explained ourselves to each other." John Adams and Thomas Jefferson died on the same day, July 4, 1826, the 50th anniversary of adoption of the Declaration of Independence. Adams's last words: "Thomas Jefferson still survives." Jefferson's last words: "Is it the fourth?"

ATLAS, CHARLES: BIRTH ANNIVERSARY. Oct 30, 1893. Charles Atlas (ex-97-pound weakling), whose original name was Angelo Siciliano, was born at Acri, Calabria, Italy. A bodybuilder and physical culturist, he created a popular mail-order bodybuilding course. The legendary sand-kicking episode used later in advertising for his course occurred at Coney Island when a life-guard kicked sand in Atlas's face and stole his girlfriend. Three generations of comic book fans read his advertisements. He died Dec 24, 1972, at Long Beach, NY.

DEVIL'S NIGHT. Oct 30. Formerly a "Mischief Night" on the evening before Halloween and an occasion for harmless pranks, chiefly observed by children. However, in some areas of the US, the destruction of property and endangering of lives has led to the imposition of dusk-to-dawn curfews during the last two or three days of October. Not to be confused with "Trick or Treat," or "Beggar's Night," usually observed on Halloween. See also: "Hallowe'en" (Oct 31).

POST, EMILY: BIRTH ANNIVERSARY. Oct 30, 1872. Emily Post was born at Baltimore, MD. Published in 1922, her book *Etiquette: The Blue Book of Social Usage* instantly became the American bible of manners and social behavior and established Post as the household name in matters of etiquette. It was in its tenth edition at the time of her death Sept 25, 1960, at New York, NY. *Etiquette* inspired a great many letters asking Post for advice on manners in specific situations. She used these letters as the basis for her radio show and her syndicated newspaper column, which eventually appeared in more than 200 papers.

"WAR OF THE WORLDS" BROADCAST: ANNIVERSARY. Oct 30, 1938. As part of a series of radio dramas based on famous novels, Orson Welles with the Mercury Players produced H.G. Wells's *War of the Worlds.* Near panic resulted when listeners believed the simulated news bulletins, which described a Martian invasion of New Jersey, to be real.

★ *Birthdays* ★

Harry Hamlin, actor ("L.A. Law," "Studs Lonigan"), born Pasadena, CA, Oct 30, 1951.
Andrea Mitchell, TV news correspondent, born New York, NY, Oct 30, 1946.

October 31

FIRST BLACK PLAYS IN NBA GAME: ANNIVERSARY. Oct 31, 1950. Earl Lloyd became the first black ever to play in an NBA game when he took the floor for the Washington Capitols at Rochester, NY. Lloyd was actually one of three blacks to become an NBA player in the 1950 season, the others being Nat "Sweetwater" Clifton, who was signed by the New York Knicks, and Chuck Cooper, who was drafted by the Boston Celtics (and debuted the night after Lloyd).

HALLOWE'EN or ALL HALLOW'S EVE. Oct 31. An ancient celebration combining Druid autumn festival and Christian customs. Hallowe'en (All Hallows' Eve) is the beginning of Hallowtide, a season that embraces the Feast of All Saints (Nov 1) and the Feast of All Souls (Nov 2). The observance, dating from the sixth or seventh centuries, has long been associated with thoughts of the dead, spirits, witches, ghosts and devils. In fact, the ancient Celtic Feast of Samhain, the festival that marked the beginning of winter and of the New Year, was observed Nov 1. A popular custom on Hallowe'en is children in costumes visiting neighbors' homes, calling out "trick or treat" and "begging" for candies or gifts to place in their beggars' bags.

MOUNT RUSHMORE COMPLETION: ANNIVERSARY. Oct 31, 1941. The Mount Rushmore National Memorial was completed after 14 years of work. First suggested by Jonah Robinson of the South Dakota State Historical Society, the memorial was dedicated in 1925, and work began in 1927. The memorial contains sculptures of the heads of presidents George Washington, Thomas Jefferson, Abraham Lincoln and Theodore Roosevelt. The 60-foot-tall sculptures represent, respectively, the nation's founding, political philosophy, preservation, expansion and conservation.

NATIONAL UNICEF DAY. Oct 31. Presidential Proclamation 3817, of Oct 27, 1967, covers all succeeding years. Many American children "trick or treat for UNICEF" on this day.

NEVADA: ADMISSION DAY: ANNIVERSARY. Oct 31. Became 36th state in 1864. Observed as a holiday in Nevada.

REFORMATION DAY: ANNIVERSARY. Oct 31, 1517. Anniversary on which Martin Luther nailed his 95 theses to the door of Wittenberg's Palace church, denouncing the selling of papal indulgences—the beginning of the Reformation in Germany. Observed by many Protestant churches on Reformation Sunday, on this day if it is a Sunday or on the Sunday before Oct 31.

★ *Birthdays* ★

Jane Pauley, TV personality, born Indianapolis, IN, Oct 31, 1950.
Dan Rather, journalist (coanchor "CBS Evening News"), born Wharton, TX, Oct 31, 1931.

November

November 1

ALL HALLOWS or ALL SAINTS' DAY. Nov 1. Roman Catholic Holy Day of Obligation. Commemorates the blessed, especially those who have no special feast days. Observed on Nov 1 since Pope Gregory IV set the date of recognition in 835. All Saints' Day is a legal holiday in Louisiana. Halloween is the evening before All Hallows Day.

AMERICAN DIABETES MONTH. Nov 1–30. American Diabetes Month is designed to communicate the seriousness of diabetes and the importance of proper diabetes control and treatment to those diagnosed with the disease and their families. Throughout the month, the American Diabetes Association holds special events and programs on a variety of topics related to diabetes care and treatment. For info: American Diabetes Association. Web: www .diabetes.org.

EPILEPSY AWARENESS MONTH. Nov 1–30. To increase public awareness that despite dramatic gains in treatment, epilepsy is a serious and chronic health condition for which there is no cure. For info: Epilepsy Foundation. Web: www .epilepsyfoundation.org.

EUROPEAN UNION ESTABLISHED: ANNIVERSARY. Nov 1, 1993. The Maastricht Treaty went into effect this day, formally establishing the European Union. The treaty was drafted in 1991. By 1993, 12 nations had ratified it. In 1995, three more nations ratified the treaty. The European Union grew out of the European Economic Community (also known as the Common Market), which was established in 1958.

HOCKEY MASK INVENTED: ANNIVERSARY. Nov 1, 1959. Tired of stopping hockey pucks with his face, Montreal Canadiens goalie Jacques Plante, having received another wound, reemerged from the locker room with seven new stitches— and a plastic face mask he had made from fiberglass and resin. Although Cliff Benedict had tried a leather mask back in the 1920s, the idea didn't catch on, but after Plante wore his, goalies throughout the National Hockey League began wearing protective plastic face shields.

LUNG CANCER AWARENESS MONTH. Nov 1–30. A month created to increase awareness of the need for screening, early detection, more research and compassion for lung cancer survivors. ALCASE is the only organization in the world solely dedicated to helping people at risk for and living with lung cancer. For info: Alliance for Lung Cancer Advocacy, Support and Education. Web: www.alcase.org.

MEXICO: DAY OF THE DEAD. Nov 1–2. Observance begins during last days of October when "Dead Men's Bread" is sold in bakeries—round loaves, decorated with sugar skulls. Departed souls are remembered not with mourning but with a spirit of friendliness and good humor. Cemeteries are visited and graves are decorated. Associated with All Saints' and All Souls' Day.

NATIONAL ADOPTION MONTH. Nov 1–30. Proclaimed annually by the president of the US.

NATIONAL ALZHEIMER'S DISEASE MONTH. Nov 1–30. To increase awareness of Alzheimer's disease and what the Alzheimer's Association is doing to advance research and help patients, their families and their caregivers. For info: Alzheimer's Association. Web: www.alz.org.

NATIONAL AMERICAN INDIAN HERITAGE MONTH. Nov 1–30. Proclaimed annually by the president of the US.

NATIONAL HEALTHY SKIN MONTH. Nov 1–30. For info: American Academy of Dermatology. Web: www.aad.org.

NATIONAL HOSPICE MONTH. Nov 1–30. To promote greater awareness of hospice care and the advantages it offers; to educate physicians and other health-care professionals about the concept of hospice; to honor patients and family members, as well as the thousands of dedicated professionals and volunteers who devote their time, love and support to the terminally ill and their families; and to educate public officials to ensure hospice care remains a key component in the health-care delivery system. For info: Hospice Association of America. Web: www .nahc.org.

NATIONAL MARROW AWARENESS MONTH. Nov 1–30. More than 30,000 Americans are diagnosed each year with leukemia or another life-threatening blood disease for which a bone marrow or blood stem-cell transplant offers hope for survival. The National Marrow Donor Program maintains a computerized registry of nearly 4 million volunteer donors. For info: National Marrow Donor Program. Web: www .marrow.org.

PEANUT BUTTER LOVERS' MONTH. Nov 1–30. Celebration of America's favorite food and number one sandwich. For info: Peanut Advisory Board. Web: www.peanutbutterlovers.com.

PRIME MERIDIAN SET: ANNIVERSARY. Nov 1, 1884. Delegates from 25 nations met in October at Washington, DC, at the International Meridian Conference to set up time zones for the world. On this day the treaty adopted by the conference took effect, making Greenwich, England, the Prime Meridian (i.e., zero degrees longitude) and setting the International Date Line at 180 degrees longitude in the Pacific. Every 15 degrees of longitude equals one hour and there are 24 meridians. While some countries do not strictly observe this system (for example, while China stretches over five time zones, it is the same time everywhere in China), this system has brought predictability and logic to time throughout the world.

★ *Birthdays* ★

Gary Player, golfer, born Johannesburg, South Africa, Nov 1, 1935.
Rachel Ticotin, actress ("American Family," *Total Recall*), born the Bronx, NY, Nov 1, 1958.

November 2

ALL SOULS' DAY. Nov 2. Commemorates the faithful departed. Catholic observance.

BOONE, DANIEL: BIRTH ANNIVERSARY. Nov 2, 1734. American frontiersman, explorer and militia officer, born at Berks County, near Reading, PA. In February 1778, he was captured at Blue Licks, KY, by Shawnee Indians, under Chief Blackfish, who adopted Boone when he was inducted into the tribe as "Big Turtle." Boone escaped after five months and in 1781 was captured briefly by the British. He experienced a series of personal and financial disasters during his life but continued a rugged existence, hunting until his 80s. Boone died at St. Charles County, MO, Sept 26, 1820. The bodies of Daniel Boone and his wife, Rebecca, were moved to Frankfort, KY, in 1845.

FIRST SCHEDULED RADIO BROADCAST: ANNIVERSARY. Nov 2, 1920. Station KDKA at Pittsburgh, PA, broadcasted the results of the presidential election. The station got its license to broadcast Nov 7, 1921. By 1922 there were about 400 licensed radio stations in the US.

HARDING, WARREN GAMALIEL: BIRTH ANNIVER-SARY. Nov 2, 1865. Twenty-ninth president of the US was born at Corsica, OH. His term of office: Mar 4, 1921–Aug 2, 1923 (died in office). His undistinguished administration was tainted by the Teapot Dome scandal, and his sudden death in San Francisco, CA, while on a western speaking tour prompted many rumors.

LANCASTER, BURT(ON): BIRTH ANNIVERSARY. Nov 2, 1913. Distinguished American actor who began his career in show business as a circus acrobat. In a career spanning 45 years, he appeared in nearly 80 films. Some of his more memorable roles are in *From Here to Eternity* (1953), *The Bird Man of Alcatraz* (1962) and *The Leopard* (1963); he received an Academy Award for his performance in the title role of *Elmer Gantry* (1961). Some of his later popular movies include *Atlantic City* (1981) and *Field of Dreams* (1989). Born at New York City, he died Oct 20, 1994, at Los Angeles, CA.

NORTH AND SOUTH DAKOTA: ADMISSION DAY: ANNI-VERSARY. Nov 2. North Dakota became the 39th state and South Dakota the 40th state in 1889.

SPACE MILESTONE: INTERNATIONAL SPACE STATION INHABITED. Nov 2, 2000. On Oct 31, 2000, a *Soyuz* shuttle left with the first crew to live in the International Space Station, consisting of American commander Bill Shepherd and two Russian cosmonauts. The flight left from the same site in Central Asia where *Sputnik* was launched in 1957, beginning the Space Age. The astronauts stayed on board the International Space Station (ISS) until March 2001, when they were replaced by a crew that arrived on the shuttle *Discovery*. Sixteen nations are participating in the ISS project. The construction of the station will be complete in 2006.

★ *Birthdays* ★

Patrick Buchanan, political columnist, born Washington, DC, Nov 2, 1938.
Dave Stockton, golfer, born San Bernardino, CA, Nov 2, 1941.

November 3

AUSTIN, STEPHEN FULLER: BIRTH ANNIVERSARY. Nov 3, 1793. A principal founder of Texas, for whom its capital city was named, Austin was born at Wythe County, VA. He first visited Texas in 1821 and established a settlement there the following year, continuing a colonization project started by his father, Moses Austin. Thrown in prison when he advocated formation of a separate state (Texas still belonged to Mexico), he was freed in 1835, lost a campaign for the presidency (of the Republic of Texas) to Sam Houston in 1836, and died (while serving as Texas secretary of state) at Austin, TX, Dec 27, 1836.

CLICHÉ DAY. Nov 3. Use clichés as much as possible today. Hey, why not? Give it a shot! Win some, lose some. You'll never know 'til you try it. [©2001 by WH.] For info: Wellcat Holidays. Web: www.wellcat.com.

DEWEY DEFEATS TRUMAN HEADLINE: ANNIVERSARY. Nov 3, 1948. This headline in the *Chicago Tribune* notwithstanding, Harry Truman defeated Republican candidate Thomas E. Dewey for the US presidency.

PANAMA: INDEPENDENCE DAY. Nov 3. Independence Day. Panama declared itself independent of Colombia in 1903.

PUBLIC TELEVISION DEBUTS: ANNIVERSARY. Nov 3, 1969. A string of local educational TV channels united on this day under the Public Broadcasting System banner. Today there are 348 PBS stations.

SANDWICH DAY: BIRTH ANNIVERSARY OF JOHN MONTAGUE. Nov 3, 1718. A day to recognize the inventor of the sandwich, John Montague, Fourth Earl of Sandwich, born at London, England. England's first lord of the admiralty, secretary of state for the northern department, postmaster general and the man after whom Captain Cook named the Sandwich Islands in 1778. A rake and a gambler, he is said to have invented the sandwich as a time-saving nourishment while engaged in a 24-hour-long gambling session in 1762. He died at London, England, Apr 30, 1792.

SPACE MILESTONE: SPUTNIK 2 (USSR). Nov 3, 1957. A dog named Laika became the first animal sent into space. Total weight of craft and dog was 1,121 pounds. The satellite was not capable of returning the dog to Earth, and she died when her air supply was gone. Nicknamed "Muttnik" by the American press.

★ *Birthdays* ★

Kate Capshaw, actress ("Duke of Groove," *How to Make an American Quilt*), born Fort Worth, TX, Nov 3, 1953.

Dennis Miller, comedian, actor ("Saturday Night Live," "The Dennis Miller Show"), born Pittsburgh, PA, Nov 3, 1953.

Roseanne, comedienne, actress ("Roseanne," *She-Devil*), born Roseanne Barr, Salt Lake City, UT, Nov 3, 1953.

November 4

KING TUT TOMB DISCOVERY: ANNIVERSARY. Nov 4, 1922. In 1922, one of the most important archaeological discoveries of modern times occurred at Luxor, Egypt. It was the tomb of Egypt's child-king, Tutankhamen, who became pharaoh at the age of nine and died, probably in the year 1352 BC, when he was 19. Perhaps the only ancient Egyptian royal tomb to have escaped plundering by grave robbers, it was discovered more than 3,000 years after Tutankhamen's death by English archaeologist Howard Carter, leader of an expedition financed by Lord Carnarvon. The priceless relics yielded by King Tut's tomb were placed in Egypt's National Museum at Cairo.

ROGERS, WILL: BIRTH ANNIVERSARY. Nov 4, 1879. William Penn Adair Rogers, American writer, actor, humorist and grassroots philosopher, born at Oologah, Indian Territory (now Oklahoma). With aviator Wiley Post, he was killed in an airplane crash near Point Barrow, AK, Aug 15, 1935. "My forefathers," he said, "didn't come over on the *Mayflower*, but they met the boat."

SEIZURE OF US EMBASSY IN TEHERAN: ANNIVERSARY. Nov 4, 1979. About 500 Iranians seized the US Embassy in Teheran, taking some 90 hostages, of whom about 60 were Americans. They vowed to hold the hostages until the former Shah, Mohammed Reza Pahlavi (in the US for medical treatments), was returned to Iran for trial. The Shah died July 27, 1980, in an Egyptian military hospital near Cairo. The remaining 52 American hostages were released and left Teheran on Jan 20, 1981, after 444 days of captivity. The release occurred on America's Presidential Inauguration Day, during the hour in which the American presidency was transferred from Jimmy Carter to Ronald Reagan.

UNESCO: ANNIVERSARY. Nov 4, 1946. The United Nations Educational, Scientific and Cultural Organization was formed.

★ Birthdays ★

Laura Bush, First Lady, wife of President George W. Bush, born Midland, TX, Nov 4, 1946.
Sean Combs, rapper known as P. Diddy or Puff Daddy, born New York, NY, Nov 4, 1970.
Matthew McConaughey, actor (*Dazed and Confused, A Time to Kill*), born Uvalde, TX, Nov 4, 1969.
Doris Roberts, actress ("Everybody Loves Raymond," "Remington Steele"), born St. Louis, MO, Nov 4, 1930.

November 5

ENGLAND: GUY FAWKES DAY. Nov 5. Anniversary of the "Gunpowder Plot." Conspirators planned to blow up the Houses of Parliament and King James I, Nov 5, 1605. Twenty barrels of gunpowder, which they had secreted in a cellar under Parliament, were discovered on the night of Nov 4, the eve of the intended explosion, and the conspirators were arrested. They were tried and convicted, and Jan 31, 1606, eight (including Guy Fawkes) were beheaded and their heads displayed on pikes at London Bridge. Parliament enacted a law establishing Nov 5 as a day of public thanksgiving. It is still observed, and on the night of Nov 5, the whole country lights up with bonfires and celebration. "Guys" are burned in effigy and the old verses repeated: "Remember, remember the fifth of November,/Gunpowder treason and plot;/I see no reason why Gunpowder Treason/Should ever be forgot."

GEORGE W. AND LAURA BUSH WEDDING: ANNIVERSARY. Nov 5, 1977. George W. Bush and Laura Welch were married at Midland, TX. They have twin daughters, Barbara Pierce Bush and Jenna Welch Bush, born in 1981.

★ Birthdays ★

Jerry Stackhouse, basketball player, born Kinston, NC, Nov 5, 1974.
Bill Walton, Hall of Fame basketball player, broadcaster, born Mesa, CA, Nov 5, 1952.

November 6

"GOOD MORNING AMERICA" TV PREMIERE: ANNIVERSARY. Nov 6, 1975. This ABC morning program, set in a living room, is a mixture of news reports, features and interviews with newsmakers and people of interest. It was the first program to compete with NBC's "Today" show and initially aired as "A.M. America." Hosts have included David Hartman, Nancy Dussault, Sandy Hill, Charles Gibson, Joan Lunden, Lisa McRee, Kevin Newman and Diane Sawyer.

"MEET THE PRESS" TV PREMIERE: ANNIVERSARY. Nov 6, 1947. "Meet the Press" holds the distinction of being the oldest program on TV. It originally debuted on radio in 1945. The show has changed its format little since it began: a well-known guest (usually a politician) is questioned on current, relevant issues by a panel of journalists. The moderators throughout the years have included Martha Rountree, Lawrence E. Spivak, Ned Brooks, Bill Monroe, Marvin Kalb, Chris Wallace and Garrick Utley with the current host being Tim Russert.

"THE PHIL DONAHUE SHOW" TV PREMIERE: ANNIVERSARY. Nov 6, 1967. The forerunner of

Oprah, Jerry, Montel and many others, this first talk show with audience participation went on the air on this date at Dayton, OH. The first guest interviewed by host Phil Donahue was atheist Madalyn Murray O'Hair. In 1970, the program went national; it moved to Chicago in 1974 and to New York in 1985. In later years the program was titled "Donahue." After winning 19 Emmy Awards, the show left daytime TV in 1996.

SAXOPHONE DAY (ADOLPHE SAX BIRTH ANNIVERSARY). Nov 6. A day to recognize the birth anniversary of Adolphe Sax, Belgian musician and inventor of the saxophone and the saxotromba. Born at Dinant, Belgium, in 1814, Antoine Joseph Sax, later known as Adolphe, was the eldest of 11 children of a musical instrument builder. Sax contributed an entire family of brass wind instruments for band and orchestra use. He was accorded fame and great wealth, but business misfortunes led to bankruptcy. Sax died in poverty at Paris, Feb 7, 1894.

★ Birthdays ★

Sally Field, actress (Oscars for *Norma Rae, Places in the Heart*; Emmy for *Sybil*), born Pasadena, CA, Nov 6, 1946.

Ethan Hawke, actor (*Dead Poets Society, Reality Bites*), born Austin, TX, Nov 6, 1970.

Thandie Newton, actress (*Beloved, Mission Impossible II*), born in Zambia, Nov 6, 1972.

Maria Owings Shriver, broadcast journalist ("Today"), born Chicago, IL, Nov 6, 1955.

November 7

"FACE THE NATION" TV PREMIERE: ANNIVERSARY. Nov 7, 1954. The CBS counterpart to NBC's "Meet the Press," this show employed a similar format: panelists interviewed a well-known guest. In 1983 the panel was changed to include experts in addition to journalists when Lesley Stahl succeeded George Herman as moderator. Though usually produced at Washington, DC, the show occasionally interviewed people elsewhere (such as Khrushchev in Moscow in 1957).

FIRST BLACK GOVERNOR ELECTED: ANNIVERSARY. Nov 7, 1989. L. Douglas Wilder was elected governor of Virginia, becoming the first elected black governor in US history. Wilder had previously served as lieutenant governor of Virginia.

GREAT OCTOBER SOCIALIST REVOLUTION: ANNIVERSARY. Nov 7, 1917. This holiday in the old Soviet Union was observed for two days with parades, military displays and appearances by Soviet leaders. In the mid-1990s, President Yeltsin issued a decree renaming the holiday the "Day of National Reconciliation and Agreement." According to the old Russian calendar, the revolution took place Oct 25, 1917. Soviet calendar reform causes observance to fall Nov 7 (Gregorian). The Bolshevik Revolution began at Petrograd, Russia, on the evening of Nov 6 (Gregorian), 1917. A new government headed by Nikolai Lenin took office the following day under the name Council of People's Commissars.

NIXON'S "LAST" PRESS CONFERENCE: ANNIVERSARY. Nov 7, 1962. Richard M. Nixon, having been narrowly defeated in his bid for the presidency by John F. Kennedy in the 1960 election, returned to politics two years later as a candidate for governor of California in the election of Nov 6, 1962. Defeated again (this time by incumbent governor Edmund G. Brown), Nixon held his "last" press conference with assembled reporters in Los Angeles at midmorning the next day at which he said: ". . . just think how much you're going to be missing. You won't have Nixon to kick around any more, because, gentlemen, this is my last press conference." Nixon was elected president in 1968.

REPUBLICAN SYMBOL: ANNIVERSARY. Nov 7, 1874. Thomas Nast used an elephant to represent the Republican Party in a satirical cartoon in *Harper's Weekly*. Today the elephant is still a well-recognized symbol for the Republican Party in political cartoons.

ROOSEVELT ELECTED TO FOURTH TERM: ANNIVERSARY. Nov 7, 1944. Defeating Thomas Dewey, Franklin D. Roosevelt became the first, and only, person elected to four terms as president of the US. Roosevelt was inaugurated the following Jan 20 but died in office Apr 12, 1945, serving only 53 days of the fourth term.

★ Birthdays ★

Jeremy London, actor ("I'll Fly Away," "Party of Five"), born San Diego, CA, Nov 7, 1972.
Joni Mitchell, singer, songwriter ("Both Sides Now," "Big Yellow Taxi"), born McLeod, AB, Canada, Nov 7, 1943.

November 8

CORTÉS CONQUERS MEXICO: ANNIVERSARY. Nov 8, 1519. After landing on the Yucatan peninsula in April, Spaniard Hernan Cortés and his troops marched into the interior of Mexico to the Aztec capital and took the Aztec emperor Montezuma hostage.

"DAYS OF OUR LIVES" TV PREMIERE: ANNIVERSARY. Nov 8, 1965. This popular daytime serial, like many others, has gone through many changes throughout its run. It expanded from 30 minutes to an hour; it went to number one in the ratings and slipped to nine out of 12 in the 1980s; and it dropped or deemphasized older characters, which angered its audience. Notable cast members included Mary Frann, Joan Van

Ark, Mike Farrell, Garry Marshall, John Aniston, Deidre Hall, Marilyn McCoo, Charles Shaughnessy and Genie Francis.

HALLEY, EDMUND: BIRTH ANNIVERSARY. Nov 8, 1656 (OS). Astronomer and mathematician born at London, England. Astronomer Royal, 1721–42. Died at Greenwich, England, Jan 14, 1742 (OS). He observed the great comet of 1682 (now named for him), first conceived its periodicity and wrote in his *Synopsis of Comet Astronomy*: ". . . I may venture to foretell that this Comet will return again in the year 1758." It did, and Edmund Halley's memory is kept alive by the once-every-generation appearance of Halley's Comet. There have been 28 recorded appearances of this comet since 240 BC. Average time between appearances is 76 years. Halley's Comet is next expected to be visible in 2061.

MONTANA: ADMISSION DAY: ANNIVERSARY. Nov 8. Became 41st state in 1889.

X-RAY DISCOVERY DAY: ANNIVERSARY. Nov 8, 1895. Physicist Wilhelm Conrad Roentgen discovered X-rays, beginning a new era in physics and medicine. Although X-rays had been observed previously, it was Roentgen, a professor at the University of Würzburg (Germany), who successfully repeated X-ray experimentation and who is credited with the discovery. He won the Nobel Prize for this work.

★ Birthdays ★

Parker Posey, actress (*The House of Yes, Best in Show*), born Baltimore, MD, Nov 8, 1968.
Courtney Thorne-Smith, actress ("Melrose Place," "Ally McBeal"), born San Francisco, CA, Nov 8, 1967.

November 9

BERLIN WALL OPENED: ANNIVERSARY. Nov 9, 1989. After 28 years as a symbol of the cold war, the Berlin Wall was opened on this evening, and citizens of both sides walked freely through the barrier as others danced atop the structure to celebrate the end of a historic era. Coming amidst the celebration of East Germany's 40-year anniversary, pro-democracy demonstrations led to the resignation of Erich Honecker, East Germany's head of state and party chief. It was Honecker who had supervised the construction of the 27.9-mile wall across the city during the night of Aug 13, 1961, because US President John Kennedy had ordered a troop buildup in response to the blockade of West Berlin by the Soviets.

CAMBODIA: INDEPENDENCE DAY. Nov 9. National Day. Declared independence from France in 1949.

EAST COAST BLACKOUT: ANNIVERSARY. Nov 9, 1965. Massive electric power failure starting in western New York State at 5:16 PM cut electric power to much of northeastern US and Ontario and Quebec in Canada. More than 30 million people in an area of 80,000 square miles were affected. The experience provoked studies of the vulnerability of 20th-century technology.

KRISTALLNACHT (CRYSTAL NIGHT): ANNIVERSARY. Nov 9–10, 1938. During the evening of Nov 9 and into the morning of Nov 10, 1938, mobs in Germany destroyed thousands of shops and homes carrying out a pogrom against Jews. Synagogues were burned down or demolished. There were bonfires in every Jewish neighborhood, fueled by Jewish prayer books, Torah scrolls and volumes of philosophy, history and poetry. More than 30,000 Jews were arrested and 91 killed. The night got its name from the smashing of glass store windows.

★ *Birthdays* ★

David Duval, golfer, born Jacksonville, FL, Nov 9, 1971.
Robert (Bob) Gibson, Hall of Fame baseball player, born Omaha, NE, Nov 9, 1935.

November 10

AREA CODES INTRODUCED: ANNIVERSARY. Nov 10, 1951. The ten-digit North American Numbering Plan that provides area codes for Canada, the US and many Caribbean nations was devised in 1947 by AT&T and Bell Labs. Eighty-four area codes were assigned. However, all long-distance calls at that time were operator-assisted. On this date in 1951, the mayor of Englewood, NJ (area code 201) direct-dialed the mayor of Alameda, CA. By 1960 all telephone customers could dial long-distance calls. Currently there are 285 area codes. Because of the proliferation of faxes, modems and cell phones, the US could run out of area codes as early as 2007. The system is administered by the North American Numbering Plan Administration. Web: www.nanpa.com.

"DR. LIVINGSTONE, I PRESUME?": ANNIVERSARY. Nov 10, 1871. Explorer Henry Morton Stanley led the expedition to find the missing missionary-explorer David Livingstone, who had not been heard from for more than two years. Stanley began the search in Africa on Mar 21, 1871, finally finding the explorer at Ujiji, near Lake Tanganyika, on this date, whereupon he asked the now-famous question: "Dr. Livingstone, I presume?"

MICROSOFT RELEASES WINDOWS: ANNIVERSARY. Nov 10, 1983. In 1980, Microsoft signed a contract with IBM to design an operating system, MS-DOS, for a personal computer that IBM was developing. On Nov 10, 1983, Microsoft released Windows, an extension of MS-DOS with a graphical user interface.

"SESAME STREET" TV PREMIERE: ANNIVERSARY. Nov 10, 1969. An important, successful long-running children's show, "Sesame Street" educates children while they have fun. It takes place along a city street, featuring a diverse cast of humans and puppets. Through singing, puppetry, film clips and skits, kids are taught letters, numbers, concepts and other lessons. Shows are "sponsored" by letters and numbers. Human cast members have included Loretta Long, Matt Robinson, Roscoe Orman, Bob McGrath, Linda Bove, Buffy Sainte-Marie, Ruth Buzzi, Will Lee, Northern J. Calloway, Emilio Delgado and Sonia Manzano. Favorite Jim Henson Muppets include Ernie, Bert, Grover, Oscar the Grouch, Kermit the Frog, the Cookie Monster, life-sized Big Bird and Mr Snuffleupagus.

★ Birthdays ★

Roy Scheider, actor (*Jaws, All That Jazz*), born Orange, NJ, Nov 10, 1935.
Sinbad, comedian, actor (*Unnecessary Roughness*, "A Different World"), born David Adkins, Benton Harbor, MI, Nov 10, 1956.

November 11

ANGOLA: INDEPENDENCE DAY. Nov 11. National holiday. Angola gained its independence from Portugal in 1975.

BONZA BOTTLER DAY™. Nov 11. To celebrate when the number of the day is the same as the number of the month. Bonza Bottler Day™ is an excuse to have a party at least once a month. For info: Gail M. Berger. E-mail: gberger5@ aol.com.

"GOD BLESS AMERICA" FIRST PERFORMED: ANNIVERSARY. Nov 11, 1938. Irving Berlin wrote this song especially for Kate Smith. She first sang it during her regular radio broadcast. It quickly became a great patriotic favorite of the nation and one of Smith's most requested songs.

POLAND: INDEPENDENCE DAY. Nov 11. Poland regained independence in 1918, after having been partitioned among Austria, Prussia and Russia for more than 120 years.

VETERANS DAY. Nov 11. Veterans Day was observed on Nov 11 from 1919 through 1970.

Public Law 90–363, the "Monday Holiday Law," provided that, beginning in 1971, Veterans Day would be observed on "the fourth Monday in October." This movable observance date, which separated Veterans Day from the Nov 11 anniversary of World War I Armistice, proved unpopular. State after state moved its observance back to the traditional Nov 11 date, and finally Public Law 94–97 of Sept 18, 1975, required that, effective Jan 1, 1978, the observance of Veterans Day revert to Nov 11. As Armistice Day this is a holiday in Belgium, France and other European countries. "At the eleventh hour of the eleventh day of the eleventh month" in 1918 fighting ceased in World War I.

WASHINGTON: ADMISSION DAY: ANNIVERSARY. Nov 11. Became 42nd state in 1889.

★ Birthdays ★

Leonardo DiCaprio, actor (*What's Eating Gilbert Grape, Titanic*), born Ridgewood, NJ, Nov 11, 1975.
Calista Flockhart, actress ("Ally McBeal"), born Freeport, IL, Nov 11, 1964.
Demi Moore, actress ("General Hospital," *Ghost, GI Jane*), born Roswell, NM, Nov 11, 1962.

November 12

STANTON, ELIZABETH CADY: BIRTH ANNIVERSARY. Nov 12, 1815. American woman suffragist and reformer, Elizabeth Cady Stanton was born at Johnstown, NY. "We hold these truths to be self-evident," she said at the first Women's Rights Convention, in 1848, "that all men and women are created equal." She died at New York, NY, Oct 26, 1902.

★ Birthdays ★

David Schwimmer, actor ("Friends"), born Queens, NY, Nov 12, 1966.
Sammy Sosa, baseball player, born San Pedro de Macoris, Dominican Republic, Nov 12, 1968.

November 13

HOLLAND TUNNEL: ANNIVERSARY. Nov 13, 1927. The Holland Tunnel, running under the Hudson River between New York, NY, and Jersey City, NJ, was opened to traffic. The tunnel was built and operated by the New York–New Jersey Bridge and Tunnel Commission. Comprised of two tubes, each large enough for two lanes of traffic, the Holland was the first underwater tunnel built in the US.

STEVENSON, ROBERT LOUIS: BIRTH ANNIVERSARY. Nov 13, 1850. Author, born at Edinburgh, Scotland, known for his *Child's Garden of Verses* and novels such as *Treasure Island* and *Kidnapped*. Died at Samoa, Dec 3, 1894.

★ Birthdays ★

Whoopi Goldberg, comedienne, actress (*Ghost, Sister Act, The Color Purple*), born New York, NY, Nov 13, 1949.

Chris Noth, actor ("Sex and the City," "Law & Order," *Burnzy's Last Call*), born Madison, WI, Nov 13, 1957.

November 14

AROUND THE WORLD IN 72 DAYS: ANNIVERSARY. Nov 14, 1889. Newspaper reporter Nellie Bly (pen name used by Elizabeth Cochrane Seaman) set off Nov 14, 1889, to attempt to break Jules Verne's imaginary hero Phileas Fogg's record of voyaging around the world in 80 days. She did beat Fogg's record, taking 72 days, six hours, 11 minutes and 14 seconds to make the trip.

DOW-JONES TOPS 1,000: ANNIVERSARY. Nov 14, 1972. The Dow-Jones Index of 30 major industrial stocks topped the 1,000 mark for the first time.

MONET, CLAUDE: BIRTH ANNIVERSARY. Nov 14, 1840. French Impressionist painter (*Water Lillies*), born at Paris. Died at Giverny, France, Dec 5, 1926.

"MURPHY BROWN" TV PREMIERE: ANNIVERSARY. Nov 14, 1988. This intelligent, timely and often acerbic sitcom set in Washington, DC, starred Candice Bergen in the title role, as an egotistical, seasoned journalist working for the fictitious TV newsmagazine show "FYI." Also featured were Grant Shaud as the show's high-strung producer, Miles Silverberg (later replaced by Lily Tomlin); Faith Ford as the former Miss America, Corky Sherwood; Joe Regalbuto as Murphy's neurotic friend, reporter Frank Fontana; Charles Kimbrough as "FYI"'s uptight anchorman, Jim Dial, and Pat Corley as Phil, owner of the local watering hole. Colleen Dewhurst appeared as Murphy's mother and Robert Pastorelli as Eldin Bernecky, perfectionist housepainter and aspiring artist (he left the series for his own show). The series ended with the May 31, 1998, episode.

NEHRU, JAWAHARLAL: BIRTH ANNIVERSARY. Nov 14, 1889. Indian leader and first prime minister after independence. Born at Allahabad, India, he died May 27, 1964, at New Delhi.

★ Birthdays ★

Prince Charles, Prince of Wales, heir to the British throne, born London, England, Nov 14, 1948.

Condoleezza Rice, US national security adviser, born Birmingham, AL, Nov 14, 1954.

Laura San Giacomo, actress (*sex, lies and videotape*; "Just Shoot Me"), born Hoboken, NJ, Nov 14, 1962.

November 15

AMERICA RECYCLES DAY. Nov 15. To promote recycling and recycled products. More than 40 states participate. For info: Environmental Defense Fund. Web: www.americarecyclesday .org.

O'KEEFFE, GEORGIA: BIRTH ANNIVERSARY. Nov 15, 1887. Described as one of the greatest American artists of the 20th century, Georgia O'Keeffe was born at Sun Prairie, WI. In 1924, she married the famous photographer Alfred Stieglitz. His more than 500 photographs of her have been called "the greatest love poem in the history of photography." She painted desert landscapes and flower studies. She died at Santa Fe, NM, Mar 6, 1986.

★ Birthdays ★

Ed Asner, actor ("The Mary Tyler Moore Show," "Lou Grant," *Roots*), born Kansas City, MO, Nov 15, 1929.
Yaphet Kotto, actor ("Homicide," *Nothing But a Man, Blue Collar, Midnight Run*), born New York, NY, Nov 15, 1937.
Sam Waterston, actor (*The Killing Fields, The Great Gatsby*, "I'll Fly Away," "Law & Order"), born Cambridge, MA, Nov 15, 1940.

November 16

OKLAHOMA: ADMISSION DAY: ANNIVERSARY. Nov 16. Became 46th state in 1907.

UNITED NATIONS: INTERNATIONAL DAY FOR TOLERANCE. Nov 16. On Dec 12, 1996, the General Assembly established the International Day for Tolerance, to commemorate the adoption by UNESCO member states of the Declaration of Principles on Tolerance in 1995. For info: United Nations. Web: www.un.org.

★ Birthdays ★

Marg Helgenberger, actress ("China Beach," "CSI"), born Fremont, NE, Nov 16, 1958.
Martha Plimpton, actress (*200 Cigarettes*, "The Defenders"), born New York, NY, Nov 16, 1970.

November 17

SUEZ CANAL: ANNIVERSARY. Nov 17, 1869. Formal opening of the Suez Canal. It had taken 1.5 million men a decade to dig the 100-mile canal. It shortened the sea route from Europe to India by 6,000 miles. An Anglo-French commission ran the canal until 1956, when Egypt's president Gamal Abdel Nasser seized it.

★ Birthdays ★

Danny DeVito, actor ("Taxi," *Twins*), director (*Throw Mama from the Train*), born Neptune, NJ, Nov 17, 1944.

Mary Elizabeth Mastrantonio, actress (*The Color of Money, Thieves*), born Oak Park, IL, Nov 17, 1958.

Martin Scorsese, director (*Mean Streets, The Color of Money, Raging Bull, Goodfellas*), born Flushing, NY, Nov 17, 1942.

November 18

DAGUERRE, LOUIS JACQUES MANDE: BIRTH ANNIVERSARY. Nov 18, 1789. French tax collector, theater scene-painter, physicist and inventor, was born at Cormeilles-en-Parisis, France. He is remembered for his invention of the daguerreotype photographic process—one of the earliest to permit a photographic image to be chemically fixed to provide a permanent picture. The process was presented to the French Academy of Science Jan 7, 1839. Daguerre died near Paris, France, July 10, 1851.

LATVIA: INDEPENDENCE DAY. Nov 18. National holiday. Commemorates the declaration of an independent Latvia from Germany and Russia in 1918.

MICKEY MOUSE'S BIRTHDAY. Nov 18. The comical activities of squeaky-voiced Mickey Mouse first appeared in 1928, on the screen of the Colony Theatre at New York City. The film, Walt Disney's *Steamboat Willie,* was the first animated cartoon talking picture.

PUSH-BUTTON PHONE DEBUTS: ANNIVERSARY. Nov 18, 1963. Push-button telephones went into service as an alternative to rotary-dial phones. Touch-tone service was available as an option at an extra charge. This option was available only in two Pennsylvania cities.

"SEE IT NOW" TV PREMIERE: ANNIVERSARY. Nov 18, 1951. "See It Now" was a high-quality and significant public affairs show hosted by Edward R. Murrow. "See It Now" covered many relevant and newsworthy stories of its time, including desegregation, lung cancer and anti-Communist fervor. One of the most notable shows focused on Senator Joseph McCarthy, leading to McCarthy's appearance on the show, which damaged his credibility. The show's premiere was the first live commercial coast-to-coast broadcast. It had premiered on radio the year before as "Hear It Now."

US UNIFORM TIME ZONE PLAN: ANNIVERSARY. Nov 18, 1883. Charles Ferdinand Dowd, a college professor and one of the early advocates of uniform time, proposed a time zone plan of the US (four zones of 15 degrees), which he and others persuaded the railroads to adopt and place in operation on this date. Because it didn't involve the enactment of any law, some localities didn't change their clocks. A year later an international conference applied the same procedure to create time zones for the entire world. US time zones weren't nationally legalized until 1918, with the passage of the Standard Time Act. See also: "Prime Meridian Set: Anniv" (Nov 1) and "US Standard Time Act: Anniv" (Mar 19).

★ Birthdays ★

Kevin Nealon, comedian, actor ("Champs," "Saturday Night Live"), born St. Louis, MO, Nov 18, 1953.

Elizabeth Perkins, actress (*Big, The Flintstones*), born Queens, NY, Nov 18, 1960.

November 19

FIRST AUTOMATIC TOLL COLLECTION MACHINE: ANNIVERSARY. Nov 19, 1954. At the Union Toll Plaza on New Jersey's Garden State Parkway motorists dropped 25¢ into a wire mesh hopper and a green light would flash. The first modern toll road was the Pennsylvania Turnpike, which opened in 1940 and which still uses people as toll collectors.

FIRST PRESIDENTIAL LIBRARY: ANNIVERSARY. Nov 19, 1939. President Franklin D. Roosevelt laid the cornerstone for his presidential library at Hyde Park, NY. He donated the land, but public donations provided funds for the building, which was dedicated on June 30, 1941.

GARFIELD, JAMES ABRAM: BIRTH ANNIVERSARY. Nov 19, 1831. Twentieth president of the US (and the first left-handed president) was born at Orange, OH. Term of office: Mar 4–Sept 19, 1881. While walking into the Washington, DC, railway station on the morning of July 2, 1881, Garfield was shot by disappointed office seeker Charles J. Guiteau. He survived, in very weak condition, until Sept 19, 1881, when he succumbed to blood poisoning at Elberon, NJ (where he had been taken for recuperation). Guiteau was tried, convicted and hanged at the jail at Washington, June 30, 1882.

HAVE A BAD DAY DAY. Nov 19. For those who are filled with revulsion at being told endlessly to "have a nice day," this day is a brief respite. Store and business owners are to ask workers to tell customers to "have a bad day." [©2001 by WH.] For info: Wellcat Holidays. Web: www .wellcat.com.

JONESTOWN MASSACRE: ANNIVERSARY. Nov 19, 1978. On this date, Indiana-born, 47-year-old Reverend Jim Jones, leader of the "Peoples Temple," was reported to have directed the suicides of more than 900 persons at Jonestown, Guyana. US Representative Leo J. Ryan, of California, and four members of his party were killed in ambush at Port Kaituma airstrip on Nov 18, 1978, when they attempted to leave after an investigative visit to the remote jungle location of the religious cult. On the following day, Jones and his mistress killed themselves after watching the administration of Kool-Aid laced with the deadly poison cyanide to members of the cult. At least 911 persons died in the biggest murder-suicide in history.

LINCOLN'S GETTYSBURG ADDRESS: ANNIVERSARY. Nov 19, 1863. In 1863, 17 acres of the battlefield at Gettysburg, PA, were dedicated as a national cemetery. Noted orator Edward Everett spoke for two hours; the address that Lincoln delivered in less than two minutes was later recognized as one of the most eloquent of the English language. Five manuscript copies in Lincoln's hand survive, including the rough draft begun in ink at the Executive Mansion at Washington and concluded in pencil at Gettysburg on the morning of the dedication (kept at the Library of Congress).

★ *Birthdays* ★

Jodie Foster, actress (Oscars for *The Accused, The Silence of the Lambs; Taxi Driver*), director (*Home for the Holidays*), born Los Angeles, CA, Nov 19, 1962.
Allison Janney, actress (*American Beauty*, "The West Wing"), born Dayton, OH, Nov 19, 1960.

Larry King, talk-show host ("Larry King Live"), born Brooklyn, NY, Nov 19, 1933.
Meg Ryan, actress (*When Harry Met Sally . . ., Sleepless in Seattle*), born Fairfield, CT, Nov 19, 1961.
Ted Turner, baseball, basketball and cable TV executive, born Cincinnati, OH, Nov 19, 1938.

November 20

HUBBLE, EDWIN POWELL: BIRTH ANNIVERSARY. Nov 20, 1889. American astronomer Edwin Hubble was born at Marshfield, MO. His discovery and development of the concept of an expanding universe has been described as the "most spectacular astronomical discovery" of the 20th century. As a tribute, the Hubble Space Telescope, deployed Apr 25, 1990, from US Space Shuttle *Discovery*, was named for him. The Hubble Space Telescope, with a 240-centimeter mirror, was to allow astronomers to see farther into space than they had ever seen from telescopes on Earth. Hubble died at San Marino, CA, Sept 28, 1953.

NUREMBERG WAR CRIMES TRIAL: ANNIVERSARY. Nov 20, 1945. The first session of the German war crimes trials started at Berlin with indictments against 24 former Nazi leaders. Later sessions were held at Nuremberg, starting Nov 20, 1945. One defendant committed suicide during the trial, and another was excused because of his physical and mental condition. The trial lasted more than ten months, and delivery of the judgment was completed on Oct 1, 1946. Twelve were sentenced to death by hanging, three to life imprisonment and four to lesser prison terms; three were acquitted.

UNITED NATIONS: UNIVERSAL CHILDREN'S DAY. Nov 20. First observance was in 1953. A time to honor children with special ceremonies and festivals and to make children's needs known to governments. Observed on different days and in different ways in more than 120 nations. For info: United Nations. Web: www.un.org.

★ *Birthdays* ★

Richard Masur, actor ("One Day at a Time," *Who'll Stop the Rain, Under Fire, Heartburn*), born New York, NY, Nov 20, 1948.

Sean Young, actress (*Blade Runner, No Way Out*), born Louisville, KY, Nov 20, 1959.

November 21

DOW-JONES TOPS 5,000: ANNIVERSARY. Nov 21, 1995. The Dow-Jones Index of 30 major industrial stocks topped the 5,000 mark for the first time.

NORTH CAROLINA: RATIFICATION DAY. Nov 21. Twelfth state to ratify Constitution in 1789.

UNITED NATIONS: WORLD TELEVISION DAY. Nov 21. On Dec 17, 1996, the General Assembly proclaimed this day as World Television Day, commemorating the date in 1996 on which the first World Television Forum was held at the UN. For info: United Nations. Web: www.un.org.

★ *Birthdays* ★

George Kenneth (Ken) Griffey, Jr, baseball player, born Donora, PA, Nov 21, 1969.

Goldie Hawn, actress ("Rowan & Martin's Laugh-In," *Private Benjamin*; Oscar for *Cactus Flower*), born Washington, DC, Nov 21, 1945.

★ *Birthdays* ★

Jamie Lee Curtis, actress ("Anything But Love," *Love Letters, A Fish Called Wanda*), born Los Angeles, CA, Nov 22, 1958.
Billie Jean King, former tennis player, born Long Beach, CA, Nov 22, 1943.

November 22

KENNEDY, JOHN F.: ASSASSINATION ANNIVERSARY. Nov 22, 1963. Thirty-fifth president of the US (1961–63), born at Brookline, MA. Kennedy was the youngest man ever elected to the presidency, the first Roman Catholic and the first president to have served in the US Navy. He was slain by a sniper while riding in an open automobile at Dallas, TX. He was the fourth US president to be killed by an assassin and the second to be buried at Arlington National Cemetery (first was William Howard Taft). Accused gunman Lee Harvey Oswald was killed in police custody awaiting trial.

LEBANON: INDEPENDENCE DAY. Nov 22. National Day. Gained independence from France in 1943.

SAGITTARIUS, THE ARCHER. Nov 22–Dec 21. In the astronomical/astrological zodiac that divides the sun's apparent orbit into 12 segments, the period Nov 22–Dec 21 is identified, traditionally, as the sun sign of Sagittarius, the Archer. The ruling planet is Jupiter.

November 23

BILLY THE KID: BIRTH ANNIVERSARY. Nov 23, 1859. Legendary outlaw of western US. Probably named Henry McCarty at birth (New York, NY), he was better known as William H. Bonney. Ruthless killer, a failure at everything legal, he escaped from jail at age 21 while under sentence of hanging. Recaptured at Stinking Springs, NM, and returned to jail, he again escaped, only to be shot through the heart by pursuing Lincoln County Sheriff Pat Garrett at Fort Sumner, NM, during the night of July 14, 1881. His last words, answered by two shots, reportedly were "Who is there?"

***LIFE* MAGAZINE DEBUTED: ANNIVERSARY.** Nov 23, 1936. The illustrated magazine *Life* debuted on this day. The first cover depicted a doctor slapping a baby with the caption "Life begins."

PIERCE, FRANKLIN: BIRTH ANNIVERSARY. Nov 23, 1804. The 14th president of the US was born at Hillsboro, NH. Term of office: Mar 4, 1853–Mar 3, 1857. Not nominated until the 49th ballot at the Democratic Party convention in 1852, he was refused his party's nomination in 1856 for a second term. Pierce died at Concord, NH, Oct 8, 1869.

★ Birthdays ★

Vin Baker, basketball player, born Lake Wales, FL, Nov 23, 1971.

November 24

CARNEGIE, DALE: BIRTH ANNIVERSARY. Nov 24, 1888. American inspirational lecturer and author, Dale Carnegie was born at Maryville, MO. His best-known book, *How to Win Friends and Influence People*, published in 1936, sold nearly 5 million copies and was translated into 29 languages. Carnegie died at New York, NY, Nov 1, 1955.

"D.B. COOPER" HIJACKING: ANNIVERSARY. Nov 24–25, 1971. A middle-aged man whose plane ticket was made out to "D.B. Cooper" parachuted from a Northwest Airlines 727 jetliner on Nov 25, 1971, carrying $200,000 that he had collected from the airline as ransom for the plane and passengers as a result of threats made during his Nov 24 flight from Portland, OR, to Seattle, WA. He jumped from the plane over an area of wilderness south of Seattle and was never apprehended. Several thousand dollars of the marked ransom money turned up in February 1980, along the Columbia River, near Vancouver, WA.

TAYLOR, ZACHARY: BIRTH ANNIVERSARY. Nov 24, 1784. The soldier who became 12th president of the US was born at Orange County, VA. Term of office: Mar 4, 1849–July 9, 1850. He was nominated at the Whig Party convention in 1848, but, the story goes, he did not accept the letter notifying him of his nomination because it had postage due. He cast his first vote in 1846, when he was 62 years old. Becoming ill July 4, 1850, he died at the White House, July 9. His last words: "I am sorry that I am about to leave my friends."

TOULOUSE-LAUTREC, HENRI DE: BIRTH ANNIVERSARY. Nov 24, 1864. French painter and designer of posters. Born at Albi, France, he died Sept 9, 1901, at Bordeaux, France.

★ Birthdays ★

William F. Buckley, Jr, editor (*The National Review*), author (*God and Man at Yale*), born New York, NY, Nov 24, 1925.
Oscar Palmer Robertson, Hall of Fame basketball player, born Charlotte, TN, Nov 24, 1938.

November 25

AUTOMOBILE SPEED REDUCTION: ANNIVERSARY. Nov 25, 1973. Anniversary of the presidential order requiring a cutback from the 70-mile-per-hour speed limit. The 55-mile-per-hour National Maximum Speed Limit (NMSL) was established by Congress in January 1974 (Public Law 93–643). The National Highway Traffic Administration reported that "analysis of available data shows that the 55 MPH NMSL forestalled 48,310 fatalities through 1980. There were also reductions in crash-related injuries and property damage." Motor fuel savings were estimated at 2.4 billion gallons per year. Notwithstanding, in 1987 Congress permitted states to increase speed limits on rural interstate highways to 65 MPH.

CARNEGIE, ANDREW: BIRTH ANNIVERSARY. Nov 25, 1835. American financier, philanthropist and benefactor of more than 2,500 libraries, was born at Dunfermline, Scotland. Carnegie Hall, Carnegie Foundation and the Carnegie Endowment for International Peace are among his gifts. Carnegie wrote in 1889, "Surplus wealth is a sacred trust which its possessor is bound to administer in his lifetime for the good of the community. . . . The man who dies . . . rich dies disgraced." Carnegie died at his summer estate, "Shadowbrook," MA, Aug 11, 1919.

DiMAGGIO, JOSEPH PAUL (JOE): BIRTH ANNIVERSARY. Nov 25, 1914. Baseball Hall of Fame outfielder, born at Martinez, CA. In 1941 he was on "the streak," getting a hit in 56 consecutive games. He was the American League MVP for three years, was the batting champion in 1939 and led the league in RBIs in both 1941 and 1948. DiMaggio was married to actress Marilyn Monroe in 1954. He died at Harbour Island, FL, Mar 8, 1999.

UNITED NATIONS: INTERNATIONAL DAY FOR THE ELIMINATION OF VIOLENCE AGAINST WOMEN. Nov 25. Women's activists have marked Nov 25 as a day against violence since 1981. On that date in 1961 the three Mirabel sisters, political activists in the Dominican Republic, were assassinated on orders of ruler Rafael Trujillo. For info: United Nations. Web: www.un.org.

★ *Birthdays* ★

Jill Hennessy, actress ("Law & Order," "Crossing Jordan"), born Edmonton, AB, Canada, Nov 25, 1969.
John Larroquette, actor (Emmy for "Night Court"; "The John Larroquette Show"), born New Orleans, LA, Nov 25, 1947.
Lenny Moore, Hall of Fame football player, born Reading, PA, Nov 25, 1933.

November 26

CASABLANCA PREMIERE: ANNIVERSARY. Nov 26, 1942. Due to the landing of the Allies in North Africa on Nov 8, the premiere and release of the film were moved up from June 1943 to Nov 26, 1942, when it premiered at New York City on Thanksgiving Day. The general nationwide release followed on Jan 23, 1943, during the Roosevelt-Churchill conferences in Casablanca.

FIRST US HOLIDAY BY PRESIDENTIAL PROCLAMATION: ANNIVERSARY. Nov 26, 1789. President George Washington proclaimed Nov 26, 1789, to be Thanksgiving Day. Both Houses of Congress, by their joint committee, had requested him to recommend "a day of public thanksgiving and prayer, to be observed by acknowledging with grateful hearts the many and signal favors of Almighty God, especially by affording them an opportunity to peaceably establish a form of government for their safety and happiness." Proclamation issued Oct 3, 1789. Next proclaimed by President Lincoln in 1863 for the last Thursday in November. In 1939 President Franklin Roosevelt moved Thanksgiving to the fourth Thursday in November.

"THE PRICE IS RIGHT" TV PREMIERE: ANNIVERSARY. Nov 26, 1956. This popular show is also TV's longest-running daily game show, surviving changes in format, networks, time slots and hosts. It began in 1956 with Bill Cullen as host and Don Pardo as announcer; four contestants had to bid on an item and the one who bid closest to the manufacturer's suggested price won the item. In 1972, after a seven-year hiatus, "The Price Is Right" came back in two versions. Bob Barker was the host of the network version, which he hosts to this day. Also on the show are attractive women who model the prizes to be won and help set up the price-guessing games. "Price" contestants are drawn from the studio audience.

TRUTH, SOJOURNER: DEATH ANNIVERSARY. Nov 26, 1883. A former slave who had been sold four different times, Sojourner Truth became an evangelist who argued for abolition and women's rights. After a troubled early life, she began her evangelical career in 1843, traveling through New England until she discovered the utopian colony called the Northampton Association of Education and Industry. It was there she was exposed to, and became an advocate for, the cause of abolition, working with Frederick Douglass, Wendell Phillips, William Lloyd Garrison and others. In 1850 she befriended Lucretia Mott, Elizabeth Cady Stanton and other feminist leaders and actively began supporting calls for women's rights. In 1870 she attempted to petition Congress to create a "Negro State" on public lands in the West. Born at Ulster County, NY, about 1790, with the name Isabella Van Wagener, she died Nov 26, 1883, at Battle Creek, MI.

★ Birthdays ★

Shawn Kemp, basketball player, born Elkhart, IN, Nov 26, 1969.
Tina Turner, singer (with ex-husband Ike: "A Fool in Love"; solo: "What's Love Got to Do with It"), born Nutbush, TN, Nov 26, 1938.

November 27

BANK BAILOUT BILL: ANNIVERSARY. Nov 27, 1991. Both houses of Congress approved legislation authorizing $70 billion in additional borrowing authority for the Federal Deposit Insurance Corporation (FDIC) because of the record number of savings and loan failures.

HENDRIX, JIMI: BIRTH ANNIVERSARY. Nov 27, 1942. American musician and songwriter Jimi Hendrix was born at Seattle, WA. One of the greatest rock guitarists in history, he revolutionized the guitar sound with heavy use of feedback and incredible fretwork. His success first came in England, then in the US after his appearance at the Monterey Pop Festival (1967). His albums included *Are You Experienced?*, *Electric Ladyland* and *Band of Gypsys*. He died Sept 18, 1970, at London, England.

★ Birthdays ★

Robin Givens, actress ("Head of the Class," *A Rage in Harlem*), born New York, NY, Nov 27, 1964.

Nick Van Exel, basketball player, born Kenosha, WI, Nov 27, 1971.

November 28

ALBANIA: INDEPENDENCE DAY. Nov 28. Commemorates independence from the Ottoman Empire in 1912.

BLAKE, WILLIAM: BIRTH ANNIVERSARY. Nov 28, 1757. English poet (*Songs of Innocence*), artist and philosopher, born at London, England. Died there Aug 12, 1827.

SPACE MILESTONE: *MARINER 4* (US). Nov 28, 1964. The first successful mission to Mars. Approached within 6,118 miles of Mars on July 14, 1965. Took photographs and instrument readings.

★ Birthdays ★

Ed Harris, actor (*The Right Stuff, Stepmom*), born Englewood, NJ, Nov 28, 1950.
Judd Nelson, actor (*The Breakfast Club, St. Elmo's Fire*, "Suddenly Susan"), born Portland, ME, Nov 28, 1959.

November 29

ALCOTT, LOUISA MAY: BIRTH ANNIVERSARY. Nov 29, 1832. American author, born at Philadelphia, PA. Died at Boston, MA, Mar 6, 1888. Her most famous novel was *Little Women*, the classic story of Meg, Jo, Beth and Amy.

★ Birthdays ★

Kim Delaney, actress ("NYPD Blue," "Philly"), born Philadelphia, PA, Nov 29, 1961.
Garry Shandling, comedian ("The Larry Sanders Show"), born Chicago, IL, Nov 29, 1949.

November 30

CLEMENS, SAMUEL LANGHORNE (MARK TWAIN): BIRTH ANNIVERSARY. Nov 30, 1835. Celebrated American author, whose books include: *The Adventures of Tom Sawyer*, *The Adventures of Huckleberry Finn* and *The Prince and the Pauper*. Born at Florida, MO, Twain is quoted as saying, "I came in with Halley's Comet in 1835. It is coming again next year, and I expect to go out with it." He did. Twain died at Redding, CT, Apr 21, 1910 (just one day after Halley's Comet perihelion).

EL SALVADOR ADOPTS US DOLLAR: ANNIVERSARY. Nov 30, 2000. El Salvador became the third Latin American country to adopt the US dollar as its official currency. Ecuador and Panama also use the US dollar and Bermuda, a British colony, uses it as well.

SAINT ANDREW'S DAY. Nov 30. Feast day of the apostle and martyr Andrew, who died about AD 60. Patron saint of Scotland.

STAY HOME BECAUSE YOU'RE WELL DAY. Nov 30. So we can call in "well," instead of faking illness and stay home from work. [©2001 by WH.] For info: Wellcat Holidays. Web: www.wellcat.com.

★ Birthdays ★

Dick Clark, longtime host of "American Bandstand," entertainer, producer, born Mount Vernon, NY, Nov 30, 1929.
Mandy Patinkin, actor (Tony for *Evita; Sunday in the Park with George*, "Chicago Hope"), born Chicago, IL, Nov 30, 1952.
Ben Stiller, actor, director (*Zoolander, The Royal Tenenbaums*), born New York, NY, Nov 30, 1965.

December

December 1

BASKETBALL CREATED: ANNIVERSARY. Dec 1, 1891. James Naismith was a teacher of physical education at the International YMCA Training School at Springfield, MA. To create an indoor sport that could be played during the winter months, he nailed up peach baskets at opposite ends of the gym and gave students soccer balls to toss into them. Thus was born the game of basketball.

50 STATE QUARTERS PROGRAM: ANNIVERSARY. Dec 1, 1997. President Clinton signed the 50 State Quarters Program Act on this date. It allows the Department of the Treasury to issue a series of quarters honoring the 50 states. Quarters are being issued in the order the states joined the Union. The first quarter issued in 1999 honored Delaware; the last quarter will be issued in 2008 and will feature Hawaii.

McCARTHY SILENCED BY SENATE: ANNIVERSARY. Dec 1, 1954. On Feb 9, 1950, Joseph McCarthy, a relatively obscure senator from Wisconsin, announced during a speech in Wheeling, WV, that he had a list of Communists in the State Department. Over the next two years he made increasingly sensational charges, and in 1953 McCarthyism reached its height as he held Senate hearings in which he bullied defendants. In 1954, McCarthy's tyranny was exposed in televised hearings during which he took on the Army, and on Dec 1, 1954, the Senate voted to silence him. McCarthy died May 2, 1957.

NATIONAL DRUNK AND DRUGGED DRIVING (3D) PREVENTION MONTH. Dec 1–31. For info: 3D Prevention Month Coalition. Web: www.3dmonth.org.

PLAYBOY FIRST PUBLISHED: ANNIVERSARY. Dec 1, 1953. _Playboy_ magazine was launched at Chicago by publisher Hugh Hefner.

PORTUGAL: INDEPENDENCE DAY. Dec 1. Public holiday. Became independent of Spain in 1640.

ROMANIA: NATIONAL DAY. Dec 1. National holiday. Marks unification of Romania and Transylvania in 1918 and the overthrow of the Communist regime in 1989.

ROSA PARKS DAY: ANNIVERSARY OF ARREST. Dec 1, 1955. Anniversary of the arrest of Rosa Parks, at Montgomery, AL, for refusing to give up her seat and move to the back of a municipal bus. Her arrest triggered a yearlong boycott of the city bus system and led to legal actions that ended racial segregation on municipal buses throughout the southern US. The event has been called the birth of the modern civil rights movement. Rosa McCauley Parks was born at Tuskegee, AL, Feb 4, 1913.

UNITED NATIONS: WORLD AIDS DAY. Dec 1. In 1988 the World Health Organization of the United Nations declared Dec 1 as World AIDS Day, an international day of awareness and education about AIDS. The WHO is the leader in global direction and coordination of AIDS prevention, control, research and education. A program called UN-AIDS was created to bring together the skills and expertise of the World Bank, UNDP, UNESCO, UNICEF, UNFPA and the WHO to strengthen and expand national capacities to respond to the pandemic. For info: American Association for World Health. Web: www.aawhworldhealth.org.

★ *Birthdays* ★

Woody Allen, actor, writer, producer (Oscar for *Annie Hall; Sleeper, Manhattan, Bullets over Broadway*), born Allen Stewart Konigsberg, Brooklyn, NY, Dec 1, 1935.

Bette Midler, singer ("You Are the Wind Beneath My Wings"), actress (*Beaches, For the Boys, Down and Out in Beverly Hills*), born Honolulu, HI, Dec 1, 1945.

Richard Pryor, actor, comedian (*Blue Collar, Stir Crazy*, "The Richard Pryor Show"), born Peoria, IL, Dec 1, 1940.

December 2

ARTIFICIAL HEART TRANSPLANT: ANNIVERSARY. Dec 2, 1982. Barney C. Clark, 61, became the first recipient of a permanent artificial heart. The operation was performed at the University of Utah Medical Center at Salt Lake City. Near death at the time of the operation, Clark survived almost 112 days after the implantation. He died Mar 23, 1983.

FIRST SELF-SUSTAINING NUCLEAR CHAIN REACTION: ANNIVERSARY. Dec 2, 1942. Physicist Enrico Fermi led a team of scientists at the University of Chicago in producing the first controlled, self-sustaining nuclear chain reaction. Their first simple nuclear reactor was built under the stands of the university's football stadium.

LAOS: NATIONAL DAY. Dec 2. National holiday commemorating declaration of the republic in 1975.

MONROE DOCTRINE: ANNIVERSARY. Dec 2, 1823. President James Monroe, in his annual message to Congress, enunciated the doctrine that bears his name and that was long hailed as a statement of US policy. ". . . In the wars of the European powers in matters relating to themselves we have never taken any part . . . we should consider any attempt on their part to extend their system to any portion of this hemi-sphere as dangerous to our peace and safety. . . ."

PAN AMERICAN HEALTH DAY. Dec 2. Presidential Proclamation 2447, of Nov 23, 1940, covers all succeeding years. The 1940 Pan American Conference of National Directors of Health adopted a resolution recommending that a "Health Day" be held annually in the countries of the Pan American Union.

SAFETY RAZOR PATENTED: ANNIVERSARY. Dec 2, 1901. American King Camp Gillette designed the first razor with disposable blades. Up until this time, men shaved with a straight-edge razor that they sharpened on a leather strap.

★ Birthdays ★

Stone Phillips, anchor ("Dateline," "20/20"), born Texas City, TX, Dec 2, 1954.
Monica Seles, tennis player, born Novi Sad, Yugoslavia, Dec 2, 1973.

Britney Spears, singer, born Kentwood, LA, Dec 2, 1981.

December 3

BHOPAL POISON GAS DISASTER: ANNIVERSARY. Dec 3, 1984. At Bhopal, India, a leak of deadly gas (methyl isocyanate) at a Union Carbide Corp plant killed more than 4,000 persons and injured more than 200,000 in the world's worst industrial accident.

FIRST HEART TRANSPLANT: ANNIVERSARY. Dec 3, 1967. Dr. Christiaan Barnard, a South African surgeon, performed the world's first successful heart transplantation at Cape Town, South Africa.

ILLINOIS: ADMISSION DAY: ANNIVERSARY. Dec 3. Became 21st state in 1818.

UNITED NATIONS: INTERNATIONAL DAY OF DISABLED PERSONS. Dec 3. On Oct 14, 1992 (Resolution 47/3), at the end of the Decade of Disabled Persons, the General Assembly proclaimed Dec 3 to be an annual observance to promote the continuation of integrating the disabled into general society. For info: United Nations. Web: www.un.org.

★ Birthdays ★

Brendan Fraser, actor (*The Mummy, George of the Jungle*), born Indianapolis, IN, Dec 3, 1968.
Daryl Hannah, actress (*Splash, Grumpy Old Men*), born Chicago, IL, Dec 3, 1961.

December 4

SPACE MILESTONE: INTERNATIONAL SPACE STATION LAUNCH (US). Dec 4, 1998. The shuttle *Endeavour* took a US component of the space station named *Unity* into orbit 220 miles from Earth where spacewalking astronauts fastened it to a component launched by the Russians Nov 20, 1998. On July 25, 2000, the Russian service module *Zvezda* docked with the station. It will take a total of 45 Russian and US launches over the next five years before the space station is complete. When finished, it will be 356 feet across and 290 feet long, and will support a crew of up to seven. On Oct 31, 2000, NASA launched the first expedition with a three-man crew to stay aloft for four months.

★ Birthdays ★

Jeff Bridges, actor (*The Fisher King*), born Los Angeles, CA, Dec 4, 1949.

Marisa Tomei, actress (*The Flamingo Kid, My Cousin Vinny*), born Brooklyn, NY, Dec 4, 1964.

December 5

AFL-CIO FOUNDED: ANNIVERSARY. Dec 5, 1955. The American Federation of Labor and the Congress of Industrial Organizations joined together in 1955, following 20 years of rivalry, to become the nation's leading advocate for trade unions.

MONTGOMERY BUS BOYCOTT BEGINS: ANNIVERSARY. Dec 5, 1955. Rosa Parks was arrested at Montgomery, AL, for refusing to give up her seat on a bus to a white man. In support of Parks, and to protest the arrest, the black community of Montgomery organized a boycott of the bus system. The boycott lasted from Dec 5, 1955, to Dec 20, 1956, when a US Supreme Court ruling was implemented at Montgomery, integrating the public transportation system.

TWENTY-FIRST AMENDMENT TO THE US CONSTITUTION RATIFIED: ANNIVERSARY. Dec 5, 1933. Prohibition ended with the repeal of the 18th Amendment, as the 21st Amendment was ratified.

VAN BUREN, MARTIN: BIRTH ANNIVERSARY. Dec 5, 1782. The eighth president of the US (term of office: Mar 4, 1837–Mar 3, 1841) was the first to have been born a citizen of the US. He was a widower for nearly two decades before he entered the White House. His daughter-in-law, Angelica, served as White House hostess during an administration troubled by bank and business failures, depression and unemployment. Van Buren was born at Kinderhook, NY, and died there July 24, 1862.

★ *Birthdays* ★

José Carreras, opera singer, one of the "Three Tenors," born Barcelona, Spain, Dec 5, 1946.
Frankie Muniz, actor ("Malcolm in the Middle," *My Dog Skip*), born Ridgewood, NJ, Dec 5, 1985.

December 6

EVERGLADES NATIONAL PARK ESTABLISHED: ANNIVERSARY. Dec 6, 1947. Part of vast marshland area on southern Florida peninsula, originally authorized May 30, 1934, was established as a national park. For info: National Park Sevice. Web: www.nps.gov/ever.

FINLAND: INDEPENDENCE DAY. Dec 6. National holiday. Declaration of independence from Russia in 1917.

GERSHWIN, IRA: BIRTH ANNIVERSARY. Dec 6, 1896. Pulitzer Prize–winning American lyricist and author who collaborated with his brother,

George, and with many other composers. Among his Broadway successes: *Lady Be Good, Funny Face, Strike Up the Band* and such songs as "The Man I Love," "Someone to Watch Over Me," "I Got Rhythm" and hundreds of others. Born at New York, NY, he died at Beverly Hills, CA, Aug 17, 1983.

MISSOURI EARTHQUAKES: ANNIVERSARY. Dec 6, 1811. New Madrid, MO. Most prolonged series of earthquakes in US history occured not in California but in the Midwest. Lasted until Feb 12, 1812. There were few deaths because of the sparse population. These were the most severe earthquakes in the contiguous US; those higher on the Richter scale have all occurred in Alaska.

THIRTEENTH AMENDMENT TO THE US CONSTITUTION RATIFIED: ANNIVERSARY. Dec 6, 1865. The 13th Amendment to the Constitution was ratified, abolishing slavery in the US. "Neither slavery nor involuntary servitude, save as a punishment for crime whereof the party shall have been duly convicted, shall exist within the United States, or any place subject to their jurisdiction." This amendment was proclaimed Dec 18, 1865. The 13th, 14th and 15th Amendments are considered the Civil War Amendments.

★ *Birthdays* ★

Dave Brubeck, jazz musician, born Concord, CA, Dec 6, 1920.
Macy Gray, singer, born Canton, OH, Dec 6, 1969.

December 7

DELAWARE RATIFIES CONSTITUTION: ANNIVERSARY. Dec 7, 1787. Delaware became the first state to ratify the proposed Constitution. It did so by unanimous vote.

PEARL HARBOR DAY: ANNIVERSARY. Dec 7, 1941. At 7:55 AM (local time), Dec 7, 1941, "a date that will live in infamy," nearly 200 Japanese aircraft attacked Pearl Harbor, HI, long considered the US "Gibraltar of the Pacific." The raid, which lasted little more than one hour, left nearly 3,000 dead. Nearly the entire US Pacific Fleet was at anchor there and few ships escaped damage. Several were sunk or disabled, while 200 US aircraft on the ground were destroyed. The attack on Pearl Harbor brought about immediate US entry into World War II, a declaration of war being requested by President Franklin D. Roosevelt and approved by the Congress Dec 8, 1941. This day is proclaimed as National Pearl Harbor Remembrance Day by the president of the US.

SPACE MILESTONE: *APOLLO 17* **(US).** Dec 7, 1972. Launched this date with three-man crew who explored the moon, Dec 11–14. Lunar landing module named *Challenger*. Pacific splashdown, Dec 19. This was the last manned mission to the moon.

SPACE MILESTONE: *GALILEO* **(US).** Dec 7, 1995. Launched Oct 18, 1989, by the space shuttle *Atlantis*, the spacecraft *Galileo* entered the orbit of Jupiter, after a six-year journey. It has been orbiting Jupiter ever since, sending out probes to study three of its moons. Organic compounds, the ingredients of life, were found on them. On May 25, 2001, it passed within 86 miles of Callisto, one of Jupiter's moons.

★ Birthdays ★

Larry Joe Bird, Hall of Fame basketball player, NBA coach, born West Baden, IN, Dec 7, 1956.

Ellen Burstyn, actress (*Alice Doesn't Live Here Anymore; The Exorcist; Same Time, Next Year*), born Edna Rae Gilhooley, Detroit, MI, Dec 7, 1932.

December 8

AMERICA ENTERS WORLD WAR II: ANNIVERSARY. Dec 8, 1941. One day after the surprise Japanese attack on Pearl Harbor, Congress declared war against Japan and the US entered World War II.

CHINESE NATIONALISTS MOVE TO FORMOSA: ANNIVERSARY. Dec 8, 1949. The government of Chiang Kai-Shek moved to Formosa (Taiwan) after being driven out of mainland China by the Communists led by Mao Tse-Tung.

FEAST OF THE IMMACULATE CONCEPTION. Dec 8. Roman Catholic Holy Day of Obligation. A public holiday in Nicaragua.

NAFTA SIGNED: ANNIVERSARY. Dec 8, 1993. President Clinton signed the North American Free Trade Agreement, which cut tariffs and eliminated other trade barriers between the US, Canada and Mexico. The agreement went into effect Jan 1, 1994.

SOVIET UNION DISSOLVED: ANNIVERSARY. Dec 8, 1991. The Union of Soviet Socialist Republics ceased to exist, as the republics of Russia, Byelorussia and Ukraine signed an agreement at Minsk, Byelorussia, creating the Commonwealth of Independent States. The remaining republics, with the exception of Georgia, joined in the new Commonwealth as it began the slow and arduous process of removing the yoke of Communism and dealing with strong separatist and nationalistic movements within the various republics.

★ Birthdays ★

Kim Basinger, actress (*The Natural, The Getaway, My Stepmother Is an Alien*; Oscar for *L.A. Confidential*), born Athens, GA, Dec 8, 1953. **Teri Hatcher**, actress ("Lois & Clark"), born Sunnyvale, CA, Dec 8, 1964.

December 9

HARRIS, JOEL CHANDLER: BIRTH ANNIVERSARY. Dec 9, 1848. American author, creator of the "Uncle Remus" stories, born at Eatonton, GA. Died July 3, 1908, at Atlanta, GA.

KELLY, EMMETT: BIRTH ANNIVERSARY. Dec 9, 1898. American circus clown and entertainer, born at Sedan, KS. Kelly was best known for "Weary Willie," a clown dressed in tattered clothes, with a beard and large nose. Died at Sarasota, FL, Mar 28, 1979.

TANZANIA: INDEPENDENCE AND REPUBLIC DAY. Dec 9. Tanganyika became independent of Britain in 1961. The republics of Tanganyika and Zanzibar joined to become one state (Apr 27, 1964), renamed (Oct 29, 1964) the United Republic of Tanzania.

★ *Birthdays* ★

Beau Bridges, actor ("James Brady Story," *The Fabulous Baker Boys*), born Los Angeles, CA, Dec 9, 1941.

Judi Dench, actress (*Tomorrow Never Dies, Iris*), born York, England, Dec 9, 1934.

John Malkovich, actor (*The Killing Fields, The Sheltering Sky*), filmmaker, born Christopher, IL, Dec 9, 1953.

December 10

DICKINSON, EMILY: BIRTH ANNIVERSARY. Dec 10, 1830. One of America's greatest poets, Emily Dickinson was born at Amherst, MA. She was reclusive, mysterious and frail in health. Seven of her poems were published during her life, but after her death her sister, Lavinia, discovered almost 2,000 more poems written on the backs of envelopes and other scraps of paper locked in her bureau. They were published gradually, over 50 years, beginning in 1890. She died May 15, 1886, at Amherst, MA. The little-known Emily Dickinson who was born, lived and died at Amherst now is recognized as one of the most original poets of the English-speaking world.

FIRST GRAND OLE OPRY BROADCAST: ANNIVERSARY. Dec 10, 1927. Grand Ole Opry made its first radio broadcast from Nashville, TN.

FIRST US SCIENTIST RECEIVES NOBEL PRIZE: ANNIVERSARY. Dec 10, 1907. University of Chicago professor Albert Michelson, eminent physicist known for his research on the speed of light and optics, became the first US scientist to receive the Nobel Prize.

HUMAN RIGHTS DAY. Dec 10. Presidential Proclamation 2866, of Dec 6, 1949, covers all succeeding years. Customarily issued as "Bill of Rights Day, Human Rights Day and Week."

MISSISSIPPI: ADMISSION DAY: ANNIVERSARY. Dec 10. Became 20th state in 1817.

NOBEL PRIZE AWARDS CEREMONIES. Dec 10. Oslo, Norway, and Stockholm, Sweden. Alfred Nobel, Swedish chemist and inventor of dynamite who died in 1896, provided in his will that income from his $9 million estate should be used for annual prizes—to be awarded to people who are judged to have made the most valuable contributions to the good of humanity. The Nobel Peace Prize is awarded by a committee of the Norwegian parliament, and the presentation is made at the Oslo City Hall. Five other prizes, for physics, chemistry, medicine, literature and economics, are presented in a ceremony at Stockholm, Sweden. Both ceremonies traditionally are held on the anniversary of the death of Alfred Nobel. First awarded in 1901, the current value of each prize is about $1 million. To date, more than 250 Americans have won Nobel Prizes.

RALPH BUNCHE AWARDED NOBEL PEACE PRIZE: ANNIVERSARY.
Dec 10, 1950. Dr. Ralph Johnson Bunche became the first black man awarded the Nobel Peace Prize. Bunche was awarded the prize for his efforts in mediation between Israel and neighboring Arab states in 1949.

TREATY OF PARIS ENDS SPANISH-AMERICAN WAR: ANNIVERSARY.
Dec 10, 1898. Following the conclusion of the Spanish-American War in 1898, American and Spanish ambassadors met at Paris, France, to negotiate a treaty. Under the terms of this treaty, Spain granted the US the Philippine Islands and the islands of Guam and Puerto Rico and agreed to withdraw from Cuba. Senatorial debate over the treaty centered on the US's move toward imperialism by acquiring the Philippines. A vote was taken Feb 6, 1899, and the treaty passed by a one-vote margin. President William McKinley signed the treaty Feb 10, 1899.

★ Birthdays ★

Kenneth Branagh, actor, director (*High Season, Henry V*), born Belfast, Northern Ireland, Dec 10, 1960.

Susan Dey, actress ("The Partridge Family," "L.A. Law"), born Pekin, IL, Dec 10, 1951.

December 11

BURKINA FASO: NATIONAL DAY. Dec 11. Gained independence from France as Upper Volta in 1958.

EDWARD VIII ABDICATION: ANNIVERSARY. Dec 11, 1936. King Edward VIII was born at Richmond Park, England, on June 12, 1894, and ascended to the English throne upon the death of his father, George V, on Jan 20, 1936, but coronation never took place. He abdicated on Dec 11, 1936, in order to marry "the woman I love," twice-divorced American Wallis Warfield Simpson. Edward was named Duke of Windsor by his brother-successor, George VI. The Duke died at Paris, May 28, 1972, but was buried in England, near Windsor Castle.

INDIANA: ADMISSION DAY: ANNIVERSARY. Dec 11. Became 19th state in 1816.

SPACE MILESTONE: *MARS CLIMATE ORBITER* (US). Dec 11, 1998. This unmanned craft was to track the water vapor over Mars, which it was scheduled to reach in September 1999. However, it burned up just before beginning to circle the planet. Its companion, *Mars Polar Lander*, was launched Jan 3, 1999, and was to land on Mars, burrow into the ground and analyze the soil. However, on Dec 3, 1999, just before landing, all communications with the craft were lost.

UNITED NATIONS: UNICEF: ANNIVERSARY. Dec 11, 1946. Anniversary of the establishment by the

United Nations General Assembly of the United Nations International Children's Emergency Fund (UNICEF). For info: United Nations. Web: www.unicef.org.

★ *Birthdays* ★

Teri Garr, actress (*Young Frankenstein, Tootsie, The Black Stallion*), born Lakewood, OH, Dec 11, 1949.

Rita Moreno, singer, actress (Oscar for *West Side Story*; Tony for *The Ritz*), born Hunacao, Puerto Rico, Dec 11, 1931.

December 12

BONZA BOTTLER DAY™. Dec 12. To celebrate when the number of the day is the same as the number of the month. Bonza Bottler Day™ is an excuse to have a party at least once a month. For info: Gail M. Berger. E-mail: gberger5 @aol.com.

DAY OF OUR LADY OF GUADALUPE. Dec 12. The legend of Guadalupe tells how in December 1531, an Indian, Juan Diego, saw the Virgin Mother on a hill near Mexico City, who instructed him to go to the bishop and have him build a shrine to her on the site of the vision. After his request was initially rebuffed, the Virgin Mother appeared to Juan Diego three days later. She instructed him to pick roses growing on a stony and barren hillside nearby and take them to the bishop as proof. Although flowers do not normally bloom in December, Juan Diego found the roses and took them to the bishop. As he opened his mantle to drop the roses on the floor, an image of the Virgin Mary appeared among them. The bishop built the sanctuary as instructed. Our Lady of Guadalupe became the patroness of Mexico City and by 1746 was the patron saint of all New Spain and by 1910 of all Latin America.

PENNSYLVANIA RATIFIES CONSTITUTION: ANNIVERSARY. Dec 12, 1787. Pennsylvania became the second state to ratify the US Constitution, by a vote of 46 to 23, in 1787.

POINSETTIA DAY (JOEL ROBERTS POINSETT: DEATH ANNIVERSARY). Dec 12. A day to enjoy poinsettias and to honor Dr. Joel Roberts Poinsett, the American diplomat who introduced the Central American plant that is named for him into the US. Poinsett was born at Charleston, SC, Mar 2, 1799. He also served as a member of Congress and as secretary of war. He died near Statesburg, SC, Dec 12, 1851. The poinsettia has become a favorite Christmas season plant.

SINATRA, FRANK: BIRTH ANNIVERSARY. Dec 12, 1915. Born at Hoboken, NJ, Frank Sinatra matured from a teen idol to the premier singer of American popular music. Known as the "Chairman of the Board" to his fans, he made more than 200 albums. His signature songs included "All the Way," "New York, New York" and "My Way." His film career included musicals (*On the Town* and *Pal Joey*) and two gritty films for which he won Oscar nominations, *From Here to Eternity* and *The Man with the Golden Arm*. Died May 14, 1998, at Los Angeles, CA.

SUPREME COURT RULES FOR BUSH: ANNIVERSARY. Dec 12, 2000. The Supreme Court effectively handed the 2000 presidential election to George W. Bush, ruling by a vote of 5 to 4 that there could be no further counting of Florida's disputed presidential votes. After five weeks of conflict over the vote count in Florida, Democratic candidate Al Gore conceded the election to Bush.

★ *Birthdays* ★

Jennifer Connelly, actress (Oscar for *A Beautiful Mind*), born Catskills, NY, Dec 12, 1970.
Robert Lee (Bob) Pettit, Jr, Hall of Fame basketball player, born Baton Rouge, LA, Dec 12, 1932.
Tom Wilkinson, actor (*The Full Monty, In the Bedroom*), born Leeds, England, Dec 12, 1948.

December 13

NORTH AND SOUTH KOREA END WAR: ANNIVERSARY. Dec 13, 1991. North and South Korea signed a treaty of reconciliation and nonaggression, formally ending the Korean War—38 years after fighting ceased in 1953. This agreement was not hailed as a peace treaty, and the armistice that was signed July 27, 1953, between the United Nations and North Korea was to remain in effect until it could be transformed into a formal peace.

SWEDEN: SANTA LUCIA DAY. Dec 13. Nationwide celebration of festival of light, honoring St. Lucia. Many hotels have their own Lucia, a young girl attired in a long, flowing white gown, who serves guests coffee and *lussekatter* (saffron buns) in the early morning.

★ *Birthdays* ★

Steve Buscemi, actor (*Fargo, Pulp Fiction*), born Brooklyn, NY, Dec 13, 1958.
Christopher Plummer, actor (Emmy for "The Moneychangers"; *The Sound of Music, Dolores Claiborne*), born Toronto, ON, Canada, Dec 13, 1929.
Dick Van Dyke, actor, comedian (*Mary Poppins*, "The Dick Van Dyke Show," "Diagnosis Murder"), born West Plains, MO, Dec 13, 1925.

December 14

ALABAMA: ADMISSION DAY: ANNIVERSARY. Dec 14. Became 22nd state in 1819.

HALCYON DAYS. Dec 14–28. Traditionally, the seven days before and the seven days after the winter solstice. To the ancients a time when fabled bird (called the halcyon—pronounced hal-cee-on) calmed the wind and waves—a time of calm and tranquillity.

SOUTH POLE DISCOVERY: ANNIVERSARY. Dec 14, 1911. The elusive object of many expeditions dating from the seventh century, the South Pole was located and visited by Roald Amundsen with four companions and 52 sled dogs. All five men and 12 of the dogs returned to base camp safely. Next to visit the South Pole, Jan 17, 1912, was a party of five led by Captain Robert F. Scott, all of whom perished during the return trip. A search party found their frozen bodies 11 months later.

★ Birthdays ★

Patty Duke, actress (Oscar for *The Miracle Worker*; Emmy for *My Sweet Charlie*), born New York, NY, Dec 14, 1946.

December 15

BILL OF RIGHTS DAY. Dec 15. Presidential Proclamation. Has been proclaimed each year since 1962 but was omitted in 1967 and 1968. (Issued in 1941 and 1946 at Congressional request and in 1947 without request.) Since 1968 has been included in Human Rights Day and Week Proclamation. The first ten amendments to the US Constitution, known as the Bill of Rights, became effective following ratification by Virginia on this day in 1791. The Bill of Rights was first proposed by James Madison in 1789.

"DAVY CROCKETT" TV PREMIERE: ANNIVERSARY. Dec 15, 1954. This show, a series of five segments, can be considered TV's first miniseries. Shown on Walt Disney's "Disneyland" show, it starred Fess Parker as American Western hero Davy Crockett and was immensely popular. The show spawned Crockett paraphernalia, including the famous coonskin cap (even though there is no evidence that Boone ever wore a coonskin cap).

PUERTO RICO: NAVIDADES. Dec 15–Jan 6. Traditional Christmas season begins mid-December and ends on Three Kings Day. Elaborate nativity scenes, carolers, special Christmas foods and trees from Canada and US. Gifts on Christmas Day and on Three Kings Day.

SITTING BULL: DEATH ANNIVERSARY. Dec 15, 1890. Famous Sioux Indian leader, medicine man and warrior of the Hunkpapa Teton band. Known also by his native name, Tatanka-yatanka, Sitting Bull was born on the Grand River, SD. He first accompanied his father on the warpath at the age of 14 against the Crow and thereafter rapidly gained influence within his tribe. In 1886 he led a raid on Fort Buford. His steadfast refusal to go to a reservation led General Phillip Sheridan to initiate a campaign against him. This led to the massacre of Lieutenant Colonel George Custer's men at the Little Bighorn, after which Sitting Bull fled to Canada, remaining there until 1881. Although many in his tribe surrendered on their return, Sitting Bull remained hostile until his death in a skirmish with the US soldiers along the Grand River.

★ Birthdays ★

Don Johnson, actor ("Miami Vice," "Nash Bridges"), born Flatt Creek, MO, Dec 15, 1949.

Alexandra Stevenson, tennis player, born San Diego, CA, Dec 15, 1980.

December 16

AUSTEN, JANE: BIRTH ANNIVERSARY. Dec 16, 1775. English novelist (*Pride and Prejudice, Sense and Sensibility*), born at Steventon, Hampshire, England. Died July 18, 1817, at Winchester, England.

BARBIE AND BARNEY BACKLASH DAY. Dec 16. If we have to explain this to you, you don't have kids. It's one day each year when Mom and Dad can tell the kids that Barbie and Barney don't exist. [©2001 by WH.] For info: Wellcat Holidays. Web: www.wellcat.com.

BATTLE OF THE BULGE: ANNIVERSARY. Dec 16, 1944. A German offensive was launched in the Belgian Ardennes Forest, where Hitler had managed to concentrate 250,000 men. The Nazi commanders, hoping to minimize any aerial counterattack by the Allies, chose a time when foggy, rainy weather prevailed and the initial attack by eight armored divisions along a 75-mile front took the Allies by surprise, the Fifth Panzer Army penetrating to within 20 miles of crossings on the Meuse River. US troops were able to hold fast at bottlenecks in the Ardennes, but by the end of December the German push had penetrated 65 miles into the Allied lines (though their line had narrowed from the initial 75 miles to 20 miles). By that time the Allies began to respond and the Germans were stopped by Montgomery on the Meuse and by Patton at Bastogne. The weather then cleared and Allied aircraft began to bomb the German forces and supply lines by Dec 26. The Allies re-established their original line by Jan 21, 1945.

BEETHOVEN, LUDWIG VAN: BIRTH ANNIVERSARY. Dec 16, 1770. Regarded by many as the greatest orchestral composer of all time, Ludwig van Beethoven was born at Bonn, Germany. Impairment of his hearing began before he was 30, but even total deafness did not halt his composing and conducting. His last appearance on the concert stage was to conduct the premiere of his *Ninth Symphony*, at Vienna, Austria, May 7, 1824. He was unable to hear either the orchestra or the applause. Often in love, he never married. Of a stormy temperament, he is said to have died during a violent thunderstorm Mar 26, 1827, at Vienna.

BOSTON TEA PARTY: ANNIVERSARY. Dec 16, 1773. Anniversary of Boston patriots' boarding of British vessel at anchor at Boston Harbor. Contents of nearly 350 chests of tea were dumped into the harbor.

"DRAGNET" TV PREMIERE: ANNIVERSARY. Dec 16, 1951. This famous crime show stressed authenticity, and episodes were supposedly based on real cases. It starred Jack Webb as stoic and determined Sergeant Joe Friday, a man whose life was his investigative police work and who was recognized by his recurring line, "Just the facts, ma'am." A new version appeared in 1967 with Webb and his new partner, Officer Bill Gannon (Harry Morgan). "Dragnet" is also known for its theme music and its narrative epilogue describing the fate of the bad guys.

MEXICO: POSADAS. Dec 16–24. A nine-day annual celebration throughout Mexico. Processions of "pilgrims" knock at doors asking for posada (shelter), commemorating the search by Joseph and Mary for a shelter in which the infant Jesus might be born. Pilgrims are invited inside, and fun and merrymaking ensue with blindfolded guests trying to break a "piñata" (papier-mâché-decorated earthenware utensil filled with gifts and goodies) suspended from the ceiling. Once the piñata is broken, the gifts are distributed and celebration continues.

★ *Birthdays* ★

Benjamin Bratt, actor ("Law & Order"), born San Francisco, CA, Dec 16, 1963.

Lesley Stahl, journalist ("60 Minutes," former White House correspondent), born Lynn, MA, Dec 16, 1941.

December 17

AZTEC CALENDAR STONE DISCOVERY: ANNIVERSARY. Dec 17, 1790. One of the wonders of the Western Hemisphere—the Aztec Calendar or Solar Stone—was found beneath the ground by workmen repairing Mexico City's Central Plaza. The centuries-old, intricately carved stone, 11 feet, eight inches in diameter and weighing nearly 25 tons, proved to be a highly developed calendar monument to the sun. Believed to have been carved in the year 1479, this extraordinary time-counting basalt tablet originally stood in the Great Temple of the Aztecs. Buried along with other Aztec idols soon after the Spanish conquest in 1521, it remained hidden until 1790. Its 52-year cycle had regulated many Aztec ceremonies, including grisly human sacrifices to save the world from destruction by the gods.

SATURNALIA. Dec 17–23. Ancient Roman festival honoring Saturnus, the god of agriculture. It was a time of merriment at the end of harvesting and wine-making. Presents were exchanged, sacrifices were offered, and masters served their slaves. Approximates the winter solstice. Some say that the date for the observance of the birth of Jesus was selected by the early Christian church leaders to fall on Dec 25 partly to counteract the popular pre-Christian festival of Saturnalia.

"THE SIMPSONS" TV PREMIERE: ANNIVERSARY. Dec 17, 1989. TV's hottest animated family, "The Simpsons," premiered as a half-hour weekly sitcom. The originator of Homer, Marge, Bart, Lisa and Maggie is cartoonist Matt Groening.

WRIGHT BROTHERS' FIRST POWERED FLIGHT: ANNIVERSARY. Dec 17, 1903. Orville and Wilbur Wright, brothers, bicycle shop operators, inventors and aviation pioneers, after three years of experimentation with kites and gliders, achieved the first documented successful powered and controlled flights of an airplane. The flights, near Kitty Hawk, NC, piloted first by Orville then by Wilbur Wright, were sustained for less than one minute but represented man's first powered airplane flight and the beginning of a new form of transportation. Orville Wright was born at Dayton, OH, Aug 19, 1871, and died there Jan 30, 1948. Wilbur Wright was born at Millville, IN, Apr 16, 1867, and died at Dayton, OH, May 30, 1912. This day is proclaimed annually as Wright Brothers Day by the US president.

★ Birthdays ★

Bernard Hill, actor (*Gandhi, Shirley Valentine*), born Manchester, England, Dec 17, 1944.
Bill Pullman, actor (*Independence Day, While You Were Sleeping*), born Delphi, NY, Dec 17, 1954.

December 18

NEW JERSEY RATIFICATION DAY: ANNIVERSARY. Dec 18, 1787. New Jersey became the third state to ratify the Constitution (following Delaware and Pennsylvania). It did so unanimously.

★ *Birthdays* ★

Christina Aguilera, singer, born Staten Island, NY, Dec 18, 1980.

Brad Pitt, actor (*Interview with the Vampire, A River Runs Through It*), born Shawnee, OK, Dec 18, 1964.

Steven Spielberg, producer, director (*E.T. the Extra-Terrestrial, Indiana Jones* movies, *Close Encounters of the Third Kind, Jurassic Park*; Oscars for *Schindler's List, Saving Private Ryan*), born Cincinnati, OH, Dec 18, 1947.

December 19

CHRISTMAS GREETINGS FROM SPACE: ANNIVERSARY. Dec 19, 1958. At 3:15 PM, EST, the US Earth satellite *Atlas* transmitted the first radio voice broadcast from space, a 58-word recorded Christmas greeting from President Dwight D. Eisenhower: "to all mankind America's wish for peace on Earth and goodwill toward men everywhere." The satellite had been launched from Cape Canaveral Dec 18.

WOODSON, CARTER G.: BIRTH ANNIVERSARY. Dec 19, 1875. Historian who introduced black stud-ies to colleges and universities, born at New Canton, VA. His scholarly works included *The Negro in Our History* and *The Education of the Negro Prior to 1861*. Known as the father of black history, he inaugurated Negro History Week. Woodson was working on a six-volume *Encyclopaedia Africana* when he died at Washington, DC, Apr 3, 1950.

★ *Birthdays* ★

Kevin Edward McHale, Hall of Fame basketball player, born Hibbing, MN, Dec 19, 1957.

Cicely Tyson, actress (Emmy for *The Autobiography of Miss Jane Pittman; Sounder*), born New York, NY, Dec 19, 1939.

December 20

AMERICAN POET LAUREATE ESTABLISHMENT: ANNIVERSARY. Dec 20, 1985. A bill empowering the Librarian of Congress to name, annually, a Poet Laureate/Consultant in Poetry was signed into law by President Ronald Reagan. In return for a stipend as Poet Laureate and a salary as the Consultant in Poetry, the person named will present at least one major work of poetry and will appear at selected national ceremonies. The first Poet Laureate of the US was Robert Penn

Warren, appointed to that position by the Librarian of Congress Feb 26, 1986.

CLINTON IMPEACHMENT PROCEEDINGS: ANNIVERSARY. Dec 20, 1998. President Bill Clinton was impeached by a House of Representatives that was divided along party lines. He was convicted of perjury and obstruction of justice stemming from a sexual relationship with a White House intern. He was then tried by the Senate in January 1999. On Feb 12, 1999, the Senate acquitted him on both charges. Clinton was only the second US president to undergo impeachment proceedings. Andrew Johnson was impeached by the House in 1868 but the Senate voted against impeachment and he finished his term of office. See also: "Johnson Impeachment Proceedings: Anniv" (Feb 24).

LOUISIANA PURCHASE DAY. Dec 20, 1803. One of the greatest real estate deals in history was completed in 1803, when more than a million square miles of the Louisiana Territory were turned over to the US by France, for a price of about $20 per square mile. This almost doubled the size of the US, extending its western border to the Rocky Mountains.

SACAGAWEA: DEATH ANNIVERSARY. Dec 20, 1812. As a young Shoshone Indian woman, Sacagawea in 1805 (with her two-month-old son strapped to her back) traveled with the Lewis and Clark Expedition, serving as an interpreter. It is said that the expedition could not have succeeded without her aid. She was born about 1787 and died at Fort Manuel on the Missouri River, Dec 20, 1812. Few other women have been so often honored. There are statues, fountains and memorials of her, and her name has been given to a mountain peak. In 2000 the US Mint issued a $1 coin honoring her.

SOUTH CAROLINA: SECESSION ANNIVERSARY. Dec 20, 1860. South Carolina's legislature voted to secede from the US, the first state to do so. Within six weeks, five more states seceded. On Feb 4, 1861, representatives from the six states met at Montgomery, AL, to establish a government, and on Feb 9 Jefferson Davis was elected president of the Confederate States of America. By June 1861, 11 states had seceded.

★ *Birthdays* ★

Jenny Agutter, actress (Emmy for "The Snow Goose"), born London, England, Dec 20, 1952. **John Spencer**, actor ("The West Wing," "L.A. Law"), born New York, NY, Dec 20, 1946.

December 21

FIRST CROSSWORD PUZZLE: ANNIVERSARY. Dec 21, 1913. The first crossword puzzle was compiled by Arthur Wynne and published in a supplement to the *New York World*.

HUMBUG DAY. Dec 21. Allows all those preparing for Christmas to vent their frustrations. Twelve "humbugs" allowed. [©2001 by WH.] For info: Wellcat Holidays. Web: www.wellcat .com.

PAN AMERICAN FLIGHT 103 EXPLOSION: ANNIVERSARY. Dec 21, 1988. Pan Am World Airways Flight 103 exploded in midair and crashed into the heart of Lockerbie, Scotland, the result of a terrorist bombing. The 259 passengers and crew members and 11 persons on the ground were killed in the disaster. The tragedy raised questions about security and the notification of passengers in the event of threatened flights. In the resultant investigation it was revealed that government agencies and the airline had known that the flight was possibly the target of a terrorist attack.

PILGRIM LANDING: ANNIVERSARY. Dec 21, 1620. According to Governor William Bradford's *History of Plymouth Plantation*, "On Munday," [Dec 21, 1620, New Style] the Pilgrims, aboard the *Mayflower*, reached Plymouth, MA, "sounded ye harbor, and founde it fitt for shipping; and marched into ye land, & founde diverse cornfields, and ye best they could find, and ye season & their presente necessitie made them glad to accepte of it. . . . And after wards tooke better view of ye place, and resolved wher to pitch their dwelling; and them and their goods." Plymouth Rock, the legendary place of landing since it first was "identified" in 1769, nearly 150 years after the landing, has been a historic shrine since.

SPACE MILESTONE: *APOLLO 8* (US). Dec 21, 1968. First moon voyage launched, manned by Colonel Frank Borman, Captain James A. Lovell, Jr, and Major William A. Anders. Orbited moon Dec 24, returned to Earth Dec 27. First men to orbit the moon and see the side of the moon away from Earth.

STALIN, JOSEPH: BIRTH ANNIVERSARY. Dec 21, 1879. Russian dictator whose family name was Dzhugashvili, was born at Gori, Georgia. One of the most powerful and most feared men of the 20th century, Stalin died (of a stroke) at the Kremlin, at Moscow, Mar 5, 1953.

★ *Birthdays* ★

Jane Fonda, actress (Oscars for *Klute*, *Coming Home*; *Julia*, *On Golden Pond*), born New York, NY, Dec 21, 1937.

Samuel L. Jackson, actor (*Pulp Fiction, Jurassic Park*), born Washington, DC, Dec 21, 1948.

Ray Romano, comedian, actor ("Everybody Loves Raymond"), born Queens, NY, Dec 21, 1957.

December 22

CAPRICORN, THE GOAT. Dec 22–Jan 19. In the astronomical/astrological zodiac, which divides the sun's apparent orbit into 12 segments, the period Dec 22–Jan 19 is identified, traditionally, as the sun sign of Capricorn, the Goat. The ruling planet is Saturn.

FIRST GORILLA BORN IN CAPTIVITY: BIRTH ANNIVERSARY. Dec 22, 1956. "Colo" was born at the Columbus, OH, zoo, weighing in at 3¼ pounds, the first gorilla born in captivity.

★ Birthdays ★

Hector Elizondo, actor (*Pretty Woman, Frankie and Johnny,* "Chicago Hope"), born New York, NY, Dec 22, 1936.

Ralph Fiennes, actor (*Schindler's List, The English Patient*), born Suffolk, England, Dec 22, 1962.

Diane K. Sawyer, journalist ("60 Minutes," "Primetime Live"), born Glasgow, KY, Dec 22, 1946.

December 23

FEDERAL RESERVE SYSTEM: ANNIVERSARY. Dec 23, 1913. Established pursuant to authority contained in the Federal Reserve Act of Dec 23, 1913, the system serves as the nation's central bank, with the responsibility for execution of monetary policy. It is called on to contribute to the strength and vitality of the US economy, in part by influencing the lending and investing activities of commercial banks and the cost and availability of money and credit.

FIRST NONSTOP FLIGHT AROUND THE WORLD WITHOUT REFUELING: ANNIVERSARY. Dec 23, 1987. Dick Rutan and Jeana Yeager set a new world record of 216 hours of continuous flight, breaking their own record of 111 hours set July 15, 1986. The aircraft *Voyager* departed from Edwards Air Force Base in California, Dec 14, 1987, and landed Dec 23, 1987. The journey covered 24,986 miles at an official speed of 115 miles per hour.

METRIC CONVERSION ACT: ANNIVERSARY. Dec 23, 1975. The Congress of the US passed Public Law 94–168, known as the Metric Conversion Act of 1975. This act declares that the SI (International System of Units) will be this country's basic system of measurement and establishes the United States Metric Board, which is responsible for the planning, coordination and implementation of the nation's voluntary conversion to SI. (Congress had authorized the metric system as a legal system of measurement in the US by an act passed July 28, 1866. In 1875, the US became one of the original signers of the Treaty of the Metre, which established an international metric system.)

TRANSISTOR INVENTED: ANNIVERSARY. Dec 23, 1947. John Bardeen, Walter Brattain and William Shockley of Bell Laboratories shared the 1956 Nobel Prize for their invention of the transistor, which led to a revolution in communications and electronics. It was smaller, lighter, more durable, more reliable and generated less heat than the vacuum tube that had been used up to this time.

★ Birthdays ★

Susan Lucci, actress ("All My Children," *Mafia Princess*), born Westchester, NY, Dec 23, 1949.

December 24

CARSON, CHRISTOPHER "KIT": BIRTH ANNIVERSARY. Dec 24, 1809. American frontiersman, soldier, trapper, guide and Indian agent best known as Kit Carson. Born at Madison County, KY, he died at Fort Lyon, CO, May 23, 1868.

CHRISTMAS BELLS RING AGAIN IN ST. BASIL'S: ANNIVERSARY. Dec 24, 1990. For the first time since the death of Lenin in 1924, the bells of St. Basil's Cathedral, on Red Square in Moscow, rang to celebrate Christmas.

CHRISTMAS EVE. Dec 24. Family gift-giving occasion in many Christian countries.

HUGHES, HOWARD: BIRTH ANNIVERSARY. Dec 24, 1905. Wealthy American industrialist, aviator and movie producer who spent his latter years as a recluse. Born at Houston, TX, he died in airplane en route from Acapulco, Mexico, to Houston, Apr 5, 1976.

LIBYA: INDEPENDENCE DAY. Dec 24. Libya gained its independence from Italy in 1951.

★ Birthdays ★

Mary Higgins Clark, author (*Where Are the Children?*, *Silent Night*), born New York, NY, Dec 24, 1931.

Ricky Martin, singer, actor ("General Hospital"), born Enrique José Martín, San Juan, Puerto Rico, Dec 24, 1971.

December 25

BOGART, HUMPHREY: BIRTH ANNIVERSARY. Dec 25, 1899. American stage and screen actor, Humphrey DeForest Bogart was born at New York, NY. Among his best remembered films are *The African Queen*, *The Maltese Falcon*, *Casablanca* and *To Have and Have Not*. Bogart died Jan 14, 1957, at Hollywood, CA.

CHRISTMAS. Dec 25. Christian festival commemorating the birth of Jesus of Nazareth. Most popular of Christian observances, Christmas as a Feast of the Nativity dates from the fourth century. Although Jesus's birth date is not known, the Western church selected Dec 25 for the feast, possibly to counteract the non-Christian festivals of that approximate date. Many customs from non-Christian festivals (Roman Saturnalia, Mithraic sun's birthday, Teutonic yule, Druidic and other winter solstice rites) have been adopted as part of the Christmas celebration (lights, mistletoe, holly and ivy, holiday tree, wassailing and gift giving, for example). Some Orthodox churches celebrate Christmas Jan 7 based on the "old calendar" (Julian). Theophany (recognition of the divinity of Jesus) is observed on this date and also on Jan 6, especially by the Eastern Orthodox Church.

CHRISTMAS FIRESIDE CHAT WARNING: ANNIVERSARY. Dec 25, 1943. In his Christmas message to the American people, Franklin D. Roosevelt warned, "The war is now reaching the stage when we shall have to look forward to large casualty lists—dead, wounded and missing. War entails just that. There is no easy road to victory. And the end is not yet in sight."

CUBA: CHRISTMAS RETURNS: ANNIVERSARY. Dec 25, 1998. Christmas was celebrated in Cuba after Fidel Castro's government announced that it was again a regular holiday in the Cuban calendar. In 1997 the government had granted a Christmas holiday in deference to Pope John Paul II, who was visiting the island the next month. Christmas had been abolished as a holiday in Cuba in 1969.

"THE STEVE ALLEN SHOW" TV PREMIERE: ANNIVERSARY. Dec 25, 1950. Talented actor, comedian, singer and musician Steve Allen hosted a number of variety shows from 1950 to 1969 (with a few breaks in between to host specials and "The Tonight Show"). For two years, his television show was similar to his radio show and featured singer Peggy Lee, announcer Bern Bennett and Llemuel the llama. His next show competed with Ed Sullivan's show, though Allen's stressed comedy. Some of his "funny men" were Don Knotts, Tom Poston, Louis Nye, Gabe Dell, Pat Harrington, Jr, Dayton Allen and Bill Dana. His other shows included a talk show, a game show, a comedy show, an educational music show and a flashback-comedy show.

★ *Birthdays* ★

Jimmy Buffett, singer ("Margaritaville"), songwriter, born Pascagoula, MS, Dec 25, 1946.
Mary Elizabeth (Sissy) Spacek, actress (Oscar for *Coal Miner's Daughter; In the Bedroom*), born Quitman, TX, Dec 25, 1949.

December 26

BOXING DAY. Dec 26. Ordinarily observed on the first day after Christmas. A legal holiday in Canada, the United Kingdom and many other countries. Formerly a day when Christmas gift boxes were "regularly expected by a postman, the lamplighter, the dustman and generally by all those functionaries who render services to the public at large, without receiving payment therefore from any individual." When Boxing Day falls on a Saturday or Sunday, the Monday or Tuesday immediately following may be proclaimed or observed as a bank or public holiday.

KWANZAA. Dec 26–Jan 1. American black family observance created in 1966 by Dr. Maulana Karenga in recognition of traditional African harvest festivals. This seven-day festival stresses unity of the black family, with a harvest feast (*karamu*) on the first day and a day of meditation on the final one. Kwanzaa means "first fruit" in Swahili.

MAO TSE-TUNG: BIRTH ANNIVERSARY. Dec 26, 1893. Chinese Communist revolutionary and "founding father" of the People's Republic of China, born at Hunan Province, China. Died at Beijing, Sept 9, 1976.

RADIUM DISCOVERED: ANNIVERSARY. Dec 26, 1898. French scientists Pierre and Marie Curie discovered the element radium, for which they later won the Nobel Prize for physics.

SAINT STEPHEN'S DAY. Dec 26. One of the seven deacons named by the apostles to distribute alms. Died during the first century. Feast Day is Dec 26 and is observed as a public holiday in Austria and the Republic of Ireland.

SECOND DAY OF CHRISTMAS. Dec 26. Observed as holiday in many countries.

SLOVENIA: INDEPENDENCE DAY. Dec 26. National holiday. Commemorates 1990 announcement of separation from the Yugoslav Union.

★ *Birthdays* ★

Carlton Ernest Fisk, Hall of Fame baseball player, born Bellows Falls, VT, Dec 26, 1947.
Alan King, comedian, actor (*The Bonfire of the Vanities*, "Seventh Avenue"), born New York, NY, Dec 26, 1927.

December 27

DIETRICH, MARLENE: BIRTH ANNIVERSARY. Dec 27, 1901. Born at Berlin, Germany, Dietrich enrolled in Max Reinhardt's drama school. Her first big break was in 1930 when Josef Von Sternberg cast her in *The Blue Angel*, the first talkie made in Germany. A year later, she and Sternberg moved to Hollywood and began a string of six films together with *Morocco*, the only film for which she received an Academy Award nomination. Some of her other films were *Destry Rides Again, Around the World in 80 Days, Touch of Evil, Judgment at Nuremberg* and *Witness for the Prosecution*. During the 1950s she was a cabaret singer in a stage revue that toured the globe. Dietrich died May 6, 1992, at Paris, France.

"HOWDY DOODY" TV PREMIERE: ANNIVERSARY. Dec 27, 1947. The first popular children's show was brought to TV by Bob Smith and was one of the first regular NBC shows to be shown in color. It was set in the circus town of Doodyville. Children sat in the bleachers' "Peanut Gallery" and participated in activities such as songs and stories. Human characters were Buffalo Bob (Bob Smith), the silent clown Clarabell (Bob Keeshan, Bobby Nicholson and Lew Anderson), storekeeper Cornelius Cobb (Nicholson), Chief Thunderthud (Bill LeCornec), Princess Summerfall Winterspring (Judy Tyler and Linda Marsh), Bison Bill (Ted Brown) and wrestler Ugly Sam (Dayton Allen). Puppet costars included Howdy Doody, Phineas T. Bluster, Dilly Dally, Flub-a-Dub, Captain Scuttlebutt, Double Doody and Heidi Doody. The filmed adventures of Gumby were also featured. In the final episode, Clarabell broke his lone silence to say, "Good-bye, kids."

PASTEUR, LOUIS: BIRTH ANNIVERSARY. Dec 27, 1822. French chemist-bacteriologist born at Dole, Jura, France. Died at Villeneuve l'Etang, France, Sept 28, 1895. Discoverer of prophylactic inoculation against rabies. Pasteurization process named for him.

RADIO CITY MUSIC HALL: ANNIVERSARY. Dec 27, 1932. Radio City Music Hall, at New York City, opened on this date.

★ Birthdays ★

Gerard Depardieu, actor (*The Return of Martin Guerre, Cyrano de Bergerac*), born Chateauroux, France, Dec 27, 1948.
Cokie Roberts, news correspondent, born New Orleans, LA, Dec 27, 1943.

December 28

IOWA: ADMISSION DAY: ANNIVERSARY. Dec 28. Became 29th state in 1846.

PLEDGE OF ALLEGIANCE RECOGNIZED: ANNIVERSARY. Dec 28, 1945. The US Congress officially recognized the Pledge of Allegiance and urged its frequent recitation in America's schools. The pledge was composed in 1892 by Francis Bellamy, a Baptist minister. At the time, Bellamy was chairman of a committee of state school superintendents of education, and several public schools adopted his pledge as part of the Columbus Day quadricentennial celebration that year. In 1955, the Knights of Columbus persuaded Congress to add the words "under God" to the pledge.

***POOR RICHARD'S ALMANACK*: ANNIVERSARY.** Dec 28, 1732. The *Pennsylvania Gazette* carried the first known advertisement for the first issue of *Poor Richard's Almanack* by Richard Saunders (Benjamin Franklin) for the year 1733. The advertisement promised "many pleasant and witty verses, jests and sayings, new fashions, games for kisses, men and melons, breakfast in bed, &c." America's most famous almanac, *Poor Richard's* was published through the year 1758 and has been imitated many times since.

WILSON, WOODROW: BIRTH ANNIVERSARY. Dec 28, 1856. The 28th president of the US was born Thomas Woodrow Wilson at Staunton, VA. Twice elected president (1912 and 1916), it was Wilson who said, "The world must be made safe for democracy," as he asked the Congress to declare war on Germany, Apr 2, 1917. His first wife, Ellen, died Aug 6, 1914, and he married Edith Bolling Galt, Dec 18, 1915. He suffered a paralytic stroke, Sept 16, 1919, never regaining his health. There were many speculations about who (possibly Mrs Wilson?) was running the government during his illness. His second term of office ended Mar 3, 1921, and he died at Washington, DC, Feb 3, 1924.

★ Birthdays ★

Patrick Rafter, tennis player, born Mount Isa, Queensland, Australia, Dec 28, 1972.

Maggie Smith, actress (*The Prime of Miss Jean Brodie, Gosford Park*; Tony for *Lettice & Lovage*), born Ilford, England, Dec 28, 1934.

Denzel Washington, actor ("St. Elsewhere," *Malcolm X*); Oscars for *Glory, Training Day*), born Mount Vernon, NY, Dec 28, 1954.

December 29

JOHNSON, ANDREW: BIRTH ANNIVERSARY. Dec 29, 1808. Seventeenth president of the US, Andrew Johnson, proprietor of a tailor shop at Laurens, SC, before he entered politics, was born at Raleigh, NC. Upon Abraham Lincoln's assassination Johnson became president. He was the first president to be impeached by the House and was acquitted Mar 26, 1868, by the Senate. After his term of office as president (Apr 15, 1865–Mar 3, 1869) he made several unsuccessful attempts to win public office. Finally he was elected to the US Senate from Tennessee and served in the Senate from Mar 4, 1875, until his death at Carter's Station, TN, July 31, 1875.

STILL NEED TO DO DAY. Dec 29. Time runs out! All those dreams you've had, all those fantasies? It's time, friend. Do it! [©2001 by WH.] For info: Wellcat Holidays. Web: www.wellcat.com.

TEXAS: ADMISSION DAY: ANNIVERSARY. Dec 29. Became 28th state in 1845.

WOUNDED KNEE MASSACRE: ANNIVERSARY. Dec 29, 1890. Anniversary of the massacre of more than 200 Native American men, women and children by the US Seventh Cavalry at Wounded Knee Creek, SD. Government efforts to suppress a ceremonial religious practice, the Ghost Dance (which called for a messiah who would restore the bison to the plains, make the white men disappear and bring back the old Native American way of life), had resulted in the death of Sitting Bull, Dec 15, 1890, which further inflamed the disgruntled Native Americans and culminated in the slaughter at Wounded Knee, Dec 29.

YMCA ORGANIZED: ANNIVERSARY. Dec 29, 1851. The first US branch of the Young Men's Christian Association was organized at Boston. It was modeled on an organization begun at London in 1844.

★ Birthdays ★

Ted Danson, actor ("Cheers," "Becker," *Three Men and a Baby*), born San Diego, CA, Dec 29, 1947.

Mary Tyler Moore, actress (two Emmys for "The Dick Van Dyke Show"; three Emmys for "The Mary Tyler Moore Show"; *Ordinary People*), born Brooklyn, NY, Dec 29, 1936.

Jon Voight, actor (*Midnight Cowboy, Deliverance*), born Yonkers, NY, Dec 29, 1938.

December 30

KIPLING, RUDYARD: BIRTH ANNIVERSARY. Dec 30, 1865. English poet, novelist and short-story writer, Nobel Prize laureate, Kipling was born at Bombay, India. After working as a journalist at India, he traveled around the world. He married an American and lived in Vermont for several years. Kipling is best known for his children's stories, such as the *Jungle Book* and *Just So Stories*, and poems such as "The Ballad of East and West" and "If." He died at London, England, Jan 18, 1936.

"LET'S MAKE A DEAL" TV PREMIERE: ANNIVERSARY. Dec 30, 1963. Monty Hall hosted this outrageous and no-skill-required game show. Audience members, many of whom wore costumes, were selected to sit in the trading area, and some were picked to "make a deal" with Hall by trading something of their own for something they were offered. Sometimes prizes were worthless ("zonks"). At the end of the show, the two people who had won the most were given the option to trade their winnings for a chance at the "Big Deal," hidden behind one of three doors. The most recent revival (1990–91) was hosted by Bob Hilton.

"THE ROY ROGERS SHOW" TV PREMIERE: ANNIVERSARY. Dec 30, 1951. This very popular TV Western starred Roy Rogers and his wife, Dale Evans, as themselves. It also featured Pat Brady as Rogers's sidekick who rode a jeep named Nellybelle, the singing group Sons of the Pioneers, Rogers's horse Trigger and Evans's horse Buttermilk. This half-hour show was especially popular with young viewers. Known as the "King of the Cowboys," Rogers was born Leonard Slye at Cincinnati, OH. His many songs included "Don't Fence Me In" and "Happy Trails to You."

USSR ESTABLISHED: ANNIVERSARY. Dec 30, 1922. After the Russian Revolution of 1917 and the subsequent three-year civil war, the Union of Soviet Socialist Republics (or Soviet Union) was founded, a confederation of Russia, Byelorussia, the Ukraine and the Transcaucasian Federation. It was the first state in the world to be based on Marxist Communism. The Soviet Union was dissolved Dec 8, 1991. See also: "Soviet Union Dissolved: Anniv" (Dec 8).

★ **Birthdays** ★

Sanford (Sandy) Koufax, former sportscaster, Baseball Hall of Fame pitcher, born Brooklyn, NY, Dec 30, 1935.

Matt Lauer, news anchor ("Today"), born New York, NY, Dec 30, 1957.

Tiger Woods, golfer, born Eldrick Woods, Cypress, CA, Dec 30, 1975.

December 31

FIRST BANK OPENS IN US: ANNIVERSARY. Dec 31, 1781. The first modern bank in the US, the Bank of North America, was organized by Robert Morris and received its charter from the Continental Congress. It began operations Jan 7, 1782, at Philadelphia.

MATISSE, HENRI: BIRTH ANNIVERSARY. Dec 31, 1869. Painter born at Le Cateau, France. Matisse also designed textiles and stained glass windows. Died at Nice, France, Nov 3, 1954.

NEW YEAR'S DESIGNATE A DRIVER CAMPAIGN. Dec 31. For info: Mothers Against Drunk Driving (MADD). Web: www.madd.org.

NEW YEAR'S EVE. Dec 31. The last evening of the Gregorian calendar year, traditionally a night for merrymaking to welcome in the new year.

PANAMA: ASSUMES CONTROL OF CANAL: ANNIVERSARY. Dec 31, 1999. With the expiration of the Panama Canal Treaty of 1979 at noon, the Republic of Panama assumed full responsibility for the canal and the US Panama Canal Commission ceased to exist.

★ Birthdays ★

Sir Anthony Hopkins, actor (*The Silence of the Lambs, Legends of the Fall*), born Port Talbot, South Wales, UK, Dec 31, 1937.

Val Kilmer, actor (*Batman Forever, Top Secret, The Doors, Heat*), born Los Angeles, CA, Dec 31, 1959.

Ben Kingsley, actor (Oscar for *Gandhi; Bugsy, Schindler's List*), born Krishna Bhanji, Yorkshire, England, Dec 31, 1943.

Bebe Neuwirth, actress ("Cheers," "Frasier"; stage: *Chicago*), born Newark, NJ, Dec 31, 1958.

Calendar Information for the Year 2003

Time shown is Eastern Standard Time. All dates are given in terms of the Gregorian calendar.
(Based in part on information prepared by the Nautical Almanac Office, US Naval Observatory.)

ERAS	YEAR	BEGINS
Byzantine	7512	Sept 14
Jewish*	5764	Sept 26
Chinese (Year of the Sheep [Goat])	4701	Feb 1
Roman (AUC)	2756	Jan 14
Nabonassar	2752	Apr 24
Japanese (Heisei)	15	Jan 1
Grecian (Seleucidae)	2315	Sept 14 (or Oct 14)
Indian (Saka)	1925	Mar 22
Diocletian	1720	Sept 12

*Year begins at sunset.

RELIGIOUS CALENDARS

Epiphany	Jan 6
Shrove Tuesday	Mar 4
Ash Wednesday	Mar 5
Lent	Mar 5–Apr 19
Palm Sunday	Apr 13
Good Friday	Apr 18
Easter Day	Apr 20
Ascension Day	May 29
Whit Sunday (Pentecost)	June 8
Trinity Sunday	June 15
First Sunday in Advent	Nov 30
Christmas Day	Dec 25

Eastern Orthodox Church Observances

Great Lent begins	Mar 10
Pascha (Easter)	Apr 27
Ascension	June 5
Pentecost	June 15

Jewish Holy Days*

Purim	Mar 18
Passover (1st day)	Apr 17
Shavuot	June 6
Tisha B'av	Aug 7
Rosh Hashanah (New Year)	Sept 26–27
Yom Kippur	Oct 6
Succoth	Oct 11–12
Chanukah	Dec 20–27

*All Jewish holidays begin the previous day at sundown.

DAYLIGHT SAVING TIME SCHEDULE—2003

Sunday, Apr 6, 2:00 AM–Sunday, Oct 26, 2:00 AM—in all time zones.

CIVIL CALENDAR—US—2003

New Year's Day	Jan 1
Martin Luther King's Birthday (obsvd)	Jan 20
Lincoln's Birthday	Feb 12
Washington's Birthday (obsvd)/Presidents' Day	Feb 17
Memorial Day (obsvd)	May 26
Independence Day	July 4
Labor Day	Sept 1
Columbus Day (obsvd)	Oct 13
General Election Day	Nov 4
Veterans Day	Nov 11
Thanksgiving Day	Nov 27

Other Days Widely Observed in US—2003

Groundhog Day (Candlemas)	Feb 2
St. Valentine's Day	Feb 14
St. Patrick's Day	Mar 17
Mother's Day	May 11
Flag Day	June 14
Father's Day	June 15
National Grandparents Day	Sept 7
Hallowe'en	Oct 31

CIVIL CALENDAR—CANADA—2003

Victoria Day	May 19
Canada Day	July 1
Labor Day	Sept 1
Thanksgiving Day	Oct 13
Remembrance Day	Nov 11
Boxing Day	Dec 26

CIVIL CALENDAR—MEXICO—2003

New Year's Day	Jan 1
Constitution Day	Feb 5
Benito Juarez Birthday	Mar 21
Labor Day	May 1
Battle of Puebla Day (Cinco de Mayo)	May 5
Independence Day*	Sept 16
Dia de La Raza	Oct 12
Mexican Revolution Day	Nov 20
Guadalupe Day	Dec 12

*Celebration begins Sept 15 at 11:00 PM, EDT.

SEASONS

Spring (Vernal Equinox)	Mar 20, 8:00 PM, EST
Summer (Summer Solstice)	June 21, 3:10 PM, EDT
Autumn (Autumnal Equinox)	Sept 23, 6:47 AM, EDT
Winter (Winter Solstice)	Dec 22, 2:04 AM, EST

Calendar Information for the Year 2004

Time shown is Eastern Standard Time. All dates are given in terms of the Gregorian calendar.
(Based in part on information prepared by the Nautical Almanac Office, US Naval Observatory.)

ERAS	YEAR	BEGINS
Byzantine	7513	Sept 14
Jewish*	5765	Sept 18
Chinese (Year of the Monkey)	4702	Jan 22
Roman (AUC)	2757	Jan 14
Nabonassar	2753	Apr 23
Japanese (Heisei)	16	Jan 1
Grecian (Seleucidae)	2316	Sept 14
		(or Oct 14)
Indian (Saka)	1926	Mar 21
Diocletian	1721	Sept 12

*Year begins at sunset.

RELIGIOUS CALENDARS

Epiphany	Jan 6
Shrove Tuesday	Feb 24
Ash Wednesday	Feb 25
Lent	Feb 25–Apr 10
Palm Sunday	Apr 4
Good Friday	Apr 9
Easter Day	Apr 11
Ascension Day	May 20
Whit Sunday (Pentecost)	May 30
Trinity Sunday	June 6
First Sunday in Advent	Nov 28
Christmas Day	Dec 25

Eastern Orthodox Church Observances

Great Lent begins	Feb 23
Pascha (Easter)	Apr 11
Ascension	May 20
Pentecost	May 30

Jewish Holy Days*

Purim	Mar 7
Passover (1st day)	Apr 6
Shavuot	May 26
Tisha B'av	July 27
Rosh Hashanah (New Year)	Sept 16–17
Yom Kippur	Sept 25
Succoth	Sept 30–Oct 8
Chanukah	Dec 8–15

*All Jewish holidays begin the previous day at sundown.

DAYLIGHT SAVING TIME SCHEDULE—2004

Sunday, Apr 4, 2:00 AM–Sunday, Oct 31, 2:00 AM—in all time zones.

CIVIL CALENDAR—US—2004

New Year's Day	Jan 1
Martin Luther King's Birthday (obsvd)	Jan 19
Lincoln's Birthday	Feb 12
Washington's Birthday (obsvd)/Presidents' Day	Feb 16
Memorial Day (obsvd)	May 31
Independence Day	July 4
Labor Day	Sept 6
Columbus Day (obsvd)	Oct 11
General Election Day	Nov 2
Veterans Day	Nov 11
Thanksgiving Day	Nov 25

Other Days Widely Observed in US—2004

Groundhog Day (Candlemas)	Feb 2
St. Valentine's Day	Feb 14
St. Patrick's Day	Mar 17
Mother's Day	May 9
Flag Day	June 14
Father's Day	June 20
National Grandparents Day	Sept 12
Hallowe'en	Oct 31

CIVIL CALENDAR—CANADA—2004

Victoria Day	May 24
Canada Day	July 1
Labor Day	Sept 6
Thanksgiving Day	Oct 11
Remembrance Day	Nov 11
Boxing Day	Dec 26

CIVIL CALENDAR—MEXICO—2004

New Year's Day	Jan 1
Constitution Day	Feb 5
Benito Juarez Birthday	Mar 21
Labor Day	May 1
Battle of Puebla Day (Cinco de Mayo)	May 5
Independence Day*	Sept 16
Dia de La Raza	Oct 12
Mexican Revolution Day	Nov 20
Guadalupe Day	Dec 12

*Celebration begins Sept 15 at 11:00 PM, EDT.

SEASONS

Spring (Vernal Equinox)	Mar 20, 1:49 AM, EST
Summer (Summer Solstice)	June 20, 8:57 PM, EDT
Autumn (Autumnal Equinox)	Sept 22, 12:30 PM, EDT
Winter (Winter Solstice)	Dec 21, 7:42 AM, EST

Calendar Information for the Year 2005

Time shown is Eastern Standard Time. All dates are given in terms of the Gregorian calendar.
(Based in part on information prepared by the Nautical Almanac Office, US Naval Observatory.)

ERAS	YEAR	BEGINS
Byzantine	7514	Sept 14
Jewish*	5766	Oct 3
Chinese (Year of the Rooster)	4703	Feb 9
Roman (AUC)	2758	Jan 14
Nabonassar	2754	Apr 23
Japanese (Heisei)	17	Jan 1
Grecian (Seleucidae)	2317	Sept 14 (or Oct 14)
Indian (Saka)	1927	Mar 22
Diocletian	1722	Sept 11

*Year begins at sunset.

RELIGIOUS CALENDARS

Epiphany	Jan 6
Shrove Tuesday	Feb 8
Ash Wednesday	Feb 9
Lent	Feb 9–Mar 26
Palm Sunday	Mar 20
Good Friday	Mar 25
Easter Day	Mar 27
Ascension Day	May 5
Whit Sunday (Pentecost)	May 15
Trinity Sunday	May 22
First Sunday in Advent	Nov 27
Christmas Day	Dec 25

Eastern Orthodox Church Observances

Great Lent begins	Mar 14
Pascha (Easter)	May 1
Ascension	June 9
Pentecost	June 19

Jewish Holy Days*

Purim	Mar 14
Passover (1st day)	Apr 13
Shavuot	June 2
Tisha B'av	Aug 3
Rosh Hashanah (New Year)	Oct 4–5
Yom Kippur	Oct 13
Succoth	Oct 18–19
Chanukah	Nov 26–Dec 3

*All Jewish holidays begin the previous day at sundown.

DAYLIGHT SAVING TIME SCHEDULE—2005

Sunday, Apr 3, 2:00 AM–Sunday, Oct 30, 2:00 AM—in all time zones.

CIVIL CALENDAR—US—2005

New Year's Day	Jan 1
Martin Luther King's Birthday (obsvd)	Jan 17
Lincoln's Birthday	Feb 12
Washington's Birthday (obsvd)/Presidents' Day	Feb 21
Memorial Day (obsvd)	May 30
Independence Day	July 4
Labor Day	Sept 5
Columbus Day (obsvd)	Oct 10
General Election Day	Nov 8
Veterans Day	Nov 11
Thanksgiving Day	Nov 24

Other Days Widely Observed in US—2005

Groundhog Day (Candlemas)	Feb 2
St. Valentine's Day	Feb 14
St. Patrick's Day	Mar 17
Mother's Day	May 9
Flag Day	June 14
Father's Day	June 19
National Grandparents Day	Sept 11
Hallowe'en	Oct 31

CIVIL CALENDAR—CANADA—2005

Victoria Day	May 23
Canada Day	July 1
Labor Day	Sept 5
Thanksgiving Day	Oct 10
Remembrance Day	Nov 11
Boxing Day	Dec 26

CIVIL CALENDAR—MEXICO—2005

New Year's Day	Jan 1
Constitution Day	Feb 5
Benito Juarez Birthday	Mar 21
Labor Day	May 1
Battle of Puebla Day (Cinco de Mayo)	May 5
Independence Day*	Sept 16
Dia de La Raza	Oct 12
Mexican Revolution Day	Nov 20
Guadalupe Day	Dec 12

*Celebration begins Sept 15 at 11:00 PM, EDT.

SEASONS

Spring (Vernal Equinox)	Mar 20, 7:34 AM, EST
Summer (Summer Solstice)	June 21, 2:46 PM, EDT
Autumn (Autumnal Equinox)	Sept 23, 6:23 PM, EDT
Winter (Winter Solstice)	Dec 21, 1:35 PM, EST

Calendar Information for the Year 2006

Time shown is Eastern Standard Time. All dates are given in terms of the Gregorian calendar.
(Based in part on information prepared by the Nautical Almanac Office, US Naval Observatory.)

ERAS	YEAR	BEGINS
Byzantine	7515	Sept 14
Jewish*	5767	Oct 4
Chinese (Year of the Dog)	4704	Jan 29
Roman (AUC)	2759	Jan 14
Nabonassar	2755	Apr 23
Japanese (Heisei)	18	Jan 1
Grecian (Seleucidae)	2318	Sept 14
		(or Oct 14)
Indian (Saka)	1928	Mar 20
Diocletian	1723	Sept 11

*Year begins at sunset.

RELIGIOUS CALENDARS

Epiphany	Jan 6
Shrove Tuesday	Mar 7
Ash Wednesday	Mar 8
Lent	Mar 8–Apr 15
Palm Sunday	Apr 9
Good Friday	Apr 14
Easter Day	Apr 16
Ascension Day	May 25
Whit Sunday (Pentecost)	June 4
Trinity Sunday	June 11
First Sunday in Advent	Dec 3
Christmas Day	Dec 25

Eastern Orthodox Church Observances

Great Lent begins	Mar 6
Pascha (Easter)	Apr 23
Ascension	June 1
Pentecost	June 11

Jewish Holy Days*

Purim	Mar 14
Passover (1st day)	Apr 13
Shavuot	June 2–3
Tisha B'av	Aug 3
Rosh Hashanah (New Year)	Oct 4–5
Yom Kippur	Oct 13
Succoth	Oct 18–19
Chanukah	Dec 26–Jan 2

*All Jewish holidays begin the previous day at sundown.

DAYLIGHT SAVING TIME SCHEDULE—2006

Sunday, Apr 2, 2:00 AM–Sunday, Oct 29, 2:00 AM—in all time zones.

CIVIL CALENDAR—US—2006

New Year's Day	Jan 1
Martin Luther King's Birthday (obsvd)	Jan 16
Lincoln's Birthday	Feb 12
Washington's Birthday (obsvd)/Presidents' Day	Feb 20
Memorial Day (obsvd)	May 29
Independence Day	July 4
Labor Day	Sept 4
Columbus Day (obsvd)	Oct 10
General Election Day	Nov 7
Veterans Day	Nov 11
Thanksgiving Day	Nov 23

Other Days Widely Observed in US—2006

Groundhog Day (Candlemas)	Feb 2
St. Valentine's Day	Feb 14
St. Patrick's Day	Mar 17
Mother's Day	May 14
Flag Day	June 14
Father's Day	June 11
National Grandparents Day	Sept 10
Hallowe'en	Oct 31

CIVIL CALENDAR—CANADA—2006

Victoria Day	May 22
Canada Day	July 1
Labor Day	Sept 4
Thanksgiving Day	Oct 9
Remembrance Day	Nov 11
Boxing Day	Dec 26

CIVIL CALENDAR—MEXICO—2006

New Year's Day	Jan 1
Constitution Day	Feb 5
Benito Juarez Birthday	Mar 21
Labor Day	May 1
Battle of Puebla Day (Cinco de Mayo)	May 5
Independence Day*	Sept 16
Dia de La Raza	Oct 12
Mexican Revolution Day	Nov 20
Guadalupe Day	Dec 12

*Celebration begins Sept 15 at 11:00 PM, EDT.

SEASONS

Spring (Vernal Equinox)	Mar 20, 1:19 PM, EST
Summer (Summer Solstice)	June 21, 8:23 PM, EDT
Autumn (Autumnal Equinox)	Sept 23, 12:02 AM, EDT
Winter (Winter Solstice)	Dec 21, 7:20 PM, EST

Calendar Information for the Year 2007

Time shown is Eastern Standard Time. All dates are given in terms of the Gregorian calendar.
(Based in part on information prepared by the Nautical Almanac Office, US Naval Observatory.)

ERAS	YEAR	BEGINS
Byzantine	7516	Sept 14
Jewish*	5768	Sept 12
Chinese (Year of the Pig)	4705	Feb 18
Roman (AUC)	2760	Jan 14
Nabonassar	2756	Apr 23
Japanese (Heisei)	19	Jan 1
Grecian (Seleucidae)	2319	Sept 14
		(or Oct 14)
Indian (Saka)	1929	Mar 20
Diocletian	1724	Sept 11

*Year begins at sunset.

RELIGIOUS CALENDARS

Epiphany	Jan 6
Shrove Tuesday	Feb 27
Ash Wednesday	Feb 28
Lent	Feb 28–Apr 7
Palm Sunday	Apr 1
Good Friday	Apr 6
Easter Day	Apr 8
Ascension Day	May 17
Whit Sunday (Pentecost)	May 27
Trinity Sunday	June 3
First Sunday in Advent	Dec 2
Christmas Day	Dec 25

Eastern Orthodox Church Observances

Great Lent begins	Feb 19
Pascha (Easter)	Apr 8
Ascension	May 17
Pentecost	May 27

Jewish Holy Days*

Purim	Mar 4
Passover (1st day)	Apr 3
Shavuot	May 23
Tisha B'av	July 24
Rosh Hashanah (New Year)	Sept 12–13
Yom Kippur	Sept 22
Succoth	Sept 27
Chanukah	Dec 5–12

*All Jewish holidays begin the previous day at sundown.

DAYLIGHT SAVING TIME SCHEDULE—2007

Sunday, Apr 8, 2:00 AM–Sunday, Oct 28, 2:00 AM—In all time zones.

CIVIL CALENDAR—US—2007

New Year's Day	Jan 1
Martin Luther King's Birthday (obsvd)	Jan 15
Lincoln's Birthday	Feb 12
Washington's Birthday (obsvd)/Presidents' Day	Feb 19
Memorial Day (obsvd)	May 28
Independence Day	July 4
Labor Day	Sept 3
Columbus Day (obsvd)	Oct 9
General Election Day	Nov 6
Veterans Day	Nov 11
Thanksgiving Day	Nov 22

Other Days Widely Observed in US—2007

Groundhog Day (Candlemas)	Feb 2
St. Valentine's Day	Feb 14
St. Patrick's Day	Mar 17
Mother's Day	May 13
Flag Day	June 14
Father's Day	June 10
National Grandparents Day	Sept 9
Hallowe'en	Oct 31

CIVIL CALENDAR—CANADA—2007

Victoria Day	May 21
Canada Day	July 1
Labor Day	Sept 3
Thanksgiving Day	Oct 8
Remembrance Day	Nov 11
Boxing Day	Dec 26

CIVIL CALENDAR—MEXICO—2007

New Year's Day	Jan 1
Constitution Day	Feb 5
Benito Juarez Birthday	Mar 21
Labor Day	May 1
Battle of Puebla Day (Cinco de Mayo)	May 5
Independence Day*	Sept 16
Dia de La Raza	Oct 12
Mexican Revolution Day	Nov 20
Guadalupe Day	Dec 12

*Celebration begins Sept 15 at 11:00 PM, EDT.

SEASONS

Spring (Vernal Equinox)	Mar 20, 7:08 PM, EST
Summer (Summer Solstice)	June 21, 2:11 PM, EDT
Autumn (Autumnal Equinox)	Sept 23, 5:51 AM, EDT
Winter (Winter Solstice)	Dec 22, 1:09 AM, EST

Calendar Information for the Year 2008

Time shown is Eastern Standard Time. All dates are given in terms of the Gregorian calendar.
(Based in part on information prepared by the Nautical Almanac Office, US Naval Observatory.)

ERAS	YEAR	BEGINS
Byzantine	7517	Sept 14
Jewish*	5769	Sept 30
Chinese (Year of the Rat)	4706	Feb 7
Roman (AUC)	2761	Jan 14
Nabonassar	2757	Apr 23
Japanese (Heisei)	20	Jan 1
Grecian (Seleucidae)	2320	Sept 14 (or Oct 14)
Indian (Saka)	1930	Mar 21
Diocletian	1725	Sept 12

*Year begins at sunset.

RELIGIOUS CALENDARS

Epiphany	Jan 6
Shrove Tuesday	Feb 12
Ash Wednesday	Feb 13
Lent	Feb 13–Mar 22
Palm Sunday	Mar 16
Good Friday	Mar 21
Easter Day	Mar 23
Ascension Day	May 1
Whit Sunday (Pentecost)	May 11
Trinity Sunday	May 18
First Sunday in Advent	Nov 30
Christmas Day	Dec 25

Eastern Orthodox Church Observances

Great Lent begins	Mar 10
Pascha (Easter)	Apr 27
Ascension	June 5
Pentecost	June 15

Jewish Holy Days*

Purim	Mar 21
Passover (1st day)	Apr 20
Shavuot	June 9
Tisha B'av	Aug 10
Rosh Hashanah (New Year)	Sept 30–Oct 1
Yom Kippur	Oct 9
Succoth	Oct 14
Chanukah	Dec 22–29

*All Jewish holidays begin the previous day at sundown.

DAYLIGHT SAVING TIME SCHEDULE—2008

Sunday, Apr 6, 2:00 AM–Sunday, Oct 26, 2:00 AM—in all time zones.

CIVIL CALENDAR—US—2008

New Year's Day	Jan 1
Martin Luther King's Birthday (obsvd)	Jan 21
Lincoln's Birthday	Feb 12
Washington's Birthday (obsvd)/Presidents' Day	Feb 18
Memorial Day (obsvd)	May 26
Independence Day	July 4
Labor Day	Sept 8
Columbus Day (obsvd)	Oct 14
General Election Day	Nov 4
Veterans Day	Nov 11
Thanksgiving Day	Nov 27

Other Days Widely Observed in US—2008

Groundhog Day (Candlemas)	Feb 2
St. Valentine's Day	Feb 14
St. Patrick's Day	Mar 17
Mother's Day	May 11
Flag Day	June 14
Father's Day	June 8
National Grandparents Day	Sept 7
Hallowe'en	Oct 31

CIVIL CALENDAR—CANADA—2008

Victoria Day	May 19
Canada Day	July 1
Labor Day	Sept 1
Thanksgiving Day	Oct 6
Remembrance Day	Nov 11
Boxing Day	Dec 26

CIVIL CALENDAR—MEXICO—2008

New Year's Day	Jan 1
Constitution Day	Feb 5
Benito Juarez Birthday	Mar 21
Labor Day	May 1
Battle of Puebla Day (Cinco de Mayo)	May 5
Independence Day*	Sept 16
Dia de La Raza	Oct 12
Mexican Revolution Day	Nov 20
Guadalupe Day	Dec 12

*Celebration begins Sept 15 at 11:00 PM, EDT.

SEASONS

Spring (Vernal Equinox)	Mar 20, 12:57 AM, EST
Summer (Summer Solstice)	June 20, 8:00 PM, EDT
Autumn (Autumnal Equinox)	Sept 22, 11:39 AM, EDT
Winter (Winter Solstice)	Dec 21, 6:59 AM, EST

Alphabetical Index

Index

Index

Index

Index

Index

Index